In(ter)discipline
New Languages for Criticism

In(ter)discipline

New Languages for Criticism

❖

Edited by Gillian Beer, Malcolm Bowie and Beate Perrey

Routledge
Taylor & Francis Group
LONDON AND NEW YORK
2007

First published 2007 by Modern Humanities Research Association and Routledge

2 Park Square, Milton Park, Abingdon, Oxfordshire OX14 4RN
52 Vanderbilt Avenue, New York, NY 10017

Routledge is an imprint of the Taylor & Francis Group, an informa business

First issued in paperback 2020

ISBN 13: 978-1-905981-13-7 (hbk)
ISBN 13: 978-0-367-60261-1 (pbk)

CONTENTS

LIST OF CONTRIBUTORS

MIEKE BAL, a well-known cultural critic and theorist, holds the position of Royal Dutch Academy of Sciences Professor (KNAW). She is also Professor of the Theory of Literature in the Faculty of Humanities at the University of Amsterdam. Her many books include *A Mieke Bal Reader* (2006), *Travelling Concepts in the Humanities: A Rough Guide* (2002), and *Narratology: Introduction to the Theory of Narrative* (1997). She is also a video artist.

GILLIAN BEER is King Edward VII Professor Emeritus at the University of Cambridge. Her books include *Darwin's Plots* (1983; 2nd edition, 2000), *George Eliot* (1986), *Arguing with the Past* (1989), *Open Fields: Science in Cultural Encounter* (1996), and *Virginia Woolf: The Common Ground* (1996). She is currently completing two books, already under contract, *Alice in Space* and *Experimental Islands*. She holds honorary doctorates from a number of universities, including the Sorbonne. In November 2003 she gave the key British Academy Lecture and in spring 2004 was at Yale as a Fellow of the Yale Center for British Art and the Beinecke Library.

VICTORIA BEST is Lecturer in French at St John's College, Cambridge. She specializes in twentieth-century literature, having a particular interest in the links between identity and narrative. Her publications include *Critical Subjectivities: Identity and Narrative in the Work of Colette and Marguerite Duras* (2000), *An Introduction to Modern French Literature* (2002), and *The New Pornographies: Explicit Sex in Recent French Fiction and Film*, co-authored with Martin Crowley (2007). She is currently writing a book on fantasy and dream in modern French literature.

MALCOLM BOWIE was, until shortly before his death in 2007, Master of Christ's College in the University of Cambridge. Previously Marshal Foch Professor of French Literature and Fellow of All Souls College at Oxford University, he co-founded and directed until 2002 Oxford University's European Humanities Research Centre. He was a Fellow of the British Academy and the Royal Society of Literature, and an Officier dans l'Ordre des Palmes Académiques. His research focused on French literature of the nineteenth and twentieth centuries, on psychoanalysis, and on the relations between literature, music, and painting. His publications include *Henri Michaux: A Study of his Literary Works* (1973), *Mallarmé and the Art of Being Difficult* (1978), *Freud, Proust and Lacan: Theory as Fiction* (1987), *Lacan* (1991), *Psychoanalysis and the Future of Theory* (1993), and *A Short History of French Literature*, written jointly with Terence Cave and Sarah Kay (2003). His book *Proust Among the Stars* (1998) was a Los Angeles Times Best Book of 1999 and won the 2001 Truman Capote Award for Literary Criticism.

GABRIELE BRANDSTETTER received her PhD from Munich University and habilitation from Bayreuth University. She served as Professor of Theatre Studies at Justus-Liebig-University, Giessen, 1993–97, and as Professor of Modern German Literature Studies at the University of Basel, 1997–2003. Since 2003 she has been Professor of Theater and Dance Studies at Freie Universität Berlin. Her research focus is on: performance theories; concepts of body and movement in notation, image and performance; dance, theatricality and gender differences. Selected publications: *Loie Fuller. Tanz – Licht-Spiel – Art Nouveau* (1989, with co-author B. Ochaim), *Tanz-Lektüren. Körperbilder und Raumfiguren der Avantgarde* (1995), *ReMembering the Body. Körperbilder in Bewegung* (2000, with co-editor Hortensia Völckers), *de figura. Rhetorik – Bewegung – Gestalt* (2002, with co-editor S. Peters), *Erzählen und Wissen. Paradigmen und Aporien ihrer Inszenierungen in Goethes 'Wahlverwandschaften'* (2003, editor), *Bild-Sprung. TanzTheaterBewegung im Wechsel der Medien* (2005), *Schwarm(E)Motion. Bewegung zwischen Affekt und Masse* (2007, with co-editors B. Brandl-Risi and K. van Eikels), and *Tanz als Anthropologie* (2007, with co-editor C. Wulf).

SANTANU DAS is currently a British Academy Postdoctoral Fellow at the School of English and Drama, Queen Mary, University of London, and will be joining the school as a lecturer in 2008. He was formerly a Research Fellow at St. John?s College, Cambridge, and his interests include early twentieth-century art and literature, the body and the senses. He is the author of *Touch and Intimacy in First World War Literature* (Cambridge University Press, 2005). He is now working on a monograph on India and the First World War, and is editing for Cambridge a volume of essays titled *Race, Empire and First World War Writing.*

CAROLIN DUTTLINGER is University Lecturer in German at the University of Oxford and a Fellow of Wadham College. She studied at the universities of Freiburg and Cambridge, where she completed her doctorate in 2003. Her primary research interests lie in the field of twentieth-century German literature and thought, with particular reference to the relationship between literature and visual culture. She is the author of *Kafka and Photography* (2007) and the co-editor of *Performance and Performativity in German Cultural Studies* (2003). She has published on such writers as Benjamin, Adorno, Freud, Kafka, Barthes, and Sebald. Her new project explores theories and practices of attentiveness (*Aufmerksamkeit*) in twentieth-century literature, thought, and culture.

PATRICK GRAY is a doctoral student in English Literature and Renaissance Studies at Yale University, working on the relationship between classical philosophy, Renaissance literature, and psychoanalysis, as well as the distinction between poetry and propaganda. He has also studied at Oxford University, the University of North Carolina at Chapel Hill, and the Université de Paris–Sorbonne (Paris IV).

ANTHONY GRITTEN is Head of Postgraduate Studies and Research at the Royal Northern College of Music, Manchester. He is the co-editor of *Music and Gesture* (2006) and a contributor to the Legenda volume *Phrase and Subject: Studies in Literature and Music* (2006). His research interests include Stravinsky, French musical and intellectual culture, performance studies, philosophy and aesthetics of music, and theory and analysis of twentieth-century music.

KATRIN KOHL is a Lecturer in German at Oxford University and a Fellow and Tutor of Jesus College, Oxford. Her books include *Rhetoric, the Bible, and the Origins of Free Verse: The Early 'Hymns' of Friedrich Gottlieb Klopstock* (1990), *Friedrich Gottlieb Klopstock* (2000), *Metapher* (2007), and a monograph on the role of metaphor in poetics from the Middle Ages to the present, entitled *Poetologische Metaphern: Formen und Funktionen in der deutschen Literatur* (2007). She has also published articles on various aspects of German poetry and poetics.

LAWRENCE KRAMER is Professor of English and Music at Fordham University (New York) and the editor of *19th-Century Music*. The most recent of his numerous books are *Why Classical Music Still Matters* (2007), *Critical Musicology and the Responsibility of Response: Selected Essays* (2007), *Opera and Modern Culture: Wagner and Strauss* (2004), and *Musical Meaning: Toward a Critical History* (2001).

JOANNE LEE is Senior Lecturer in Fine Art at Nottingham Trent University where she was Programme Leader for the BA Fine Art course until 2006. She is currently on sabbatical leave in order to complete an improper study of aesthetic education. Her work investigates questions of attention, curiosity, wonder, imagination, interpretation, and resourcefulness. This is pursued through writing and visual practice and frequently has an explicit link to issues of pedagogy in Fine Art. Most recently she has collaborated with the sculptor Julie Westerman to produce *Drafts/Draughts*, a book for Artwords Press which documents a conversation exploring the migration of ideas between real and imagined, conceptual and material.

CATHERINE M. LORD is a University Lecturer in Media and Culture at the University of Amsterdam. As well as lecturing on topics connected with intermediality, literature, and film, she has a special interest in the relation between artistic practice and academic theory. In 1999 she published *The Intimacy of Influence: Narrative and Theoretical Fictions between the Works of George Eliot, Virginia Woolf and Jeanette Winterson*. She has written articles containing her own fiction and poetry, and is currently publishing short stories that can be read as taking on the role of a scholarly essay. In 2006 she premiered her short fiction film, *She's Back Again*, in Amsterdam and New York. She worked on the film *Raak* (*Contact*), premiered at the 2006 Utrecht film festival and to be shown internationally, and is now writing two short films. She is co-editor of *Essays in Migratory Aesthetics: Cultural Practices between Migration and Art-Making* (2007).

TIM MEHIGAN is foundation Professor of Languages and Head of the Department of Languages and Cultures at the University of Otago, New Zealand. Tim has published widely on German literature and thought since the Enlightenment, notably on Heinrich von Kleist and Robert Musil. His most recent publications include *Robert Musil* (Reclam 2001), *The Critical Response to Musil's 'Man Without Qualities'* (Camden House 2003), and, as editor, *Heinrich von Kleist und die Aufklärung* (Camden House 2000), *Frameworks, Artworks, Place: The Space of Perception in the Modern World* (Rodopi 2008), and, as guest editor with the journal *Seminar*, a collection of essays under the title 'Image, Body, Text' (2007). Tim Mehigan was elected Fellow of the Australian Academy of Humanities in 2003.

Beate Perrey is Senior Lecturer in Critical Musicology and Analysis at the University of Liverpool. She studied at Munich, Harvard, and Cambridge where she completed her doctorate with *Schumann's 'Dichterliebe' and Early Romantic Poetics* (2002). A Research Fellow at Trinity, Christ's College, Cambridge, and UCL, she was Visiting Professor at the École Normale Supérieure rue d'Ulm in Paris 2003–04. As a trained pianist, she is particularly interested in 19th–21st century Austro-German music. She edited *The Cambridge Companion to Schumann* (2007) and recent articles explore Kurtág, Francis Bacon, Celan, Schubert, Heine, Adorno and Glenn Gould. Her new project is about Music, Poetry and Sense Experience. Together with Gillian Beer and Malcolm Bowie, she co-directed, from 2002 to 2006, the research project *New Languages for Criticism: Cross-Currents and Resistances* at Cambridge University out of which this book has grown.

Adam Phillips, formerly Principal Child Psychotherapist at Charing Cross Hospital, and member of the Guild of Psychotherapists, works as a psychoanalyst in private practice in London. He is the author of *On Kissing, Tickling and Being Bored* (1993), *On Flirtation* (1994), *Terrors and Experts* (1995), *The Beast in the Nursery* (1998), *Darwin's Worms* (1999), *Promises, Promises: Essays on Literature and Psychoanalysis* (2001), *Houdini's Box: On the Arts of Escape* (2001), *Equals* (2002), *Going Sane* (2005), and *Side Effects* (2006). He is also the editor of the new Penguin translation of Freud. His new *Winnicott* (Fontana Modern Masters) appeared in 2007.

Katy Price teaches English Literature and Creative Writing at Anglia Ruskin University in Cambridge and is Communications Officer for History of Science at the BA Festival of Science. She has published on William Empson's astronomy love poems in *Interdisciplinary Science Reviews* (2005) and *Some Versions of Empson* (2007), edited by Matthew Bevis.

Daniel Rosenberg is Associate Professor of History in the Robert D. Clark Honors College at the University of Oregon. With Susan Harding, he is editor of *Histories of the Future* (2005). His current project is entitled *The Graphic Invention of Modern Time*.

Lucia Ruprecht is Lecturer in the department of German at the University of Cambridge and Fellow of Emmanuel College. She is the author of *Dances of the Self in Heinrich von Kleist, E. T. A. Hoffmann and Heinrich Heine,* and co-editor (with Carolin Duttlinger and Andrew Webber) of *Performance and Performativity in German Cultural Studies*. Her research is placed at the intersection of literature, dance, and cultural theory, with a focus on the nineteenth and twentieth centuries. Her current project, carried out in collaboration with the research centre Kulturen des Performativen at Free University Berlin, deals with charisma and virtuosity as key terms of an aesthetic of performance around 1900.

Peter Szendy teaches aesthetics in the Philosophy Department at the University of Nanterre (Paris X). He is also programme adviser for the concert hall Cité de la Musique in Paris. His books include *Écoute, une histoire de nos oreilles* (2001, with a foreword by Jean-Luc Nancy), *Membres fantômes: des corps musiciens* (2002), *Wonderland: la musique, recto verso* (with Georges Aperghis, 2004), and *Sur écoute: esthétique de l'espionnage* (2007). His book *Les prophéties du texte-Léviathan: lire selon Melville* (2004) became the libretto of the opera *Avis de tempête* by Georges Aperghis.

Gillian Beer, Beate Perrey and Malcolm Bowie
in front of Christ's College Master's Lodge, University of Cambridge, February 2003
Photograph © Lucia Ruprecht

PREFACE

❖

This book represents the proceedings of the international conference 'In(ter)-discipline: New Languages for Criticism' hosted by the Faculty of Music and Sidney Sussex College at the University of Cambridge, 20–21 September 2003. The conference was one of a series of events and activities organized by the research project *New Languages for Criticism: Cross-Currents and Resistances*, initiated in 2002 and co-directed by the three editors of this volume until 2006. The project greatly benefited from the sponsorship granted by the Centre for Research in the Arts, Social Sciences and Humanities (CRASSH) at the University of Cambridge. Comprising lightly edited versions of papers presented at the conference, this volume reflects the aim of the research project as a whole: to stimulate discussion about the diverse critical languages employed in today's scholarship and criticism, and also to explore the challenge of using language to investigate non-linguistic artistic media. The increasingly interdisciplinary research within modern humanities demands new methods and can yield fresh insights, as well as presenting some tonic difficulties.

The book thus brings together the work of some of the most distinctive voices in criticism, both established and upcoming, from across a wide range of disciplines within the humanities. The contributors are active as international scholars in fields centring on aesthetics, the visual arts, music, dance, history, literature, science writing, philosophy, and psychoanalysis. While each contributor pursues a particular concern, all show a commitment to comparative thinking within a wider interdisciplinary perspective and to elaborating the links and analysing the conceptual interfaces between different forms of cultural expression. Many of the essays aim in both topic and chosen style to reach beyond the academic domain. They stimulate a kind of critical writing and thinking that engages the wider public readership, seeking to reach beyond the jargon and the epistemological constraints of individual disciplines while remaining coherent and incisive. Some of the contributors have already had a powerful impact in this regard through the very nature of their work, and the conference offered an exceptional opportunity to debate these approaches.

Within two generations, interdisciplinary studies have revolutionized and energized scholarship, teaching, and research worldwide, perhaps more so than any other recent intellectual or academic trend. No longer is it possible (if it ever was) even to attempt to 'master' one discrete field as a wholly independent inquiry, each with its own unique and peculiar diagnostic, analytical, and lexical tools, not to mention historiographical traditions. This was never the case in reality, but there was a reluctance and shyness, perhaps born of a fear of intellectual hubris, about the possibilities of looking beyond the boundaries of one's own field, or faculty.

One of the great benefits that has come from the post-modern dissolution of these departmental boundaries, between high and popular culture, between the academy and the marketplace, between scholarship and the mass media, has been an awareness (and sometimes a willingness to embrace) the interconnectedness of the arts, humanities, and sciences and their methodologies. This in its turn has demanded recognition of the ways in which aesthetic discourses are not only continuous, similar, and comparable, but also sometimes un-exchangeable, incompatible, and exclusive. Hence the name of the project: *New Languages for Criticism: Cross-Currents and Resistances.* We have been concerned with aesthetic, linguistic, and conceptual cross-currents, in the sense of intermittent or continuous confluence, as well as seeking to explore instances of non-adaptability or open conflict between the different areas of research, their subject matters, and forms of discourse. Other questions concern critical style. Many critics feel it proper to avoid a personal style of writing. But might a more immediate and individualized description of our responses, possibly in the spirit of 'close reading', lead to more piercing and more sympathetic analysis? Or is the outcome of such an approach likely to be merely atomism?

With these concerns in mind, the reader will be interested to know that the original inspiration for the project *New Languages for Criticism: Cross-Currents and Resistances* came from a critical text which seemed to raise, through its unconventional tone, thought-structure, and line of argument all those intricate issues that interdisciplinary criticism holds in store: Theodor W. Adorno's musico-philosophical essay of 1928 on the composer Franz Schubert.[1] This text became the focus of the first conference organized by the project. What brought together the three directors of the project was, perhaps above all, their shared passion for music. Other affinities included European literature and poetry, philosophy, psychoanalysis, and the visual arts. The first members joining the project in its initial year 2002–03 and mostly coming from Cambridge University widened the range of disciplines even further to explore questions of interdisciplinary research in fortnightly meetings, often through discussion of challenging texts from different disciplines. By means of study days and conferences in the subsequent three years, the project provided a unique framework for bringing together many more scholars of different generations and different humanities disciplines to explore the critical languages currently in use in each of their specialist areas, and to experiment with the possibilities for constructive exchange between these languages. One of the project's main aims has been to create, via such public events, forums through which it becomes possible to promote public debate concerning the very nature of research in the arts, social sciences, and humanities. Another aim was to contribute to current discussions about the place of the 'humanities research culture' in society today, in Britain and beyond. The hope has been to contribute to a better public understanding of university-based research and to allow that research fruitful public outcomes.

During its four years of existence *New Languages for Criticism: Cross-Currents and Resistances* generated altogether nine conferences. Some of these meetings took place at the invitation of and in collaboration with academic and cultural institutions in Britain and France, thus reaching beyond the halls and walls of Cambridge, though setting out from as well as returning to it:

1. *Adorno's Schubert*, focusing on the kind of critical language the German philosopher used in his essay on the composer: King's College, Cambridge University, 22 February 2003.[2]
2. *In(ter)discipline: New Languages for Criticism*, which forms the topic of this book: Sidney Sussex and Faculty of Music, Cambridge University, 20–21 September 2003.[3]
3. *The Uncanny Day*, exploring the phenomenon and idea of Freud's Uncanny in music, literature, philosophy, and art: in collaboration with Tate Liverpool and the University of Liverpool, 5 March 2004.[4]
4. *Music and Literature I*, on verbal evocations of music: Christ's College, Cambridge University, 7 May 2004.[5]
5. *Theodor W. Adorno et l'avant-garde artistique*, on Adorno's critical writings about modernism: in collaboration with the Centre de Recherches sur les Arts and le Langage (CRAL) of the École des Hautes Études et Sciences Sociales (EHESS) in Paris, 28 May 2004.[6]
6. *Writing Dance*, an exploration of the journalistic and theoretical critical languages used in dance studies: in collaboration with the Laban Centre of Dance, London, 10 September 2004.[7]
7. *Music and Literature II*, focusing on the use of musical language and musical analysis in literary critiques: in collaboration with the Institute for Advanced Studies in the Humanities at the University of Edinburgh, 20 November 2004.[8]
8. *Music, Poetry and Sense Experience*, a bilingual conference on the sense of the senses in music, literature, poetry, and the cognitive sciences: in collaboration with CRAL at the EHESS, Paris, 10–11 June 2005.[9]
9. *Why Art Matters*, a conference on the function and role of art in society, and a tribute to Malcolm Bowie: Clare Hall, Cambridge University, 12 December 2005.[10]

The interdisciplinary approach we fostered through the project is realized in the scope of this book. We hope the reader will be able to find inspiration in the writings assembled here. They are all, in one way or another, reflections on the nature of translation and affect: how can we transmit facts and interpretations, sense and sensations between the disciplines, between different artistic media, between cultures, and across the private as well as the public sphere? What are the advantages, the difficulties and risks involved? If single disciplines have come to produce their own technologies of reading and writing, may that result in too well established modes of thinking? How can we investigate the process of looking for, asking, and answering (or failing to answer) questions which may at times have gone stale? How does one break the routine to propose and practise alternative critical languages?

Acknowledgements

Neither this book nor a project such as *New Languages for Criticism: Cross-Currents and Resistances* could have materialized, or thrived, as the project did over four years, without the enthusiasm, engagement, and commitment of a great number of people who all contributed to its success. Thanks go above all to the three directors of the Centre for Research in the Arts, Social Sciences and Humanities at Cambridge University: Ian Donaldson, its first director from 2001, Ludmilla Jordanova, director between 2003 and 2005, and Mary Jacobus, its present director; also to its excellent administrative team for their continuous help and generous support. Special thanks go to those who, in addition to providing fascinating intellectual contributions, played key roles in co-organizing, hosting, and sometimes securing significant additional funds for some of our events: Esteban Buch and Jean-Marie Schaeffer, directors of the Centre de Recherches sur les Arts et le Langage at the École des Hautes Études en Sciences Sociales (EHESS) in Paris; Peter Dayan from the University of Edinburgh; Christoph Grunenberg, director of Tate Liverpool; Jean Khalfa (Trinity College), Nick Marston (King's College), and Lucia Ruprecht (Emmanuel College), University of Cambridge. Thanks also go to Christopher Prendergast for his encouragement.

Gillian Beer, Malcolm Bowie, Beate Perrey

Malcolm Bowie's untimely death in 2007 robbed us and many others of a dear friend and collaborator. This volume is in a real sense the outcome of his inspiration.

Our particular thanks go to Alison Finch for making available to us the manuscript of Chapter 7, for her thoughtful editing, and for her help throughout the months when this book finally began to take its present shape. Thanks also go to Legenda Press, Oxford, to Ritchie Robertson, Graham Nelson, and Polly Fallows, as well as to Holger Stüwe, for their skill and kind assistance in the making of this book, and to Liverpool University for offering crucial financial assistance.

Gillian Beer, Beate Perrey

Notes to Preface

1. Adorno's essay has been published in a new English translation prepared by Jonathan Dunsby and Beate Perrey with an introduction and commentaries by Kofi Agawu, Esteban Buch, Scott Burnham, Jonathan Dunsby, Richard Leppert, and Beate Perrey in *19th-Century Music*, 29 (2005–06), 3–63.
2. Many colleagues have been part of the project as speakers and discussants at the various events we organized, all of which were devoted to the theme of *In(ter)discipline*. Though their papers may not appear in this book, to these many friends, colleagues, and former students we are much indebted even as their names appear only in the form of plain alphabetical lists. Speakers at the Adorno Day included Nikolaus Bacht, Musicology (King's College, Cambridge), Jonathan Dunsby, Music Theory (Eastman School of Music, University of Rochester), Lydia Goehr, Philosophy (Columbia University), Simon Jarvis, Literature, Philosophy, Theory (University of Cambridge), Andreas Mayer, History and Philosophy of Science (University of Cambridge), Ben Morgan, German intellectual history (University of Oxford), Max Paddison, Music Aesthetics (University of Durham), Christian Thorau, Music Theory (Musikhochschule Frankfurt).

3. We are grateful to Hugo Azérad, French Poetry (University of Cambridge), Scott Burnham, Musicology (Princeton University), Ingo Berensmeyer, English Literary, Cultural, and Media Studies (University of Siegen), Simon McBurney, Artistic Director of the Théâtre de Complicité, London, Bruce Robbins, Cultural Theory (Columbia University), Derek Scott, Popular Musicology (University of Leeds), Elinor Shaffer, Comparative Literature and Criticism (School of Advanced Study, University of London), Marilyn Strathern, Anthropology (University of Cambridge), Stephen Thomson, Literature and Science (University of Reading), Catherine Toal, Literary Theory (European College of Liberal Arts Berlin).
4. Thanks go to Stephen Clark, Philosophy (University of Liverpool), Penny Florence, Art History and Theory (Slade School of Fine Art, University College London), Alyce Mahon, Art History (University of Cambridge),
5. Thanks go to Suzie Clark, Music Theory (University of Oxford), Natasha Goldberg, Music and European Languages (University of Cambridge).
6. Thanks go to Jean-Paul Olive, Music Aesthetics (Université de Paris VIII), Makis Solomos, Musicology (Université de Montpellier III), Jean-Marie Schaeffer, Art History (CRAL, EHESS).
7. Thanks go to Valerie Briginshaw, Dance (University College Chichester), Ramsay Burt, Dance History (De Montfort University), Emilyn Claid, Choreographer and Dance Artist (Dartington College of Arts), Martin Hargreaves, Dance Critic (Laban Centre of Dance, London), Dee Reynolds, Performance Studies (University of Manchester), Ana Sanchez-Colberg, Choreographer (Laban Centre of Dance, London).
8. Thanks go to Martin Dixon, Music and Philosophy (University of Glasgow), David Evans, Modern French Poetry (University of St Andrews), David J Gascoigne, Modern French Fiction (University of St Andrews), Mikhail Karikis, Media Art <http://www.mikhailkarikis.com/index.html>, Janina Klassen, Musicology (Musikhochschule Freiburg), Angela Leighton, English Poetry and Literature (Trinity College, Cambridge), Emma Sutton, Literature and Music (University of St Andrews).
9. Thanks go to Jérôme Dokic, Philosophy and Cognitive Sciences (École des Hautes Études en Sciences Sociales, Institut Jean-Nicod), Martin Kaltenecker, Musicology (CRAL, EHESS), Laura Odello, Philosophy (Université de Paris VIII / University of Trieste), Susan Stewart, Poetry and Criticism (Princeton University).
10. Thanks go to Peter de Bolla, Cultural History and Aesthetics (University of Cambridge), Rachel Bowlby, English Literature and Psychoanalytic Theories (University College London), Marian Hobson, Philosophy (Queen Mary, University of London), Brian Hurwitz, Art and Medicine (King's College London), Roger Pearson, Modern French Literature (University of Oxford), Jacqueline Rose, Psychoanalysis, Feminism, Literature (Queen Mary, University of London), Clive Scott, European Literature (University of East Anglia), Adam Thirlwell, Literature (All Souls College, Oxford), John Tusa, Arts, Society and Politics (Barbican Centre, London).

CHAPTER 1

❖

What If? The Language of Affect

Mieke Bal

Imagine three huge video screens between which you are standing. For thirteen and a half minutes you are immersed in a world partly like your own — enough to fool you into considering what you see as possible — and partly radically different — enough to make you feel uneasy. The predominant colour is green. No music accompanies the single, female voice, which speaks without ostensive emotion. You don't understand the spoken language and so resort to the subtitles. I take this work as an entrance into the question of art criticism today.

Eija-Liisa Ahtila's three-screen video installation *The House* (2002) raises numerous questions, all of which ultimately concern the work's own status and modes of legibility. Together they ask what matters in the relationship between art and the world from which it emerges, to which it responds, and to which it returns its reflections. I will examine how this complex, multiple questioning is performed, then take this 'how' as a kind of model for the new language of criticism — in other words, I will take this work as a 'theoretical object'. In particular, I will explore how it proposes *affect* as a basis for interacting with art. This may seem paradoxical for a piece whose main character appears particularly affect-less. But I argue that this paradox is precisely the point of affect, as the basis for an art that heeds Brecht's lessons *against* identification and *for* commitment. Although the character's 'affect-less' diction and appearance preclude emotional identification and thoughtless empathy, this emptiness leaves the artwork open for an affective encounter of a third kind.[1]

The legibility of this video installation is hampered by a kind of super-legibility. Straightforwardly accessible in imagery and soundtrack, *The House* speaks clear languages — but, indeed, in the plural. The sight of a toy car driving across a living-room wall, a cow walking into an unremarkable house, and a woman flying through the trees, it is easy to think of such fairy-tale-like stories as Astrid Lindgren's *Pippi Långstrump* (*Pippi Longstocking*). After all, Pippi had a horse in her living room. And Pippi's namesake, Pippilotti Rist, deployed this profoundly satisfying discursive mode in her 1997 video *Ever Is All Over,* where a dreamy-looking young woman smashes car windows with a huge flower. When we realize that this fairy-girl is Rist herself, and after we have seen a police officer turn from a threat into a winking, supportive woman, we know that, in their mode of representation, fairy tales can hide an undercurrent of darkness.[2]

This will be a useful reminder if we consider the fairy-tale genre as a code for Ahtila's work, and, conversely, if we consider her work as a commentary on that genre. This — the first of five readings that I will give of Ahtila's video installation — is obviously both right and wrong. It is right because it helps counter the darker mood that the work also elicits; as a recasting of a literary genre, it prepares us for the increasing complexity that its successive layers of meaning generate; and as an activation of a traditional linguistic genre, it raises the issue of interdisciplinarity. It is wrong, though, because this issue is raised with a specific clarity, in that the fairy-tale aspects of the installations are primarily visual, emerging more from what we see than from what we hear the woman in the video say, whereas the original fairy-tale genre belongs to the literary domain. Moreover, beyond the question of the imbrication of genre and medium, this installation's struggle with legibility embodies interdisciplinarity in specific ways that I hope to clarify. The various readings that *The House* elicits, then rejects as too limited, succeed, merge, contradict, and compete with one another all at the same time.

Each of the multiple layers of meaning, I will argue in presenting my own five readings, bleeds out of the previous one, which continues to flow in and through its successor. Together they thus build up to form, in the end, the political aesthetic of the work: its affect-based commitment. The question 'What if ...?' sums up this aesthetic. Imagine this question as suddenly being uttered mentally by the viewer, who is holding her breath, while at the same time uncertainty about meaning and its displacement produce a suspense that is not about what happens next in the story but about what happens within us — we who are caught in the interstices between the image and the reality on which it impinges.

Affect as a Medium

'What if ...?' suggests play, play-acting, the unreality of fiction, a resonance of 'once upon a time'. As the polyphony of the installation's tone suggests, fairy tales should not be underestimated. The fantasy of being able to fly, with birds singing all around you, plays on an almost universal desire for liberation from all the natural and conventional restraints placed upon human life, such as the force of gravity. It both appeals to and activates deeply buried affective childhood memories in each viewer. The car that defies gravity and conspires with your contrary wish to defy your parents' sense of order is, likewise, so attractive that seeing such marvels on video screens can enable the viewer to enter the mind of the child within us all; what if the wished-for omnipotence of the child were to become real?

Mediating between the fictional figure on the screen and the viewer's own memories, desires, and disappointments, these images, which recall fairy tales, can be qualified as *affection-images*. This Deleuzian term need not be, as it often is, associated with the human — or digital, 'posthuman' — face. Rather, it refers to images which neither mediate (Deleuze uses the significant verb 'translation') between the viewer and the image nor lead to action but which elicit a temporary conflation of subject and object. As Mark Hansen argues in a different but related context, Deleuze identifies the affect-image he spotted in the close-ups of classical cinema not only *with* but *as* the face. Deleuze wrote:

> There is no close-up of the face. The close-up is the face, but the face precisely in so far as it has destroyed its triple function [individuation, socialization, communication] [...] The close-up turns the face into a phantom [...] The face is the vampire.[3]

The view of the close-up image qua face, standing in as *face* instead of the human face, becomes increasingly relevant as Ahtila's installation continues. In this chapter I will suggest that the flying woman is just such a 'face', without even being a close-up of the object represented; it is a close-up of and to the viewer that collapses subject with object.

For Hansen, this Deleuzian view leads affect away from the viewer's body. In contrast, in what Hansen calls 'digital-facial-images' (DFI), the viewer's body is directly addressed and hence mobilized, not into action but into affective response. Regardless of the relevance of oppositional reasoning here, the viewer's body, although not forced into motion as in interactive video, is swept into the motion that is observed and within which the three-screen installation has positioned it. The sensations of flying among the treetops, of weightlessness, and of becoming a child again are (albeit very slightly) experienced as though real — at least by this viewer.[4]

Except that ... the narrator and central character of the story is an adult woman. This discrepancy between childish fantasy and adult presence is not easily overcome. Nor does the woman have the dreamy-eyed cheerfulness and ethereal appearance of Rist's character. But if the fairy tale disappears at the very moment it emerges, what, then, are we to make of these fantastic events? The fugitive nature of this interdiscourse — its inescapable participation yet minor role in *The House* — sets in motion an increasingly complex bundle of indexes of interdiscursive references that initially confuse the viewer, some of which remain literary. To start with, the house in *The House* is a haunted house. In this respect, it has something in common with the nineteenth-century genre of the fantastic, although it lacks the bleak darkness of that genre. Importantly for this installation, the fantastic is a genre that wavers between the real and the imaginary, the possible and the impossible, and which occurs outside subjectively imagined events.[5]

What, then, is the point, for a reflection on art criticism, of this invocation of 'alien' discourses? According to the published information on *The House*, the story emerged from something that is the opposite of childish wish-fulfilment in tales of wonders. The story is based on interviews with women who have experienced the trauma of psychosis. This makes much more sense, though not straight away, or unambiguously. Like the fairy-tale elements, the psychotic state is not revealed immediately. Both creep up on the viewer after a rather ordinary beginning — ordinary enough, that is, to reassure us, so that the expectation of 'naturality' (that everything happens according to the natural flow) makes our understanding lag behind our perception. This discrepancy creates space for the operation of affect as a medium.

The status of affect as a medium in and of itself suspends the relevance, though not the presence, of the heterogeneity of visual imagery and literature. Instead, something like 'mood' becomes the 'language' through which the work speaks. For between the childhood memories invoked through the fairy-tale elements and the anguish that defines the experience of psychosis, an uneasy mixture of two opposing moods fills the interaction between the work and the viewer with affect. Affect as a medium, then, will remain in place throughout the installation.

The Camera as Narrator

The woman around whom the story evolves, Elisa, drives her car, parks it, and enters her house: all entirely ordinary, everyday actions. That the car drives back and forth for a while is strange, but whether this is a phenomenon from a fictional world or a disturbed perception of the real world is not immediately clear. At first, when the sound of her footsteps continues after Elisa has left the three screens on which her images are projected, even this appears quite normal. Keen to understand the installation as a work of visual art — as a work of, specifically, the digital moving image of video — we expect this continuation to be an aural transition that will allow the camera to pick up the image of the woman once she is inside. This video-technical response is one element in the interdisciplinary merging whereby it becomes impossible to respond to this work from a 'pure' visual-art perspective. That the transition, through a cutaway shot from the woman outside to the woman inside, does not happen, that the house is empty and the ticking of the clock takes over from the sound of the footsteps, is only the slightest bit odd; then it becomes normal again. After all, clocks do tick, whether someone is at home or not.

At this point, we can make a first leap to what would have been called, in the old days of methodological optimism, a 'meta-language' — a term that I will ultimately avoid. The 'meta-language' here would be the one not of literature itself but of the narrative theory deployed to analyse and understand literature. The reasoning would run somewhat as follows: so far, the camera functions as *narrator*; that is, the visual medium takes upon itself a role traditionally reserved for linguistic subjects, by whom narrative statements are uttered. The language of art criticism uses this term quite freely, in the same way as it deploys the terms 'visual language', 'idiom', and 'discourse'. Although this transfer from one discipline to another can be productively examined for its methodological consequences, for now I will simply point it out as a first site of theoretical reflection, and consider the term 'meta-language' as a conceptual metaphor.[6]

But such a meta-language is useful only if it helps us in our need to be specific — that is, to understand *this* artwork. How does the camera act *here*, in its role as narrator? The story unfolds with the woman, Elisa, at its centre. The camera represents her at a distance, whether the shots are long, medium, or close-up. The enduring centrality of one character is good reason to extend Deleuze's thoughts on the close-up *as* face to this work. Ongoing centrality can be considered a temporal version of the close-up. Even invested with narrative power, the camera obeys the rule of the 'affection-image' thus installed. With this initial situation in mind, the notion that the camera is a narrator becomes specific: its operation is drawn into the character's orbit.

This becomes clear as soon as we follow the video's lead, of which the camera is but one embedded element. The beginning of the video functions like a so-called 'third-person narrative' (where we follow a character who does not intervene in her own representation). She drives, walks, sits, lies down, and sews and hangs black curtains. But the conceptual metaphor of the camera as narrator takes a decisive turn when the camera and voice begin to intersect, in other words, when visuality gives way to intermediality. When Elisa's voice begins to tell her story, in the grammar of the first-person narrative, the distance that seemed so 'normal' is disrupted, broken.[7]

This is also the moment when the interdiscourse of psychosis enters the scene and a second reading of this installation becomes possible. While we see oddities happen, the woman tells us about things that only a state of psychosis can explain. Slowly, as she takes over from the distancing mode of narration, everything we consider 'normal' or 'natural' slowly falls away and Elisa's world comes to appear as delusional. She explains that her car and her garden enter her living room. The autonomously driven car becomes a character, which we can still accept if we activate the genre of the fairy tale, especially as the car crawling over the wall is given the miniature dimensions of a toy car. But a garden? Later, sounds and images enter her mind. Hearing voices, hallucinating, is, indeed, the key symptom of psychosis.

Elisa is quite lucid about what is happening to her: she is looking out of her window and sees her car and the trees. Then she takes a step to the left, behind a striped curtain, and, she says, can no longer see these things. Well, this is to be expected when your gaze is blocked by a screen, isn't it? Different places offer different views, or 'shots': long, medium, close-up, or even totally blank. Elisa's vision, far from incoherent, may appear psychotic precisely because it is so 'unnaturally' consistent here, and because vision acts as a narrator. It enacts a Deleuzian perception; far from being a passive absorption of the visual field, according to Deleuze's source Bergson, perception is an active selection and isolation of the interest of life.

The move behind the curtain, to 'explain' how vision is always actively limited, is, moreover, prepared by an earlier shot. There, a following shot across the space of Elisa's living room was necessary in order to keep centring on her as she gets up from the sofa and starts walking. The moving living-room space, set off against the central image of the moving body, entirely normal and routine for the experienced cinema viewer, becomes in retrospect utterly strange here, where Elisa proposes limited vision as a phenomenon of estrangement. Her move behind the curtain and the shot that makes the room in which she stands move behind her are partners in a discussion on perception. No wonder it is not so easy for the viewer to declare her 'mad'.

In this particularly striking shot — striking because we recognize it as normal cinema fare, suddenly estranging because it matches Elisa's experience of estrangement — the narrating camera espouses the Deleuzian movement-image as a literalized 'travelling concept'. The shot is conceptual because it theorizes perception; it travels because it transforms standard views of that act; the travelling is literalized through the background tracking of the next shot. But it is through the interaction with Elisa's analysis of her perception and its limits that the shot is endowed with this theoretical relevance. All fixity is gone. The shot comes to embody a de-naturalized, impossible perception. In the very act of centring, the image de-centres, unfixes, unmoors the 'natural' surrounding in which the figure bathes To cite Paola Marrati, this is an instance where 'la mobilité de la caméra, la variabilité des angles de cadrage réintroduisent toujours des zones acentrées et décadrées par rapport à n'importe quel "sujet percevant"' [the mobility of the camera, the variability of the angles of framing always reintroduce acentric zones, de-framed in relation to whatever 'perceiving subject'].[8] Taking narration into her own hands, Elisa's self-doubt compounds our own doubt about the metaphorical use of the term *narrator.*

But this is not a competition between the visual medium (the camera) and the linguistic medium (Elisa's voice). At this point the woman's voice describes what can be seen as different positions of *focalization*. The voice estranges us from what we consider normal shifts in visual representation, thus foregrounding a self-reflexivity of the medium through an estrangement that begins to suggest mental disturbance. When the sound of the car's engine is louder than would seem possible from behind closed doors, something appears to be wrong. Is it the woman, the film's sound engineer, or the viewer's own ears that are slightly discrepant? Too loud, too long, too close. Otherwise, all is well inside this house.

The process of psychological shifts from normal to deviant continues to operate hand in hand with increasingly complex questions about the mixed medium of video. For example, Elisa looks up from her sewing, sees a man outside with a dog, then tells us that the dog came inside to sniff her. Bizarre, but even stranger, is her level, quiet voice: 'By chance', she adds. This small addition brings up an entire metaphysical thought system that she starts talking about a little later. Causality is suspended: 'By chance', she says, followed by: 'It came [...] into the same space, where there were no longer any walls.' Despite a flicker of doubt due to the philosophical resonances of the phrase 'by chance', the assumption that we are looking at a psychotic experience is increasingly strongly confirmed.[9]

Singularizing the Senses: Destroying Time-Space

Elisa hangs the black curtains, she says, to 'shut out the images. When I don't see anything, I'm where the noises are. In the street, on the shore, on the ship.' Seeing hinders being. Hearing and seeing can no longer occur simultaneously, and being has to align itself with one of the two. Elisa chooses sound over images. For a short time, then, it is relatively easy to view this video installation as an account of psychosis. Its triptych form makes it easy for our senses to identify with the experience of seeing images and hearing sounds, and the unsettling discrepancies between them. Standing between the three screens, we are inside Elisa's head. This second interpretation, based on psychosis, makes more sense than the first one, based on the fairy tale, while also accommodating those elements (the toy car driving across the wall, the cow walking into the house, the woman flying across the treetops) that suggested that genre. But the second reading does not push away the first; rather, it absorbs it. The continued presence of the first reading within the second maintains a tension that is internal to the installation.

This tension requires a reflection on the work's modes of legibility, while at the same time it keeps any attempt to answer with an unambiguous decision at bay. I consider this to be the critical moment in the installation's theorizing of issues of interdisciplinarity, and in the difficulty of developing a meta-language in the face of the complex relationship between artwork and, say, the 'real world'. As will become clear, this work of theorizing is continued throughout the thirteen-and-a-half-minute duration of the installation. But as the work advances, it 'thickens' intellectual theorizing with something I will end up calling the 'language of affect'.

If the question is whether we are watching a fairy-tale work of fantasy or a mentally disturbed woman, we are confronted with the impossibility of deciding. This impossibility is an intellectual challenge, bound up with an implicit critique of binary opposition as the predominant mode of thought in Western cultures. But given the stark difference in mood between the two choices, the dilemma begins to affect our own sense of 'having a grasp'. It becomes doubtful whether this is an intellectual challenge only. On the one hand, if an intellectual Westerner is asked to understand the mental processes of a psychotic patient, he may feel this is not easy, but at the same time, aided by the usual technical resources, he may realize that this intellectual understanding is not impossible. On the other hand, having the experience of psychosis requires a disturbing kind of 'tourism' many will baulk at.

The invitation to 'tourism', in turn, becomes questionable when we realize that psychosis may be at issue. But the character herself is not psychotic in any obvious way. True, the psychotic patient experiences sense perceptions and thoughts as both bodily and located in outside objects. This matches the states and events Elisa tells us about. We see, after all, the car on the wall and hear the loud sounds of a paddleboat, and she tells us about a ship in the harbour while the friend she is having dinner with fades into inaudibility. But there is also no sign of pain, of suffering, whereas a psychotic experience of unchecked falling or disrupted sense perception is terrifying, unbearably so.

Just as there is no overt expression of joy, so there is no overt expression of pain. The slow-motion flying among the trees looks more like dream-imagery than like the agony of an unmoored personality. When the woman has finished sewing the blackout curtains, she appears to have trouble walking, as if the floor, too, has lost its natural solidity. In this brief moment, Ahtila's work evokes other experiments with perception in contemporary art (such as, for example, Ann Veronica Janssens's light installations) rather than the anxiety of mental illness.[10] Moreover, once she has hung up the curtains, Elisa steps down from the windowsill in a normal, natural movement. Clearly, her action has dealt with the problem quite efficiently. And although it lacks the light-hearted cheer of Rist's character, her face never expresses anxiety either. Here I wish to suggest that the affect-less appearance and performance at the moments of heightened psychotic content do not deprive this work of affect. On the contrary. Since we can deal with the strange events only by assuming the psychotic state of the character, but at the same time cannot settle into an easy visual match for that state, the installation puts the burden of affective response on the viewer. It is the viewer, not the character, who is tortured by the increasing number of uncertainties and shifts.[11]

Since sounds are so central to *The House* that they take on a certain autonomy and narrative agency, thus further complicating the extension of the term 'narrator' from discourse to camera to — now — sound, the quality of Elisa's voice is a significant gear shift for a move to a third interpretation, in which the work questions its own status as narrative. Like the fairy-tale elements, the psychotic state is represented and told in an even, philosophical, exploratory mode, both visually and orally, a philosophical tenor that has already been announced through the modernist key term 'by chance'.

Elisa looks and talks normally. So does the medium through which her story is cast: the trees, and her living room, look normal. Whatever happens — and strange things do happen — the aesthetic of these magnificent visual and aural images is rigorously realistic. No spectacular special effects are used, for example. This is not to say that the work espouses the *rhetoric* of realism, which is, after all, a special effect put in the service of a belief in the constructed world as natural.[12] Here the realistic mode or style of representation has its own meaning, although it is not so easy to understand what this meaning might be. Perhaps the two discourses, the textual genre and the discourse of mental disturbance, are traps. Both, in opposite ways — the one as wish fulfilment, the other as terror — put us on the wrong foot, that is, if we seek to use them to 'translate' the work into a readable meaning. But they put us on the right foot if their apparent incompatibility makes us endorse the reluctance to translate, to understand too fast, and to declare meaning at the cost of the work's complexity. For untranslatability and the concomitant focus on the 'remainder' lie in the seams between these discourses. This is a second theoretical moment — the one where the idea of a meta-language as distinct from the object-language is presented as rigorously impossible. It is also the moment where the search for meaning is checked, suspended, and redirected towards ambiguity and multiplicity. It is the moment, in other words, where the boundary between intellect and affect breaks down.

As I suggested earlier, both the textual genre and the discourse of mental disturbance genres have a tendency to produce an affect — one light, one dark — that touches us only slightly, enough to arouse wonderment but not enough to cause joy or pain. Enough, though, to prepare us for the profound philosophical questioning that both the child and the psychotic can inspire. What if this work is not at all 'about' fantasy or psychosis but only uses those discourses to do something else altogether? If this is the case, then the 'meta-language' of art lies in art's heterogeneity itself. Moreover, translation becomes a constant, inherent activity that can never end in a so-called 'target-language'.

Together, what the two genres do, I submit, is pose rather than answer the questions of legibility and of the registers involved in reading. Thus they fold the work onto itself, and pose the question of how to make a meaning that does not foreclose the work in its recalcitrant otherness or in its reluctance to limit its speech to the intellectual register.

In this third reading, then, the work questions its own status as narrative. The conceptual metaphor — of the camera and sound as narrators — is put in jeopardy.

Again the indications of this self-reflective enfolding of the work onto itself are subtle and slow to hit home. While Elisa is confronted with the disappearance of her protective walls, the viewer wonders about the voice-over's wavering use of verb tense. We see the dog, but she tells the story — not only in the present, but also, at times, in the past. Some of the most clearly 'psychotic' episodes are told as an ordinary story. 'The car didn't stay completely parked in the garden today', she says, with a clear awareness of temporal specificity. Similarly, Elisa specifies both space and time when she states the radical dissociation of sound from image in one of the most explicit sentences: 'Yesterday I was sitting with a friend at a restaurant table eating, and I started hearing the sounds of a paddleboat [...] I didn't actually always hear my friend even though I could see her opposite me.'

This keen detailing of the time-space specificity, together with the disturbing melting of the walls and the severance of the sound from the image, is a first indication that it is storytelling itself that is at stake here. Traditional storytelling is accompanied by its simultaneous impossibility. As if responding to the primal deception of storytelling (the phrase 'once upon a time', which safely sets the story-world in a different time frame), when the walls fall away — she says — 'everything is now simultaneous, here, being'. Being and time, *Sein und Zeit*, are torn apart. This severance makes narrative as we know it impossible.[13]

What if ...? poses the question what would storytelling be if the natural, normal, ordinary time of the subject were no longer valid? At one level, the central, focal character remains the holder of the point of view, while at the same time being inside her own focalization. In first-person narrative this is quite normal, although in the present case the structure suspends the logic of focalization, however subliminally. For example, the loud sounds, disconnected from visual perception, 'formed', she says, 'another space in my head, where I was simultaneously'. On the other hand, the sounds *are* detached from the image — in our perception as well as hers. They raise the question of where, who, is the subject? What if ... she was right and I was wrong? This question induces a profound self-doubt, which cannot but entail an affective sense of our own being falling away, an affective encounter that skirts the abyss of where the boundaries between self and other melt into air.

Overdetermined by its long history in Western art, and by its connection to religion in altarpieces that gives it a solemn importance, the triptych form of the installation serves one of its multifaceted functions here. Standing between the screens, surrounded by the sounds of the boat, we are inside that sound-generated space. But, like Elisa, we lose hold of our subjectivity. The specificity — of both the noun and the sound, the tense and the perception — of the paddleboat assaults our sense of stability.

Why so specifically a paddleboat? As we shall see below, boats overwhelmingly signify the contemporary phenomenon of the refugee. In the context of a bygone time, however, and taken, with its descriptive precision, to denote riverboats on the Mississippi in the Southern USA, the paddleboat is also reminiscent of a past that we have interpreted, perhaps too easily, in terms of its past-ness: slavery. Refugees on ships, constantly in mortal danger yet unable to stay where they lived before, challenge temporal sequentiality. Sometimes they stay at sea, sometimes they are forced to return, sometimes they drown or manage to get ashore. They also challenge the development narrative created by the Enlightenment. After slavery — freedom?, the paddleboat seems to ask. 'After' becomes a decidedly ironic preposition.

Similarly, space — both spatial distance and orientation — are put under pressure. When we see Elisa floating among the treetops, our distance from her increases and we are kicked out of that newly created inside-space. It is no longer so clear that the fictional space of the story is inside Elisa's head. From the moment the sound starts to disconnect itself from the images and to move through the temporary halting place to become our spatial surrounding, the fictional space, in its stubborn refusal to satisfy our sense of what is normal, our sense of 'naturality', becomes a character in its own right. With that emancipation of sound, the unity of time and space in which stories are usually set, or chronotope, as well as the unity of vision and hearing in perception that holds the subject together, are definitively exploded.[14]

All the 'natural' — that is, conventional — elements of narrative founder in this work. But this foundering does not occur without difficulty. It is foregrounded, since Elisa comments on it, and interrupted in turn, when temporal and spatial specificity is, for brief moments, restored — lest we forget what naturality looks like and how it can disappear. The unity of the chronotope resonates only as a shadow of the naturality of storytelling that is lost, the past shadow of our ease with stories, visual and verbal. Lost is the centrality and privilege of character, when sound becomes invested with anthropomorphic autonomy and cars and dogs traverse walls on their own. Lost is causality, the meaningfulness of living in a chronology where prior events determine the present, and present occurrences explain the past. Lost is the bond between human existence and a time and space whose proportionate scales envelop the subject. Lost is the logic by which we live, figured here together with the solidity of the ground we walk on. But these explorations, and this ensuing exploding of narrative, are not confined to this discursive mode alone. In its consequences, this exploration, by means of the disruption of the conventions of storytelling, tips over into a philosophical inquiry that questions the assumptions on the basis of which we live. Hence, this third mode of reading — the meta-theoretical probing of narrativity — spills over into a fourth.

Being in Time?

Here we enter another disciplinary domain, one that has often struggled with its own position as meta- or inter-discipline, namely philosophy. As an intellectual domain or (inter-)discipline, philosophy stands for high theory. But in its guise of ontological questioning, it impinges on our deepest sense of who we are, a sense involving affect as no longer separate from intellect. 'Things that occur no longer shed light on the past', says Elisa, philosophizing about time. This is a reversal of the routine Enlightenment notion that the past clarifies the present, and that the present must learn from the past. The temporal relationship of near-collapse, between the refugees on the paddleboat and the slaves they invoke, becomes even more alarming in light of this reversal.

What would happen if spatial and temporal existence were to lose their structures by being divorced from time and with space invading being? Symmetrical to the walls of the house falling away, Elisa's subjective wholeness becomes permeable and, like time, spreads out like a thin pudding suddenly deprived of its container. 'I meet people', she says. 'One at a time they step inside me and fill all the space.' This space, interior to Elisa, accommodating lots of people, must be magical (as in fairy tales, or *Alice's Adventures in Wonderland*), mad, post-humanist, post-logical, a baroque space where play with scale causes space to be no longer measurable or reliable because the representation has cut the space out of an unknown totality and leaves the frame out of sight. Here *The House* shows its 'baroque' hand, for it responds to and resonates with Caravaggio's art. (This play with scale is the profound, philosophical meaning of Caravaggio's scenes of spatial confinement, often attributed to a lack of spatial skills.)[15]

The utterance 'everything is now simultaneous' follows hard on the heels of the story of the dog that '*came* into the room' so that 'outside a new order *arose*, one that *is* present everywhere'. This narratological lack of clarity regarding past and present tense points to a profound disquiet concerning being in time. Symmetrical to this temporal confusion of past and present and time's flattening in simultaneity, the intermittent use of the past tense of storytelling precludes too close an identification with Elisa's temporal experience. As a result we cannot know for sure whether subjective experience — of the psychotic or unnatural existence, in a philosophical experiment — is at stake. Not knowing how to read this work is what Ahtila's installation wants for us, in its greedy, encompassing exploration of 'what if ...?'

'Being in time' is reversed to become 'Time being' in 'her', or 'me', if we play the game of affective enfolding that the work solicits. Kaja Silverman, speaking of Heidegger's notion of 'care', formulates this as a paradox: 'we are only really in the world when it is in us'.[16] We will see, towards the end of the thirteen-and-a-half-minute duration of the video installation,that literalizing this paradox is a way of acquiring political agency. Her work, then, philosophizes beyond philosophy. Such affectively laden thought-experiments instantiate the artwork's mission as theoretical object for a third time.

But however important a philosophical interpretation this thought-experiment may be, it does not suffice, and it is this inadequacy that may well be the work's primary philosophical thrust. Such an interpretation falls short of this specific work in one crucial sense. True, it helps to involve the viewer and unsettle the distancing that fantasy or mental illness continue to allow. This is truly paradoxical: far from being an exercise in thinking only, philosophy works affectively, even bodily. Moreover, this involvement in turn gives significance to the experiment with the explosion of narrative form, and hence to narrative as a cultural form. This is a second way, after that of acquiring political agency, in which the work lures philosophy outside its own boundaries. But this fourth, philosophical, interpretation, like the three interpretations that precede it and stay inside it, still fails our desire to 'get it'. For it leaves one key aspect of the work unexplained. That aspect is, to put it simply, the house.

That the work is named after, is set in, and unsettles a house cannot be taken lightly. Here the issue of gender comes in. After all, Elisa is a woman, and so is the artist. Moreover, the interviewees who provided the heuristic tool of psychosis were women, whereas psychosis also occurs in men. The setting of the fiction is a house, woman's traditional domain, which, like time, space, character, and focalization, is part of our naturalizing baggage when we confront cultural artefacts such as narratives or video installations that tell stories. The house, like the family, is a building block of Western individualist society, which, we might now surmise, drives its imprisoned inhabitants to psychosis. *The House*: the work's title suggests enclosure, as does its form of the enveloping triptych. It is the house whose walls fade. This might be thought of as the failure of protection. But what if there is another aspect to it — the liberation from individual confinement? The outside world enters Elisa's being — experience or reality. Or does the difference between those two also fall away? This house-aspect is reminiscent of Louise Bourgeois's series of works — drawings, engravings, and sculptures — called *Femme Maison*, in which the body of a woman merges into a house, forcefully suggesting the confining aspect, but also the domestic power, of women's lives.[17]

But adopting or endorsing this questioning of the house, and of the ideology pertaining to it, is not simply a thematic reference, as both art history and literary analysis might be tempted to assume. The outside world permeates the house, and thus also negates its very power to confine — from the inside, so to speak. Like gender, the outside world here is rather more specific than philosophy would normally permit. A first indication of this over-specification occurs when the cow walks quietly into the living room, just after we have heard a news reporter on the television talking about some disaster or crisis. In the era of mad cow disease and foot-and-mouth infection, the evocation of the disastrous bond between ecology and economy acutely inserts 'real-life' politics as a politics of domesticity into the representation of a woman whose psychotic tendencies have allegedly cut her loose from reality. Together the television and the news of crisis connect the medium of television with the chronotope, or specific time-space, of the contemporary world.

This invasion of politics into the artwork and of world matters into Elisa's destroyed privacy occurs a second time, at the moment when the paddleboat returns to haunt us. Later in the work, Elisa says: 'The ship you see on the horizon is the same ship as all the other ships. And this ship is full of the refugees who come to every shore.' Two separate philosophical statements are made here. First there is the collapse of individuation, which suspends boundaries. Or, to put it differently, the merging of token and type, of particularity and generality: one ship is every ship, one person is every person, one shore is all shores. As soon as one ship is singled out, it is already the generalized allegorical ship that brings refugees to *all* shores. This is not the delusion of a crazy person, but an extended examination of what happens if narrative is turned inside out and the concept of 'person' opened up. It is the logical consequence of the disappearance of walls and the expansion of simultaneity. Where time and space lose their boundaries and their reassuring ordering, Heidegger's 'care' enters the stage — again, literalized.

This generalization in particularity makes all people, including all refugees, everyone's concern. It is *The House*'s theory of *translation*, as opening up closed spaces without simply forgetting difference in an illusion of transparency. Instead, the speaking subject is transformed into someone literally affected by others who enter her space and thereby drastically morph it into a different ontology. All people exist at the same time and all are inside Elisa. This insideness, this creation of internal space, is the second philosophical statement uttered here. It brings us from psychosis as illness to psychosis as wisdom. For here the psychotic structure becomes a tool for the kind of reading that matters. It is about more than just concern: it is about identity, literally being-withness, everyone being part of everyone('s world).[18]

Strangely, though, temporal differentiation returns when we least expect it. 'Some of them only for a moment', she says, 'some stay'. Beyond what the model of mental illness allows us to imagine, and also beyond the generalizations of philosophy, what enters into Elisa's being is the world of others: refugees, people who come, some to stay, some to move on. Standing among Elisa's images, we are caught in this history of the present. Here lies the relevance of the mix of past and present tense, of simultaneity and of the present's failure to shed light on the past. Refugees inside you — what clearer image could there be of the impossibility of social, political indifference? This is, indeed, a key image of this work, an image of its own critical position. More than an image in the sense of representation based on a reflection on social issues, this key image of refugees as 'psychosis' poses an aesthetics of *ethical non-indifference*.[19]

Affect as a Language

Elisa's alleged psychosis now becomes the *medium* for philosophy. Given that this ethical aesthetic is embodied in a character who, on all counts, acts as if she is psychotic, the mood mentioned earlier as both dark and uninscribed on the figure of the woman now becomes the instrument of the affective encounter between the viewer and the artwork. Mood is affective: it can be conveyed in an affective transference. The affective blankness of the character of Elisa precludes identification on the level of mood, thus opening up the space for a different kind of use of the medium of affect. The point of this installation is obviously not to make us all feel tortured by psychotic delusions. Rather, if we are to be affected by Elisa's forceful 'thrownness into the world', we must, like her, somehow grasp the diversity of perspectives that make up the 'Being' of others who are there. Psychotic behaviour is an effective metaphor for this engagement with the world.[20]

As mentioned earlier, the word Heidegger uses for this engagement is *care*. He, too, shuns identification in any facile sense; that is, any sense in which either the other is reduced to a clone of ourselves, or we melt into sentiment and lose our agency.[21] The struggle against indifference as the sole alternative that results from this anti-identificatory politics retains its full actuality today. Silverman formulates the resulting paradox as follows: 'it is only by embracing other people and things that we can free them to be themselves — only by enfolding them within our psychic enclosure that we can create the space where they can emerge from concealment'.[22] This paradox, she writes, 'is resistant to all rationalizing gestures'. Perhaps art can do what thought and its writing in criticism, theory, and philosophy cannot. I submit that Ahtila's installation gives shape to this struggle. To place us in a spatial relationship of affective permeability with a woman who speaks like a delusional patient, who acts sometimes like an omnipotent child, and who shows us a blank face on which we are invited to project affect is her creative proposition towards a solution of the Heideggerian paradox.

Mood is essential to our being in the world, to our potential to envelop others in care without devouring them by stripping them of their diverse otherness. At the end of an explanation of mood in *Being and Time*, Heidegger writes emphatically: '*Essentially, a state-of-mind implies a disclosive submission to the world, out of which we can encounter something that matters to us.*'[23] It is because mood, the viewer's mood, is so essential that Elisa is put in charge, not of suffering from psychosis and eliciting our compassion, but of deploying psychotic perception as an (imaginative) means to demonstrate a possible way out of the paradox of 'care'. The installation itself — its three-screen enclosure, the immensity of the screens, the quality of the sound and images — is the conduit, or medium in the material sense, through which the resulting mood can be transferred to the viewer.

People enter Elisa while Elisa's images, voice, and experiences of discrepancy surround us. At this point, the screens, one after the other, turn red, blue, and green, not the black of the curtains that was meant to stop visual images from entering the room and that, simultaneously, locked us up in the dark movie theatre of Elisa's sound images. After all, that blackness was not really intended to keep out the world, but rather to cohabit with the sounds of the world. But the amorphic, monochromic screens are emptied of form, to become not black but colourful, literally so. And if the description of the people inside Elisa might sound frighteningly alienating for a brief moment — 'They set up wherever they want to and take my facial expressions or my leg's resting position' — we cannot but give the final words she speaks their full weight as 'conclusion': 'I shake and say to myself for a long time: good, really good.'

Interdisciplinarity

What strikes me immediately in this ending of the video installation is how far it is removed from the suffering of the psychotic. The fairy tale with which I began is also far away. Or is it? We have just witnessed an account of the literalized, physicalized metaphor of care, made possible by mood; it is this that is judged 'really good'. According to psychoanalytic theories, most famously that of Bruno Bettelheim, fairy tales are no lighter, no more inconsequential than the affect-laden works of contemporary art. Bettelheim's argument that the child needs to experience the fright and thrill of its own fantasies so as to be equipped to deal with adult life receives unexpected resonance here. Despite shortcomings in his study of fairy tales (among which an overemphasis on sex and a pronounced gender-indifference are the most blatant), the notion that children need affect as a homoeopathic dose of the poison of adult life could be seen as acquiring a literal, hyperbolic reality in *The*

House. Indeed, this claim may well be the primary contribution of the fairy-tale aspect to this work.[24]

Except that (to use this argumentative turn once again), for a change, this installation is not about sex. In this respect it is markedly different from Ahtila's earlier installation, *When 6 is 9*. In *The House*, gender, or what the outside world makes out of sexual difference, pushes sex to the side. The fairy-tale body free of gravity holds on to the roof of the house in order to get back onto the ground, to get a grounding, however precarious. But when Elisa walks into her living room to hang the curtains, her hesitant steps demonstrate that certainty is gone, including, I suggest, the certainty that this can be about individual life, as both psychotic and psychoanalytic versions of sex would imply. Nor can a single reading suffice to account for this installation's power to unsettle. All the readings I have evoked here — and more — are necessary to constitute a cacophony of 'voices' of which the psychotic who 'hears voices' is a model. 'Hearing voices' — polyglossic, inside one's head, affecting who one is, and non-indifferent to feeling — can be seen as a conceptual metaphor for affect in the encounter with art.[25]

But, as we now come to my fifth reading, of affective interdisciplinarity — which declares philosophy insufficient because it is too generalizing, after first declaring self-reflection too narrow — we cannot, either, disavow the way the probing of narrativity, through the destruction of its 'naturality', tips over into a philosophical inquiry into metaphysics and ethics. All of these readings continue to matter, although they only 'really' begin to do so when we reach the outside world. This human existence, our being-in-time, is impossible without a connection to the outside world — of refugees and ships arriving at all shores. Like Heideggerian 'care', care for the art we write about requires the paradox of respecting the diversity and otherness of the work, while at the same time enveloping it with our 'disclosive submission'.

This connection between the individual (here, the woman, who is the only figurative character in the work) and the outside world (evoked through her perception, selected and isolated according to a Bergsonian–Deleuzian version of that act and the welcomed entrance of people into Elisa's body) is crucial, total, and irreversible. *The House* posits that this connection is total because the world and the subject are simultaneously both inside and outside. This is what it means to be affect-ed, by art, by the world, by others. Standing between the three screens, and surrounded by sounds that are a little too loud, too subjective, and too worldly for comfort, nothing in this exercise in 'unnaturality' could appear more natural.

This is why the ultimately realist aesthetic of this video about the failure of reality is the one and only appropriate visual mode. Reaching back to the child's omnipotence from beyond a philosophy that is still too self-enclosed, Elisa's final words, 'Good, really good', with an unexpected emphasis on 'really', echo 'happily ever after'. If only ...

That a realist aesthetic is used to drive home the point that hosting refugees inside your mind, or house, or house-mind is the form psychosis takes, suggests what the purpose of criticism and the art it helps to speak today can be. Criticism serves not the artist but the relationship between the artwork and its audience. Criticism is an activity of mediation. This is not to say that critics 'translate' art presumed difficult for an audience seen as incapable of understanding it on its own. First, there is no singular meaning that art can be purported to harbour and criticism thought to translate. Secondly, audiences are free to spend as much time and energy, as much intellectual and affective engagement, with works of art as they like. Thirdly, and most important, what defines art is relationship, not autonomy. Hence the contribution of each viewer to that relationship escapes the control of the critic.

Therefore, instead of translating, of reducing the artwork to meaning, criticism's mission is to open it up to translation of a different kind, where space becomes shared and affect can flow. Among the many facets of an artwork that help open it up to a diverse public, the most important one for me is the specific mode of theorizing art that art itself is capable of. Unbound by logic and linearity, and in ways our academic disciplines cannot, art can foreground the simultaneous operations of aesthetics and politics, discourse and ethics, and popular and highbrow genres and modes of thinking. And, because art appeals to the senses as much as it does to the intellect, its recalcitrance to the divisions of academic disciplinarity offers a model of how interdisciplinary thinking can enrich each of the participating disciplines.

In this chapter I have attempted to speak 'through' Ahtila's installation. In this sense I have taken it as a model. Viewing it as theoretical object, I have tried to argue that its mobilization of a number of different disciplinary fields is neither encompassing nor arbitrary. In this specific polyphony of disciplines, the one boundary most in need of melting is that between intellectual and affective work. The thirteen and a half minutes of the installation take its viewers through a number of specific and highly pointed theoretical 'arguments' about the cultural role of discourses, about aesthetic modes and, above all, about the intense and painful bond between 'art' — representation, fantasy, imagery, and imagination — and 'life' — psychosis and the loss of certainty, childishness and sensations of omnipotence, disaster and the profound need of hospitality — lest refugees drown when they are sent back to sea. It is this bond that is 'good, really good'.

Notes to Chapter 1

1. Bertolt Brecht, 'A Short Organum for the Theatre', in *Brecht on Theatre: The Development of an Aesthetic*, ed. and trans. by John Willett (New York: Hill and Wang, 1964), pp. 179–205; (first publ. as 'Kleines Organon für das Theater', *Sinn und Form*, special issue: Bertolt Brecht (1949)); for commentary, see Theodor Adorno, 'Commitment', in *Can One Live after Auschwitz? A Philosophical Reader*, ed. by Rolf Tiedemann, trans. by Shierry Weber Nicholson (Stanford: Stanford University Press, 2003), pp. 240–58.
2. Seen at the Ydessa Hendeles Art Foundation in Toronto, in a superb exhibition aptly titled *Realities* (14 March 1999).
3. Gilles Deleuze, *Cinema 1: The Movement-Image*, trans. by Hugh Tomlinson and Barbara Habberjam (Minneapolis: University of Minnesota Press, 1986), p. 99.
4. The theoretical opposition suggested here by Hansen is, to my mind, somewhat misleading, since the distinction pertains to the examples each author adduces and to their historical positions, and Deleuze's examples — Griffith and Eisenstein — are alien to the digital images that Hansen discusses. See Mark B. N. Hansen, 'Affect as Medium, or the "Digital-Facial-Image"', *Journal of Visual Culture*, 2 (2003), 205–28. For a skilful explication of affection-images, see Patricia Pisters,

The Matrix of Visual Culture: Working with Deleuze in Film Theory (Stanford: Stanford University Press, 2003), pp. 66–71, and Paola Marrati, *Gilles Deleuze: cinéma et philosophie* (Paris: PUF, 2003), pp. 46–52. An excellent in-depth study of Deleuze's cinema books referenced by both these texts is D. N. Rodowick, *Gilles Deleuze's Time Machine* (Durham, NC: Duke University Press, 1997). For an important theoretical discussion of affect as a medium, see Ernst van Alphen, 'Affective Operations in Art and Literature', in *Res* (in press).

5. See Sorin Alexandrescu, 'Le Discours étrange, à propos de *La Nuit* de Maupassant', in *Sémiotique narrative et textuelle*, ed. by Claude Chabrol (Paris: Larousse, 1973), pp. 55–95. This genre is discussed in terms that bring it closer to psychotic delusions in Deborah Harter, *Bodies in Pieces: Fantastic Narrative and the Poetics of the Fragment* (Stanford: Stanford University Press, 1996).
6. For a point-by-point mapping of the moves implicated in this transfer, see my *Reading 'Rembrandt': Beyond the Word–Image Opposition* (New York: Cambridge University Press, 1991), esp. pp. 158–60. On conceptual metaphors, see Teri Reynolds, 'Case Studies in Cognitive Metaphor and Interdisciplinary Analysis: Physics, Biology, Narrative' (unpublished doctoral dissertation, Columbia University, New York, 2000).
7. For the terminology of narrative theory, see my *Narratology: Introduction to the Theory of Narrative*, 2nd edn (Toronto: University of Toronto Press, 1997).
8. *Gilles Deleuze*, p. 51.
9. Chance is a major issue in modernist fiction. See Robert Caserio, *The Novel in England, 1900–1950: History and Theory* (New York: Twayne, 1999).
10. See Ann Veronica Janssens, *Une image différente dans chaque oeil / A Different Image in Each Eye*, ed. by Laurent Jacob, French trans. by Daniel Vander Gucht (Liège: Espace 251 Nord, 1999); Ann Veronica Janssens *An den Frühling* (Köln: Dumond Verlag, 2007).
11. For a succinct explanation of psychosis, see Jean Laplanche and Jean-Baptiste Pontalis, *The Language of Psychoanalysis*, trans. by Donald Nicholson-Smith (London: Karnac Books, 1988), pp. 370–72. I am indebted to an unpublished paper by Mary Jacobus, 'Prometheus on the Couch: Wilfred Bion and the Language of Terror', for a keen sense of the 'nameless dread' that characterizes psychosis (lecture, 14 July 2003, School of Criticism and Theory, Cornell University).
12. For more on the rhetoric of realism in the construction of the world, see my *Double Exposures: The Subject of Cultural Analysis* (New York: Routledge, 1996).
13. The allusion is to Martin Heidegger, *Being and Time*, trans. by John Macquarrie and Edward Robinson (New York: Harper and Row, 1962). Paul Ricoeur has analysed the implications of Heidegger's conception of 'ordinary time' for narrative in *Time and Narrative*, trans. by Kathleen (McLaughlin) Blamey and David Pellauer, 3 vols (Chicago: University of Chicago Press, 1984–88), III, 60–88. For a masterly analysis of Heidegger's text in relation to visuality, see Kaja Silverman, *World Spectators* (Stanford: Stanford University Press, 2000). That philosophy is relevant for Ahtila's work has been forcefully demonstrated by Silverman in her interpretation of *Anne, Aki and God*: see 'How to Stage the Death of God', in *Eija-Liisa Ahtila: Fantasized Persons and Taped Conversations* (Helsinki: Museum of Contemporary Art, 2002), pp. 189–95.
14. On the triptych in the work of Francis Bacon — comparable in that Bacon, too, deploys a classical form for questioning the tradition from which it comes into the present — see Ernst van Alphen, *Francis Bacon and the Loss of Self* (London: Reaktion Books, 1992). Bakhtin defined *chronotope* as 'the intrinsic connectedness of temporal and spatial relationships that are artistically expressed in literature' ('Forms of Time and of the Chronotope in the Novel', in *The Dialogic Imagination: Four Essays by M. M. Bakhtin*, trans. by Caryl Emerson and Michael Holquist, ed. by Michael Holquist (Austin: University of Texas Press, 1981), pp. 84–258 (p. 84)). For a discussion of the relevance of the concept for contemporary culture, see Esther Peeren, *Intersubjectivities and Popular Culture: Bakhtin and Beyond* (Stanford: Stanford University Press, 2007).
15. On the probing of scale — its reversal and suspension — as baroque, in Caravaggio in particular, see my *Quoting Caravaggio: Contemporary Art, Preposterous History* (Chicago: University of Chicago Press, 1999).
16. *World Spectators*, p. 29.
17. See my *Louise Bourgeois' Spider: The Architecture of Art-Writing* (Chicago: University of Chicago Press, 2001).

18. For this concept of translation, see Gayatri Chakravorti Spivak, 'Translator's Preface and Afterword to Mahasweta Devi's *Imaginary Maps*' and 'Subaltern Talk', in *The Spivak Reader*, ed. by Donna Landry and Gerald MacLean (New York: Routledge, 1996), pp. 267–86, 287–308.
19. The phrase 'caught in this history of the present' is an allusion to Ernst van Alphen's *Caught by History: Holocaust Effects in Contemporary Art, Literature, and Theory* (Stanford: Stanford University Press, 1997). This book discusses contemporary art related to the Holocaust and its traumatic aftermath, in ways that I consider to be relevant as an 'after-image' of these subliminal allusions to disaster in the present which I read — perhaps read into — Ahtila's work. For an elaboration of the idea of an ethical non-indifference, see my book *Loving Yusuf* (Chicago: Chicago University Press, in press). See also Rukmini Bhaya Nair, *Lying on the Postcolonial Couch: The Idea of Indifference* (Minneapolis: University of Minnesota Press, 2002).
20. Silverman, *World Spectators*, p. 26.
21. The former would be what Silverman theorizes elsewhere as idiopathic identification, or what she calls a form of psychic cannibalism (*The Threshold of the Visible World* (New York: Routledge, 1996)). The latter is the object of dismissal for Brecht, 'A Short Organum'. For a critical discussion of Brecht, see Adorno, 'Commitment'.
22. *World Spectators*, p. 55.
23. Heidegger, *Being and Time*, p. 177 (emphasis in text); quoted in Silverman, *World Spectators*, p. 60.
24. Bruno Bettelheim, *The Uses of Enchantment: The Meaning and Importance of Fairy Tales* (New York: Knopf, 1976).
25. After I had given an oral presentation of this interpretation, one listener came to me and proposed that the people coming to inhabit Elisa's body were metaphors for sexual penetration, validated into orgasm by the final words. In the event that some readers may feel moved in the same direction, let me say the following. This hyperbolic view of penetration as the primary form of sex sits oddly with a female character. It has been sufficiently pointed out that women are not necessarily or automatically as obsessed with penetration per se as some men appear to be. Moreover, such interpretations must, first, ignore all the evocations of the boat — aural, verbal, metaphorical — that immediately precede this ending, and secondly, import sex into a work where not a single mention of this topic is made. Frankly, I would draw the line at such an unsubstantiated over-interpretation.

CHAPTER 2

❖

Nuisance Value

Adam Phillips

'Interesting philosophy', Richard Rorty writes in *Contingency, Irony and Solidarity,*

> is rarely an examination of the pros and cons of a thesis. Usually it is, implicitly or explicitly, a contest between an entrenched vocabulary which has become a nuisance and a half-formed new vocabulary which vaguely promises great things [...] It [the half-formed new vocabulary] says things like, 'try thinking of it this way' — or more specifically, 'try to ignore the apparently futile traditional philosophical questions by substituting the following new and possibly interesting questions'.

For there to be a change (whether or not it is considered to be progress), Rorty suggests, something has had to begin to feel like a nuisance. But this entrenched vocabulary has to begin to seem like a nuisance — to seem like an irritant, or an obstacle, or a saboteur — for something new to happen. Clearly, at least in philosophy, people have to be able to have the nuisance experience. Either this vocabulary becoming a nuisance is itself an inspiration; or inspiration — or Rorty's version of inspiration that he calls redescription — is spurred by the nuisance experience. It is as though one is frustrated into experimentation — try thinking of it this way; or that the old entrenched vocabulary makes some new things sound baffling or implausible. The nuisance effect of the entrenched vocabulary is that it makes one want to ignore it — its apparently futile traditional philosophical questions — and start replacing it with new questions. Certain vocabularies make certain sorts of questions possible. It is not working through that Rorty recommends, it is ignoring and substitution; not mourning, but moving off and moving on.

Something about what Rorty calls, in his blandly tendentious phrase, 'interesting philosophy' needs a nuisance. So it is worth wondering what it might be about an entrenched or familiar vocabulary that would make it into a nuisance. You might feel, for example, that there was something that mattered a great deal to you that you couldn't get, or get at, in the vocabulary available; but this old vocabulary would have to exist for you to have this feeling. You would be dependent on the way in which it frustrated you; because this very frustration would be a prompt. The old vocabulary would pester you with what it couldn't do for you, with the roads not taken by that set of words. Indeed the thing about nuisance is that, by definition, it won't leave you alone; you can't ignore it until you come up with a way of ignoring that works. If a substitute is a constant reminder of what it is substituting for — if a new lover becomes a compulsory and compulsive allusion to the one you have lost — it is a mixed blessing. When we are talking about something or someone becoming a nuisance, we are trying to describe a specific kind of conflict that is called up in us; we are describing being set a task, but a discomfiting one. We don't tend to make claims for our nuisances — people often describe children as nuisances, but ideally no one wants a nuisance, or to be one. What Rorty is drawing our attention to is how the interesting philosopher needs to be able to notice the nuisance value of an entrenched vocabulary. Whether a nuisance is an invitation or an opportunity or more obviously an annoyance, it is a demand. We may not want to be a nuisance — though why we don't is worth wondering about; but we do, Rorty implies, need to be able to have the nuisance experience. It is a nuisance when we are made to attend to something that we would rather not. Clearly nuisance and the notion of resistance, of preferring not to, go together. But whether the nuisance is, to use an entrenched vocabulary, the cause or the consequence of resistance — whether we resist something because it is a nuisance, or it is a nuisance because we resist it — is never so clear. How we make something or someone a nuisance, and what we use nuisances to do, and what, if anything, this might have to do with what was called (in an older entrenched vocabulary) appreciation of the arts, is the gist of this paper.

Rorty's blithe and impressively light-hearted solution to the nuisance of an entrenched philosophical vocabulary is to regard its traditional questions as apparently futile, ignore them, and replace them with new and possibly more interesting questions. And psychoanalysis is of a piece with this kind of jaunty pragmatism, in so far as one of the things Freud showed us was just how inventive we are at ignoring things we don't like and substituting things we prefer. The only difference is that for Freud this is often the problem rather than any kind of solution; from a psychoanalytic point of view, it has always been the best and worst thing about us that we are able to replace a negative hallucination with a positive hallucination, that we can turn pain into pleasure, at least for the time being. Nuisance, we could say, is the compliment we give to the unacceptable when we want it to be merely annoying; the nuisance never lets go, but it doesn't drive us mad (we don't describe stalkers as a nuisance; we don't say, unless we are characters in an Evelyn Waugh novel, that it is a nuisance to fall in love, or a nuisance when people die). Nuisance, in other words, makes us think of the inconvenient rather than the repressed; and therefore, perhaps, it is not suitable as a term of art. We may at least claim to like art that disturbs us, but we don't tend to describe a poem or a painting or a piece of music as a nuisance, even if their makers often are. We use the word nuisance when there is something that we don't want to be bothered by, but are. The relative blandness of the term is reassuring; it reminds us of our passion for convenience, the narcissism of small conflicts, the wish to be left alone. As a determined pragmatist, Rorty, in passing, also wants us to use nuisance. If something becomes a nuisance, you can do something about it. And doing something about it, for Rorty, is doing without it. If a nuisance is something you can't ignore, then at its best it will prompt you to find more productive ways of ignoring, better substitutes.

And yet what is odd about the contest Rorty describes between the new more interesting philosophy and the older entrenched vocabulary is that it is a contest in which one party is encouraged to ignore the words of the other. And, of course, a nuisance is something by definition that you can't ignore; if you could ignore it, it wouldn't become a nuisance. Indeed, that peculiar act of trying to ignore someone or something — the act of seeing and then having to persuade yourself that you haven't really seen, or don't really need to look — is what you start doing with a nuisance. A nuisance is nothing if not good at engaging you; and then at having to deal with all the ways in which one resists being engaged. A nuisance is someone who does and doesn't take no for an answer. But there is, as Rorty intimates, a contest of sorts — an albeit ignoble or mock-heroic one — whenever there is a nuisance around. Though what is striking about nuisance, and so of some interest, is that unlike the artworks we would prefer to make and admire, the nuisance, the nag, and the pest don't tend to bring out the best in us, or in themselves. On the whole, no one wants to be a nuisance; and yet there are clearly situations, predicaments, in which it may be necessary to be able to be one; or, as we say, put up with one.

We don't think of the users or promoters of an entrenched vocabulary as trying or wanting to make a nuisance of themselves, though, given how unacceptable it is to be a nuisance, perhaps we should begin to notice just how much nuisance artfulness is there to conceal or make more pleasing (the word obsession, one could say, pathologizes nuisance just as the word preoccupation aestheticizes it). Every child has to learn how to be a nuisance and how not to be, because nuisance is one of the forms demand takes, even if we think of it as a peculiarly unimaginative, monotonous, and insistent form. All children have to make whatever is insistent about them more winning. It is clearly very difficult, for example, to grow up in an environment in which appetite is considered to be a nuisance, an interruption, rather than something taken for granted. The child's appetite, one would think, will only be a nuisance if treated as such by the adults upon whom he is dependent; but if it is treated as a nuisance by the adults, then the child will have to take on being a nuisance in order to survive. In the face of exasperation and impatience and avoidance, he will have to persist; so wherever we make a nuisance of ourselves — or notice that we are trying not to make a nuisance of ourselves — there is some kind of unmet or unrecognized need (as the psychoanalyst André Green says, in a different context: wherever a grievance is, there was a trauma). In this picture, to be unable to complain would be to have abolished one's history. Nuisance and wanting go together even if we prefer them separate. If nuisance is need insufficiently transformed — the bad art of wanting — if nuisance, like many repetitions, is the sign of something thwarted or blocked or stalled, then it would be worth wondering what would have to happen for someone to never need to be a nuisance, or, perhaps more interestingly, for them never to experience someone or something else as a nuisance. Or to put it the other way round, which are the predicaments in which nuisance is a necessity? Whenever there is impoverishment and a kind of hopeless hope that it can ever be met — or turned into something else — we will find nuisance abounding. The nuisance, in other words — and the nuisance in oneself — is an interesting figure because of the assumptions he makes. He is living as if he knows exactly what he wants but for all sorts of reasons the other person doesn't want to give it to him. So it is easy for us to think of children, often benignly, as making a nuisance of themselves, and more difficult for us to think this of, say, people begging, who, broadly speaking, we experience as a nuisance but try extremely hard to make them and ourselves feel that they are not. If we don't give money to people begging in the street, are we withholding something that belongs to them? People divide significantly around their answers to this question, which is also about what it means to find someone else a nuisance, or to manage one's response to them by experiencing them as a nuisance. If someone begging on the street weren't a nuisance, what would he be?

In his chronicle *Down and Out in Paris and London*, published in 1933, George Orwell asks the question, 'Why are beggars despised?'.

> I believe it is for the simple reason that they fail to earn a decent living. In practice nobody cares whether work is useful or useless, productive or parasitic; the sole thing demanded is that it shall be profitable. In all the modern talk about energy, efficiency, social service and the rest of it, what meaning is there except 'Get money, get it legally, and get a lot of it'? Money has become the grand test of virtue. By this test beggars fail, and for this they are despised [...] A beggar, looked at realistically, is simply a businessman, getting his living like other businessmen, in the way that comes to hand.

In Orwell's view, we despise beggars because they don't earn through work, and because they are poor. If money has become the grand test of virtue, we will be unduly suspicious of those who don't have it. Of course, as Orwell knows, we are duly suspicious of those who have a lot of it. But the point Orwell is keen to make — which seems slightly odd — is that we despise beggars because what they do is not profitable, because they are not good at what they do. Orwell stresses that there is no 'essential difference between beggars and ordinary working men'; it's just that beggars, like children, don't work and don't make money. And this is so despicable that the state makes begging illegal; to get money the beggar has to seem to be actually doing something. 'As the law now stands,' Orwell writes,

> if you approach a stranger and ask him for twopence, he can call a policeman and get you seven days for begging. But if you make the air hideous by droning 'Nearer, my God, to Thee' or scrawl some chalk daubs on the pavement, or stand about with a tray of matches — in short, if you make a nuisance of yourself — you are held to be following a legitimate trade and not begging. Match-selling and street-singing are simply legalized crimes.

There are in fact several pages in the book about a street-artist, pages in which Orwell is clearly wondering what so-called artists, including himself as a writer, are actually doing now in this pre- and post-war society in which money has become a grand test of virtue, and in which virtue has a quite different kind of purchase on the imagination. But in Orwell's calculated list of match-sellers, street-singers, and pavement artists — who are, in his view, on a continuum with all the other businessmen in the culture — it is only by these people making a nuisance of themselves that they can be 'held to be following a legitimate trade and not begging'. You have to make a nuisance of yourself to remain within the law; but also, Orwell implies, this is what all businessmen are doing, which is why this has become a test of the legitimacy that is legality. Everyone in this society has to force himself on other people's attention and sell them something they don't really want, let alone need. You have to make a nuisance of yourself to get on. Business is like bad art — hideous droning, scrawling daubs on the pavement; someone makes a nuisance of himself and gets away with it. The picture Orwell conjures — which, as always with Orwell, is far subtler than he is telling us that it is — is of people paying off these people in order to be able to forget about them. To use Rorty's word, the police can ignore the beggar if he is droning or scrawling or selling matches; and the passers-by give them money so they can pass them by. Beggars make a nuisance of themselves so people will give them money to stop them being a nuisance. Making a nuisance of yourself is an invitation to other people to do something that will stop you being a nuisance. We have to find legitimate ways of begging, of asking for what we need. Orwell is saying that in the society he lives in, everyone is a beggar, but in order to distract us from this hideous fact, we have to be seen to be selling something; and to do that — to, as they say, make money — you have to find a way of making a nuisance of yourself. What the real beggars in the culture make patent is how, in this culture, making a nuisance of yourself has to be redescribed — as being an artist, or being a businessman, or indeed being a policeman — to make it sufficiently acceptable. The beggar who makes a profitable nuisance of himself is Orwell's representative modern person. In this exchange, the beggar gives the nuisance he has made, of himself, for money. It is as though a nuisance is the most minimal thing one can make of oneself. The starkest gift. At the raw end of the spectrum there is being a nuisance; at the cooked end there is being a nuisance without seeming to be one. Criminals, Orwell seems to imply in the book, are the people we punish for being a nuisance; artists are the people we reward for being a nuisance; successful businessmen are criminals disguised as artists.

In *Down and Out in Paris and London*, Orwell uses art and artists, including himself, to talk about poverty; both its provenance and its effects. For the people Orwell describes and lived with, poverty was not a metaphor; it was not a useful analogy, as it could have been for Orwell himself, who was not without means. It is, in a sense, the project of the book to stop poverty being used as an analogy, to undo his and our horrified voyeurism of the poor. And the poor, Orwell suggests, are forced to make a nuisance of themselves, and to be seen only as a nuisance. Successful artists and businessmen — Orwell's other two categories that he wants to lump together — have to make a nuisance of themselves, but in a way that makes them seem to be something other than a nuisance. The artist is the person for whom making a nuisance of himself works. Indeed, works so well that nuisance would be the last word we would use about the work (if not about the artist). So we might ask: what kind of nuisance is this particular work of art, and why don't we want it to be one? How have we and the artist conspired to stop it being a nuisance so that it could be something else more satisfying? And this would not be to assume that any artwork could be reduced to its nuisance value, so much as to draw attention to the nuisance value of the art. Because once we can find the nuisance — like Rorty's interesting new philosopher stuck with the old entrenched vocabulary — we can ourselves begin to get to work. A nuisance, if we can do something with it, gives us something to be going on with.

In a talk given in 1945 called 'Home Again', about children returning home after being evacuated during the war, the psychoanalyst and paediatrician D. W. Winnicott wrote of how these children needed to test the home environment in order to rediscover its reliability. After all, if one has been sent away once, one could be sent away again. The child, Winnicott writes,

> begins to be cheeky, to lose his temper, to waste your food, to try to worry you and to interfere with your other interests. He may very likely try out a little thieving, testing how true it is that you are really his mother, and so in a sense what is yours is his. These can all be signs of a step forward in development — the first stage of a sense of security, although maddening from your point of view. The child has had to be his own strict father and mother while he has been away, and you may be sure that he has had to be over-strict with himself to be on the safe side [...] Now, however, at home with you, he will be able to take holidays from self-control, for the simple reason that he will leave the business of control to you. Some children have been living in artificial and overdone self-control for years, and it can be assumed that when they begin to let mother take over control once more they are going to be a bit of a nuisance from time to time.

Winnicott is describing the developmental necessity of the returning child's freedom to be a nuisance. If the child enacts his personal repertoire of anti-social behaviour and the parents still love him and keep him — if he gives the environment what Winnicott calls 'the full blast of his hatred', and it and he remain in touch and remain intact — then he has discovered a home he can trust in, and entrust himself to. If the parents can't allow the child to be a bit of a nuisance, the child cannot find his way back to the parents. Being a nuisance is the way the child makes a home to return to. But this involves not the parents' so-called unconditional love and acceptance, but the parents' being able to experience the child as a nuisance — hate him for it, if need be — and giving the child time to become lovable again. In Winnicott's view, the object becomes real by being hated; we can only love real people, or discover people to be real, when they have withstood our hatred. Nuisance is the nice word for the hateful exchange that a relationship can survive, and by surviving can become resilient rather than merely wishful.

So what Winnicott calls 'the nuisance value of the symptoms' is always a sign of hope in the child. If the child is prepared to be difficult, he is at least hoping that there is a world he can live in as himself, with all his love and hate. 'The nuisance value of the anti-social child', Winnicott writes, 'is an essential feature, and is also, at its best, a favorable feature indicating again a potentiality for recovery.' All the child's so-called anti-social behaviour, one could say — all his stealing, lying, incontinence, and so on — are simply the form his entitlement to have parents takes. The child is living as if, living in hope that, people can recognize, meet and where necessary withstand his need. It is the child who can't be difficult, the child who is too fearful to make a nuisance of himself, that we should be really worried about. The child who is a bit of a nuisance wants more life, wants the better life that can include whatever his development is going to be. The child who is no trouble may have given up hope. For Winnicott, the mother's 'willingness to meet the claims arising out of frustration, claims that begin to have a nuisance value', gives the deprived child somewhere to start from again.

But it is clear from this picture that what Winnicott calls the nuisance value of the symptom only exists if the environment both experiences the nuisance and comprehends it as a message, a message about a deprivation. Being a nuisance, in other words, is a precarious process; it demands a great deal of the environment it makes around it. And it is a considerable act of faith. The nuisance value of the symptom resides in the symptom being given value in the way it is responded to. When a nuisance is experienced merely as a nuisance, when a nuisance is taken too literally, when a nuisance goes on being a nuisance, it is a missed opportunity. In an older entrenched language, one could say, it takes courage to make a nuisance of oneself — the kind of courage that is involved in being prepared to try and make the kind of world that one can actually live in. For Winnicott, given that deprivation is endemic to human development, the capacity to be a nuisance and the capacity to bear with a nuisance are tantamount to the capacity one has to live one's own life. And this involves a willingness to interrupt and be interrupted. So taken is Winnicott by the notion of nuisance that he wants to posit it as a need of what he was keen to call human nature. 'It has often been said', he says in a paper of 1957 entitled 'Integrative and Disruptive Factors in Family Life', 'as a joke and with truth that children are a nuisance; but coming at the right time in a relationship they are the right kind of nuisance. There seems to be something in human nature that expects a nuisance, and it is better that this nuisance should be a child than an illness or an environmental disaster.' Expecting a nuisance, of course, is different from needing one. It is as if Winnicott is referring to a kind of magic; we expect a nuisance and if we are lucky it will be just that, not a catastrophe. It's a bit like saying we expect to be interrupted, to have our lives disrupted, but preferably by good things. Expecting a nuisance, ideally, is like expecting a child. And expecting nuisance as part of human nature is presumably expecting things not to be as we want them to be, expecting our lives not to be as we expect them to be. For Winnicott nuisance, unlike trauma, is potentially just the right amount of unsettlement.

But to call something or someone a nuisance — and I think Winnicott may be alluding to this — is to be uncertain of its significance. Do we use the word nuisance to reassure ourselves that we have domesticated a trauma, that we have transformed something shocking into something irritating, that nuisances don't link us to our losses and our lapses? Or is a nuisance what we say it is, a low-key disturbance, not a derivative or an echo or a clue to something graver? It is possible that we call things or people nuisances precisely when they baffle that distinction, or when they provoke us into ignoring it. A nuisance puts us in this difficult position, the position of wanting something to go away, the position of being forced to take something seriously that one doesn't want to be serious about. When Strachey's Freud in 'The Question of Lay Analysis' refers to 'the fact that neurotics are a nuisance and an embarrassment for all concerned — including the analysts', he is also referring to the fact that even psychoanalysts who had found a new way of valuing neurotics didn't necessarily like them. Nuisance may be inspired — by memory, by the meaning that is desire. Being able to be a nuisance may be necessary to survival; so-called nuisance value may be another way of describing the individual's stubborn ambivalence about recognition, the baffled nature of his insistent appeal. And yet nuisance, by definition, creates a resistant if not actually hostile environment; it invites the avoidance it fears. Perhaps being a nuisance is wanting to start again; or nuisance is the sign of something that wants to get started. After all, an old entrenched vocabulary can be a nuisance, but nuisance always speaks in an entrenched vocabulary.

Note to Chapter 2

This chapter first appeared in *The Threepenny Review*, no. 99 (Fall 2004) <http://www.threepennyreview.com/samples/phillips_f04.html>. Full details of works cited are given in the bibliography on p. 222.

CHAPTER 3

❖

Borges's Blindness and Giacometti's Eyes

Beate Perrey

What is red? Red depends on our eyes...
JORGE LUIS BORGES, *The Total Library*

In this chapter I shall explore the challenge that criticism faces when approaching a non-linguistic artistic medium such as sculpture or painting. My hypothesis rests on the notion that visual art corresponds to a person's potential blindness in its blank spaces, analogous to silences in music. These visual or aural open spaces inspire vision in the first place, and thus generate critical commentary. Poetic critical writing, however — unlike ordinary critical writing, which tends to cover open spaces or 'blind spots' of potential insight with commentary — is able to open up the artwork once more. Criticism, I shall argue, may gain from allowing itself to close its eyes, as it were, that is from an inward view to reinvent the works it talks about through a poetic critical language. In the course of this essay, as it seems to invite such connections, I shall indirectly draw on an idea articulated by Adam Phillips in his essay 'Nuisance Value': and the theme of art and poverty expressed in the language of poetry.[1] I shall make use of Orwell's reported invitation to consider the artist as the person who is making a nuisance of him- or herself. The artist whose work I shall explore is the Italian sculptor and painter Alberto Giacometti. In discussing the artistic approach and practice of his ways of seeing,[2] I shall focus on one of his best-known sculptures, *Tête sur tige*, as well as on one of his painted portraits, *Caroline*, of 1965. I shall deflect these sculpted and painted views of seeing with views *about* seeing by the blind Argentinian writer and critic Jorge Luis Borges, and by David Sylvester, Giacometti's best critic. In thinking about Giacometti's work, and these two chosen portraits in particular, I shall try to respond, again only indirectly, to one of the questions Phillips put to us so intriguingly: 'What kind of nuisance is this particular work of art, and why don't we want it to be one?'[3]

Both art and criticism may indeed, as Phillips suggests, sometimes seem like a nuisance. But that is so for these two forms of expression only, I would argue, at moments when they don't seem to 'work', or at least don't seem to work for us;

that is, when one feels that one might be better off without them — when either the work of art or the piece of criticism seems to spoil something by its presence, something that, for want of a better word, we might call atmosphere or ambiance. What I would like to explore in this essay is the way in which criticism does manage to 'do its work' as well as how it 'works', at least for me, as well as under what conditions it may do its work rather well and yet *not* seem like a nuisance even though it might nevertheless be spoiling something. Put more simply, I would like to consider the kind of written criticism that the reader finds enriching rather than impoverishing.And which, like a work of art itself, 'contributes' to an aesthetic experience in the sense of adding to the original one of seeing (or listening or reading); and, finally, to talk about the finding of words, of a vocabulary and a whole critical language for what one sees, as well as about what actually happens in the process of seeing, and of finding words for this process. No doubt there are links between the activity of seeing, of seeing in, of empirical observation and insight, and so it is of interest to explore the role of the observer and critic in relation to the artwork. What interests me particularly, from my own perspective as musician and music-analyst or critic, is the silence out of which the sculpted or painted artwork grows through contemplation and which it re-establishes in turn, again through contemplation, and of which the art critic, like any listener, forms part. In music too, of course, the moments of silence are often the most crucial. It is during the music's pauses, its intermittent silences as well as the silence after the music has actually stopped, that meaning crystallizes and that music is often also at its most intense — in silence. But the idea of communicating in silence, without words, in order for words to emerge, defines more obviously, it seems to me, the reading experience as well as the experience of looking. Hence my focus: Borges's blindness and Giacometti's eyes.

Borges's Blindness

Communicating in silence, I suggest, is a kind of blindness. Yet the kind of blindness known at first hand by the writer and poet Jorge Luis Borges (1899–1986) was also, as we shall see, a kind of wordlessness as well as a way into poetry. In Borges's case, blindness and poetry meant the rediscovery of an earlier personal and professional preoccupation, as well as a whole new way of life. Ironically, Borges's physical blindness coincided with his years of public recognition and international fame. In 1955 he took up the prestigious post of director of the National Library in Buenos Aires, which famously housed nearly a million books that Borges, by then almost completely blind, could — despite being their official guardian — no longer read. He commented with style in his *Poem of Gifts*:

> Nadie rebaje a lágrima o reproche
> esta declaración de la maestría
> de Dios, que con magnífica ironía
> me dio a la vez los libros y la noche.[4]

[Let neither tear nor reproach | tarnish this declaration | of the mastery of God | who, with magnificent irony, | at once gave me the gift of books | and the night.]

It was also in 1955 that Borges was appointed professor of English and American Literature at the University of Buenos Aires. After receiving in 1961 his first significant literary prize, the International Publishers' Prize (Prix Formentor), which he shared with Samuel Beckett, his work began to be widely translated, and this led to growing international recognition. Most importantly, however, Borges's blindness brought about a radical change in his working method. No longer able to compose lengthy and intricate pieces of prose, let alone novels which would necessitate the writing down and reworking of drafts, he returned to poetry after twenty years of neglecting the genre. As his blindness slowly deepened, he moved progressively from prose to free verse, and thence to metrical verse.[5]

Superficially speaking one could say that criticism becomes interdisciplinary as soon as it begins to concern itself with matters other than words: with music, art, emotions, sensations, or nature, for instance. Here a fundamentally different, non-verbal material encounters the material of language, and above that the distinctive material of the language of criticism. Here the artistic object, and the critic's relation to it, passes into language. It fell to Borges above all to reflect on this process and to open up the theme of blindness as a crisis of language linking image to word:

> But I hope some day — I am following a treatment — to improve and to be able to see that great color, that color which shines in poetry, and which has so many beautiful names in many languages. Think of *scharlach* in German, *scarlet* in English, *escarlata* in Spanish, *écarlate* in French. Words that are worthy of that great color.[6]

Borges, once deprived of physical sight, dreamt of finding 'that great color' red through the names and shades and overtones that different languages could accord it. And what he is also saying, intriguingly, is that he wanted to discover the word rather than the 'thing' behind the word; in other words, Borges was keen to discover what a word might hold inside itself, and so come to see what kind of red *scharlach* or *escarlata* might possibly be. In this sense Borges the poet (more than the blind man) had a greater belief in words than in things. He was more committed to words than to things for he was convinced that it is the word *scharlach* that could bring about the 'thing', the colour, rather than the other way around. What Borges is also saying is that he is trying to become a better poet, trying to 'improve' as he put it, while 'following a treatment': blessed with the gift bestowed upon the man who has gone blind, and by turning failing eyesight into insight, Borges hopes to see a multitude of reds come alive in poetry, and in poetry alone. It is not things or objects that we can see, Borges says, but words. Blindness, by virtue of its signifying impact on life, on seeing, and being, recasts seeing itself.

Giacometti's Eyes

A similar kind of blindness, the kind that recasts seeing, is central to the work of Giacometti, and in particular to what we can see in the eyes of his sitters. Here blindness has become the key to sculpting or drawing a face. Along with Mieke Bal I shall argue for, as she puts it so eloquently in her book on Rembrandt, 'an interpretation of the theme of blindness as the acceptance of not-being-able-to-see,

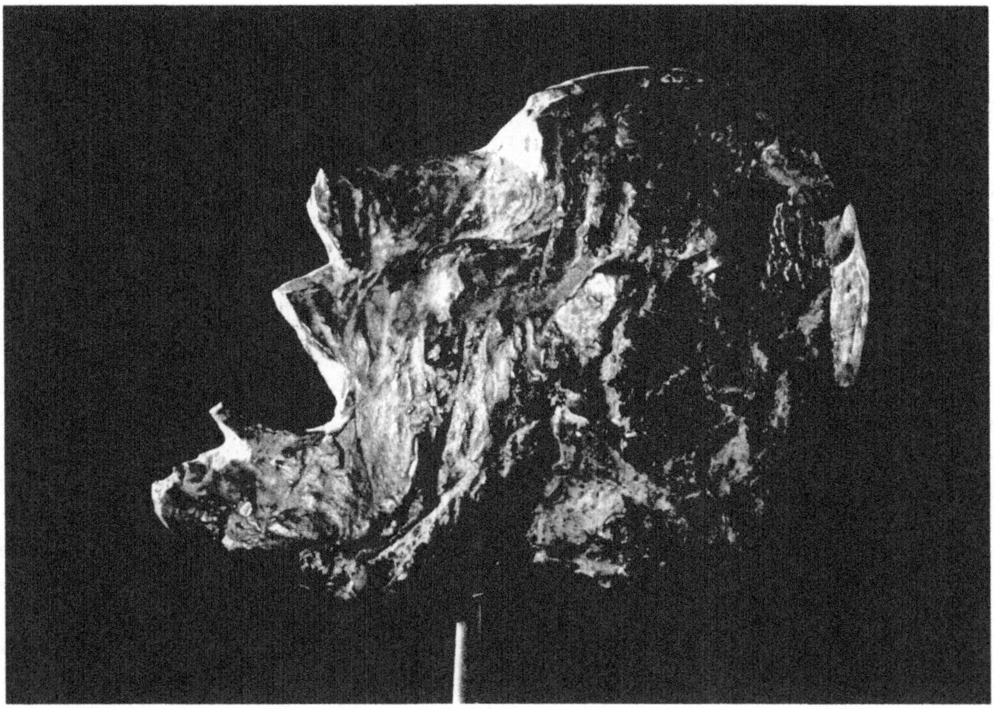

Figure 3.1. *Tête sur tige* (*Head on Rod*), Alberto Giacometti, 1947.
Bronze, 61cm. © Photo Galerie Maeght, Paris, and DACS, London 2007

which is required in order to achieve insight'.[7] Giacometti himself reflected on the potential gains of experiencing inability: 'I don't know if I work in order to do something or in order to know why I can't do what I want to do.'[8]

Giacometti's professed aim was to 'copy reality and nothing else', 'simply to copy, so as to take account of what one sees'.[9] But in the process of copying, he was interested as much in inachievement ('to know why I can't do what I want to do') as in achievement ('I work in order to do something'), as long as the experience of inachievement would yield some kind of insight. As with most of his portraits, whether drawn, painted, or sculpted, Giacometti's *Tête sur tige* (*Head on Rod*) of 1947 doesn't inhabit a place. Suspended in the air and isolated, it is a haunting image of what looks at first sight like a blind man. Or is it the vision of a dead man? Radiating in the flickering reflection of the surrounding light, the head is falling backwards as well as pointing forward and up, as if at once in a state of thriving and in a state of decline. With eyes wide open or eyes wide shut — perhaps full of expectancy? or perhaps full of revolt? — this man seems to be struggling with life as much as with death, as if one were the other, one coinciding with the other. A closer look, however, eventually dispels the ambiguity: with eyes like these, appallingly unnatural, as if scooped out, this is more like a dead man's head. In sustained contemplation, one begins to feel one's own eyes to be scooped out. Disturbing, they compel our gaze to fix on what the dark blank sockets stand for:

the loss of vision. For this image to emerge, a single head is all there need be, is all with which this world that Giacometti has brought before us begins and ends. Yet it is precisely the beginnings and endings of this world, the striking vacillation between the solid and earthy matter of which this head of clay is made and the translucent air surrounding it which begin to intertwine. For the rough and restless surface structure of the head makes its whole appearance nervous and the reflections of light render the head's true boundaries uncertain. But this seemingly unfinished, 'broken' surface structure, as Sylvester puts it,[10] is also what makes it particularly susceptible to interpretation. We are being let in.

Those who have seen any of Giacometti's sketches, drawings, or paintings will recall that the artist was in the habit of producing countless variations on the same sitter, the same pair of eyes, whence the theme of blindness. In later years, the darkness of sculpted, painted, or drawn eyes, while still signifying disappearance, began to expand and spread across the whole of a face, and soon also across much of the canvas or paper. There are many examples; among the most striking are the portraits of Caroline, painted in 1965 not long before Giacometti's death, the following year (Figure 3.2).

Giacometti draws us into the gaze he tried to depict and in doing so raises the whole question of seeing and being seen. But by literally drawing into his images a real sense of blindness he produced works that redirect the question of seeing and viewing from the painter as 'active' onlooker to the viewer as 'passive' contemplator. The act of looking turns into one of empathetic participation, a seeing through the artist's eyes, and a seeing that may well also result in blindness. Seeing, his paintings seem to imply, is never a one-way process, for the assumption that the eyes we see are also the ones that see us corresponds to the relatively blind way of seeing that the negation of blindness encourages. The resulting critical narrative presents a more complex account of both blindness and seeing, of seeing as well as being seen by the painter, the viewer, and the critic. In this series of successive mirrors, different pairs of eyes exchange glances in a thoroughly collaborative process of meaning-making. That critical narrative, however, and the verbal criticism of such portraits, will itself be characterized by the tension between these different, and differently seeing, eyes. It is the ensuing conversation[11] between the viewed object's 'other' or 'others' brought to life by the sculpture or painting at the very moment of seeing that makes for the story's complexity.[12]

But Giacometti's eyes, of which the eyes in the Caroline portrait and those of the *Tête sur tige* are only examples, add to this complex dynamic of visuality as I have described it yet another and more problematic sense: if these portraits are indeed about simultaneousy seeing and not seeing, they clearly create an acute sense of loss. In Giacometti's portraits we find a myriad of brush-strokes sometimes covering the represented face almost entirely in the artist's intense effort to create one. Here a tightly-knit web of traces covers not only the canvas but the very face that is represented while mysteriously allowing it nevertheless to reveal its defining features. Eventually, however, as Giacometti's determination to totally copy a face intensified in later years, the facial features begin to disappear in a sea of paint strokes. This can be seen in the portrait *Caroline* of 1965, but also in many

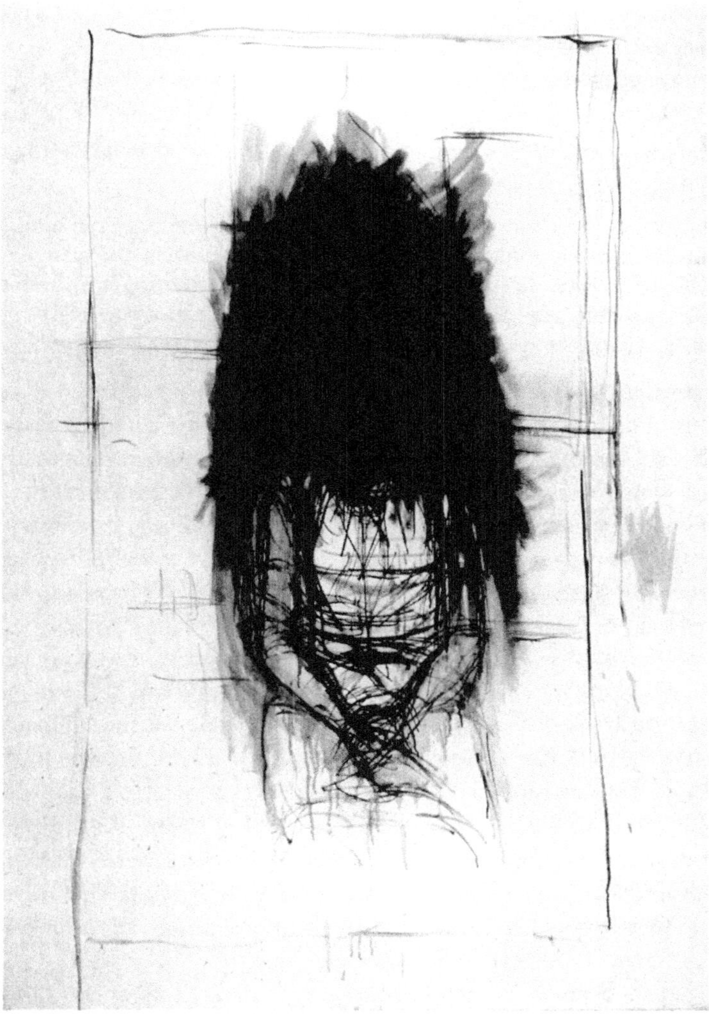

Figure 3.2. *Caroline*, Alberto Giacometti, 1965. Oil on canvas (92 × 73 cm)

portraits drawn well before this date. If the scooped-out eyes of *Tête sur tige* (see Figure 3.1) compel us as viewers into real involvement, it is therefore not only what Giacometti paints that affects us but, even more so, how he does it. As we contemplate his sculptures and paintings, calmly viewing the result of what must have been an impressive scene of restless and relentless activity, we are drawn right in. No longer observing from a distance, we find ourselves tied up with the making of the portrait, its eyes, and its gaze — to become a part of it, in a brief moment of a complete seeing eye to eye. But to return to my original focus on silence and blindness, to the breaks, suspensions, and pauses in music and the blank spaces in painting, embodied in Giacometti's portrait of Caroline with its darkly absent eyes while darkness has taken over the face as a whole, let us note that this portrait is a vision of loss, once more. In creating eyes that are not really there, and in drawing a face that seems about to disappear, Giacometti left us the most poignant and haunting idea of what the human face can never be seen to be.

What is set forth instead is a vision of the ungraspable. The moment of a perceptible risk of disappearance is made visible. One of Giacometti's own remarks is rather telling:

> One never copies anything but the vision that remains of it at each moment, the image that becomes conscious. You never copy the glass on the table; you copy the residue of a vision ... You see it as if it were disappearing, coming into view again, disappearing, coming into view again — that's to say, it really always is between being and not being. And that is what one wants to copy.[13]

What is interesting is that Giacometti's claim to 'copy reality and nothing else' is at odds with his work — including the minuscule figures a few centimetres high, the tall and emaciated bodies of his sculptures, and of course the lost looks of his painted sitters through their carved-out, absent-minded eyes. Giacometti's verbal insistence on the objective nature of his undertaking, however, as if it were a truly scientific enterprise, clearly played on his own personal sense of progress and discovery. For Giacometti certainly believed that he was moving closer to what he conceived to be a scientific truth, a kind of 'reality' when painting a face while endlessly trying to reach the essence of its appearance. And yet he wasn't. These paintings, like his tiny sculptures and painfully thin torsos, have hardly anything to do with 'truth', or 'essence', so little do they seem to bear any likeness to human beings. But what Giacometti did bring to these visions instead were all the possibilities of an appearance, all the different faces that a face can have, and that he wanted his visions of a face to contain. All of them. And none. No doubt, like Borges's desire to be able to see 'that great color' in as many splendours as there may be words and languages out there and available to speak it, Giacometti's way of seeing was determined by looking at phenomena rather than objects. His were visions of imaginary appearance and disappearance.

The critic David Sylvester captures this in his book *Looking at Giacometti*:

> I found increasingly that the paintings with which I spent the most time, hypnotized by their gaze, were the large portraits of Caroline seated, painted in the 1960s [...] works in which more and more of the effort went into solidifying the face and its aura while leaving the rest of the picture almost untouched [...] hallucinatory visions of figures in space [...]. The radiant intensity with which he could realize a single standing nude isolated in space was sustained and increasingly refined in complex interior and exterior scenes where a luminous space floods the image as if voids were the positive and solids the negative [...]. Fluidity of vision is reconciled with a crystalline clarity of structure. A precise tentativeness in recording facts is warmed by an intoxicating breath of the sublime. Michelangelo's belief that the sculptor brings to light a form buried in the marble he is carving becomes a metaphor for the act of drawing, even to the contrasts between totally polished parts and parts that are still emerging from the block. Solid bodies of an uncanny lightness are locked into space charged with a buoyant, exhilarating, numinous energy and filled and filled by light.[14]

Here in the final cadential paragraph of Sylvester's remarkable book, the paintings are seen as 'hallucinatory visions of figures in space' where solid matter and the void surrounding them become superimposed. A distinct lightness of tone and the factor of a sublime force are elicited to widen and heighten the semantic reach of Giacometti's vision. Sylvester's writing exerts the kind of hypnotic power that the critic himself confesses to have experienced when being seized and held by the very gaze of the portraits he contemplated. This last paragraph, clearly devoted to a poetic language of criticism, is written in an unusually metaphoric style. More evocative than informative, it is a celebration of seeing. Sylvester virtually inhabits the painting and in the process loses his blindness. All at once Sylvester's criticism turns into art itself, able to show us the art of another.

This is more than mere hyperbole. While one of the registers available to Sylvester's critical voice takes us into the ethereal sphere of abstract thought and associative reflection, another, just as present and compelling at other moments in his book, recalls the realities of the painted canvas as well as the material consequences of Giacometti's overzealous brush-strokes. In layering these differently pitched commentaries about production and interpretation onto the works he talks about, Sylvester combines observation and perception with description and reinvention to capture the moving, fugitive impressions forming while looking at an objectively unchanging work of art. He adopts Giacometti's hypnotized gaze for us, and we in turn do the same through that of Sylvester's. As Giacometti once noted,

> If the gaze, that is to say life, becomes what matters most, then there is no doubt: it's the head that is essential. The rest of the body is reduced to antennae which make life for its agents possible — a life which takes place in the brainbox.[15]

A life that takes place in the brainbox is something to which Giacometti was completely committed, as was Borges, for both Borges's Blindness and Giacometti's Eyes are about inscape and inwardness rather than about outlook, view, or perspective. But this closing in on inwardness, this life in the mind, dramatizes the notion of insight, whether artistic, critical or otherwise, and the means of expression in the midst of the deeply private experience of seeing and being seen.

Notes to Chapter 3

1. See above, Chapter 2, pp. 24–31.
2. To evoke the title of John Berger's influential book *Ways of Seeing* (London: BBC and Harmondsworth: Penguin Books, 1972).
3. See above, p. 28.
4. Borges, 'Poema de los dones', *El hacedor* (1960), in *Obra poética, 1923–1977* (Madrid: Emecé/ Alianza, 1993), p. 119. My translation.
5. See Emir Rodríguez Monegal, *Jorge Luis Borges: biographie littéraire* (Paris: Gallimard, 1983), pp. 502–10, and Marcel Le Goff, *Jorge Luis Borges: l'univers, la lettre et le secret* (Paris: Harmattan, 1999), p. 53.
6. Jorge Luis Borges, 'Blindness', *The Total Library: Non-Fiction 1922–1986*, trans. by Esther Allen and others (London: Penguin Books, 2001), pp. 473–83 (p. 474).
7. Mieke Bal, *Reading 'Rembrandt': Beyond the Word–Image Opposition* (Cambridge: Cambridge University Press, 1991), p. 348.
8. David Sylvester, *Looking at Giacometti* (New York: Owl Books, 1997), pp. 76–77.

9. Ibid., p. 106.
10. See David Sylvester, *About Modern Art: Critical Essays, 1948–97*, updated, 2nd edn (London: Pimlico, 1997), p. 54.
11. Mieke Bal wrote interestingly about the notion of polyphony when exploring the meeting and melting of different affective and intellectual factors in interdisciplinary work. See above, Chapter 1, p. 21.
12. A sophisticated account of the interrelations of verbal and visual discourse-strategies of representation can be found in Bal, *Reading 'Rembrandt'*.
13. Quoted in Sylvester, *Looking at Giacometti*, p. 77.
14. Sylvester, *Looking at Giacometti*, pp. 119–21.
15. Quoted in *Alberto Giacometti: Le dessin à l'œuvre*, ed. by Agnès de la Beaumelle (Paris: Gallimard/Centre Pompidou, 2001), p. 153. My translation.

CHAPTER 4

❖

Wittgenstein's Chopin: Interdisciplinarity and 'the Music Itself'

Lawrence Kramer

The object of study constructed by musical scholarship, familiarly known as 'the music' or 'the music itself', has traditionally served to maintain a rigid separation between musical knowledge and worldly knowledge, music and the world. The going assumption was that music could only be understood from the inside out; Virgil Thomson once expressed the result by saying that communication about music was possible only among musicians. The past twenty years has changed all that. Impelled by both a rising awareness of critical theory and the demand to historicize, musical scholarship has become interdisciplinary to the core. Once-firm disciplinary foundations have felt tectonic shifts; familiar concepts such as the musical work have come under critical scrutiny, and the distinction between musical composition and musical performance has blurred. But there has still been relatively little reflection on how this change to a musical in(ter)discipline changes the very concept of music, or on how that change affects the continued presence of the music itself and the means and ends of our departures from it.

As a start on those tasks, this paper offers a cycle of reflections on a phrase, a trope, and an idea. *The music itself*, which is all three, has long served as a disciplinary means to circumscribe musical knowledge on the one hand and the community formed about that knowledge on the other. Anyone with expert knowledge of music knows the gratifying feeling of immediate contact that ensues when a stranger is revealed as sharing that knowledge. The contact invokes a fellowship, which is also a part-ownership, of the semi-sacred object designated by the term or idea *the music* (itself! not some other thing!). This localizing and exclusionary effect is no doubt a property of disciplinarity in general, but the case of music exaggerates it in an exemplary way, promotes it to the level of myth and ideology, because it sets music against the whole rest of the world and, as if that were not enough, against the whole sphere of semantic specification and referential cognition.

The result might be described as a recovery of the aura that Walter Benjamin famously ascribed to art before the age of mechanical reproduction. Regardless of its means of reproduction, music allows — has historically allowed — the establishment of a cult value at odds with both critical and hermeneutic modes of thought and practice on the one hand, and the exercise of everyday worldly rationality on the other. That this amounts to the denial of the obvious permeation of music by worldly phenomena could until quite recently be upheld as an ideal, for example by Heinrich Schenker:

> The entire content of a musical composition [is] one unit of background-depth and foreground-breadth. Within the mystery of such a connection also lies the complete independence of music from the outside world [...] that distinguishes music from all the other arts.[1]

One presumably unintended consequence has been the almost total lack of authority on worldly matters granted to thinkers about music unless, as in the case of Adorno, they already have credentials as thinkers about something else. Such authority, where it exists, is funnelled into the cult value conferred on musicians by their fans.

It follows that to have worldly knowledge of music, and for music to contribute to the broader projects of worldly knowledge and reflection, it is necessary to break with the disciplinarity of music. Musical understanding must focus on some object of a different kind from the music itself, or, as I have put it elsewhere, the music's itself, the 'itself' of music.[2] Not that the musical phenomenon is to be neglected or forgotten; far from it. But to know music in any genuine sense it is necessary to know more than music, and not only that, but to know that music knows more than music. Music, which so easily becomes intermedial, demands an understanding that becomes, if not so easily, interdisciplinary.

It is important, though, to say just what this means and what it does not. It does not mean combining and reconciling the vocabularies and procedures of two different disciplines. It means, rather, precisely operating *between* them, in a perennially transitional, hard-to-regulate space wherein the terms of each discipline move metonymically in the direction of the other until their tether runs out. The movement corresponds to the sinuous flow of conceptual transformation, of symbolic substitution, and, in the classic Lacanian formulation, of desire. This space is not undisciplined, but it does not yield to the discipline of the disciplines that flank it. It is perhaps best conceived as a conceptual equivalent to the space of hybridity described by Homi Bhabha as the core condition of twenty-first-century cultural formation. The description draws out the implications of a liminal symbolic space that is also an everyday object:

> The hither and thither of a stairwell, the temporal passage that it allows, prevents identities at either end of it from settling into primordial polarities. This interstitial passage between fixed identifications opens up the possibility of a cultural hybridity that entertains difference without an assumed or imposed hierarchy.[3]

The stairwell winds between levels, identities, disciplines; motion along it, and under it, behind stairs, affords a continuous shifting of perspective and orientation. The disciplines bridged by the *inter* are historical legacies, impossible either to ignore or to follow blindly. They are not abolished under the conditions of the inter, nor yet integrated into a higher unity, but continually recast as the boundary forces and seedbeds of subsequent knowledge-projects.

My effort here will be to enter such an interspace between two fields chosen precisely for their lack of rich prior connections: musicology and the philosophy of mind and language, the former represented by the disciplinary icon *the music itself*, the latter by an icon of philosophical heroism, Ludwig Wittgenstein. I will try to use observations by Wittgenstein to reconfigure the music itself in ways that help both clarify and dissolve its defensive, anti-mundane force. I will also try to adapt Wittgenstein's procedures to form a model of interdisciplinary inquiry: to form, in effect, a personified figure for the work and pleasure of thinking between, enjoying between, and living between the disciplines. Wittgenstein's modes of defamiliarization, lapidary writing, and thought-experiment can contribute to the formation of a model of interdisciplinary inquiry both into music and beyond it.

The cognitive result I propose to call 'descriptive realism'. It is this which is the ultimate issue here, especially, but not exclusively, as it is reached — perhaps reached best — by the proximate issue, the experience of music. At stake is an entry in the ongoing debate about realist versus constructivist modes of understanding that is perhaps the dominant trope of knowledge in the academic world today and the primary source of the (in)famous conflict of the faculties. More broadly, the stakes are those of struggles over the status and sources of truth that seem increasingly to pervade social and political life on a global scale, but with a complexity that must here remain only penumbral. What I will try to propose, via music, via Wittgenstein, is a small piece of an unaccomplished whole, a Wittgensteinian language-game, if you like. The speech-acts involved have the aim, not of producing realistic descriptions in the familiar empirical sense, but of recognizing how descriptions help produce realities that are, nonetheless, independent of every particular description. Such realities are fully capable of serving as points of reference against which the interpretative claims of the descriptions can also be understood as what Jürgen Habermas calls validity claims.[4] This is something possible only in the inter space, never merely the inner space, of the disciplines.

One more word about the dramatis personae. Wittgenstein is a figure so mythical and so protean that he really has become a figure, that is, a trope: everyone has a different Wittgenstein. The one I invoke here is the aphoristic thinker who was deeply imbued with the musical culture of the late-nineteenth-century Vienna in which he grew up, and where his family often entertained the likes of Brahms, Mahler, and Bruno Walter: a thinker to whom the musical 'classics' were second nature but who, unlike Theodor Adorno, rarely let them sound through his philosophical work. The exceptions, though, are remarkable, and far more resonant than their casual appearance suggests. In one of them, discussed below, Wittgenstein makes a seemingly offhand but actually quite telling reference to Chopin, who will gradually emerge as a figure too, this one for the secret imperative of music not, at all costs, to remain itself.

The music itself resists interpretation. So we are told. It is a commonplace to say that no interpretation, no matter how rich, can fully represent even the simplest piece of music. The statement is not wrong, but the wrong conclusion — that the true, musical meaning remains unaccounted for, a secret of the music itself lost to the imperial force of language — is consistently drawn from it.

What would happen if we examined the commonplace according to the Wittgensteinian mandate: if we didn't take it for granted, but regarded it as something remarkable that no interpretation can fully represent a piece of music?

Imagine an interpretation that does tell us something we can hear in a piece, even as we always, necessarily, hear more. Let it be something simple, say that a piece by Chopin is meditative, reflective. What must be the relationship between the interpretation, qua meaning, and the piece? The piece would appear as that uninterpreted substrate in which the meaning is embedded. It would be that which had the meaning, regarded apart from the meaning, though it could only manifest itself as such once the meaning had been discerned. This substrate would not be an abstraction, like its counterpart in the interpretation of a text. It is not a hole through which understanding falls and disappears. It is a material sensuous form; it is a source of pleasure; it is an incitement to listen, an invitation to interpret anew with the promise of being both rewarded and evaded by the resulting change of aspect. Heard amid this lived, dynamic process, the music itself is what will always have been something more; it is the threshold of that becoming other on which it is also pleasant to linger. One way to define music is precisely as the material remainder of interpretation.

Music in the realm of Western listening must thus be described before it can be interpreted: in that respect it is like everything else. But there is also a respect in which music must be described even before it can be heard. It can be heard intelligibly only 'under a description' in the philosophical sense of the term. (A 'description', in this special sense, is the answer to the question 'What are you doing?' The question, of course, does not actually have to be put into words, but it does have to be understood. It makes a difference whether I am snapping my fingers to call a dog, express impatience, or insult someone.) Apart from such descriptions, whether potential or actual, there is no 'work' of music, no music itself, though there may be musical sounds in abundance. Music must always be reconstituted in order to be constituted in the first place. The case is suggestively similar with dreams, which have to be put into textual form not just in order to be interpreted, but in order to be remembered. Like unvoiced dreams, the music itself can only show itself and vanish.

The music itself has the force of expression or description without the substance. It is like a seemingly grammatical sentence that says nothing: 'Colourless green ideas sleep furiously' is the standard example. Like a figure on a staircase drawn by Escher, you can never get to where it leads. Why do we take this strange thing so much for granted? And what would happen if we didn't?

Wittgenstein wondered, too:

> Couldn't we think that a man who has never known music and who comes to us and hears someone playing a reflective [piece by] Chopin, that he would be convinced that this is a language and we just want to keep the meaning secret from him?
>
> In verbal language there is a strongly musical element. (A sigh, the intonation of a question, of an announcement, of longing, all the numberless *gestures* [Gesten] of intonation.)[5]

Wittgenstein's tone-deaf guest doesn't know how to recognize the music itself, and just for that reason he perceives something true about it that is normally glossed over. The music itself is hiding something; it has a hard edge. Those who know music have learned how to treat this hiding not as a lack but a gift. For them — 'us' — the music itself reveals and conceals the meaning at the same time, so that we get an inkling of the meaning in the moment it eludes us, which is every moment. And knowing music, we know that the little semantic vortex that results is supposed to be giddy with pleasure.

Wittgenstein links this experience to the sphere of inflection rather than articulation: music flows in and out of the continuously fluctuating tonality of speech, here figured as a strongly physical as well as a strongly musical medium, one in which, or *that* in which, knowledge (sought in a question, found in an announcement) and desire (even the unlimited desire of romantic longing) blend into a continuum.

But there is more to the music itself than this, more *in* it than this. Wittgenstein does not speak here about just any music, but about music by Chopin, and more particularly about reflective music by Chopin — even such music 'as' Chopin per se: 'a reflective Chopin' [nachdenklichen Chopin] is the exact phrase. Unlike the tone-deaf guest, those of us who know music do not hear the music itself when it is Chopin that someone plays. What we hear are the music's gestures of intonation — a question, an announcement, longing — knitted together by a process of reflection that lies transparently open before us. To hear just the music itself would be an obstacle to this full and open hearing. Chopin's particular gift is to sweep the music itself out of our way so that feeling and reflection can come through.

Wittgenstein's presentation of 'someone' playing a reflective Chopin is remarkably close to Jane Welsh Carlyle's impression of Chopin himself doing so in 1843:

> [Chopin's music] is not a specimen of art offered to the general admiration. [...] It is rather a reflection of part of his soul, and a fragment of his life lavished on those who have ears to hear and a heart to understand.[6]

Wittgenstein's tone-deaf guest hears only the specimen of art — the music itself. But because he does not know music by ear or by heart, because he does not, in Wittgensteinian terms, know how to do anything with or say anything about what he hears, he cannot make the leap to the fragment of life lavished on him. So he responds to the music's Cheshire-cat purr — its message with a vanishing meaning like a smile with a vanishing face — with resentment. And in a way he is right to do so, because he is right about the music itself, and this music itself, even though he is wrong about both in a larger sense. Chopin's reflective music, the paradigm of musical reflectiveness in general, really is a kind of secret language, a paradigm for the secretiveness of language in general. But the secret kept by language is always an open secret, the action of which, disclosed without disclosure, is itself a form of meaning.

Chopin's role in the history of feeling thus blends with Wittgenstein's inquiry into the lived character of language. It blends, indeed, with the feeling of that inquiry's own lived character, its own musical gesture of intonation, much as it might have done in the Wittgenstein mansion in *fin de siècle* Vienna where someone would so often come and hear someone playing.

One of Wittgenstein's key preoccupations was with what it meant to perceive an object 'as' something. The question was initially a matter of simple perception, famously illustrated by the duck-rabbit, a line drawing that could be seen as either animal but not both at once. But from simple perception the question branched out to embrace fiction, metaphor, and what might broadly be called perceived conception. What goes on, Wittgenstein wanted to know, when I perceive a chair as a fort? What about when I perceive a smile now as an invitation, now as a threat, now as true, now as false? What happens when I hear a melody as a lament?

These questions were not looking for explanations of subjective phenomena; a leading theme in Wittgenstein's later writings is the futility of just that. The questions were meant to elicit descriptions of human actions and the forms of life embodied by them. How, exactly, do I act when I perceive an object 'as' something? How does the perception act on me? What do I want from the object and it from me? What happens?

Wittgenstein responds by talking about changes in 'aspect'. When I see a smile as a threat rather than a greeting, a different aspect of the smile comes to the fore: it is, so to speak, switched on while another aspect is switched off. The change of circumstance or interpretation is realized by the 'lighting up' — *Aufleuchtung* — of an aspect. The new aspect is not discernible in itself. We see by it, but do not see it. Nor does it correspond to a physical or material change, or even to a change in appearance. 'But what is different?' Wittgenstein asks, 'My impression? My point of view? — Can I say? I *describe* the change like a perception quite as if the object had changed before my eyes.'[7] There is nothing above or beyond that description, which is neither literal nor metaphorical but merely truthful. 'The expression of a change of aspect is the expression of a *new* perception, simultaneous with the expression of an unchanged perception' (*PI* 196). I see nothing new in the object; I just see the object in a new way. Yet there is nothing paradoxical about this experience. It is the most familiar, most natural thing in the world. If it baffles us, that is only because we allow ourselves to forget that its remarkable qualities are part of the fabric of our ordinary experience and need to be neither explained nor demystified, but only investigated.

When does that investigation lead us to music? What aspect of music does it end by lighting up?

Wittgenstein habitually identifies perceiving-as with seeing-as, as if unconsciously swayed by the general tendency in Western thought to equate knowledge with vision. Yet he does observe, even if he does not quite acknowledge, a difference between seeing-as and hearing-as. His examples suggest that seeing-as is usually instantaneous; that it usually jumps abruptly from seeing an object now this way, now that; and that what we see is usually seen as unambiguously present. His definition of aspect-change embraces all these tendencies: 'I contemplate a face, suddenly I notice its similarity to another. I *see* that it hasn't changed; and still see it otherwise' (*PI* 193). Elsewhere, still more forcefully: 'We don't see facial contortions and now *infer* (like a doctor making a diagnosis) joy, sadness, boredom. We describe a face immediately as sad, radiantly happy, bored, even when we aren't able to give another description of the facial features' (*Z* 41). Breaks in this visual immediacy have a threatening quality, as if they endangered the texture of phenomenality itself. The examples given are few and disconcerting: a familiar object made unrecognizable by unfamiliar lighting or position, the inability to recognize someone after a lapse of years or in a crowd (*PI* 197).

Hearing-as is altogether different. Wittgenstein's examples, most of them involving music, suggest that hearing-as usually involves a deferral; that it usually marks a transition from *not* hearing-as, that is, from nonsense to sense rather than from sense to sense; and that what is heard is only ambiguously present in — but this is my term, not his — the music itself.

Let us take these things up one at a time.

(1) For Wittgenstein, hearing-as in music is modelled on performing-as; musical expression is to the ear what expressive performance is to the hands (the implied medium is usually the piano). This process takes time. In principle it involves sorting through alternatives until the right one presents itself: 'I have a theme repeated to me and each time played in a slower tempo. Finally I say "*Now* it's right", or "*Now* at last it's a march", or "*Now* at last it's a dance"' (*PI* 206). The right aspect lights up in an abruptly enhanced present moment: the italicized *Now*. The Now of seeing-as is typically much less marked, less sharply distinguished from the time before it.

(2) The time before hearing-as is expressively indefinite. Before one hears the repeated theme as a march or a dance, one doesn't hear it as much of anything. Wittgenstein imagines someone deficient in seeing-as whom he calls aspect-blind; we might suggest that a period of being aspect-deaf is built in to the experience of music.

Insofar as hearing-as moves from the sound of some mute pre-intelligible substance to the music of an aspect, as if the aspect were lit up in the auditory dark, hearing-as is the Ur-form of perceiving-as. Before it is heard as something, music embodies the 'it' of the phrase 'it makes sense' apart from any sense it might make. This separation, however, is not absolute, which is why, luckily for us, music is never 'absolute', either. Although, as Wittgenstein says, one can hear a musical phrase apart from the special feeling or sentiment (*Empfindung*) that it gives us, what one hears in that case is not yet music. One cannot hear the music itself until one hears it as something else. Only from the perspective of that 'as' can one even speak of the music itself. This is not a purely conceptual formulation, but a description of what the experience is like. Where visual uncertainty brings anxiety, the uncertainty of the music itself brings pleasure, or, more precisely, *repeats* the pleasure that *follows* it. The music itself is always that which will have become the music-as.

Conversely, the music-as is that which may have been, and may yet become, the 'it' of the music itself. When, as sometimes happens, I hear music *as* something right off, the possibility of losing the *-as* remains as part of the horizon of my listening. The music may even seek to install that loss the better to induce the pleasure of music in between the *it-* and the *-as*, and the richer to make the *-as* when it comes to me and I to it. This primordial play of pronouns has a meaning and a music of its own.

(3) The content of musical expression is neither in the music nor outside it. Unlike seeing-as, hearing-as does not give its outcome a *place*. If see a face as sad, I know how to locate the sadness in the person whose face it is. If I hear a melody as sad, the sadness 'belongs' only to the melody. 'Sad' is simply what the melody is. Yet there is no lack here, not even an absence; although we have no term for it, the non-locality of musical expression is a positive quality. It becomes even more so when one goes beyond blunt terms like 'sad' and enters the arena of modern musical hermeneutics, where one might hear a melody, or whatever, as, say, nostalgic for the utopia of a form that its own construction renders ideologically remote.

Wittgenstein plays out the non-locality of musical expression through the ambiguities of the loaded word *Empfindung*, which can mean 'sensation', 'feeling', 'perception', and 'sentiment', and in the case of the last carries long-standing connotations of refinement and emotional quickness:

> Just think of the expression: 'I heard a lamenting [klagende] melody'! And now the question: 'Did he *hear* the lament?'
>
> And if I answer: 'No, he didn't hear it; he only got a feeling of it' [er empfindet es] — what does that accomplish? One certainly can't pretend even once to name a sense organ for this 'feeling' [Man kann ja nicht einmal ein Sinnesorgan dieser 'Empfindung' angeben].
>
> Some might now reply: 'Of course I hear it!' — Some: 'I don't really *hear* it.'
>
> But conceptual distinctions can be established. (*PI* 209)

The last statement notwithstanding, no conceptual distinctions *are* established, either here or elsewhere. On the contrary, it is the futility of such distinctions, rendered here in the Janus-faced identity of hearing and not hearing, that gives us the feeling, *die Empfindung*, of hearing-as.

Wittgenstein sometimes treats understanding speech and understanding melody as essentially the same activity:

> Understanding a sentence in speech is more closely related to understanding a theme in music than one might suspect. [...] Why should dynamics and tempo move in just *this* line? One would like to say: 'Because I know what it all means.' But what does it mean? I wouldn't know how to say. To 'explain' I could only compare it with something else that had the same rhythm (I mean the same line). (One says: 'Don't you see, it's as if a conclusion were being drawn', or 'That's like a parenthesis', etc.) (*PI* 143)[8]

The meaning comes from anywhere but the sentence itself, the theme itself. It comes from a rhythm, a line of action traced in time, that becomes fully perceptible only when I make, that is, perform, a certain kind of description, a persuasive comparison. The sentence itself, the theme itself, mean precisely nothing. In fact, these supposedly solid and familiar entities may not even make sense as phenomena. How exactly, does one experience the sentence itself?

Historical acts of musical understanding often look misguided or irresponsibly 'subjective' to later interpreters, but reveal their rationality when placed in historical context. What were once successful ordinary descriptions evolve into failed extraordinary ones. Most of Wittgenstein's own descriptions seem old-fashioned at the distance of half a century. Even something as simple, as seemingly neutral, as calling a passage 'glorious' can sound a little embarrassing in the ironic, pastiche-laden postmodern world. Most descriptions, most interpretations of any kind, can expect at best to be destined to this kind of obsolescence. But they do not on that account become invalid or illegitimate, nor stand exposed as mere semantic barnacles encrusting the pristine surface of the music itself. The process of understanding evoked by Wittgenstein involves a sort of situational body heat based on the urgencies of time, place, and circumstance. When the performative urgency cools, meaning hardens and shrinks, as if turning to stone. But it can be brought back to life in a vivid enough retrospect.

Consider the constant nineteenth-century habit of assigning emotions expressed in music to the person of the composer, especially if the emotions are painful. The animating context is the double one of the era's inability to conceive of subjectivity apart from an actual subject, except in the uncanny form of the automaton, and the idealization of suffering as a sign of spiritual distinction. Hence Heine's remarks on Meyerbeer:

> How it is that an artist [...] destined far more than any mortal artist for good fortune — how is it that he has nonetheless felt that enormous pain that sobs and sighs out to us from his music? For what he has not felt himself, the musician cannot express so powerfully, so shockingly [...]. The artist is that child of whom the fairy tale relates that its tears become pure pearls.[9]

For Heine, pain cannot be expressed powerfully unless it is sincere, so it is safe to assume its sincerity on the basis of its power. The same expressive power and power of expression is the magical means by which the pain is embodied and revalued, by which tears become pearls. We know, all appearances to the contrary, that Meyerbeer must have suffered enormously because the music itself says so by the sobbing and sighing that suddenly speaks to Heine. What makes such past commentary as his viable is not only our ability to recover the historical moment of its viability, but its real relationship to the music, which it understands — correctly — as courting description as a person might court love or understanding.

During his tour of England and Scotland in 1848, deeply depressed and correctly convinced that his own death was near, Chopin repeatedly played 'a funeral march' — presumably the famous March from his Op. 35 Sonata — when asked to perform in private.[10] Evidently he needed to hear something in this music, needed to hear it as something: perhaps as the survival of his sensibility after his body's death, now palpably near, perhaps as the tragic dignity of his passing, or perhaps as something darker and more tortured, the self-consuming substance of his depression. On one occasion, whatever it was he heard become appallingly clear, though only to him. Or so we are told: the incident is reported by a collector of Chopiniana with a good reputation, but the original source, a letter, is supposed to have been destroyed.[11] But the story makes sense even if it is only a fiction about Chopin, which in a way it remains even if it really happened.

This is what Chopin is said to have said:

> I had played the Allegro and the Scherzo [of the B flat minor Sonata] more or less correctly. I was about to attack the March when suddenly I saw arising

> from the body of my piano those cursed creatures which had appeared to me one lugubrious night [in Majorca]. I had to leave for one instant to pull myself together, after which I continued without saying anything.[12]

Chopin had been desperately ill in Majorca some ten years before and described the small 'cell' where he slept as 'shaped like a coffin'.[13] The 'cursed creatures' he encountered again as revenants seem to be harbingers of death, bearers of portent like the banshee or incubus. As they arise, they identify the body of the piano with Chopin's own body. It is 'my piano', he says, and whose body could be more identified with the piano than his? Whereupon the creatures turn these bodies into vessels of death, the coffins, graves, crypts of a gothic churchyard. Displacing the music but also expressing its spirit, the cursed creatures intrude a terrified silence on the music that is doubly mortal for Chopin, the silence of his death as both man and musician, the silence, the horror, of an ear that can no longer hear, a hand that can no longer play.

Chopin hears the music as what these cursed creatures embody; the creatures are tropes, figures, allegories, gargoyles, for what the music becomes — not expresses, but becomes — in this hearing. But the shape of this becoming, in the form of the creatures, is separated from the music, whose onset the creatures block. On this one occasion, Chopin hesitated to release the power of hearing-as; he acted to protect the music from becoming the advancing march of his death. But in so doing he lost something he did not yet know he had, the power of the music to protect him from the very creatures whose silence it reversed. To hear the music as his death was bad; not to hear it as his death was worse. Just to hear the music itself, without the death it harboured, was to hear nothing, a sound more void than silence. So Chopin withdrew a moment to pull himself together: to compose himself, so to speak. And this in turn enabled him to consign his own voice to the music, both in the immediate present and the posthumous future, so that he could keep silent about what had happened to him: so that he could silence the silence.

Or did he just tell himself not to be ridiculous, to forget about things that go bump in the night and just go back and play the music 'more or less correctly'? If so, was he coming to his senses or denying them? Would it even have been possible for *him*, above all, to hear *this* music, above all, without hearing it as something burdened with mortality? At what point, in this whole fantastic scene, could Chopin have played the music itself?

Notes to Chapter 4

1. From Heinrich Schenker, 'Rameau oder Beethoven? Erstarrung oder geistiges Leben in der Musik?', in *Das Meisterwerk in der Musik*, 3 vols (Munich, 1925–30), III, 11–24; translation from Sylvan Kalib, 'Thirteen Essays from the Three Yearbooks, *Das Meisterwerk in der Musik* by Heinrich Schenker: An Annotated Translation' (unpublished doctoral dissertation, Northwestern University, 1973), p. 512 (first sentence italicized in original).
2. In my *Classical Music and Postmodern Knowledge* (Berkeley: University of California Press, 1995), p. 232.
3. Homi K. Bhabha, *The Locations of Culture* (New York: Routledge, 1994), p. 4; the stairwell is part of an installation by the artist and writer Renée Green.

4. Jürgen Habermas, 'What Is Universal Pragmatics?', in *Communication and the Evolution of Society*, trans. by Thomas McCarthy (London: Heinemann, 1979), pp. 1–68 (pp. 1–3, 28–31).
5. Ludwig Wittgenstein, *Zettel*, ed. by G. E. M. Anscombe and G. H. von Wright, trans. by G. E. M. Anscombe (Berkeley: University of California Press, 1970), no. 161. This volume (hereafter *Z*) is a collection of writings from the post-1945 period of the *Philosophical Investigations*. My translation here and throughout.
6. Quoted in Arthur Hedley, *Chopin* (London: Dent, 1963), p. 323.
7. Ludwig Wittgenstein, *Philosophical Investigations*, 2nd [bilingual] edn, trans. by G. E. M. Anscombe (New York: Macmillan, 1958), p. 195; hereafter *PI*. Again, my translation here and throughout.
8. 'Das Verstehen eines Satzes der Sprache ist dem Verstehen eines Themas in der Musik viel verwandtner, als man etwa glaubt. Ich meine es aber so: dass das Verstehen des sprachlichen Satzes näher, als man denkt, dem liegt, was man gewöhnlich Verstehen des musikalichen Themas nennt. Warum sollen sich Stärke und Tempo gerade in *dieser* Linie bewegen. Man möchte sagen: "Weil ich weiss, was das alles heisst." Aber was heisst es? Ich wüsste es nicht zu sagen. Zur "Erklärung" könnte ich es mit etwas anderem vergleichen, was denselben Rhythmus (ich meine, dieselbe Linie) hat. (Man sagt: "Siehst du nicht, das ist, als würde eine Schlussfolgerung gezogen" oder: "Das ist gleichsam eine Parenthese", etc.)'
9. *Poetry and Prose of Heinrich Heine*, ed. and trans. by Frederick Ewen (New York: Citadel Press, 1948), p. 753.
10. Jeremy Siepmann, *Chopin: The Reluctant Romantic* (Boston: Northeastern University Press, 1995), p. 211.
11. See Jeffrey Kallberg, 'Chopin's March, Chopin's Death', *19th-Century Music*, 25 (2001–02), 3–26 (pp. 22–23).
12. Quoted in Siepmann, p. 217.
13. Letter of 28 December 1838; quoted in Siepmann, p. 140.

CHAPTER 5

❖

Preserving the Performance: Scholarship as Art?

Gabriele Brandstetter

It is typical of our ways of talking about theatre studies and theories of performance to speak of productions as ephemeral events. The 'fleeting', the 'never-to-be-recaptured', 'the unique moment' — as our topos would have it — somehow does not pertain to the concrete and lasting reality of the work of art, but it occurs only once within the space-time in which performers and audience share one single event. Productions, and also the art of the producer — irrespective of their content and their specific form — need to be perceived. This perception occurs within a horizon of expectations and as an experience of time present. Recent critical discourses have invoked the ideas of 'the production of presence' (Hans Ulrich Gumbrecht)[1] or 'making presence a staged event' (Martin Seel).[2] Hence various discussions have centred on concepts of production, event, and 'presence'. They have raised questions about the temporality of what is ephemeral, of what can never be recaptured: the paradoxical 'present absence' of the production as an event. This whole body of critical discourse is marked by an almost melancholy longing for what has been lost. Evanescence, that aspect of the production which is already lost in the moment of its realization, a complexity of structures that memory is powerless to retain in its entirety: it is this emotional factor which, in my experience, leads to an affective overemphasis on production, while the recording and preserving of these events is forced to take a secondary role.

But recording and preserving gives rise to a complementary topos of its own: the media and forms that can be applied to the task, the fixing of momentary events in writing, image, and film. Related to this topos are discourses and cultural techniques that serve as aids to recall: transcription, documentation, safeguarding in archives.

'Presence versus representation': so runs the current formula that sums up the complex of questions that cluster around the themes of 'event' and 'aesthetics'. These questions are at present of some urgency, not only in theatre studies but also in such interdisciplinary fields as 'cultural studies' in its several senses. For this one formula: presence and representation — or, as Gumbrecht terms it, the opposition and interweaving of 'cultures of presence and cultures of signification' — calls other antitheses into existence. Thus we speak of the paradoxical antitheses of production and preservation, of event and documentation, of perception and memory in the aesthetic sphere, of movement which enacts and the stylized annotation that holds it in time.

My intention in what follows is to try to make such strong and uncompromising oppositions and their rigid, hierarchical structures modulate into a 'weak' configuring of the relationship between production and preservation. To that end I shall present the positions of artistic performance and its preservation, of production and its re-scription, in a different perspective from that usual in critical discourse. I shall not be breaking up the configuration of production and preservation, but rather enforcing on it an inversion of terms. The focus of attention will thus not be the question whether there is an 'art of production'. Equally, I do not wish to raise the question of preservation by embarking on an analysis of its different modes. What does interest me is the question of an 'art of performance' in its theoretical and performative ambivalence — that is to say, in the tension that arises between production as art and preservation as scholarship and criticism. To invoke this tension immediately opens the way to conceptual puzzles, one being whether preservation cannot itself be regarded as production; then there is the complementary question whether theory itself may not open up an evidential scenario which is — in essence — performative.

It would be a major undertaking to pursue such issues in detail and, finally, to their conclusions. For present purposes, I may thus perhaps be forgiven for cutting such a discussion down to a few key terms and hypotheses. Taking them in sequence, I shall treat the following issues:

(1) Theatre Studies and their Ephemeral Object: 'Production'
(2) A New Vogue for 'Understanding'?
(3) *Evidentia*; or, Scholarship as Art?
(4) *Réécriture*; or, Preservation as Gesture (in the sense of Roland Barthes and Giorgio Agamben)

Underlying all these considerations of the coupling together of performance and preservation there is, I must confess, one constant assumption. It is not often spelled out as a sine qua non of such discussions and thus remains immune to scrutiny. It is the assumption that a faithful translation from one medium to another is possible at all. For we may counter this assumption by contending that, in the act of preserving, translating, in the crossing from one medium to another, there is already an implicit element of transformation. Whether we are speaking in terms of image, script, or video — media whose potential modes of preservation must be viewed differently — the transition from one medium to another is always a factor in the process of recording. To demonstrate and reflect on this effect would be, in my view, an essential element in any description that sets out to comprehend the recording and the episteme of recording as 'art', which is to say: in the sense of *techné*.[3] Indeed I would go further in my intransigence and insist that it must be possible to identify a form of representation which registers the element of hiatus in the transition from one medium to another and thereby allows the gap marking the process of translation to become visible within the transcription itself. Could

this be one way of binding meaningfully together the 'art of production' and the practice of preservation? Of demonstrating *tempus* (in Harald Weinrich's sense):[4] the 'time apart' and 'space apart' of the recording in its paradoxical and dual nature? For, on the one hand, it is clear: the retrospective quality of preserving events in writing or by technical means imparts its own kind of temporality to any such recording in terms of the stratification and interruption of time-sequences. Thus it reveals itself as a reconstructive discourse, a discourse permeable to other time-sequences and one that — of necessity — contains lacunae. On the other hand, we must acknowledge the existence of what I term the pre-positional quality of recording, and this in a twofold sense: first, in a temporal sense, because a recording or written text always comes before the production — 'performance and/as pre-scription'.[5] Secondly, I understand recording in the sense of a 'pro-posal': a placing before, hence a proposal for that re-scription (*réécriture*) of what is to be preserved — a process that can never fully keep what it promises. Hence I ask that 'proposal' be understood in the sense of a persistent, but ultimately never quite successful, approximation to the event of the production.

There is a certain diffuseness about the relationship between production and preservation: if you will allow me the metaphor, a 'grey zone'. How can I make the diffuseness of such a 'grey zone' perceptible in such a context as the present one? To do this, I have chosen to interpolate eight brief visual segments which — corresponding to the etymological affinity between *theoria* and *theatron* — are to be understood in their original sense of the opening of a viewing-space. Thus, the segments will also create such openings, beginning with Gerhard Richter's installation *Acht Grau* (*Eight Grey*).[6]

Segment: first image

'To offer for viewing': pre-script in the pro-scenium:

Entrance fee 3 euros. The cashier asks whether we have been fully informed: the exhibition consists of only this one room with eight pictures. There have been cases of visitors storming out in anger and demanding their money back.

On view: *Acht Grau*.

Theatre Studies and their Ephemeral Object: 'Production'

The question as to how the transient event of a production can be made into a transmissible object of scholarship through various systems and methods of recording has always been a central issue in theatre studies. In recent times, discussion of it has become so intense that we may well call it the main issue of the discipline. And this is not simply a question of methodology. Rather the question penetrates to the core of the discipline, since the way in which theatre studies understand and define themselves essentially depends on the processes by which — and, apparently, also the success with which — this re-production of the discipline's object may be realized. There has long been a need to subject theatre studies to a historical and methodological re-examination in this perspective.[7] Looking at those areas of research and strategies of discussion that are of most vital interest today, there is an interesting observation to be made. To put it simply: hermeneutics are back in fashion. This fact emerges from the ground-breaking studies undertaken in the interdisciplinary context of the conferences organized in Berlin on the field of research 'Kulturen des Performativen', around issues of performance and performativity, on the relation between presence and representation, and on temporality and the perception of time with a view to devising a theory of the event. And, significantly, what is emerging is a hermeneutics of production. Understanding and interpreting are suddenly the new shibboleths of a newly discovered — or rather, recently revived — debate.

Segment: second image

'This is no image.' — Gerhard Richter's *Acht Grau*: an installation that oscillates between established genres: photograph, painting, sculpture, architecture.

'Is this an image?' An image of an image?

In delivering this paper I chose to show transparencies; I could have used a Powerpoint reproduction instead. What can be glimpsed here of the possibility of a perception such as might disclose itself within the installation *Acht Grau*?

An intensification of the doubt that what we see corresponds to the reality of what is perceived.

A New Vogue for Understanding?

The debate to which I have been referring has been conducted mainly with reference to dance — for instance, in a series of articles in the periodical *ballettanz*: 'How can we understand the art of dancing?' or 'Why should we understand dance'[8] — and how? Should we read books about it? Yet again we see at issue the opposition and tension between body and script, between performance and analysis. The claim is made for 'dance' that it is 'a complex semantic system, that is: one that "structures meanings"',[9] and such claims frequently include an appeal to have recourse to 'hermeneutics, the art of understanding' — something that is, however, 'far too precious to be subjected to theory-wars'.[10] So 'dance' as such is elevated in an obviously over-generalized, indeed essentialist manner to signifying the ephemeral par excellence. 'Dance' is globalized to the extent that it is used to exemplify all modes of 'production' and is endowed with ontological status as a 'mighty discourse-generating mega-puzzle'.[11]

I do not wish to engage here with the conceptual and methodological questions that are endemic in this debate, which is by no means novel. Nor do I wish to address the opposition which is claimed in these articles to exist between 'dance-dance', 'dance as pure dance', and 'dance as concept'.[12] Although these essays do not, on the whole, address any specific production, it is none the less clear from them that — in setting out to define how we may 'understand' dance — they still draw a clear line between production and observation, between enactment and interpretation.

SEGMENT: THIRD IMAGE

At the request of Gerhard Richter, the opaque glass of the windows in the room for the exhibit was replaced by transparent panes which afforded a view of the boulevard Unter den Linden.[13] The enamelled panels of Richter's *Acht Grau* echo the form of these windows. They reflect the interior, the visitors, and the urban exterior which is admitted through the transparent panes.

An environment that entraps the observer: windows and opaque mirrors evoke in this interaction the blind spot in perception and understanding. I quote a remark made by Gerhard Richter in 1996 on glass as a symbol: 'see all; understand nothing'.[14]

Is it not time we simply dissolved any sharp distinction between the art of production and the scholarly discipline of describing it?

The avant-garde of the twentieth century, as we well know, said farewell to a concept of the theatre that defined it as an enclosed representation in which some ultimate meaning (be this God, the author, or some other final sense) simply saw itself doubled on stage. In its place models arose — both as theory and in the most diverse forms of theatrical practice — which had the observer become a participant in the staged action. Accordingly, the barrier between observer and observed simply collapsed. Thus, a shift of paradigms from hermeneutics to deconstruction occurred, in the course of which the concepts of a pre-determined mode of understanding and the universalization of meaning had become suspect. This shift makes itself felt once more in the debate that now flourishes on issues of 'production and preservation'. But it is not conducted using a concept of understanding or analysis which presupposes a substantial semantic identity of the object in question — 'dance' as such, for example — or which concretizes production in the sense of an object under examination.

What I would like to emphasize at this point and in direct contrast to the mode of thought I have just been outlining is the important factor of the blurring of perception.[15] For this surely has a place in any discussion of production. Blurring occurs through the incorporation of the observer into the space-between, the grey area which is common to production and preservation and which rules out any sharp distinction between emotionally engaged observation and a perspective that observes this same observation. Using Roland Barthes's terminology, the process that obliterates the border between observer and performance, between a production and the means by which it is recorded, could be called a *sismologie*.[16] By this we may understand a radical destabilizing of the position of observer, one that is indissolubly bound up with both the blurring of perspective onto any production and also with the elusiveness of the event itself. For example, the contingent quality of perception and memory in the process of perceiving and remembering within the act of observation itself could be seen as just such a destabilizing factor. It thus shatters the complacency of an understanding of the processes of preservation which is derived in purely verbal terms. Barthes replaces it with a concept of notation guided by the body, by the movement of the hand that records, as the manual tracing of script.

SEGMENT: FOURTH IMAGE

Grey. A coming to terms with the paradoxical mediation of two apparently incompatible epistemes of the plastic arts: the picture as a 'transparent window onto the world' and, beside it, the 'picture as opaque object, as a monochrome relief'.[17]

What are the implications of identifying the insertion of the observer into what is observed for a theory of the relationship between production and preservation? This question brings me to the third main point of my discussion, and once again I can only sketch in an answer.

Evidentia; or, Scholarship as Art?

In what way does the question as to an 'art of production' impinge on theory, on the scenography of notation?

Two aspects of the implied relation between an observer and the event observed seem especially relevant to me: on the one hand, the turning away from the contemplation of structures towards a foregrounding of the transience of the event. This change of position is accompanied by a new orientation towards process — not merely towards the processuality of the observed 'occurrence', the production, but also in an intensified awareness of temporality as it undergoes a delaying effect and is — as one might say — 'corroded' by virtue of the recording that reconstitutes it. Only in this way can that complex of focused and thus contingent perceptions be articulated that is reassembled via the medium of a fragmented memory into a recorded likeness. Such a complex consists of several textual and temporal strata, discloses its own performativity in layered form, and makes no attempt to disguise this in ways we know only too well from traditional hermeneutic or semiotic analyses of productions. Rather, it reveals itself as a mode of writing, speaking, recording which makes its own temporality visible as an interaction of closeness to and distance from the event that is the production and transposes these in a sensuous, at times sensual, manner into the arena of theory.[18]

SEGMENT: FIFTH IMAGE

Acht Grau. The monochrome effect and aesthetic withdrawal:

Grey (here I quote Gerhard Richter): 'In the grey images there is a lack of differentiation, nothingness, nullity, the beginning and the end. In the glass panes there are analogies with postures and possibilities; in coloured panels chance prevails, everything is possible, or rather: form is nonsense.'[19]

The perception of a production and the retracing of it through the medium of memory get in each other's way at those points where the aim is to realize evidentiality. For here we have to do with different forms and modes of 'evidence'. The area of intersection becomes visible as that region where the immediate experience of the event, the performance which appeals to a variety of sensory modes, is transposed into the field of coordinates which constitutes the act of preservation and thereby takes on a different kind of visibility: precisely that of *evidentia* in Quintilian's sense of a verbal rendition of events as they occur which is so vivid that we are more inclined to believe we are seeing them than hearing them.[20] It would thus be the task of the process of recording to develop just such a correspondence to a visual confrontation: as the art of 'writing into seeing' (*ekphrasis*). This would amount to producing *evidentia* within a scenario of scholarship: one that would not exhaust itself through codifying a performance by its structures, settings, traditions, and modes of discourse, but rather one which — within the conspectus of its 'viewing-space', of its *demonstratio* — would integrate into the very act of recording an awareness of both the conditions of its own processes of observation and the forms and lacunae present in the conventions of perception and representation to which it adheres.

Segment: sixth image

Acht Grau: monochrome reflecting surfaces

An act of separating colour, surface, and the textures produced by painting; what used to be seen as an image in terms of 'painting', shapes, and texture disappears in Richter's glass panels. Now only the observer serves as the conduit through which it enters into both the arena and the process of representation. It thereby becomes a 'spectral kinetic manifestation', a 'shadow and reflex' — and vanishes once more with the observer's departure, leaving behind a 'traceless, monochrome field'. [21]

How might it be possible for such a realization of *evidentia* — as an act corresponding to the production itself — to be made manifest in its preservation? This question has no answer, at least in the sense of a method or set of rules to be applied. Rather, *evidentia* — to the extent that it is the result of such a process of preservation — always has an emergent status. I mean this to be understood in the sense of Niklas Luhmann's definition that emergence is the coming into being of something which, in retrospect, always appears as a likely outcome without its ever having had the status of being the sole predictable result.[22] I would argue that this is also a viable definition of creativity. Such a definition of emergence and the hypothesis of a co-emergence of subject and object in the sphere of scholarship would also afford us 'a dimension of self-awareness within which scholarly observation may be organised'.[23]

A further possibility of making manifest such *evidentia* as an element of emergence in the process of preservation would be to include corporeality: to implicate the body — in its dual role as agent and as the material vehicle of the processes of perceiving and recording — in the reflective process as well. The aim would therefore be to conceive of and implement an experimental approach to the art of preservation: as a mode of transcribing a production, in the sense of an ephemeral and untranslatable event, which is not fixed in the act of preservation, but which marks in a trace that emphasizes the fleetingness of the very act of recording as one of its intrinsic qualities. Such a mode would also make clear that this layered process of retrospectivity in the act of recording is emphatically not meant to make up for a loss of those elements of the production that have inevitably already been taken by transience but, rather, to restore something to it.

Segment: seventh image

Acht Grau. The construction of the panels, the alignment of the monochrome glass surfaces, shows: the opaque mirrors are not smooth reflecting surfaces; they are locked into place in different angles of inclination to the wall, each surface warped into itself. Thus what seems an ordering of static elements into a series becomes a mutable, genetically interacting mirror-space — not the stasis and closedness of the glass surface, as might appear at first sight, but rather a rotation and refraction of the reflected shape.

And does this not also amount to a critique of reflection itself? Of the exhibition and specular immersion of the observer?

Réécriture; or, Preservation as Gesture

A mode of recording oriented to so great an extent towards the manifestation of *evidentia* must necessarily exhibit an awareness of its own paradoxical structure and constitution and make this part of the preserving process itself. In this way, the process is revealed as, on the one hand, the act of anchoring contingent elements of the production as a fixing which also transforms what it fixes, while on the other it is also manifest as the act of transposition itself, as a bodily, material medial act which could also be apprehended as a performative event in its own right. It would be a process of transcription in which the act of writing would no longer be obsessed with combating by verification the fleetingness and elusiveness of a production, but would rather put its own transitory nature on open display and, in the process, put its own strategy at risk as something which is also in motion and transient. Preservation would thus be released from its compulsion to supplement what is lost, namely the loss of the never-to-be-recovered, evanescent production.

The experiment to which a theory of recording necessarily leads, as well as its status of *evidentia* as artistry of scholarship, is thus grounded in the representation of the process of preservation itself: as production or as performance — and in this sense as a corporeal act manifesting itself in the temporality of movement. It would be a *gesture* in the terms in which Giorgio Agamben defines the term. For Agamben contends that gesture defines the status of the image in modernity by annulling its mythical immobility and transporting it into another viewing-space, so that it becomes — to borrow a term from Gilles Deleuze — a series of 'images in motion'.[24] Gesture, which belongs to the 'sphere of action', is, in Agamben's formulation, 'the staging of a mediacy, the becoming-visible of the means as such. It makes manifest human existence as being always within a medium'.[25] In this sense, the moving trace of a written record, the act of writing, transposing, constellating — while always retrospective — can be effective as gesture: an action and direct-pointing which, in its action, recovers the very object of transcription.

Segment: eighth image

Acht Grau. 'Emptiness', 'the image withdrawn', 'manifest lack of affect':[26] such qualities are attributed to Gerhard Richter's monochrome glass panels again and again. But is not the experience, the *evidentia* of the viewing-space, at the same time beyond it? In a perceptual space of manifold corporeality, of the opening of the possible?

An art of production in the sense of academic study as an art-form does not purport to claim some rough equating of production and recording; it is important that there be no misunderstanding here. Rather, it means taking seriously what is observed. But it means taking the scholarly process with equal seriousness: as a renewed and self-renewing concentration of the act of observing — 'observing as recapitulation'. It is not my intention to introduce a didactic element at this point, or any prescriptions for the analysis of productions. Rather this recapitulation is to be thought of as practice, as action in transposition. It makes the mediality of the process, of the 'gesture' as Agamben defines it, the theme of its own action and demonstration. Thus a balance is created, a 'mutual exposition' as Agamben phrases it, that is 'not stasis', 'but a simultaneous oscillation of potentiality in the act and of the act in potentiality'.[27]

In this sense, the recording of a production (of a dance, for example) is the gesture of the gesture. Thus I give Giorgio Agamben the last word, for — as he puts it — 'The gesture is a potentiality that does not realize itself in the act so as to be exhausted thereby, but to preserve itself as potentiality in action — and dance within it.'[28]

Notes to Chapter 5

This chapter was first published, as 'Aufführung und Aufzeichnung: Kunst der Wissenschaft?', in *Kunst der Aufführung — Aufführung der Kunst*, ed. by Erika Fischer-Lichte, Clemens Risi, and Jens Roselt (Berlin: Theater der Zeit, 2004), pp. 40–50. The title of the German original of the chapter has connotations that no single English rendition can preserve. *Aufzeichnung* may have in German the sense of a pictorial or written record, such as notes or memoirs, as well as meaning the recording by technical means of a musical or staged event. *Aufführung* can refer to a single public performance of a work such as a ballet or an opera, or else to a whole production by a single choreographer, director, or conductor, which is repeated many times. *Wissenschaft* in German subsumes such categories as scholarship, in the sense of philology or academic study, but also 'science' in meanings normally limited in English to abstract, exact, or empirical sciences. These connotations mean that the terms of the title are sometimes rendered differently in different parts of the text. Hence such terms as 'scholarly' may also have such connotations as 'philosophical' or 'scientific'.

1. See Hans Ulrich Gumbrecht, 'Produktion von Präsenz, durchsetzt mit Absenz: über Musik, Libretto und Inszenierung', in *Ästhetik der Inszenierung*, ed. by Josef Früchtl and Jörg Zimmermann (Frankfurt a.M.: Suhrkamp, 2001), pp. 63–76.
2. See Martin Seel, 'Inszenieren als Erscheinenlassen: Thesen über die Reichweite eines Begriffs', in *Ästhetik der Inszenierung* (see Gumbrecht, above), pp. 48–62.
3. At this point I am emphatically not referring to the custom of adding to descriptions of recorded performances the annotation that a videotape was used as an ancillary resource for the analysis of dance or theatrical performances.
4. Namely, the 'endowing with form' of a 'narrated world' — hence a process that throws a narrative production into relief. See Harald Weinrich, *Tempus: besprochene und erzählte Welt*, 5th edn (Stuttgart: Kohlhammer, 1994).
5. Hans-Friedrich Bormann, 'Theatralität als Vorschrift: zu Michael Frieds Kunst und Objekthaftigkeit', in *Diskurse des Theatralen*, ed. by Erika Fischer-Lichte and others (Basel and Tübingen: Francke, 2004), pp. 91–101.

6. *Gerhard Richter: Acht Grau*, ed. by the Solomon R. Guggenheim Foundation (New York: Guggenheim Museum Publications, 2002). The 'segments' that punctuate my text represent the images seen in the exhibition, transparencies of which were shown at the conference New Languages for Criticism.
7. See also Isa Wortelkamp, *Sehen mit dem Stift in der Hand: die Aufführung im Schriftzug der Aufführung* (Freiburg i.Br.: Rombach, 2006).
8. Franz Anton Cramer, 'Wie darf ich Tanz verstehen?', *ballettanz*, 2003.3 (March), pp. 28–31; Arnd Wesemann, 'Warum Tanz verstehen?', ibid., pp. 36–37.
9. Cramer, 'Wie darf ich Tanz verstehen?', p. 29.
10. Ibid., p. 31.
11. Wesemann, 'Warum Tanz verstehen?', p. 37.
12. Cramer, 'Wie darf ich Tanz verstehen?', p. 30.
13. See Benjamin H. D. Buchloh, 'Gerhard Richters *Acht Grau*: zwischen Vorschein und Glanz', in *Gerhard Richter: Acht Grau* (see note 7, above), pp. 13–29.
14. *Gerhard Richter: Acht Grau*, p. 9.
15. See Wolfgang Ullrich, *Die Geschichte der Unschärfe* (Berlin: Wagenbach, 2002).
16. Roland Barthes, cited in Gerhard Neumann, 'Theatralität der Zeichen', in *Szenographien: Theatralität als Kategorie der Literaturwissenschaft*, ed. by Gerhard Neumann, Caroline Pross, and Gerald Wildgruber (Freiburg i.Br.: Rombach, 2000), pp. 65–112 (p. 68). For further reading on the phenomenon of 'blurring', see Gerald Wildgruber, 'Theorie und Chor', ibid., pp. 391–452 (pp. 443–44).
17. Buchloh, 'Gerhard Richters *Acht Grau*', p. 14.
18. That interpretation should also evince a quality of 'agency' reveals logic as no longer (solely) inherent in the paradigm of writing but also as the performative aspect of a mode of practice: as a form of action productive of *evidentia*. See Sibylle Peters, 'Performative Writing 1800/2000? Evidenz und Performanz in der medialen Refiguration des Wissens', in *Performativität und Ereignis*, ed. by Erika Fischer-Lichte and others (Basel and Tübingen: Francke, 2003), pp. 99–116.
19. Gerhard Richter, cited in Buchloh, 'Gerhard Richters *Acht Grau*', p. 18.
20. See 'Evidentia, Evidenz', in *Historisches Wörterbuch der Rhetorik*, ed. by Gerd Ueding, 7 vols (Tübingen: Niedermeyer, 1992–), III (1996), pp. 33–47 (p. 44: 'es ist dann nicht mehr, als ob die Dinge erzählt, sondern als ob sie selbst aufgeführt würden').
21. *Gerhard Richter: Acht Grau*, pp. 19, 20.
22. See Hans Ulrich Gumbrecht and others, 'Emergence: A Manifesto for Risk Taking Interdisciplinarity' (unpublished document in possession of Gabriele Brandstetter, 2002), esp. p. 6.
23. Ibid., p. 8.
24. See Giorgio Agamben, 'Noten zur Geste', in *Postmoderne und Politik*, ed. by Jutta Georg-Lauer (Tübingen: Edition Diskord, 1992), pp. 97–107 (p. 101).
25. Ibid., p. 103.
26. *Gerhard Richter: Acht Grau*, p. 16.
27. Agamben, 'Noten zur Geste', p. 107.
28. Ibid., p. 106.

CHAPTER 6

❖

Echoing the 'Mortal Ear': Orfeo's Indiscipline

Peter Szendy

Standing once again on the threshold of what might be considered the first opera — Monteverdi's *L'Orfeo*, on a libretto by Alessandro Striggio[1] — I am about to follow in some of Orpheus's footsteps, watching them intently, in a sort of close reading (or close listening) of some of the traces he left on his way through the realm of Music.

I dimly remember — and hence foresee — various motifs, shadows, movements, or figures lurking out there: there are gestures of inversion, interruptions, strange echoes, and even the damaged and defective contour of an ear ...

On this very threshold where I stand, in the prologue, enters *Music itself* and its songs, ushered in by a toccata and a couple of solemn orchestral ritornellos. There it sounds, onstage. *It* sounds, indeed. For, although Music borrows the voice and the silhouette of a woman, I do not know who or what is singing; I can only tell that *it* sounds, without deciding between an impersonal meaning (as if I were saying: 'it rains') and the embodied presence of Music itself, or herself, in person, in front of me.

But what does Music sing? What does *she* say? What does *it* mean?

Music — Music says — comes from a river: 'Dal mio Permesso amato a voi ne vegno.' The Permessos was a Greek river where the Muses lived (a river whose name, in the Italian libretto, also sounds like 'permission'). If we please, then, Music — Music says — comes to us from, or in the shape of, a *flow*.

Music, alone and sovereign in this prologue, sings of its sovereignty. When it sounds, when it flows or rains — Music says — even the rivers and the creeks have to be mute:

> Or mentre i canti alterno, or lieti or mesti,
> Non si mova augellin [...],
> Né s'oda in queste rive onda sonante.
>
> [Now while I am alternating my songs, now gay, now sad, | May the birds be still [...], | May we not hear waves near these shores.]

In Music's absolute realm, or in the realm of absolute music, there is — Music says — there has to be, silence around her sovereign singing. Even her mythic origin (the river from which she comes) should be silent — and here in the score, there is a conspicuous and emphatic pause.

What is the nature of this pause? To what discipline does it belong? Is it the musical expression of an absolute listening, the sort of listening that would be attuned to Music's sovereignty? Is it an example, an edifying illustration of what absolute music expects from its listeners? Or is it, rather, a blank space waiting to be filled by some unmusical or amusical traces?[2] At this point, on the threshold, it is difficult to tell. Let us wait and see what happens, see (and listen to) what other pauses or interruptions occur on Orpheus's sonorous way. They might shed some light backwards, so to speak, on this one.

It is precisely in the midst of this sovereign flow of words and sounds surrounded by silence that, still in the prologue, Music utters a strange and arresting expression: *mortal orecchio*, 'mortal ear'. 'Io,' says Music, 'su cetera d'or, cantando soglio | mortal orecchio lusingar tal'ora' [I, singing to the golden lyre, am wont | Sometimes to delight the mortal ear]. Were I to keep on listening to it beyond its immediate context, this 'mortal ear' would turn out to be a sort of internal prophecy within the opera. Indeed, mortal listening is the very motif of Orpheus's disobedience or indiscipline. Already subtly announced on the threshold of the prologue, it is this finite, this weak or defective, ear that makes Orpheus turn around, in the fourth act, after having heard a noise. Thus he loses his beloved for the second time, and, in the fifth act, is bound to hear no more than his own mournful lamentations, echoed back to him in a fragmentary way.

This underlying thread, to which the prologue alludes so discreetly, will prove to be a sort of subtext, running as it were under the plot. I 'prehear', or perhaps 'fore-hear', in it an implicit discourse on listening. A kind of impersonal discourse that, in substance, would say: by being represented as structurally *flawed* (i.e. mortal or finite and faulty, undisciplined) in the opera, listening may no longer belong to the exclusive realm of Music; listening may even take place as an interruption of Orpheus's (and Music's) power; in short, it may be that listening happens only if and when there is *a flaw in the flow.*

Let me jump forward, now, to the fourth act. Why does Orpheus turn around, disobeying Pluto's divine law and order? Why such indiscipline?

This crucial revolution in the opera (a revolution in the almost literal sense of an about turn, a volte-face or a reversal) happens in the midst of Orpheus's doubts, doubts that seem to be caused by the fact that *he sings*. Just before disobeying, while singing about singing, Orpheus sings: 'Ma *mentre io canto*, ohimè, chi m'assicura | Ch'ella mi segua [...]?' [But *while I am singing*, alas, who assures me | That she is following me? (my emphasis)] To Orpheus, singing, his own singing, his very power as a musician, seems somehow suspect. And surely it is not a mere coincidence that, a few bars later, after a sudden noise *offstage* (i.e. outside the musical scene), Orpheus exclaims: 'Ma che odo?' [But what do I hear?] His mortal, his defective and suspicious ear is distracted from the sovereign self-listening of Music and its songs. (Indeed, by allowing his musical confidence to be undermined by his doubts, Orpheus was already opening his ear to distraction before hearing the noise — that is, before this positive interruption of Music's flow from offstage.)

The consequence is well known: Orpheus immediately turns around to see his beloved, thereby losing her once again.

Orpheus's ear (i.e. the ear of the musician par excellence) is thus mortal in two ways: it kills his beloved; and it belongs to a finite being, hence to a being unprotected against his own flaws. Orpheus's ear is full of doubts, even about Music itself. It is a curious and suspicious ear because it does not know or 'fore-hear' what happens. Undisciplined to, or by, Music, Orpheus's ear wants to *see*.

Such mortal ear is the signature of the opera, the mark of its singularity when compared to its antique sources. In the tenth book of Ovid's *Metamorphoses*, Orpheus and Eurydice walk surrounded by a silence that no voice troubles. In Book iv of Vergil's *Georgics*, the main source of Striggio's libretto, it is only after Orpheus's about turn that a great noise resonates three times in the underworld. It seems, then, that Monteverdi and Striggio reversed the order of cause and effect by making the noise sound before the revolution of this volte-face, as if it were the very reason for that revolution. The consequence, I would suggest, is that in their version or inversion, mortal listening (i.e. 'our' listening, open as it is to distraction) is structurally undisciplined and doomed to fail. Mortal listening is unruly and therefore disruptive.

What I would like to call the 'revolutionary motif' of the volte-face subtly pervades the opera's musical structure, as if variously disseminated melodic inversions were foretelling, or 'fore-sounding', the dramatic catastrophe (itself another word for revolution).

In the third-act aria, *Possente spirto*, for example, Orpheus's plea to Charon is accompanied by two violins, then by two cornetti (from measure 193), and finally by a harp (*arpa doppia*, from measure 217). While the violins and the cornetti respond to Orpheus's singing by simply echoing it, the harp part reverses the melodic fragments: the ascending ones become descending, and vice versa.

This reversal, or inversion, happens immediately (one measure) after the occurrence of the verb *voltare*, which means in Italian 'to turn': 'A lei volt'ho il cammin' [To her I have turned my path]. In this section of the opera, there is indeed a dense accumulation of all sorts of turns, both literary and musical. In some lines, Orpheus seems almost to sing and speak backwards: 'Orfeo son io che d'Euridice i passi seguo', he says; let me translate word by word, step by step, the right (and therefore wrong) way round: 'Orpheus am I who Eurydice's steps follows.'

But the revolution of Orpheus's mortally undisciplined listening is not only foreshadowed, or 'fore-echoed', in the music and the libretto; it also has a lasting aftermath; it gives repeated echoes in the fifth and last act, when Orpheus bemoans the catastrophe of his own volte-face.

In the last act, symmetrical with the first, a second allegorical figure appears. Enter, not Music, but Echo. These two characters are the only ones that are neither human nor divine. I am therefore tempted to consider Echo as a sort of replica of Music itself. A ruined or a damaged repetition of it. Leaving aside the problem raised by the opera's ending (happy or tragic, as there are two versions of it, both by Monteverdi), Echo clearly seems to have been substituted for Music, as its fragmentary version or reversion. Echo is a sort of mortal copy of Music itself, deprived of, or expelled from, its sovereignty.

What Echo does with Orpheus's lamentations, in fact, is at the same time musical and totally unmusical. It is not merely a matter of silence or pause in the musical flow, as in the prologue. Indeed, while repeating fragments of the musical flow (and I will not elaborate here on whether repetition is an interruption or a continuation), Echo is writing another text, on another sheet or plane. Without staves, without sounds.

For example, when Orpheus sings 'E mai sempre darommi, ahi doglia, ahi pianto!' [And for ever I will endure suffering and, alas!, crying] (measures 45–49), Echo repeats the sounds musically enough, but mutely reorders the letters. Echo silently rewrites: 'hai pianto', it says, instead of 'ahi pianto!', shifting the *h* and inaudibly re-spelling *ahi* as *hai*; thus, 'for ever crying' becomes 'you have cried'.

To Orpheus's mortal ear, Echo's repetitions are both musically faithful (he *hears* no difference) and secretly subversive in their literality. Echo discreetly undermines Orpheus's performative promise, by *turning* the future ('and for ever I will') into a past ('you have cried'). Echo is perhaps the ultimate and inaudible occurrence of the mortal volte-face in the opera.

To conclude, I have tried briefly to outline a hidden — or at least often overlooked — subtext or countertext that runs through *L'Orfeo*. I have tried to overhear it, so to speak.

What I have called the 'revolutionary motif' of Orpheus's volte-face cannot be apprehended as a purely musical phenomenon, or a purely literary one. Its effects are disseminated across the borders of this very distinction — not only because *L'Orfeo* is an opera, and, as such, interlocks various regions, but because the sovereignty of the realm in which we expect them to unite, the sovereignty of Music, is questioned, indeed subverted. And this in a work that is generally considered as celebrating Music's unlimited power.

Hence, rather than applying an 'interdisciplinary' reading to Monteverdi's opera, I wanted to show that the indiscipline already at work in Orpheus's listening — not to speak of ours — ruins the absolute autonomy or sovereignty of Music. Indiscipline (or interdiscipline, if we cannot do without this worn-out notion, which also has the disadvantage of presupposing the boundaries of the very disciplines it seeks to question), indiscipline, I say, does not occur to the musical work from outside. It happens (if and when it happens) by staying closest to its self-distant inside.

Notes to Chapter 6

1. *L'Orfeo, favola in musica da Claudio Monteverde*, ed. by Denis Stevens, corrected edn (London: Novello, 1968).
2. On the history of 'absolute listening', its limits and its paradoxes, see Peter Szendy, *Écoute: une histoire de nos oreilles*, with foreword by Jean-Luc Nancy (Paris: Éditions de Minuit, 2001).

CHAPTER 7

Is Music Criticism Criticism?

Malcolm Bowie

These few remarks are offered as a contribution to a still-young discussion on the usefulness or otherwise of the literary arts to those who write about music, whether critically, historically, or analytically. I already have a hunch that my comments may in due course turn into something of a diatribe on the theme of lost opportunities, and that they will dwell particularly on the art of writing as a neglected resource for those who go into print about musical structure or effect, but I do not for a moment want to suggest that writers on music cannot write, for some of them certainly can. Here is Gerald Abraham, for example, discussing Chopin as melodist in 1939:

> It would be a disastrous mistake to regard the melodies of the nocturnes and Chopin's nocturne-like melodies in general as mere echoes or imitations of Italian song-melody. [...] [He] had an instinct amounting to genius for inventing melodies that would be actually ineffective if sung or played on an instrument capable of sustaining tone but which, picked out in percussive points of sound each beginning to die as soon as born, are enchanting and give an illusion of a singing that is often lovelier than singing itself. In other words, Chopin's melody, in so far as it is Italian, is not an imitation but a stylisation of Italian *bel canto*.[1]

The contrast between the continuous cantilena of, say, Bellini's melodies and the broken continuity of Chopin's has found its way into Abraham's syntax and given his main sentence its own tune. He works hard to combine the technical description of sound-production with a lively account of musical pleasure being sought and, after a tantalizing movement of deferral, found.

Or consider Tovey writing about the finale of Beethoven's Op. 111 piano sonata:

> Hitherto Beethoven's static and ecstatic visions in this sublime mood have been aloof from action. In such variation movements as those in Op. 57, the B flat trio, Op. 97, and the Violin Concerto, the slightest intrusion of foreign chords can dispel the vision, the more roughly the better. But now in Op. 111, and afterwards in the Ninth Symphony, the E flat Quartet, Op. 127, and the C sharp minor Quartet, Op. 131, Beethoven finds ways of modulating which bring action harmoniously into the contemplative vision. This kind of passage demonstrates the highest power of mastery of form.[2]

After many pages of technical description, the singularity of Beethoven's achievement in these late works comes down to a contrast and an improbable reconciliation between the *vita activa* and the *vita contemplativa*. Thanks to the discreet ingenuity of Tovey's writing, that is to say, an existential choice that figures prominently in the works of the Church fathers and in the history of European monasticism has been brought to bear, in a miniaturized and intensified form, on three bars of keyboard music. The momentousness of late Beethoven has by stealth been reinserted into a long European history. An active power has been rediscovered inside a timeless ecstasy.

And a similar rhythm of expansion and contraction is to be found throughout the work of Charles Rosen, an admirer of Tovey's who has inherited his great predecessor's sense of music belonging at once to itself and to a larger social and historical order. Rosen's music criticism is informed, as many readers will know, by a keen sense of drama at all levels of argument and analysis. Whether he is discussing the social conditions in which sonata form was consolidated in the late eighteenth century, the clash between different styles within 'Romantic' musical culture, or the build-up and discharge of tension during a single symphonic movement, his attention is always drawn to the placing and timing of key events within complex processes of development. *The Classical Style* is a masterpiece in which precise textual observation is combined with bold speculative criticism, and it is Rosen's dramaturgical imagination that holds these two elements together. Music that matters is always seen in the drama of its temporal unfolding, and in the grip that it exerts, in the flow of time, on the mental powers, sensuous, intellectual, and emotional, of executant and hearer. (Rosen's account of Haydn's 'Oxford' Symphony is a compelling example of this 'criticism as drama'.[3])

Yet despite these wonderful things, these excellent instances of a richly expressive and precisely focused critical language directed at major works and complex issues, there is still something dispiriting, because stunted and half-hearted, about much modern writing on music. One disappointment is to find that so much analysis is defensively or self-denyingly intent on technical description to the exclusion of all but a bleached and dried-out after-image of musical experience proper, and another disappointment is to discover that when a music writer has gone off to literary studies to find a language for, shall we say, the articulation of narrative design as it appears in Bruckner's symphonies or Chopin's ballades, he or she has often come back with terminological gadgetry and little more. One group seems to fear that any departure from technical rectitude is in danger of enveloping the reader in a purple haze of fine writing, or of settling for mere programme notes, and the other seems to think that figures and tropes borrowed from the literary lexicon are somehow by themselves able to restore musical experience to the minds of real listeners in real time. There is another lesson to be learnt from criticism, and one that could produce something stranger and finer and harder-to-do for music writing, but this is not to be found in manuals or glossaries or all-embracing theories of narrative.

The question has really to do with the rhythm, drive, and momentum of artistic meaning, and with the bifurcations, simultaneities, and stratifications that occur inside a single time-bound artistic process. And in order to get help or inspiration in the endeavour to articulate this, this the ever-changing plenum of meaning, as it were, this plenum with its ballooning vacuities caught up inside it, we probably need to go not to the literary technicians or theory-builders but to writer-critics of the front rank. I shall indulge myself for a moment or two by quoting from one of the most remarkable tributes ever to have been paid by one great writer to another. This is from Mandelstam's 'Conversation about Dante', written in the Crimea in 1933, but first published, in English translation, only in 1965, and in Russian two years later. Mandelstam begins by talking about poetry as a hybrid process, in which two main axes are occupied at once — one of them involving the prosodic instruments themselves and the other the intonational and phonological performances that such instruments permit. He calls out to music for his working definitions of poetry, from the first paragraph onwards. But more remarkable than the nods and courtesies that pass between different art-forms in his writing are the strong outward references to artisanship, to the multitude of crafts and trades that lie beyond the professional concerns of the poet or composer. He follows Dante in his adherence to ordinary life and daily work. Already on the second page of his great essay, the reader of poetry as he or she negotiates rhyme, metaphor, and sentence structure is taken out into the open air:

> The quality of poetry is determined by the speed and decisiveness with which it embodies its schemes and commands in diction, the instrumentless, lexical, purely quantitative verbal matter. One must traverse the full width of a river crammed with Chinese junks moving simultaneously in various directions — this is how the meaning of poetic discourse is created. The meaning, its itinerary, cannot be reconstructed by interrogating the boatmen: they will not be able to tell how and why we were skipping from junk to junk.[4]

We do of course all pause from time to time to ask the boatman where we are going as we pass through the sometimes excessively busy communicative channel that is a work of art in its many-stranded unfolding. Sometimes the busy river works us too hard, and we look for a resting place. Rather than read Dante we begin to worry about his classical, biblical, or Thomistic sources; rather than listen to Mozart we step sideways into questions of patronage or performance practice or period style. And sometimes of course attention paid to these extraneous matters pays handsome rewards when it comes to the act of playing or listening to a given work. Alan Tyson's remarkable work on paper-types and watermarks, for example, tells us new things about the order of composition of Mozart's late works,[5] and this in turn may suddenly bring previously unsuspected features of a given composition into our field of hearing for the first time. But often in musical scholarship one finds that the return journey to works in performance, or to works seen in their intrinsic formal elaboration, is never seriously attempted once the external frame of reference has been established as an autonomous object of inquiry. The work in its coherence, integrity, or splendour exists as a guarantee that scholarly exertion is worthwhile, but exists remotely, as a talisman, an inscrutable and unaccountable radiance cast over the world of academic toil. It does not call attention to itself, and it does not readily call criticism to action.

An example of this strange yet somehow highly principled removal of the work itself from the field of inquiry is to be found in Tovey's account of Mozart's Symphony No. 40 in G minor, K.550. He writes with his customary brilliance about the opening bars, and takes to task those commentators — already a multitude by the 1930s when these programme essays were first collected — who talk loosely about tragedy in the context of this work: 'Mozart's whole musical language is, and remains throughout, the language of comic opera.'[6] If the darkness and disconsolateness of the piece are to be defined, we need to approach the task through the lightness and grace of this operatic idiom. To reinforce the point, and the difficulty of the undertaking, Tovey points to the similarities between the opening bars of the symphony and those of Rossini's *Barbiere di Siviglia* overture. (Others have pointed out that the rhythm of the opening phrase of the symphony's first subject is identical with that of Cherubino's 'Non so più' in *Le nozze di Figaro*, written two years earlier.) But Tovey, having issued this challenge, having called for a new definition of tragedy in music, abandons analysis altogether: 'We can learn to know them', he says of the symphony's four movements, 'as we know friends whose deepest feelings are not hidden from us because we tacitly agree not to press on them with heavy words.'[7] Thus does a loquacious and eloquent critic fall unrepentantly silent.

I want to spend a little time on Mozart's first movement, in order to sketch out some possible paths for criticism. The tonal architecture of the movement, and indeed of the symphony as a whole, has been well described. It is one of the best written about of Mozart's orchestral works. (Neal Zaslaw provides a selective reading list in his major book on Mozart's symphonic corpus.[8]) But what has not been fully caught is the intellectual velocity of the writing, its rhythmic and motivic complexity and its argumentative toughness — to say nothing of what I shall take a chance and call its 'poetics'. Certain elements of this astonishing music are dwelt on, and perfectly properly, in the commentaries: its indebtedness to Baroque formulae of one kind or another, and the background presence of Baroque ritornello form as its sonata argument proceeds; its links both with Mozart's chamber music and, as we have noted, with comic opera; the shape of its themes; and the improbable routes that Mozart's modulations take, especially in the brief and compressed development section. Stanley Sadie, writing on the last of these matters, for example, says of the development that it 'begins with an abrupt, disorientating shift of key, to F sharp minor — very remote indeed from the home key, and the effect of remoteness is heightened as the music seems to slip, as if beyond control, through other keys'.[9]

For the most part these topics are separately considered, and the affective complexity of the music — the combined action within it, for example, of lyric grace on the one hand and rage and violence on the other — is stippled in with an adjective or two here and there. The force of an aesthetic experience is held at arm's length, and the combinatory mechanism itself, with its active power of sustaining and dramatizing ambiguity, gets short shrift. It does not in fact require a significant departure from conventional analysis, nor the importation of fanciful quasi-technical terms from other disciplines, to begin getting a clearer sense of Mozart's overall integrative process. Just as a disparate array of source-materials flow into Dante's *terza rima*, and find themselves realigned and re-energized by its syntactic and metrical constraints, so Mozart's references outwards to other compositions and other styles of composition are reprocessed by the internal economy of his symphonic argument. And in the same way this active transformative power, audible at once to listeners who are reasonably familiar with Mozart's works at large and those of his immediate predecessors, serves us well when we come to the internal thematic transformations from which the movement is built. Each theme is a mnemonic device by which we retain a sense of the music's past states even as we career and swerve with it into its unfolding futures. The similarity between the themes enhances this quality of known and unknown jointly at play, of forward-flung remembrance, of a mobile *multum in parvo.* As the themes move from bass to treble, and from woodwind to strings, and as they are stretched and compressed, played against alternative versions of themselves, an extraordinary sensation of cornucopian fullness is created, in the development section, but not there alone, for the movement is developmental even up to the brink of its final cadence. In Mandelstam's terms, we are aided in finding our way across this river not because there is a boatman to guide us but because all the craft are indeed junks. This would be a very different river if some only of the craft were junks, and others were steamers, schooners, dredgers, or trawlers.

I should like to dwell for a moment longer on the development proper, for it seems to me that our old-fashioned talk of exposition, development, and recapitulation, which is fine for many plain descriptive purposes, is seriously limited when we come to talk about the time-bound process that music is, or about the rhythms of differentiation and de-differentiation that govern its moving architecture. Alfred Einstein wrote of the developments in the last three symphonies that they are 'plunges into the abyss of the soul, symbolized in modulations so bold that to Mozart's contemporaries they must have seemed to lose their way entirely, and so distant that only Mozart himself could find the path back from them into the light of day'.[10] The G minor's first movement is one of those special cases among Mozart's final works — one thinks also of the string trio K.563 and the last B flat piano concerto K.595 — where the development reaches an extreme of compression, expressive intensity, and harmonic originality. What seems to me uncertain, however, in the present case is precisely the return to the light of day of which Einstein speaks. To be sure, the tonal architecture view of the piece will insist that closure has been achieved, the return journey to the home key completed, and a last reminiscence just before the end of loss and disintegration satisfactorily dissolved by the final partial reassertion of the opening theme. Sonata form exists, in this view, to protect us from the abyss. Edward Said offers an extreme version of this view in his remarkable *Musical Elaborations*, when he identifies the sonata principle with an entire range of objectionable political attitudes. Vienna, in its music and not just in its notorious imperial arrangements, gave us a structure that was dominative, coercive, authoritative, combative, overtly administrative and executive. Thus do Said's adjectives rain down upon the musical form crystallized and made famous by Haydn, Mozart, and Beethoven. Said, in what is in other ways a subtle-minded study, caricatures the role of the development section — it is 'the space opened up between two strongly marked poles, the inaugural declarations, which is where the theme first gets stated, and at the end, which is where a final cadential formula winds things up'[11] — and has nothing to say about the extremes of tonal uncertainty and waywardness that the great Viennese composers discovered there. But he is stating in hyperbolic form a commonly held opinion, to the effect that sonata movements are all about closure, and provide long-range echoes of an altogether encouraging kind between early and late moments in the passage of musical time. We should be closer to the mark, in speaking of these late Mozart developments at least, if we said that they introduce a crucial and cruel asymmetry between the strongly marked poles that lie on either side of them, and that in so doing they introduce an ironic counterweight to the rhetoric of authority and control. The act of remembrance that the hearer is invited to perform involves a spoiled echo between start and close. Even where the recapitulation includes a good deal of note-for-note repetition, the dangerous tonal landscapes traversed in between mean that the same material is now no longer quite the same. It knows latterly what it did not know early on. The world has changed. Reassertion of an earlier state of affairs begins to resemble a salvage operation or at best a Pyrrhic victory. We have been given the wherewithal to see through it. The music has already told us too much about its own disempowerment for last gestures, however 'coercive' in intent, to carry full conviction. The daylight still has the dark caught inside it. Literary texts train their readers in the perception and long-breathed articulation of ambiguities, contradictions, and semantic dissonances of this kind, and in so far as literary criticism makes good use of this training it has something of worth to offer writing about music.

And there is another thing that literature can help us do. Good criticism is an art of translation — from language to language, or from level to level, or idiom to idiom, within a given language. Literature, and criticism in its wake, are all to do with meaning on the move, in transit, in transformation from moment to moment inside a signifying flux. It would be unhelpful in the extreme to stabilize this by reference to a master language, a great code, a super-theory of textuality or narrativity, that answered all the questions in advance, and reduced the transformative energies of the text to a series of pro forma transactions. Music, being its own language and its own meta-language too, has seemed not to need to know about criticism, or not to need to know much about it. The best analysis of a work of music could just be another work of music, we are sometimes told. And a version of this much in favour among writers on music is that analysis needs a single technical language, and no expressive frills. Music is a pure thing and must be protected from the taint of loose verbalization. What I have been suggesting is that a willingness on the part of writers on music to use a more varied verbal palette can actually bring us closer to the real world of musical experience, and to the wonderfully impure acts of translation, of provocation, of risk-taking, and of abyssmanship that musical experience involves. Were I a betting man, I would suggest that criticism of the kind that I have been calling for can do much better than better-behaved monolingual or monological musical discourse in talking about certain pieces. In talking, for example, about the interplay between martial rhythm and quietly confiding lyricism in the first movement of the C major concerto K.467. This is a strange and magical co-presence, and as things stand a certain kind of literary criticism seems better prepared than strict musical analysis to characterize it.

Notes to Chapter 7

1. Gerald Abraham, *Chopin's Musical Style* (London: Oxford University Press, 1939), p. 64.
2. Donald F. Tovey, *A Companion to Beethoven's Pianoforte Sonatas* (London: Associated Board, 1931), p. 294.
3. Charles Rosen, *The Classical Style: Haydn, Mozart, Beethoven* (London: Faber and Faber, 1971), pp. 159–62.
4. Osip Mandelstam, 'Conversation about Dante', in *Osip Mandelstam: The Collected Critical Prose and Letters*, ed. by Jane Gary Harris, trans. by Jane Gary Harris and Constance Link (London: Collins Harvill, 1991), pp. 397–442 (p. 398).
5. Alan Tyson, *Mozart: Studies of the Autograph Scores* (Cambridge, MA: Harvard University Press, 1987).
6. Donald F. Tovey, *Essays in Musical Analysis*, 6 vols (London: Oxford University Press, 1935–39), I: *Symphonies*, 192.
7. Ibid., p. 195.
8. Neal Zaslaw, *Mozart's Symphonies: Context, Performance Practice, Reception* (Oxford: Clarendon Press, 1989), pp. 569–600.
9. Stanley Sadie, *Mozart Symphonies* (London: Ariel Music, 1986), p. 87.
10. Alfred Einstein, *Mozart: His Character, his Work*, trans. by Arthur Mendel and Nathan Broder (New York: Oxford University Press, 1945), p. 235.
11. Edward W. Said, *Musical Elaborations* (London: Vintage, 1992), p. 100.

CHAPTER 8

❖

Modernist Futures

Gillian Beer

At the end of his autobiography *Blasting and Bombardiering*, covering the period 1914–26, Wyndham Lewis turns briefly to the present moment of his Conclusion:

> I don't know how such a book as this ought to end: I feel inclined just to shut it down now. But I'm told, by people who seem to know, that I ought to drag in the present (Autumn 1937, time of writing.) [...]
>
> The Zeitgeist, as I said three hundred pages back, is getting clear of the wash, or the undertow, kicked up by the Great War; we've got a new Zeitgeist, almost. It's almost as if a new guy had got into the landscape. I can hear him and smell him — there are new crepitations in the air, as yet unexplained. I believe he will be a great improvement, from my point of view, on the last one.[1]

Lewis's buoyant welcome for the coming 'new guy' is rare among writers of the late 1930s. But his reasons are intriguing: 'There is [among literary men] an agreeable alteration in accent. Words fall with a more businesslike, a bleaker click' (341). 'A bleaker click': the acrid humour in that description, and the emphasis on bodily sensation in the previous passage ('I can hear him and smell him'), are typical of Lewis's pungent dissent from all orthodox positions, including his own. Here, he positions himself as an optimist in the face of the gathering gloom of the late 1930s. Perhaps there is still an impulse of Futurist energy in that hope to swim free from the 'wash, or undertow, kicked up by the Great War'. In 1931 in his book entitled *Hitler* he presents his subject as 'a man of peace', and not until he had visited Germany again later in 1937 did he revise his views. In 1939, at last, he writes an attack on *The Hitler Cult*. Wyndham Lewis, Vorticist, is always a troubling node in any map that attempts to inscribe literary modernism as a coherent movement. He is an innovator as well as a reactionary.

I want here to investigate four novels of the 1930s that together, I hope, will raise some questions about the category 'modernism' and its relation to the public world. The novels are Aldous Huxley's *Brave New World* (1932), Harold Nicolson's *Public Faces* (1932), Henry Green's *Party Going* (1939), and Virginia Woolf's *Between the Acts* (1941). Huxley and Nicolson's 1932 novels are set in the future. Nicolson and Woolf's novels are both set in June 1939. Green's novel is deliberately dated at the end with its place and years of composition: London. 1931–38. All four of them are preoccupied with the future (which may of course require them to dwell on the past).

Before I turn to these particular texts let us note some of the significations of modernism in the late twenties and thirties in Britain. Evolutionists sought to combine genetics and natural selection, and what Julian Huxley names 'the modern synthesis' reached its fruition in Theodosius Dobzhansky's *Genetics and the Origin of Species* in 1937. Genetics is essentially a study of the future by means of past selective processes, and during the 1920s and 30s the popular interest in eugenics had become eager and widespread (the recoil against the movement was for a time total in the wake of Nazi horrors in the 1940s). Eugenics seeks to control human fertility in the service of specific social ideologies and for the advantage of the present and next generation. It is a future-based enterprise. I shall say more about it when I turn to Aldous Huxley's *Brave New World*.

In theology, too, 'modernism' became a key term with a broad audience. For example, in the *Listener* in its first year of publication, 1929, there are advertisements for books on Theological Modernism. That movement emphasized that things had changed since the time of Christ: one must keep one's mind open to new knowledge and its implications, and not rely on authority. The public world of history and the private world of sensibility have shifted the forms of belief into new shapes. Its premises were thus quite closely in accord with literary modernism, which emphasized experiment and novelty.

In retrospect we group our modernists as particular literary writers, but:

> Your modernist, then, describes nature in terms of a four-dimensional conception, which is neither space nor time, but a complete union of both [...]. Whether the space-time continuum is regarded as a very efficient diagram or whether it is regarded as an accurate model of reality is perhaps a matter of choice rather than of argument.

Not a description of Joyce or Woolf, or indeed of J. B. Priestley with his time-warp plays, but (as the reference to diagram and model perhaps reveals) to what the writer calls those 'ultra-modernists' 'Jeans, Eddington, Einstein'. The quotation is from C. W. R. Hooker's *What is the Fourth Dimension?* (1934).[2]

So the terms 'modern' and modernism' were widely dispersed, with overlapping significations, across a whole range of inquiries by the 1920s and 30s, perhaps most influentially of all — because most fully integrated with daily life — in the 'modern movement' in architecture, with its emphasis on function over decoration. Writers responded to the new uncertainties that physics offered, for example. They responded also to the shared dilemmas of daily experience: the General Strike, the Depression, the rise of fascism and of communism. They reached out through new technology, such as radio. But did the writers themselves know whether they were modernists or not? In many cases, no.

For example, take Harold Nicolson. We would never now in any conventional genealogy of modernism find a place for him. The husband of Vita Sackville-West, yes, but part of the orthodox world of diplomacy and order. Indeed, I am not seeking to squeeze him under the fence into the enclosure of modernism but rather to suggest that too much gets left out if we take a coterie view of the movement (if it is a movement). Perhaps it might help if we thought of it less as a curriculum subject and more in the terms that Nicolson himself used in the title of his series of radio talks in December 1931: 'The New Spirit in Literature'. In these talks he praises and discusses Auden and Woolf and Joyce and he offers a translation into and out of Joyce, taking a passage to show what he calls the 'old-fashioned' 'inferential' narrative version and the new Joycean. Nicolson is here acting as emissary and interpreter for the new spirit in literature.

In the next year, 1932, he published a novel *Public Faces* prefaced by an epigraph from W. H. Auden:

> Private faces in public places
> Are wiser and nicer
> Than public faces in private places.[3]

This novel is in a number of ways astonishing, though it keeps to what he had called 'old-fashioned', 'inferential' narrative methods. It is a near-future novel, set around 3 June 1939, and it details the onset of an atomic war, in which Britain alone possesses the bomb. Most commentary on life in the 1930s that I have read has always asserted that people were unaware of the possible development of such a bomb, but here in 1932 it is the premise of the entire novel that such a bomb has been developed (or, perhaps, more exactly, will have been developed over the seven years between 1932 and its setting, 1939). The tone is a disturbing mixture of high comedy and chill prophecy. The novel demonstrates how far momentous decisions may depend on personal small animosities, on the weariness of the committee room with a long agenda, on keeping the other party out (here, the dreaded imagined *predecessor* 'Churchill Government'), on the exact language and translation of diplomatic texts, and on the absurdities of daily living (little vanities, the fatal decision to have a day in the country, or to walk rather than take a car to a meeting): 'Those eddies of chance, those swirls of foolishness, those whirlpools of inadvertence'. Most of the characters fail to notice that (as the omniscient narrator suggests)

> if in fact there be any current of events, it can be likened, not to the continuous streaming of a river, but to the more recondite currents of the greater seas. Shifting, discontinuous, submerged, the flux and reflux of these hidden influences veer with wind and tide; nor can the little knowledge of man suffice to foretell the force or destination of such energies. (124)

This novel offers a bleak vision of the collapse towards war through having too much power. England has acquired a monopoly on the chemical needed to produce the bomb, and so all the other powers are lined up against her. And within the pacifist Cabinet there is one minister bent on power who, half-unwittingly, sends rockets across Europe and on to the USA. But Nicolson emphasizes always that the Abu Saad dispute, which threatened to turn an initially quite trivial problem into 'a world conflict',

> was determined, neither by the anxious endeavours of the well-meaning, nor yet by the sinister purposes of those who thought in terms of war, but by the interaction of several human frailties, and by the intrusion of the tiny pebbles of chance. (125)

That sense of chanciness seems to be resisted in the love story of the book, though that too is flipped upside down at the conclusion. There are new gender negotiations in the book — the scene where John Shorland, a relatively junior civil servant but major character in the book, is introduced to us opens with a paragraph thus:

> John Shorland had, at that very moment (it was 8.40pm on Thursday, June 2, 1939), realised that he was in love. He was not only in love, he was desperately in love. He was in love with the Parliamentary Under-Secretary of State. (23)

I have to admit that I was trapped by the joke. My immediate thought was: 'I didn't realize you could be so open about homosexuality in the thirties'. The 1932 reader was expected to blench. But of course, because this is seven years in the future, Nicolson imagines, with an undertow of satirical improbability, that the Under-Secretary of State is a young woman, Jane Campbell, 'a woman of tact, gaiety, and determination' (26) who, together with John Shorland, eventually saves the day at the end of the novel and pulls the world back from the brink.

The source of the crisis is Persia, or Iran, and that remains the problem at the end, with Russian troops invading Persia. The novel freely mingles actual people — Hore Belisha, Aneurin Bevan, Winston Churchill in 1936 alliance with Oswald Mosley, and what the doorman thinks of as 'the sweeter, simpler period of Mr. Neville Chamberlain' (65) — with the members of the fictional 'Pacifist cabinet' whom Nicolson conjures up. It is sometimes dizzying to remember that all this is being written before the coming to power of Hitler, before the appeasement policy, or the outbreak of the Second World War in September 1939 . This novel foresees with icy accuracy the time of the actual war's onset.

The last chapter comprises (fictional) extracts from newspapers of the next few years, the 1940s, including two on the climate changes produced by the exploding of the atomic bomb in June 1939: *Country Life*, July 1942, reports that the President of the Royal Horticultural Society 'has definitely come down on the side of those who believe that the Gulf Stream has been permanently diverted. He has transformed three of his orchards at Angley Manor into vineyards' (245). Nicolson appears to have a happier idea than ours of what would happen if the Gulf Stream is diverted — now we expect it to bring permanent cold! — but he includes also an extract from a (fictional) wireless talk by the (very real and omnipresent) 1930s commentator Gerald Heard in September 1943, wondering where all the eels have gone: 'the eel has formed a distaste for our present hot summers and dry winters' (245). The reach of Nicolson's satire and of his prophecy is long indeed.

The novel is both hilarious and despairing. It builds a dense and compelling picture of how diplomacy works, and fails to work: how nations drive themselves reluctantly towards war and how all the good will in the world can only by sheer good fortune avert catastrophe. The satire is directed at how history is written, as well as at the venal appetites that propel humankind. A last turn in the book's jokes is the pseudo-introduction at the end to the fictional second edition of the work in 1978, written purportedly by Nicolson's grandson in a gruesome new English spelling. He has decided to republish it because it 'provides admirabl instans muddleheadedness of last to kapitalist dekades' but repudiates his grandfather's 'long-windedness' 'his fawls valyoos, his kompleet lak of enni narrativ gifts' (247).

In that same year, 1932, Aldous Huxley published a now far more famous vision of the future, *Brave New World,* set in 'this year of stability, A.F. 632', that is After Ford, the car manufacturer, so in about AD 2485. The time distance gives Huxley more liberty, though he uses it to hone his criticism of the present tendencies of his society through a fantastic society of the future and an atavistic society of the past. Wyndham Lewis had written a future novel, *The Childermass*, set outside heaven, in 1928. But Huxley is more in the mode of *Gulliver's Travels*. The book is partly a satire on the future as represented by the USA and its advanced technologies and their inevitable inroads into European culture: 'The future of America is the future of the world.'[4] But the two worlds set up within the novel are neither of them Utopias that the reader can accept. The first is the sybaritic, standardized, sex-driven, disease-free yet entirely ungenerative society of the World State, with its hatcheries, and its identical citizens whose status and role is inscribed before their birth in their genetic controls in the 'Social Predestination Room' (117): 'We also predestine and condition. We decant our babies as socialized human beings, as Alphas or Epsilons' (10).

The other world is that of the Lawrentian American Indian reservation where there is 'A mother, and all this dirt, and gods, and old age, and disease ...' (106). Bernard Marx, visiting from the World State and appalled by the idea of the bloody rituals of the Reservation, finds that 'his conditioning had made him not so much pitiful as profoundly squeamish. The mere suggestion of illness or wounds was to him not only horrifying, but even repulsive and rather disgusting' (120). In the Reservation there is dancing and drugs and sex and crafts, reproduction and jealousy, and a community as fiercely bound together as the World State is banal and orderly. But like the World State it is deeply intolerant of any deviation, any aberrant individual. Here John, elsewhere called the Savage, has lived all his childhood, unhappily, always in a state of semi-exclusion: 'If one's different, one's bound to be lonely' (119). That is Bernard Marx's condition too: 'If one happens to be decanted different ...' (119).

So is there any pathway between these two repellent states of being? It is to be found, if anywhere, in John, the young 'savage' born of a 'civilized' mother Linda, whose entire upbringing has been brought about through Shakespeare's language. His speech and his experience are saturated with wonderful insights and inappropriate reactions to the conditions in which he finds himself. He is a kind of Miranda, utterly innocent and unprepared for the world beyond.

> Bernard couldn't help laughing.
>
> John also laughed, but for another reason — laughed for pure joy.
>
> 'O brave new world', he repeated. 'O brave new world that has such people in it. Let's start at once.'
>
> 'You have a most peculiar way of talking sometimes', said Bernard, staring at the young man in perplexed astonishment. 'And, anyhow, hadn't you better wait till you actually see the new world?' (121)

But unlike Shakespeare's Miranda, John finds that appalling disillusionment is to be his lot, a disillusionment that betrays the violence he harbours within him. When

Lenina strips naked and offers herself to him he is stricken and 'thrust[s] her roughly away at arm's length' (170). The scene mingles absurdity and Grand Guignol. It is funny but dismaying.

> Outside, in the other room, the Savage was striding up and down, marching, marching to the drums and music of magical words. 'The wren goes to't, and the small gilded fly does lecher in my sight.'

And he is off in a grand amalgam of Lear and Othello's words ending in the repeated 'fat rump and potato finger'.

> 'John.'
> 'What is it?' he asked gruffly.
> 'I wonder if you'd mind giving me my Malthusian belt.' (172)

Eugenics again. Standardizing, regulating, controlling: all these dismal aspects of the World State are set against the irruptive power of sex and reproduction. Near the book's end the Controller describes how this State came to be and how it deals with aberrant citizens. It banishes them to an island, with their kind.

And now another force enters the argument: the wars of the past and the need to control the violence unleashed by scientific discoveries. Happiness, the Controller argues, matters more than truth and beauty in such periods.

> And, of course, whenever the masses seized political power, then it was happiness rather than truth and beauty that mattered. Still, in spite of everything, unrestricted scientific research was still permitted. People still went on talking about truth and beauty as though they were the sovereign goods. Right up to the time of the Nine Years' War. *That* made them change their tune all right. What's the point of truth or beauty or knowledge when the anthrax bombs are popping all around you? That was when science first began to be controlled — after the Nine Years' War. People were ready to have even their appetites controlled then. Anything for a quiet life. We've gone on controlling ever since. (201)

Here we hear the genuine horror of an approaching future being foreknown by Huxley in the early thirties. Did it come about? Are we its inheritors? Not quite. But catastrophe breeds indifference. And the point of this fable, and its constant oscillation, is on the question of freedom. Human beings cannot be free because they are driven by appetites. Human beings cannot be free because they are corralled by societies. Human beings cannot be free because they do not want to be. All these statements seem implicit in Huxley's grim humour. The last scenes of the book, with the media rampage around John, the Savage, are brutal, and he is brutalized. He takes the only route out left to him, and the dangling feet are described with compass points, seeming to indicate the World State, in the final paragraph:

> Slowly, very slowly, like two unhurried compass needles, the feet turned towards the right; north, north-east, east, south-east, south, south-south-west; then paused, and, after a few seconds, turned as unhurriedly back towards the left. South-south-west, south, south-east, east ... (229)

It may seem a far cry from this stark fable to the subtle innuendos of Henry Green's *Party Going* (1939) and so indeed it is. But I include this novel with its marvellously devious inscription of the moment-by-moment waverings of emotion because of the bold narrative shape that Green devises to evoke dread in the reader and a sense of revolutionary futures lying in wait. 'Party going' promises arrival. Going to a party is a preliminary to being there. But here the group of upper-class passengers are trapped in a hotel on Waterloo station, waiting for the fog to lift so that the trains can go again. They plan to be in the south of France. They do not set out within the span of the novel. They scheme, chat, make erotic moves, take baths, while below the great mass of people stand and surge, always — according to the fears of these passengers — about to break into the hotel in hordes. The massive crowd is one bulwark of the novel. The other is the frail, ill, perhaps demented aunt with her inexplicable concern for a dead pigeon with which the novel opens:

> Fog was so dense, bird that had been disturbed went flat into a balustrade and slowly fell, dead at her feet.
>
> There it lay and Miss Fellowes looked up to where that pall of fog was twenty feet above and out of which it had fallen, turning over once. She bent down and took a wing then entered a tunnel in front of her, and this had DEPARTURES lit up over it, carrying her dead pigeon.[5]

The gloom never lifts from the surroundings throughout the book despite the anxious high spirits of some of the characters. Fear, longing, sexual tension, a sense of being lost in a massive event that will not yield to the will: all these haunt the pages. Max the host, with his bullying and emphatic hospitality, draws all the others to him — especially the women. These are rich people. There is a strange atmosphere as of a last-ditch stand against the future, even while the actual business of the day is simply the nuisance of delayed trains in a fog. The fear of the crowd breaking in ebbs and flows, and the rush never happens, but always threatens. The word 'revolution' is uttered once, and haunts the text beneath the line in turns such as:

> 'Max is upstairs with Amabel, darling.'
> 'Oh no, Alex, how revolting', she said, and gave herself away. (517)

The aunt, Miss Fellowes, troubles consciences and, with the suggestion that she may be dying — or she may just be drunk — unsteadies all their responses: 'I think what we are both afraid of', said Evelyn, 'is that parcel she had and what was inside it' (p. 503).

What was inside it was a dead, washed pigeon. It is without signification. It is simply a dead, washed pigeon. That is what disturbs them, and us. It is also what produces the grim merriment of reading this novel. It seems full of distant thunder. It is both packed with the present and yet leans endlessly towards a future that may never happen, and that promises nothing better. Green wrote it throughout the thirties, from 1931 to 1938, so that it catches up tenuous anxieties and nameless dreads.

Those dreads are more nameable in Virgina Woolf's last novel *Between the Acts*, published after her death in 1941[6] and first stirring as she worked on the proofs of *Three Guineas* in April 1938. She sets the work over twenty-four hours, from evening to evening, in mid-June 1939 (fictionally, about a fortnight after the date of Nicolson's international crisis). And she worked on it up to the time of her death, in the midst of air raids and rumours of invasion. So the future war which the characters in the novel half foresee has come about before she finishes writing. Like Nicolson, she weaves actual events and people into her fiction: old Bart reads *The Times*: 'M. Daladier', he read, finding his place in the column, 'has been successful in pegging down the franc ...' (19). And so indeed he had, for a while. He was the French prime minister at the Munich agreement that gave Europe for a while the delusion of peace, remembered in Neville Chamberlain's announcement of 'peace in our time' on his return. Giles, his son, who commutes between the tranquillity of the country estate Pointz Hall to his work in the city of London, is the only one of the characters to realize how close war is. He is exasperated by the insouciance of the others.

> Giles nicked his chair into position with a jerk. Thus only could he show his irritation, his rage with old fogies who sat and looked at views over coffee and cream when the whole of Europe — over there — was bristling like ... He had no command of metaphor. Only the ineffective word 'hedgehog' illustrated his vision of Europe, bristling with guns, poised with planes. At any moment guns would rake that land into furrows; planes splinter Bolney Minster into smithereens and blast the folly. He, too, loved the view. (66–67)

In *Between the Acts* Woolf gathers the history of England together in the form of pastiche, setting the village pageant at the book's centre and stringing it through the text to suggest both the depth of the past and its terrible frailty. She had no faith in Europe's continuance: in a letter to Vita Sackville-West on 29 August 1939 she wrote: 'We pour to the edge of a precipice ... & then? I can't conceive that there will be a 27th June 1941.' Calendar time itself is to be obliterated. There is no future imaginable, or sustainable. Woolf was dead before that impossible date of 27 June 1941 arrived, but arrive it did. This novel engrosses itself in the present and sweeps up the past as a ballast against the tenuousness of the future. 'You cannot escape Fate,' wrote Leonard Woolf much later, in the second volume of his autobiography, *The Journey not the Arrival Matters* (1969), 'and Fate, I have always felt, is not in the future, but in the past.'[7] Between the acts of the pageant people gossip (the dots between statements are in the text and indicate voices heard in fragments):

> 'But you must remember', the old cronies chatted, 'they had to do it on the cheap. You can't get people, at this time o' year, to rehearse. There's the hay, let alone the movies. ... What we need is a centre. Something to bring us all together ... The Brookes have gone to Italy, in spite of everything. Rather rash? If the worst should come — let's hope it won't — they'd hire an aeroplane, so they said ...'.

'Don't bother about the plot: the plot's nothing', a nameless person says (109). 'Peace was the third emotion. Love. Hate. Peace. Three emotions made the ply of human life', Isa thinks (111). The newspapers presage a future of prosperity: a refrigerator in every house, but the surge of the book is towards a shattered world or a world at the beginning again. The repeated acts — the annual pageant, the sexual congress of husband and wife, the phatic sayings and clichés, the pike rising, rhymes, the starlings' ecstatic chatter at evening — all hold off the future that insistently creeps in: 'I agree — things look worse than ever on the continent. And what's the channel, come to think of it, if they mean to invade us?' (232). In the evening at the book's end old Lucy Swithin and younger Isa stand together in the dining room.

> 'Did you feel', she asked, 'what he said: we act different parts but are the same?'
> 'Yes', Isa answered. 'No', she added. It was Yes, no.
> Yes, yes, yes, the tide rushed out embracing. No, no, no, it contracted. The old boot appeared on the shingle.
> 'Orts, scraps and fragments', she quoted what she remembered of the vanishing play. (251)

Only on the final page does the hope of longer survival declare itself anew, first through Lucy's reading about primitive man 'half-human, half-ape, [who] roused himself from his semi-crouching position and raised great stones' (255); then through the encounter of wife and husband. The book's final words are:

> The house had lost its shelter. It was night before roads were made, or houses. It was the night that dwellers in caves had watched from some high place among rocks.
> Then the curtain rose. They spoke. (256)

Darkness renews the primordial. The onward rush to the precipice is momentarily stayed as night swings round again, bringing unchanging darkness to the world. Take what comfort we will from that silence, that gentleness, at the end of the novel, and from the unheard speech framed just beyond its last words: 'They spoke', yet the sense of a future lost, shattered, cannot be allayed. Woolf, after all, never knew that the war ceased.

These four novels, so diverse in their narrative methods and each so idiosyncratic in temper, do not all fit classic definitions of modernism. Instead they indicate how novelists work their own seams and do not cohere as a 'movement', except in retrospect, and by leaving aside discussion of outstanding works. But what does join all four is dread: a sense that the oncoming world may not endure and that the future is not something to be embraced but something to be staved off, by all the means available to fiction.

Notes to Chapter 8

1. Wyndham Lewis, *Blasting and Bombardiering* (1937) (London: Calder and Boyars, 1967), p. 340. Further references are given after quotations in the text.
2. C. W. R. Hooker, *What is the Fourth Dimension? Reflections Inspired by a Pair of Gloves* (London: A. & C. Black, 1934).
3. Harold Nicolson, *Public Faces* (1932) (Harmondsworth: Penguin Books, 1944). The Penguin edition has a prefatory note: 'If the careers of some still living characters have not turned out entirely as prophesied the reader will remember that this book was first issued in 1932.' Further references are given after quotations in the text.
4. Aldous Huxley, *Brave New World* (1932), Introduction by David Bradshaw (London: Vintage, 2004), p. vii. Further references are given after quotations in the text.
5. Henry Green, *Loving, Living, Party Going* (1939) (Harmondsworth: Penguin Books, 1993). Further references are given after quotations in the text.
6. Virginia Woolf, *Between the Acts* (London: Hogarth Press, 1941). Further references are given after quotations in the text.
7. Leonard Woolf, *The Journey not the Arrival Matters: An Autobiography of the Years 1939–1969* (London: Hogarth Press, 1969). Further references are given after quotations in the text.

CHAPTER 9

Conversation, Sport, or Hatchet Job? Criticism and the Power of Metaphor

Katrin Kohl

In an article entitled 'Critics on Reviews' published in the American magazine *Poets & Writers* in 2003, Mary Gannon concludes that critics share with authors 'a deep desire to maintain a culture that values reading and writing'.[1] Her interviewee Sven Birkerts has reviewers participating in 'the cultural conversation' (56) while interviewee Gail Caldwell sees them trying 'to enhance the dialogue of the culture' (59). For the critic Michael Dirda, this discourse also works diachronically, 'to keep reading going, to keep the excitement of books alive for another generation or two' (61). Criticism, understood as comment on contemporary work, here connects with the activity of the literary historian, who brings the work of past generations into current conversation.

The roles played out in Gannon's article indicate that literary critics see themselves and their colleagues not simply in terms of the individual at a desk, writing a text about another text, but as participants in a cultural enterprise. The roles they adopt then direct the tone and thrust of their reviews. Critics come in the guise of dialogue facilitators, positioning themselves in an imagined space with authors and readers as embodied interlocutors. They appear as literature-lovers engaged in a 'humane and human endeavor'[2] and as 'career-killers' (56) churning out 'wit for wit's sake' and 'hostility for hostility's sake',[3] as partisans 'championing certain writers or schools' (58), and as cogs in a commercially driven 'recommendation machine' powered by the financial interests of big business (61). The critic's project may be motivated by 'honesty' (57) or sheer 'sensationalism',[4] by Platonic 'higher ideals', or by the sympathetic urge 'to try to understand, on a very localized level, what a certain book is trying to do, even if it does it badly'.[5]

The role chosen by the critic matters, for it determines the critic's relationship with the work under discussion and the reader. It affects every aspect of the critic's writing: the choice of register, the use of speech acts indicating subjective involvement or objective distance, the selection or avoidance of emotive language and first-person pronouns, the rhythm. A vital part is played by metaphor, since this allows the imagined role to be projected in language, and to work in turn on the reader's imagination.[6]

Dirda, who is motivated by his 'love for literature, [...] love for the word on the page, love for wit and humor and style', is disinclined to be 'highly critical', favouring a 'descriptive' approach: 'Let me tell you what is there, let me quote you some examples of the prose, let me tell you how I respond and what I think of this.'[7] As a faithful mediator of the work, he shares his response for the benefit of literature and ultimately humanity. In demanding that 'love is what should activate your work',[8] he embeds the act of reviewing books in a tradition of literature that is informed by Christian values; the reviewer as mediator does for literature what Jesus did for humankind. The author and critic Dale Peck similarly 'cares' about literature 'more than anything else' but prefers to promote it with fire and brimstone.[9] In an article in *The Observer* written a few months before the publication of his collected reviews under the title *Hatchet Jobs*,[10] Kate Kellaway comments that Peck 'emerges as a fighter with the evangelical zeal of a Jehovah's Witness for whom the End of the Novel is Nigh'.[11] Having variously attacked one unfortunate author as 'the worst writer of his generation',[12] called for 'the end of gay literature', lambasted 'the vogue of black women's fiction',[13] and dismissed 'the diarrhoeic flow of words' that makes up *Ulysses*,[14] Peck acknowledges the part played by hyperbole in the presentation of his judgements, but stresses his urge to 'tell the truth'[15] and impart his superior knowledge of the author's true destiny:

> When I write these book reviews and I seem to get all hopping mad and angry, it's because I *am* all hopping mad and angry. I tend to get more angry with people that I really think are just dicking around with their talent.[16]

Whereas Peck focuses on the relationship between critic and author, Gannon finds most critics agreeing that 'readers' needs should determine the nature of book reviews' (60), and this can entail a more mundane role. Birkerts points out that 'the working book reviewer, quotidian book reviewer, has to understand that they are really serving a consumer-advice function to a significant degree'.[17]

The choice of role determines the space in which the critic interacts with the author and reader, and implies structured hierarchies. As consumer advisers, critics serve in the impersonal marketplace; as lovers of literature, they move among like-minded equals; as judges or preachers, they place themselves above authors and readers, embodying the values of the institution or discipline they represent. While presenting criticism as a 'labor of love', Gannon emphasizes that her interviewees are members of an established profession who 'take their vocation seriously' (61): they work for reputable newspapers and journals, with several having gained the public recognition afforded by the Pulitzer Prize in Criticism.[18] She places them, accordingly, at the centre of the cultural dialogue. Yet there are hints of crisis when Birkerts laments that major books no longer land 'squarely in the middle of the culture' and reviews have ceased to command 'the large-circulation zones of life'.[19] While he elsewhere envisages the act of reviewing as 'playing the culture sport',[20] he now suggests destabilization and impending chaos using a political metaphor: a 'balkanized sense of a literary culture'[21] is emerging, allowing the power vacuum to be filled by commercialization. Reader orientation makes the critic potentially redundant: for example 'Amazon straw poll reviewing'[22] gives status to the opinions of amateur readers simply by disseminating them in the market. Any consensus on standards within the profession loses its force if there is no public consensus that the value of criticism depends on professional expertise.

This sense of crisis helps to explain why Dale Peck has caused such a sensation as the 'scourge of literary America'.[23] His title *Hatchet Jobs* revives a stock metaphor to powerful effect, not least because of its potential for development through visual image and symbolism. The title 'Hatchet Man' for Kellaway's article on Peck's forthcoming book is in fractured letters, above a photograph showing Peck clad in a rage-red T-shirt and clutching a hatchet, while the introduction to the article extends the American debate to Britain with the question, 'Is aggression a critical virtue, and should British reviewers follow his lead?'.[24] Embodiment of the metaphor in a heroic individual claiming privileged access to the one and only literary truth, holding a hatchet as symbol of execution, endows Peck with the aura of a moral leader. Aggression is an improbable 'virtue', yet in a culture that threatens to render professional criticism redundant, Peck's voice of righteousness holds the promise of salvation.

Diverging models of criticism are not confined to the literary sphere. In art criticism, the tensions are if anything more acute because there is no consensus on the status of writing with respect to the critic's engagement with the artwork. In an article entitled 'The Dysfunction of Criticism', the artist and critic J. J. Charlesworth contributes to an extended debate on criticism and the role of the critic in *Art Monthly* by deriding the focus of that debate: instead of providing 'a politics of criticism, and a discussion over the desirable future of art and culture', it focuses 'on what the most appropriate relationship between a writer, his/her writing and the work of art should be'.[25] Lambasting a current 'preoccupation with criticism's specifically literary dimension', he identifies 'pluralism' and 'relativism' as 'corrosive intellectual trends' that 'diminish art criticism to the level of mere art writing' (4). The parlous state of criticism today, when 'no one can much agree on any clear mission for art writing, criticism or the role of the critic', is contrasted with earlier decades when there was a shared assumption that 'the theorisation and criticism of art were possible, desirable and necessary' (2). Where Gannon claims a consensus among literary critics that unites the activities of authors, critics, and readers in a common culture of reading and writing, Charlesworth demands that the work of art be validated with reference to an order that is superior to language. In fact, the tensions highlighted in his article shed light on the issues within literary criticism that Peck has brought to the fore as arbiter of an absolute literary truth. These issues gain urgency in art criticism owing to the difference between the visual medium of the artwork and the linguistic medium of the critical response — the 'always-present gap between words and seeing' highlighted by John Berger in *Ways of Seeing*.[26] It is neither self-evident that the spectator needs the critic's words in order to respond appropriately to the work of the artist, nor obvious that artist and spectator, critic and reader should share a concern for writing beyond its usefulness as a means of straightforward communication.

While Charlesworth's polemic makes for crude distinctions, the binary oppositions that structure his article usefully highlight central issues in debates about criticism. He assumes two distinct types of critic, profiling them against a background of deteriorating confidence among intellectuals in the possibility of social change. On the one hand there is the art critic proper, prominent in

	Art critic (critical)	*Art writer (belletristic)*
Human faculties involved	rational faculties reflection	emotions sentiment, sensitivity
Mode of discourse	contestative, polemical	beautiful, literary
Purpose of discourse	criticism interventionist political	writing affirmative aesthetic
Relationship with reality	objective truth authentic	subjective taste inauthentic
Relationship with artwork	exerting authority dominating judging distanced	on a par, complementary serving interpreting immediate
Relationship with other critics	contestative	unengaged
Relationship with reader	controlling or ignoring	mediating
Relationship with society	active transformative accountable	passive conformist unaccountable
Context and orientation	public social, political oriented outward	private cultural, commercial oriented inward

TABLE 9.1. Characteristic qualities of the art critic and the art writer, as contrasted by J. J. Charlesworth

the 1980s, whose writing constitutes a 'critical intervention in how art is given value', and on the other hand the current art writer, who has emerged in the last decade to produce a 'belletristic form of art writing'.[27] The art critic laid claim to 'authority' and 'general truth' (4), passed 'value judgments' (3), and confidently required art to be 'other than it is' (2) in order to 'change things for the better' (4) in culture and society. The art writer by contrast reduces 'critical choice to the level of unaccountable subjective taste' (4), is 'uncomfortable about being generally or brilliantly oppressive',[28] shows 'obsessive deference to the primacy of the work' and provides 'a subordinate, complementary service of sensitive interpretation' (2–3). Whereas the art critic was concerned with the cultural and political significance of art (4), the art writer appears in various guises ranging from 'pop-cultural *flâneur*' to 'dandified copywriter' (3), producing 'beautiful writing about beautiful objects and their beautiful makers'[29] and pandering to 'unreflective cultural sensibilities' (3). Instead of operating in a 'coherent public sphere' marked by 'open enquiry and debate', art writing now serves a 'market driven by fashion' (3). The art critic's deployment of 'writing's polemic and contestative potential' has given way to the art writer's 'inward'-looking, 'passive', 'privatised', 'affirmative' articulation of 'immediate sentiments' (2–3).

Table 9.1 shows schematically how Charlesworth contrasts the 'art critic' proper with the belletristic 'art writer'. As is indicated in Charlesworth's reference to dandyism, and in his quick dismissal of 'Postmodernism's once-dynamic, politicised proliferation of criteria' (4), the profiles that emerge from his article gain meaning from a much wider Western discourse about writing and culture. The thrust of his argument is that art criticism is in danger of losing both its authority and its function — a similar point to that put forward by Sven Birkerts. This is not because art as such is in crisis: Charlesworth acknowledges the 'ever-expanding world' of contemporary art and the 'booming success' of contemporary painting (2). The reason for the potential redundancy of criticism lies in the fact that 'everything seems to happen without explanation, as if the realm of contemporary art were simply following the rule of some natural order' (2–3), while 'relativism' and 'pluralism' undermine the project of offering 'generally valid criticism' (4). His rationalist concept of criticism here becomes particularly apparent, along with its limitations. Charlesworth assumes both the superiority of criticism over a work that requires explanation, and the critic's privileged access to the truth of the work, locating that truth beyond the immediate critical process with its 'banal prerequisites' of 'looking at art, stringing words together and acknowledging your reader — as if they were the essence of its being' (2). His postulate of an 'essence' beyond the world of art, language, and fellow human beings smacks of a Platonic Idea, which would make it an enterprise instrinsically hostile to art and inclined to devalue language, the medium of criticism: when the poets were banished from Plato's Republic, painting was implicated,[30] and language defined as but 'a copy and subsequent reflection of the mental condition'.[31] Charlesworth's stock metaphor defining the language of criticism as 'stringing words together' is congruent with his rationalist approach since it separates the material words, which he considers irrelevant to the essence of criticism, from the abstract ideas, which hold that essence. Yet his article demonstrates the efficacy of language not only as a means of expressing his rational concept of criticism, but as a shaping force. By envisioning language as a physical 'string' of words and contrasting this with the 'essence' of criticism's 'being', he constructs criticism as ontologically and spiritually superior to language — metaphorically animating the concept of criticism. Determining the extent to which the linguistic metaphors of the 'string' and 'essence' shape or express his concepts of language and criticism would be a futile exercise. On the basis of a cognitive approach to language, 'metaphors as linguistic expressions are possible precisely because there are metaphors in a person's conceptual system'.[32]

The philosophical tendency to separate thought and language has come under attack from many quarters, not least from philosophy itself and in the projects of poststructuralism. With respect to art, in particular, it is more fruitful to assume that

> thought is *imaginative*, in that those concepts which are not directly grounded in experience employ metaphor, metonymy, and mental imagery [...]. It is this imaginative capacity that allows for 'abstract' thought and takes the mind beyond what we can see and feel.[33]

If processes of thought, imagination, and language are taken to be interactive, criticism gains much wider scope in responding to art and communicating that response, for there are then no necessary gaps between the artwork, the critic's cognitive, imaginative, and linguistic response, and the reader's reception. The relationship between art and criticism ceases to be defined hierarchically, permitting open interplay — with poststructuralist displays of performative criticism as only one possibility. If criticism is defined along the lines of Charlesworth's 'banal prerequisites' as *the critic's response to the work of art communicated in written or spoken language to the reader*, this allows criticism to incorporate, adjust to, interact with, or intervene in other discourses, offering comment, interpretation, analysis, or evaluation depending on the project and theoretical reference point. While such a modest and dull definition exhibits the 'relativism' and 'pluralism' Charlesworth so detests, it overcomes the danger facing his account: that criticism is reduced to ranting from self-imposed margins. A relativistic, pluralistic account has the advantage of giving criticism continued lively existence as a multi-perspectival, multi-vocal discourse that has the capacity to interact with art and change through time.

By protesting against reflection on the premises of criticism, Charlesworth seeks to mask the instability of the concept of criticism. Another side of the debate in *Art Monthly* is represented by the critic and editor Alex Coles, who in an earlier article had advocated an interactive model of criticism where language comes more strongly into play: he sees the difference between critics turning on 'how the critic relates to the artwork through the texture and tenor of their prose'.[34] Whereas Charlesworth demands critical intervention and locates the 'essence' of criticism beyond both the artwork and the critic's written text, Coles inclines towards the belletristic approach (though without adopting that term) and advocates ensuring that 'something of the gist of the artwork finds its way into the register of the writing' (9). Rather than foregrounding the critic's relationship with society, he focuses on the relationship between critic and artwork, using metaphors of time and space to signal the need for criticism to adjust to the work. He distinguishes between the 'critic of the study' who 'just stands still in front of [the work]' and 'lifts the artwork out of time to examine it', and a more involved type of critic who 'shuffles in parallax' with it, 'experiences it in time', and 'moves to the same rhythm as the work' (7–9). In highlighting the need for art critics to respond to the 'appropriation-based and site-sensitive practices' of contemporary art (8), he points to the interdependence of the critic's conceptual approach and the perspective this gives on the work: a critic willing to permit interdisciplinary connections and shifting positions is likely to be more responsive to a work that requires such connections and shifts from the spectator, and correspondingly more inclined to mediate such requirements and their effect to the reader.

Charlesworth's dismissal of Coles's 'obsession with the literary subtleties of art writing' (4) fails to address the fact that subtleties of language — and above all subtleties of metaphor, that most poetic of literary phenomena — fulfil a central role in any type of criticism. Indeed, by aiding the process of developing concepts into verbal arguments and vice versa, metaphor contributes to the very aim he considers paramount: it allows the critic to become effective as an 'agent through which what is critical in art is publicly put into play between artwork, spectatorship and readership — critical in the sense of what is "of decisive importance in relation to the issue"' (4). Where Charlesworth is mistaken is in assuming that the critic is 'the agent' achieving this, for the work is surely capable of communicating directly, without explanation. Moreover, 'what is critical' is a matter of ongoing negotiation between originator, work, spectators (or listeners), and readers, and hence inherently unstable not just among contemporaries, but also in the process of reception through time. Nevertheless, especially with respect to non-verbal art forms, criticism may serve an important role in giving linguistic and hence mental definition to the effect of a work, enriching its meaning for the viewers or audience in a more fundamental and less exclusive way than Charlesworth envisages. When Coles foregrounds the 'texture and tenor' of the critic's prose, he is right to emphasize the important role of language, but he places too much emphasis on the critic's style, failing to clarify the issues raised by Charlesworth not least because he ignores the roles of reader and spectator in the critical process. Metaphor is a prime means by which the critic, in response to the artwork and its context, shapes the reader's view of 'what is critical' about the artwork, to the point of inspiring the reader to become a spectator, or discouraging the reader from engaging with the artwork directly at all. Whether critics project themselves as the primary authority charged with the task of disseminating the objective truth about the artwork, or as facilitators encouraging subjective engagement with a work that forms the primary focus of the critical process, will affect the critic's conceptual approach to the work, the language by which this is communicated, and the conceptual response by the reader. The critic therefore needs to attend to the implications of every part of the critical process.

The power of metaphor to influence transmission of meaning deserves attention from the critic not least because it can inhibit understanding. A brief passage from a book review by Adrian Clark in *The British Art Journal* — 'the research journal of British art studies' — may serve as an example. Clark's review of Mel Gooding's monograph on the Welsh artist Ceri Richards (1903–71) ends with a two-sentence 'paean of praise' for the book and the impressive stature of this 'fascinating and important artist', yet focuses attention throughout on the failure of book and artist to meet the reviewer's expectations.[35] According to Clark, Gooding's study has 'no hint of criticism', 'doesn't act as a proper biography', and leaves 'unsatisfied the historian's wish to categorise and grade'. Lumping Richards in with 'that plethora of British artists of the 20th century who have not yet found their level amongst the still-shifting sands of critical reputations', Clark defines the artist's work solely by evaluation according to established names and categories:

> Richards's work breaks down into some loose groupings. The illustrations to Dylan Thomas' poetry are beautiful, clever things, but they are 'merely' illustrations; the original trigger of artistic creation has been pulled by the poet first. The works tinged by surrealism are unusual in an English context [...], but they are derivative in their inspiration. There is a heavy dose of Ernst about them. [...] Later there is a difficult 'series' of works, based on Debussy's 'La Cathédrale Engloutie', in which the artist tried to show in paint the way in which music influences the senses. These are not entirely satisfactory pictures. The artist has had an idea based partly on reading Kandinsky and partly on his own love of music, and he has tried to intellectualise that idea in paint. He does not succeed; not perhaps, because he fails where others succeed, but because the idea cannot be transferred to this medium.

Clark employs some stylistically striking metaphors, but they tend to distract from his points. The 'heavy dose of Ernst' is incongruously clichéd and the 'trigger of artistic creation' comically inappropriate. The metaphor 'tinged' wrongly suggests that surrealism defines itself with reference to colour. The natural metaphor of the 'still-shifting sands' conflicts with culturally dependent 'reputation', negates the natural processes invoked by implying that the sands will shortly cease to shift, and misleadingly suggests that artists 'find' 'their level' themselves and remain there. While these metaphors clutter the argument, others work more subtly and consistently to devalue Richards's work, which Clark causes to disintegrate into a sum of parts that make less than a whole, reinforcing the devaluation implied in the metaphor 'breaking down' by suggesting generic incoherence in 'loose groupings'. The low value accorded the illustrations presupposes the traditional subordination of this genre to 'original' painting proper, while the label of 'surrealism' serves only to support the claim of derivativeness. The works responding to Debussy are denied the status of a genuine 'series', and judged 'difficult' on the basis of their failure to observe genre boundaries. The dictum that Richards's assumed 'idea' 'cannot be transferred' to the medium of painting forms the basis of Clark's negative assessment, which he elaborates by making the 'idea' into a hybrid in terms of genre (painting, music), authorship (Kandinsky, Richards), and mental process (intellectual assimilation of professional theory, amateur emotional response to practice). By interpreting Richards's project nonsensically as 'intellectualising' the idea, Clark devalues it implicitly with reference to the Romantic assumption that true art cannot emerge from the rational faculties. Moreover, the 'idea' is then assumed to be confined to a place that is separate from the area in which the paint is applied, so that impossibility of transferral confirms the misguided nature of Richards's work.

Clark's rigid concepts preclude coherent understanding of Richards's work and give the reader no sense of Gooding's perspective on Richards. Clark's own failure to respond to Richards's work is couched in the form of an authoritative assessment of the artist's objective worth that claims superiority over both the artist and the author of the monograph. The metaphors that inform Clark's judgements establish boundaries and hierarchies that inhibit the process of communication between Richards, his work, and the spectator, and counteract Gooding's project. The review prevents the work from communicating ways of seeing to the reader that might differ from the ways that have been established by academic convention. Criticism is here confined within a discipline that sees its function as confirming its own categories in perpetuity, without entering into communication with other discourses. The language of such criticism renders the work of art incoherent.

The potential of metaphor to transcend disciplinary boundaries and evoke the effect of art through the 'texture and tenor' of prose is evident by contrast in a review by Justin Davidson, staff writer for the daily *Newsday*, who was awarded the Pulitzer Prize for Criticism in 2002 'for his crisp coverage of classical music that captures its essence'.[36] In the following paragraph concluding a review of Brahms's *Ein deutsches Requiem* performed by the New York Philharmonic, he conveys a sense of the performance by setting it vividly in context: it was a memorial concert by the

New York Philharmonic held on 20 September 2001, benefiting the World Trade Center disaster relief fund. Yet he avoids sensationalism, balancing the immediate pressure of experienced reality with a historical perspective that gives the work a new artistic immediacy. In contrast to Clark, he projects himself as emotionally involved, though without pathos. He provides his assessment of the performance not by objective classification or measurement against static criteria, but by using narrative pace, dynamic metaphors, parallelism, alliteration, and rhythm to evoke the work in process. Davidson sets the scene for comments on the concert's musical qualities in a context of silence, emphasizing the unusual absence of noise from the city in the aftermath of the disaster:

> So the Philharmonic's return to the stage after a period of quiet echoed an earlier day, when concerts were rare and more momentous, and music was a live art. Brahms' Requiem can be a distant, brooding work, but this performance was detailed and fluid and full of motion, as if sculpted out of still-warm wax. Soprano Heidi Grant Murphy was exquisitely seraphic. Baritone Thomas Hampson supplied thoughtful thunder. And the orchestra discovered a trembling and fire I had not heard in this piece before. As a chorister told me on the subway afterwards: 'The meaning of this piece has changed. It's not just about abstract death.'[37]

Davidson connects the performance to the real-life disaster by the metaphor of the orchestra's 'return' after the event, and the chorister's response foregrounding actual death as a revitalization of the work. The power of the music emerges gradually out of the 'quiet', with the 'echo' evolving into 'music' and then 'thunder', culminating in the passionate 'trembling' and 'fire' of the orchestra. Human interpretation is subtly introduced when 'thunder' is balanced by 'thoughtfulness' and the orchestra is credited with 'discovery'. Davidson uses the resonances of death to foreground the redemptive force of the Requiem, brought out by the vitality, movement, and transformative power of the performance: the music is experienced as 'a live art', as 'fluid' and 'full of motion'. The spiritual dimensions of the Requiem gain force in metaphors that connect sound with biblical symbolism: the 'seraphic' voice of the soprano, the 'thunder' of the baritone, and the 'trembling and fire' of the orchestra. The wax simile daringly compares music to a material medium, yet it works because the metaphor of 'sculpting' remains within the field of art, suggesting powerful creation of a well-formed whole while also conveying a process in time, with the metaphor of warmth reinforcing the sense of vitality. The simile takes the rhythmically strong tricolon 'detailed and fluid and full of motion' to a climax, drawing attention to its poetic force with alliteration and three strong stresses on 'still-warm wax', but this is no end in itself. The phrase 'as if' invites the reader to engage the imagination, in order to understand the transformed and transforming meaning of the music.

The metaphors convey the critic's complex response to the performance as a listener activating his intellectual, emotional, and imaginative faculties. His knowledge of the work and its performances is supplied not as superior expertise, but in the form of experience that allows him to understand and convey the special quality of this performance: not 'distant' but immediate, not 'brooding' but vibrant.

While Davidson uses binary oppositions, he keeps both sides active and interactive, enriching them by association with other metaphors, especially metaphors of movement. Avoiding static boundaries, he holds extremes in play and conveys tension as an activating force, above all the tension between death and life that forms not only the theme and purpose of the work but also the present experience of the audience. The last words gain immediacy in the direct speech of the young boy, simultaneously a respondent to the work and an originator of the performance. Emerging from a conversation in the mundane heart of New York, scene of the disaster that took on associations with the Day of Judgement, his comment captures the interaction of life and art.

The reviews by Clark and Davidson suggest that the 'literary dimension' is central to the enterprise of criticism, for better or worse. In all forms of discourse about the arts, reflection on the language of criticism is an indispensable part of the critic's work. Criticism at its best exploits the possibilities of natural language to convey the infinitely rich variety of art. In contrast to philosophical ideals of a perfectly logical language based on individual correspondence between word and meaning,[38] natural languages allow metaphor to facilitate imaginative transfer processes across boundaries that are thereby shown to be in flux. The complex connections between the mental, emotional, linguistic, and physical processes involved in the production and reception of works of art are as yet poorly understood in scientific terms, but it is clear that those connections hold tremendous potential for the artist to create hitherto unseen and unheard-of forms, and for the public to understand them both contemporaneously and in later times. Automatic adherence to established mental divisions and linguistic conventions will tend to inhibit the critic's response to an 'original' work and consequently prevent appreciation of the very creativity our culture considers essential to the 'creative arts'. If criticism is to live up to the standards set by the works it purports to engage with, it needs to foster imaginative language.

Notes to Chapter 9

1. Mary Gannon, 'Critics on Reviews', *Poets & Writers*, 31.5 (September–October 2003), 54–61 (p. 61). Further references to this article (other than citations from interviews) are given after quotations in the text.
2. Dirda, quoted ibid., p. 61.
3. The novelist and editor Heidi Julavits, quoted ibid., p. 57.
4. Birkerts, quoted ibid.
5. Julavits, quoted ibid.
6. Metaphor is here understood as both linguistic and cognitive. The seminal work establishing a cognitive theory of metaphor is George Lakoff and Mark Johnson, *Metaphors We Live By* (Chicago and London: University of Chicago Press, 1980).
7. Quoted in Gannon, 'Critics on Reviews', p. 61.
8. Quoted ibid.
9. Quoted ibid., p. 57.
10. Dale Peck, *Hatchet Jobs: Writings on Contemporary Fiction* (New York and London: New Press, 2004).
11. Kate Kellaway, 'Hatchet Man', *Observer*, 23 November 2003, Review section, pp. 1–2 (p. 1).
12. Rick Moody; see Kellaway, 'Hatchet Man', p. 1. See also Gannon, 'Critics on Reviews', p. 57.

13. According to Birkerts, quoted ibid.
14. Quoted in Kellaway, 'Hatchet Man', p. 1.
15. Quoted ibid.; see also Gannon, 'Critics on Reviews', p. 57.
16. Quoted ibid.
17. Quoted ibid., p. 60.
18. Jonathan Yardley in 1981, Dirda in 1993, and Caldwell in 2001.
19. Quoted in Gannon, 'Critics on Reviews', p. 61.
20. Quoted ibid., p. 56.
21. Quoted ibid., p. 61.
22. Quoted ibid.
23. Kellaway, 'Hatchet Man', p. 1.
24. Ibid.
25. J. J. Charlesworth, 'The Dysfunction of Criticism', *Art Monthly*, no. 269 (September 2003), 1–4 (p. 2). The contributors to the debate in *Art Monthly* refer in turn to earlier debates in Britain and the USA.
26. John Berger and others, *Ways of Seeing* (London: BBC and Harmondsworth: Penguin Books, 1972), p. 7.
27. Charlesworth, 'The Dysfunction of Criticism', p. 3. In defining his types, Charlesworth refers to a debate in the American art theory journal *October*.
28. Charlesworth, 'The Dysfunction of Criticism', p. 2, quoting Matthew Arnatt.
29. Ibid., p. 3, quoting Suzanne Perling Hudson.
30. Plato presents both poetry and painting as mere imitations, at two removes from reality; Plato, *Republic*, trans. by Robin Waterfield (Oxford and New York: Oxford University Press, 1998), pp. 345–49 (596a–598d). See also p. 356 (603a–b).
31. Ibid., p. 78 (382b). For Plato's view of language see also the dialogue *Cratylus*.
32. Lakoff and Johnson, *Metaphors*, p. 6. The relationship between thought, language, and the world has of course received considerable attention in recent decades. Within the context of the cognitive sciences and specifically linguistics, Ray Jackendoff concludes that 'the proper formulation of reference is as a relation between linguistic expressions and the world *as conceptualized by the language user*' (*Foundations of Language: Brain, Meaning, Grammar, Evolution* (Oxford: Oxford University Press, 2002), p. xvi). With respect to speech act theory, he traces 'theorists' concentration on truth value' back to Plato, noting that it 'blinds us to the full vivid range of possibility' (p. 328).
33. George Lakoff, *Women, Fire, and Dangerous Things: What Categories Reveal about the Mind* (Chicago and London: University of Chicago Press, 1987), p. xiv. Rationalist accounts of thought are increasingly coming under scrutiny in the cognitive sciences; Susan Greenfield, for example, holds emotion to be 'inextricable from consciousness itself' but to be surprisingly underresearched by neuroscientists (*The Private Life of the Brain* (London: Penguin Books, 2001), p. 16).
34. Alex Coles, 'The Bathroom Critic', *Art Monthly*, no. 263 (February 2003), 7–10 (p. 7).
35. Adrian Clark, review of Mel Gooding, *Ceri Richards* (Moffat: Cameron & Hollis 2002), *British Art Journal*, 4.2 (summer 2003), 99.
36. 'The Pulitzer Prize Winners, 2002, Criticism' <http://www.pulitzer.org/year/2002/criticism>.
37. Justin Davidson, 'Philharmonic Benefits its Audience, Too', *Newsday*, 22 September 2001.
38. See Umberto Eco, *The Search for the Perfect Language*, trans. by James Fentress (Oxford: Blackwell, 1995), esp. Chapter 15: 'Philosophic Language from the Enlightenment to Today', pp. 293–316.

CHAPTER 10

❖

Set Adrift in Style: The Scholar as Fiction and Film-Maker in *Jacob's Room*

Catherine M. Lord

Set Adrift

How far can a scholarly presentation voyage out on those styles that are poetic, fictional, painterly, or filmic, and traditionally associated with the artwork? To approach this question, I shall make a critical reading of Virginia Woolf's third, experimental novel *Jacob's Room* (1922).[1] This elegy foretold features Jacob Flanders, a scholarly young man who will die on the First World War battlefields. The myriad characters who wrap their imaginations around Jacob, who focalize him for us, will never entirely know him, never entirely touch him. This act of reaching out for elusive intimacies finds its correlate in the novel's 'style', or what is an aesthetic force field navigating between an array of media. The novelist and critic Lawrence Norfolk refers in his Introduction to the 'intensely cinematic' quality of Woolf's narrative (p. vii). The literary scholary Francesca Kazan has noted the novel's 'pictorial compositions that seem to interrupt the text in an arbitrary fashion and cut through the reflections and the dialogue'.[2] The novel is replete with references to artworks from diverse media, from the Elgin Marbles to modern painting, from the music of Bach to early theories of intermediality that connect sound, colour, and light. There are frequent references to Jacob's reading of literary classics, from the Greeks to the plays of Shakespeare and Marlowe to the poetry of John Donne. Woolf's novel provides a richly mediated expanse to develop a conceptual metaphor for style. By 'conceptual metaphor' I refer to Mieke Bal's suggestion that concepts 'emphasise the concrete quality of all concepts'.[3] Certain metaphors carry aesthetic content, which also performs theoretical work. For Bal concepts are on the move.[4] As a conceptual metaphor, style sets itself adrift through spaces between media. Their coordinates will become reconfigured. Traversing different theories of mediality, style reshapes and reinvents itself.

My critique of Woolf's novel will combine three distinct but interrelated practices: the scholarly article, one short extract from my fiction work-in-progress *Imagine Jacob* (2003), and an analysis of my short film *Jacob's Storyboard* (2003). The last was made especially for the conference New Languages for Criticism.[5] The conference presentation extended itself into the miniature fiction and the film. To a degree, *Imagine Jacob* is inspired by Michael Cunningham's novel *The Hours*, one section of which cites but remakes the Clarissa of Woolf's *Mrs Dalloway* (1925) by recasting her as a publisher in the New York of 2002.[6] Cunningham's novel can be read as a critique of its model, *Mrs Dalloway*, while *Imagine Jacob* aims to be an imaginative analysis of *Jacob's Room*.

Setting Jacob and his friends in the London of 2003, just after the outbreak of the war in Iraq, *Imagine Jacob* portrays a protagonist similar to his precursor. Both are avid readers of classic texts from Shakespeare to Donne. But whereas the Jacob of Woolf's novel writes out his citations by hand, the latter-day Jacob cites texts with his digital camera. From the citations, he makes collages and models which he then montages into an amateur film. While the film could not be fully viewed at the conference but only in selected illustrations, I will convey it through ekphrasis. Jean Hagstrum recognized that the once narrow sense of this term, traditionally defined as giving voice to a voiceless art object, might be expanded to encompass a description which could 'bring person, place, picture, etc. before the mind's eye'.[7] Description can do more than bring the object to the mind's eye: it can illuminate how this site breathes with verbal tissue.

Close reading Woolf's novel at the coded edges between word and image is a route to an adventure of high stakes. Experiments in combining academic and artistic work in the same space require giving the envelope of current interdisciplinary practices a significant push. Critical practices of the future could do more than perform the 'inter' of exchanging discourses between disciplines. To put the case for interrelated practices more radically, the scholar could now be defined as the practitioner who mixes her media and carves out a style through liminal, or intermedial, spaces.

Indeed, the concept of intermediality relies on the idea that artworks come into being in the gaps between media, the space between providing an opportunity for inter-art innovation. The polyartist Dick Higgins coined the term *intermedia* in 1963,[8] without recourse to Marshall McCluhan's over-cited phrase that 'the content of any medium is another medium'.[9] Higgins defined intermedia as 'works that fall conceptually between already established works from known media'. This sense of falling between implies the presence of intermedial lacunae.

In Woolf's novel, the narrator and characters explore the gaps between media, building strips of theory and fiction to communicate across the divide.[10] So often, though, an epistemologically charged loneliness prevails. On a boat journey from the Isles of Scilly, Jacob and the narrator wonder 'What's the use of trying to read Shakespeare, especially in one of those little thin paper editions whose pages get ruffled, or stuck together with sea-water?' (41). Oddly, the written medium is represented as unreadable because the intervening medium, the sea water, has glued up the copy. Paper, print, and even sea water are anything but transparent. The Shakespeare will subsequently be knocked overboard. Submerged, love's knowledge will be lost. Literary thoughts may console, but the abyss remains. Jacob will be frustrated with his lover Florinda, for 'Beauty', his focalizing thoughts surmise, 'goes hand in hand with stupidity' (76).[11] Artworks may fall short of fulfilling intimacies. Jacob will feel but a tepid affinity for Cruttendon's modern paintings. If Jacob is himself a 'piece of work', then Bonamy, who 'couldn't love a woman', will think of little else but the enigmatic protagonist (135).

The novel confronts its fractures by making yet more. Media are to be held together in fractured tension. The novel cuts up and collages aesthetic and scholarly discourses including poetry, art history, and cosmology. Collage is defined as the activity of cutting out and assembling disparate parts, of 'pasting, sticking, or gluing'. As Herta Wescher emphasized in her extensive study of the topic, collage requires that different materials be transferred from one context to another.[12] The media scholar Yvonne Spielmann has comprehensively explored the close affinity between collage and montage. Both involve cutting and juxtaposing disconnected or discontinuous elements, but whereas in collage the emphasis lies in spatial arrangements, in film montage the connections between unrelated shots occur through time. Among many concise definitions of montage, that of Sergei Eisenstein, one of its chief architects, specifies that it is produced by taking two shots in juxtaposition and splicing them together to produce a third term. From this, the spectators can make intellectually strong third meanings.[13] Spielmann underlines that the concepts of collage and montage overlap, also producing a 'third'. In digital special effects and experimental editing, thirdness can evolve through reversals of time, through temporal suspension, or through effects of speeding up or slowing down. In such cases, the emphasis will be on spatial grammars.[14]

Collage and montage can be used as critical lenses to read Woolf's modernism. Adorno's famous statement about modernism in his letter to Walter Benjamin, in March 1936, argues that high art and the products of mass culture 'bear the stigmata of capitalism [...] Both are torn halves of an integral freedom, to which, however, they do not add up.'[15] Woolf's narrative unknowingly avows the protagonist's destiny when the narrator lets slip descriptions of battleships that 'ray out over the North Sea'. Next appears a bird's-eye view of wounded soldiers who, eerily, 'agitate up and down like fragments of broken match-stick'. War makes humans dispensable, like matches to be discarded. The progression of juxtaposed shots, from ships to broken bodies to a man whose strength is not 'diverted into sudden impulses', suppresses all ordinary logic (151). Interpretative 'wholes' are refused. Remediation may be the course towards integration.

Media in tension can be read as uneasy collaborators. The theorists of new media Jay David Bolter and Richard Grusin have argued that one medium will necessarily remediate another for significant reasons. No one medium can operate as an island. Historically, successor mediums remediate precursors to bring their forerunners into the future: digital algorithms have continued to technically improve the work on perspective achieved by sixteenth- and seventeenth-century inventors of the camera obscura.[16] Remediation functions as 'reform' when it aims to 'refashion or rehabilitate other media [...] as a process of reforming reality'.[17] While following Bolter and Grusin's insight that one medium can remedy the shortcomings in another, I will be cracking open their theory by arguing for the importance of recognizing the gaps between the media themselves.

In other words, remediation can be theorized as a process of healing rifts in critical, aesthetic, and emotional value systems. The broken matchsticks of soldiers need to be re-energized by the committed traffic agent. Montage heals the suspended agony of the matchsticks. The external narrator will move from these shots to make a comment on the techniques of the fiction writer. Between apparently impersonal focalization and the 'voice' of authority a tension is always present, just as Woolf's novel maintains a constant friction and intimacy between the verbal showing and the visual telling.

Torn Ribbons

The visual and verbal can be teased apart but remain constantly enmeshed. Eisenstein made copious readings of cinematic montage in written text. Even in his analyses of novelistic or theatrical dialogue he finds juxtapositions that demand the intervention of intellectual montage, in the absence of a movie screen.[18] His aesthetic theory is extreme. A short paragraph from *Jacob's Room*, following on from the passage of matchstick bodies and the undisturbed 'force of will' of an individual directing traffic, provides an alternative theory. Woolf's external narrator remarks: 'It is thus that we live, they say, driven by an unseizable force. They say that the novelists never catch it; that it goes hurtling through their nets and leaves them torn to ribbons. This, they say, is what we live by — this unseizable force' (151). Here, the written words are composed of the signs of different materials, namely nets and ribbons, and these are all collaged into the same printed space.

The poetic dimension of the language, with its iambic and anapaestic rhythms, subverts the external narrator's claims that novelists cannot use their nets to capture styles in motion. Here I recall Giorgio Agamben's citation of Paul Valéry's persuasive suggestion that poetry can be defined as a 'prolonged hesitation between sound and sense'.[19] According to Agamben, poetry is possible in this tension between prosodic sense and poetic sounds. In Woolf's passage, the rhythmic repetition of 'they say' drives the lines forward, but the 'unseizable force' cannot be reined in. Sounds and pace contradict lexical sense. Poetry remediates prose but perhaps not with the intention of producing greater immediacy. Should the force be too immediate, too great, the net and the ribbon would be torn to shreds.

Torn ribbons bring to mind Orson Welles's famous declaration that 'a film is a ribbon of dreams'. The very celluloid materials that allow a movie to exist — 35- and 16-millimetre film formats, to name but two — can feel, in the hand, like a trail of large ribbons. I am not, however, saying that the nets signify written text, and the ribbons the visual. Woolf's passage refuses such separation. The nets may get torn to ribbons — and yet, the metaphors have been named, and their names are separate: nets and ribbons. Both can be ruptured by unseizable forces.

It is through the rupturing that the terms collage and montage can be re-examined in the light of Woolf's work. To recall Spielmann, the customary distinctions between collage and montage emphasize spatial connectedness in the former and temporal connection in the latter. The binary opposition between the two may prove usefully unstable. One example can be found when Woolf's Jacob makes his pilgrimage to Greece, where he becomes romantically entangled with a married woman, Sandra Wentworth Williams. Young man and middle-aged woman ascend the Acropolis. The narrator uses the adverbial *now* for two purposes, one being to intensify the narrative pace: 'Now the agitation of the air uncovered a racing star. Now it was dark. Now one after another lights were extinguished. Now great towns — Paris — Constantinople — London — were black as strewn rocks' (156). Different pieces of geography — Paris, Constantinople, London — are written into the same space. So too are the effects of diffuse and back lighting: the racing star, and the lights that go to fade, one by one. All are attached through the adverbial 'now' which intermediates the different strips of light, and their cinematographic yield, with the verbal effects of rhythm which, in turn, allows the images to become part of the pacing. Yet the sense of sequence, the now, then now, and then (what next?) cracks open a temporal dimension. Spielmann suggests that a close interconnection of collage and montage can be termed cinematic collage. The passage quoted above provides an example of collage and montage, fused yet separate — not in the literal sense that we are watching a film, but that a visually mediated reading of the written text provides a visual field, an intermediated space of 'sudden vision'.

In this sequence of discreetly conveyed passion between Jacob Flanders and Sandra Wentworth Williams, the different media attempt to come, as it were, simultaneously, though whether the same can be said for the two lovers is another matter. Do they kiss, touch silently, utter words of John Donne — Jacob will give Sandra a copy of the poet's verse — do they really 'reach it' out there, on the Acropolis? The narrator reports that the two have gone missing in amorous combat: 'They had vanished. There was the Acropolis; but had they reached it? The columns and the Temple remain; the emotion of the living breaks fresh on them year after year; and of that what remains?' (156). Curiously, it is as if this hypothetical rapture is implied to have always been there, eternally, for new emotions to 'break fresh' upon them. Here is a roller-coaster between two temporalities, brought into the same site, and between two media. Hypothetically, the actors could have been removed. The breaking waves provide a space for the reader's projections, lingering with questions that montage the remains of the day.

Below is a short extract, inspired by the Woolf scene on the Acropolis, from *Imagine Jacob*. In the autumn of 2003, Jacob has returned from his travels. He is still waiting for a reply to his emails and digital attachments. He is still waiting for that reply from Sandra Wentworth Williams.

> The world has heated up; even in Hyde Park. Jacob on grass; Jacob cut on the edges of sun, or so it seems to Bonamy, walking back from the publishers, looking at the man who never sees him. Jacob stares at his laptop. Bonamy imagines calling up tidal waves of grass that would uproot trees; and still Jacob would survive, indifferent.
>
> On Jacob's liquid screen, Sandra Wentworth Williams, strips of eye and forehead, her long digits, as she called them; brown hair, tangled in sea anemones. Or so Jacob will make it with his computer palette. Had he just been another scalp on her spear?
>
> Men and women are obsessed with their mobile phones, a horse rips through

> Hyde Park's page of green. The Acropolis, before sunset, the sharp shadows of Jacob Flanders and Sandra Wentworth Williams. Between them lie Donne's poems, spine broken, pages salted and loosened. The skeletons lie well wrapped in skin.
>
> Those we most want we most fear. The wind knows no discretion and the pages of John Donne scatter like moths.
>
> Sandra Wentworth Williams catches one; it reads:
>
> 'A bracelet of bright hair about the bone'.

Hair wrapped around bone would represent an uncanny extreme of montage. The postmodern Jacob may be remediating his experiences with word-processing software in a desperate attempt to reclaim an intimacy never to be recovered. The fantasy of the hair on the bone suggests penetration. The skin ripped off, the hair triumphantly close, mourning replaced by eternity. According to Bolter and Grusin, remediation implies facing the transitory and incomplete powers of any one medium. The metaphysical conceit of the hair about the bone becomes a conceptual metaphor for an attempt to stall remediation and time, to make poetry fuse with language and visuality. But no conceptual metaphor will ever be final. It can only be a temporary ploy to stave off melancholia and its inevitable journey into mourning.

A Strip of Pavement over an Abyss

Reflecting in her diary during the writing of *Jacob's Room*, Woolf wonders: 'Why is life so tragic; so like a little strip of pavement over an abyss?'.[20] Implicitly, she sets in tension associations between her novelistic experiment and her experience of melancholy. In a splendid essay on the 'significant form' of *Jacob's Room*, the literary and cultural critic Kathleen Wall reads the novel's significance as its practice of elegy and ekphrasis. Closely following Julia Kristeva's influential work on melancholy[21] and Kazan's observation that the novel's array of visual images often breaks open the flow of narrative and dialogue, Wall argues that just as elegy responds to mourning, filling the gap with an aesthetic act, so too can loss be textually performed when written discourse gives way to images. She phrases the visually inflected object that replaces the lost object as an 'elegiac memorial'.[22] Despite the porous membranes between word and image, gaps occur between the two. Between lies a space for mourning. Ekphrasis can provide the visual supports to temporarily breach the gaps.

When the chasm is filled, however, when remediation will not go quietly into the melancholic night, but cries out regardless, Woolf's novel responds in a volley of synaesthesic adjectives. Jacob walks down a London street with Florinda, the woman with whom he is only ambiguously together. In his desire for her, his emotions and intellect remain broken apart. Between Jacob and external focalization, a meltdown occurs: 'The voices, angry, lustful, despairing, passionate, were scarcely more than the voices of caged beasts at night. Only they are not caged, nor beasts. [...] What does one fear? — the human eye. *At once the pavement narrows, the chasm deepens*' (75; my emphasis). The narrowing of the pavement resonates with the 'strip of pavement' from Woolf's diary. As the abyss threatens, the prose reaches out for the poetic rhymes of 'night' and 'eye' and produces parallel rhythms of 'At once the pavement' and 'the chasm deepens'. The eye, the purveyor of paint and image, becomes a source of fear. The external narrator's grasp of generalizing comments melts under the pressure of a poetic current. What is slowly unleashed is visuality from beyond the brink. The animals may not be 'real' but the imaginations of the eye are clearly a threat.

Remediation becomes a matter of survival and defence against onslaughts foretold. Elegiac visuality is less a matter of monuments that look backwards than one of talismans that either provoke anxiety or remain anxiously watchful. As though continuing to stave off the threats of further fracture, Woolf's novel provides scenes which act as miniature essays on the intermedialities that attempt to connect the arts, and people.

The often-thwarted attempts of major and minor characters to provoke Jacob's care, or even his incidental attention, perform the paradox inherent in acts of remediation. Any one medium attempts to cover over lacunae by drawing on its potential to become manifest through another medium. Despite this, the gaps and inconsistencies return like the proverbial repressed. One minor character in *Jacob's Room*, Miss Marchmont, dressed in a dissonant collage of clashing colours, devotes her life to confirming her philosophy that 'colour is sound — or, perhaps, it has something to do with music' (100, 102). By implication, Miss Marchmont is considering how certain media are interrelated. Yet her first breakthroughs stall. Indignant in the face of capitalist and cowardly publishers who may not accept her book, and in an unwitting act of attention-seeking behaviour, Miss Marchmont elbows a pile of books in Jacob's direction. The response: 'Jacob remained quite unmoved' (100). Tragically, in terms of the semiotics of her appearance, actions, conversation, and behaviour, Miss Marchmont cannot produce a style that would navigate the abyss of her loneliness. What she preaches she cannot extend into her daily practice. In this particular scene between the narrator and the heroically determined minor character, style can be read as a quest for human intimacy that finds a model of philosophical discourse bereft of the visual poetics of human contact. In which case, mourning and its reality effect may be repressed.

While ekphrasis might heal, the novel represses its liberal use. Putting into words the painting, the photograph, the video clip, or the installation might produce a remediated artwork never before seen. Dialogue is one device that remoulds the traditional notion that ekphrasis primarily involves the act of verbally picturing the otherwise mute art object. Jacob compliments his painter friend Cruttendon in lukewarm terms, declaring him to be a 'pretty competent painter' (122). Cruttendon longs for acknowledgement. Excited, he brings out his most recent painting. Cruttendon needs to defend his work: 'That's it. That's more like it. That's ...'. Dialogue dominates and ekphrasis is subdued. Jacob offers his opinion that the work is 'solid', then ends with the confusing plea 'But what I wish you'd explain ...' (123). Thus does he damn his friend's work with faint praise. In this passage, a sequence of montaged shots or collaged times and geographies is significantly absent. The failed artwork cannot be mourned. Miss Marchmont's academic pursuits and kitsch sartorial collages aim for, but fail at, connection. The 'strip across the pavement' would be less perilous if Jacob's responses were unmediated. But the focalizations of the human psyche are themselves mediators, simultaneously reaching out and yet failing to do so. As one conceptual metaphor for style, the strip of pavement conveys a sense of intellectual paradox; for every gain there can only be a loss.

The Scholar Makes Ribbons

The strips across the pavement allow for little stillness. Intermedial practice requires that metaphors keep moving, not just between media, but also between the substances from which artistic discourses are formed. I return to the passage from *Jacob's Room* which introduced the conceptual metaphors of ribbon and nets, where the concept of text as verbal material cannot be disentangled from its visual texture. A further entanglement can take place within film, and in a more technical sense than film's historical capacity to have absorbed the media of painting, sculpture, theatre, and photography. Yvonne Spielmann identifies the place in which collage and morphing techniques combine as digital photography and film. Morphing describes the technique of special effects, from changing the colour of the pixels in any particular shot to adding special effects. In *Jacob's Storyboard*, I aimed to take the aesthetic basis of collage from Woolf's novel and conduct a more extreme experiment. Film can shoot the combination of different materials. Furthermore, as I made a digital film, I experimented with the connections between montage, collage, and morphing by using a 'blue screen' technique. This means superimposing another object, usually moving, onto an entirely different shot. The morph might be described as an extreme collage, in which the resulting space can be adjusted, re-coloured and re-cut using digital editing programs. The process might appear to be the reverse of ekphrasis. By turning a written text into images of text, I could further examine to what extent my filmic interpretation condensed aesthetic and political themes from Woolf's novel, making them more contemporaneous through a conceptual metaphor for style.

Connected to the fiction pieces from *Imagine Jacob*, the motivation for the film is the idea that the Jacob of 2003 makes *Jacob's Storyboard* as a digital and poetic essay for Sandra Wentworth Williams. He does so knowing that the affair is over. The film is a memorial, a digital badge of mourning. The film begins at dusk with a shot of paving stones crumbling in a heap. The pieces of a disappointed love are to be picked up. Life goes on. The following shot with the film's title reveals in deep perspective the criss-cross lines of an ordinary pavement (Figure 10.1).[23] This still picture then gives way to another pavement, this time made from paving stones cut out from a printed copy of Woolf's novel, set on a black and sandy surface. Stone, sand and paper, and real glue are all juxtaposed, as we see scissors cutting up the printed page. Destruction becomes a requisite for modernist reinvention. Ribbons of paper are torn. In film, shots and images are 'cut'. The printed word has been turned into a visual icon, in Charles Sanders Peirce's sense of the word.[24] Then *Jacob's Storyboard* sets adrift the words of the book, having torn them in half.

When Bolter and Grusin theorize remediation as an impulse towards one medium's attempt to strengthen and improve another, I would suggest that more

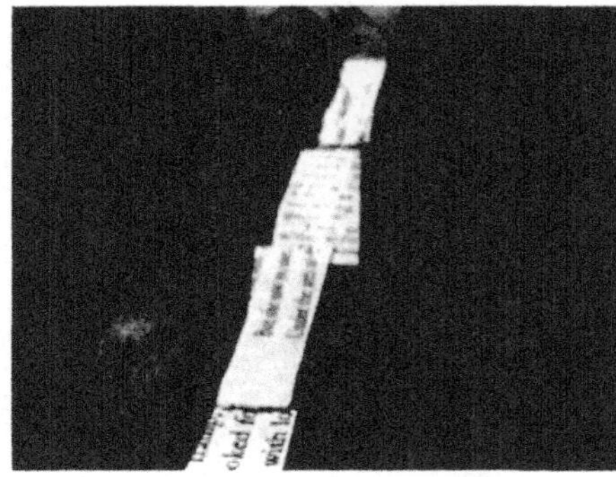

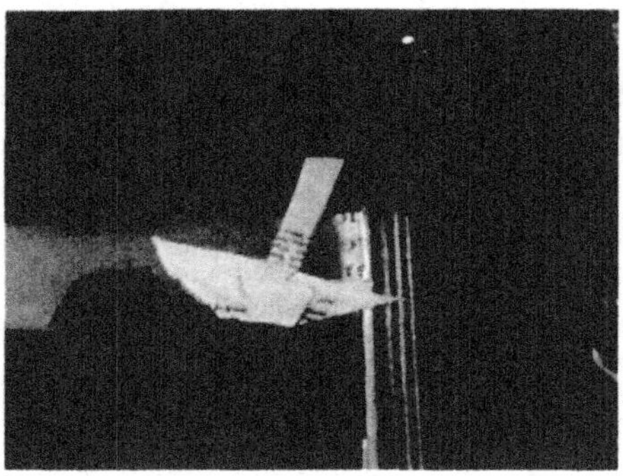

FIGURE 10.1 (above left). *Jacob's Storyboard*: film title shot.
FIGURE 10.2 (above right). Perspectives, identities, and modernisms.
FIGURE 10.3 (below left). Special effects in the house of modernism.
FIGURE 10.4 (below right). Journeys and their negatives.

attention can be paid to how this can occur through a medium's techniques of editing. In my film, I explored how one material can lend sustenance to another through the editing device of 'superimposition'. This is a stronger version of fading one image in as another disappears from the scene over a short period, be it from a few seconds to six frames. Two shots can appear to overlap. Equally well, one shot can appear ghostly as it emerges from within another. This now accepted trope of film-editing was, in the early days of the medium, regarded as a special effect. The sense of 'magic' brought audiences a feeling of immediacy. Spectators were fascinated by the film's first experiments in optical illusion. They enjoyed the montage of film as they would the magic of the circus illusionist. Bolter and Grusin underscore remediation as that which heightens the spectator's sense of the artwork's immediacy while covertly drawing attention to its artificiality. In this vein, *Jacob's Storyboard* critiques Woolf's novel through a visual reading that deploys cuts, collages, and superimpositions. All three devices can be read as acts of reading; interpretation is made incarnate through juxtapositions.

Remediation functions as an 'intimacy of influence' between past and present, when tropes and themes in the precursor work can be given more focus — can, indeed, find themselves magnified through the lens of a contemporary work. The countless references to trees and animal life provide *Jacob's Room* with its impulsive and energetic clauses, which often cascade into a debris of nouns and noun phrases at the end of sentences. The rhythm enacts volleys of acute energy followed by dissipation. The result: the novel thereby harnesses its constant preoccupation with life and its prescience of death, a foretelling which makes the quest for a life-force more urgent.

Jacob's Storyboard reasserts the themes of life and death through tropes that crack open sections of Woolf's novel. Shots of cut-out trees and piled logs appear in the collage. The photograph of the tree graphically matches and becomes superimposed on the cut-out strips of paper pavement. Once the film has set up shots of these thin strips of print, the hand-held tracking shots of their layout give the viewer a dynamic sense of perspective. The shots of the thin strips of paper pavement fade into the shot of a headless man in a suit, with a tie, holding a light bulb (Figure 10.2). Perhaps moths could meet their death at his hands. The shot could be a painting or a photograph. Thus, two media are ambiguously implied, and the difference not resolved. According to Spielmann, such combinations of the painterly and filmic, digitally rendered, constitute a 'morph'. In this example, remediation is a reminder of literary modernism as a force challenging early, twentieth-century capitalism. Fredric Jameson's work in this area has emphasized how literary modernism has pitted itself against the 'reifying' systems of capitalism, as they infiltrated the novelist tradition.[25] In the film, the 'stuffed shirt' with the bulb is an icon of late capitalism. The next shot reveals Magritte's painting of a man looking in a mirror, the reflection the back of his head (*Not to Be Reproduced*, 1937). No gaze is afforded; voyeuristic escape is not an option. Two backs of the heads struck me as an apt visualization of Woolf's Jacob, the man who is so difficult to fathom. Then another shot of logs gives way to a photograph of the back of a soldier's head. The staged shot, intended to imply an American or British soldier in Iraq, reveals print coming through from behind the photograph. The written word, the report, is one style, the war photo another. Yet both get stuck together, each element refusing the other the escape of reification. The climax of the film is a rapid-fire montage of strips of Woolf's novel being cut into tiny strips that then quickly form a paper boat. Using blue-screen superimposition techniques, this boat is set adrift and sets sail through a collage of the photographs I have just enumerated: the early-twentieth-century reproduction of a Magritte painting, juxtaposed with contemporary shots of trees under threat, a soldier in Iraq, a city gent (Figure 10.3). Adorno's 'torn halves' cannot be lined up so that our gaze catches those of the characters. At the heart of the collision between capitalist consumption, clock time pitted against nature, ancient history, is the knowledge of and the blindness to the inevitability of death.

By experimenting with both written fiction and film-making as modes of interpretation, I aimed to bring the themes of *Jacob's Room* into a contemporary context of global capitalism and the environment in crisis. The ribbons of paper made a boat to glide between media, perhaps in seach of a space outside global capitalism. But there is no escape, for the pavement will return. Thus, *Jacob's Storyboard* critiques twenty-first-century capitalism as environmentally destructive and linked to global capitalism. Collage and montage, and the film's project to keep the two practices superimposed, enables aesthetic remediation to expose the political, environmental, and mortal dangers of global capitalism. The paper boat was both model and conceptual metaphor for a style adrift, as it negotiates both tradition and, to tilt Jameson's celebrated phrase, the political pre-conscious of global capitalism.

Conclusion

As a conceptual metaphor, the boat not only travelled, it came into being through hand-made and cinematic collage. The boat was formed from different, and disconnected, printed pages cut out of a copy of *Jacob's Room* and glued together. These assorted cutouts constituted the boat's materiality. Moreover, the icon of a sailing device provided metaphors as concepts for the different manifestations of style.

As the boat travelled through photographs, paintings, and their juxtaposition, it acted as more than a metaphor for style, for it was acted upon. The digital medium of blue-screen special effects allowed the boat to produce the illusion of floating through the frame. In other words, the conceptual metaphor of 'style is movement between media' is itself a fabrication, the result of a montaged collage. The concept driving the metaphor of the boat argues that style moves between media that are already connected. In Woolf's novel, the scene on the Acropolis between Jacob and Sandra Wentworth Williams provides an example of the indissoluble connection between word and image, as do the encounters of Miss Marchmont, Cruttendon, and the external narrator with Jacob himself. The gaps in the media appear, then disappear. The strip of pavement does not act so simply as to bridge gaps when the chasm appears: it may choose to disappear at the moment it is being crossed.

During mourning, images can provide fetishes or temporary pieces of driftwood for the act of relinquishing a desire for the lost object. But these liminal sites of striving for all that is lost cannot be directly perceived; these spaces can only be inferred, or theorized. In my film, I did not stage the boat floating in empty space. In the penultimate shot, the boat crosses a pavement which has been coloured to give the impression of a photographic negative. Even the abyss requires the visualization of a medium (Figure 10.4). In the *Tractatus logico-philosophicus*, Wittgenstein analysed the limits of thought in terms of what could be pictured. Even abstract thought requires images. Tropes from the sciences also rely on metaphors and models.[26] The concept of 'cracks' between the solid points of meaning is itself a metaphor, a concept for what can only be pointed to but not entirely visualized. The moving, transforming conceptual metaphor for style is indeed a miniature theory as fiction.[27]

My scholarly experiment of mixing media and producing different collages of styles has confirmed for me the importance of understanding the gaps between the media and of respecting the distinctions between scholarly and artistic discourses. Fiction can theorize, just as theories can make from themselves aesthetic 'boats' for journeys to the edge of current practices. But it still remains important to keep distinctions between discourses, between media, and between theory and practice. Without such separations, there would be no liminal spaces. The 'concrete' aspect of a conceptual metaphor may need to fall overboard and drift away, be dissolved, re-crystallized or simply lost during the voyage. For it is this willingness to lose concepts and metaphors, to jettison the neurotic's desire to hold on at all costs to an established practice or style, that allows the boundaries of any scholarly or aesthetic practice to push forwards. Paradoxically, the movement onwards constantly pays its respects to tradition, to what has been and shall be reinvented, to what is forever lost. The capacity to mourn is a prerequisite for aesthetic experiment and for style as an unseizable force.

Notes to Chapter 10

1. Virginia Woolf, *Jacob's Room* (London: Vintage, 2000). Further references to this edition are given after quotations in the text.
2. Francesca Kazan, 'Description and the Pictorial in *Jacob's Room*', *ELH*, 55 (1988), 701–19 (p. 702).
3. Mieke Bal, *Travelling Concepts in the Humanities: A Rough Guide* (Toronto: Toronto University Press, 2002), p. 110. Bal credits extensive work done on conceptual metaphors in Teri Reynolds, 'Case Studies in Cognitive Metaphor and Interdisciplinary Analysis: Physics, Biology, Narrative' (unpublished doctoral dissertation, Columbia University, New York, 2000). By crediting Teri Reynolds, Bal also suggests a thread towards the work of Lakoff and Johnson, for whom conceptual metaphors imply a cluster of metaphors dovetailing with the same concept. See George Lakoff and Mark Johnson, *Metaphors We Live By* (Chicago: University of Chicago Press, 1980).
4. Bal takes her cue from *D'une science à l'autre: des concepts nomades*, ed. by Isabelle Stengers (Paris: Éditions du Seuil, 1987).
5. Catherine M. Lord, *Jacob's Story Board*, produced by Catherine M. Lord (Amsterdam: John Donne Productions, 2003). Premiered at the conference New Languages for Criticism, Cambridge, 20 September 2003.
6. Michael Cunningham, *The Hours* (London: Picador, 1999).
7. Jean H. Hagstrum, *The Sister Arts: The Tradition of Literary Pictorialism and English Poetry from Dryden to Gray* (Chicago: University of Chicago Press, 1958), p. 18.
8. Dick Higgins, 'Intermedia', *Leonardo*, 34 (2001), 49–54.
9. Marshall McLuhan, *Understanding Media: The Extensions of Man* (New York: McGraw-Hill, 1964), pp. 23–24.
10. See Catherine M. Lord, *The Intimacy of Influence: Narrative and Theoretical Fictions between the Novels of George Eliot, Virginia Woolf and Jeanette Winterson* (Amsterdam: ASCA Press, 1999), in which I develop a series of concepts including that of 'theoretical fiction'. Not only do narratives provide theories of life and perception; similarly, theories offer themselves as narrative, with asymmetrical aspects of analysis and fantasy.
11. For theories of focalization, see Mieke Bal, *Narratology: Introduction to the Theory of Narrative*, 2nd edn (Toronto: Toronto University Press, 1997).
12. Herta Wescher, *Collage*, trans. by Robert E. Wolf (New York: Harry Abrams, 1968), cited in *Encyclopedia of Aesthetics*, ed. by Michael Kelly, 4 vols (New York and Oxford: Oxford University Press, 1998), I, 41–42.
13. This point is asserted throughout Sergei Eisenstein, *The Film Sense*, trans. and ed. by Jay Leyda (London: Faber, 1943). See also Karel Reisz and Gavin Millar, *The Technique of Film Editing*, 2nd edn (Guildford: Focal Press, repr. 1991), pp. 33–40.
14. Yvonne Spielmann, 'Aesthetic Features in Digital Imaging: Collage and Morph', *Wide Angle*, 21.1 (January 1999), 131–48 (pp. 138–48).
15. Theodor W. Adorno, *Aesthetic Theory*, trans. and ed. by Robert Hullot-Kentor (Minneapolis: University of Minnesota Press, 1997), cited in *Encyclopedia of Aesthetics* (see Wescher, above), I, 383.
16. Jay David Bolter and Richard Grusin, 'Remediation', *Configurations*, 4 (1996), 311–58 (pp. 318–19).

17. Ibid., p. 346.
18. Sergei Eisenstein, 'Through Theatre to Cinema', *Focus on Film and Theatre*, ed. by James Hurt (Englewood Cliffs, NJ: Prentice Hall, 1974), pp. 116–29.
19. Giorgio Agamben, 'The End of the Poem', in *The End of the Poem: Studies in Poetics*, trans. by Daniel Heller-Roazen (Stanford: Stanford University Press, 1999), pp. 109–15 (p. 109).
20. Virginia Woolf, *A Writer's Diary* (London: Triad Grafton, 1978), p. 49 (25 October 1920).
21. Julia Kristeva, *Black Sun: Depression and Melancholia*, trans. by Leon S. Roudiez (New York: Columbia University Press, 1992).
22. Kathleen Wall, 'Significant Form in *Jacob's Room*: Ekphrasis and the Elegy', *Texas Studies in Literature and Language*, 44 (2002), 302–23 (pp. 305–06).
23. The stills reproduced here as Figures 10.2, 10.3, and 10.4 may be viewed at <http://home.medewerker.uva.nl/c.m.lord/> by clicking the link to 'nieuw'; the still shown on the website as Figure 1 is the opening, not the title, shot. My thanks are due to Tom van Klingeren and to Bruce Grey of the Practicum Department of the Media and Culture Department of the University of Amsterdam, for their technical assistance and patience in the making of film materials for presentation at the conference.
24. Charles Sanders Peirce, 'Logic as Semiotic: The Theory of Signs', in *Semiotics: An Introductory Anthology*, ed. with introduction by Robert E. Innis (Bloomington: Indiana University Press, 1985), pp. 4–23.
25. Fredric Jameson, *The Political Unconscious: Narrative as a Socially Symbolic Act* (Ithaca, NY: Cornell University Press, 1981).
26. For a thorough study of metaphor and models in the natural sciences, see Evelyn Fox Keller, *Making Sense of Life: Explaining Biological Development with Models, Metaphors, and Machines* (Cambridge, MA: Harvard University Press, 2002).
27. In addition to my own work on theoretical fictions in *The Intimacy of Influence*, I am indebted to Malcolm Bowie's study *Freud, Proust and Lacan: Theory as Fiction* (Cambridge: Cambridge University Press, 1987).

CHAPTER 11

❖

Languages for Learning to Delight in Art

Joanne Lee

The theory and criticism of art has, in recent years at least, been defined by its apparent interdisciplinarity. Our critical language is derived variously from aesthetics, semiotics, cultural studies, identity politics, psychoanalysis, psychology, and reception theory amongst very many others. In a manner fitting Adam Phillips's description of psychoanalysis as 'more of a grab bag of culture and history than a vision or system', writers, thinkers, and indeed artists themselves, have tended towards a working methodology best defined as eclectic.[1] To me, this curiosity about diverse models seems healthy; it marks a real interest in the world and, done well, it is a model for engaging with the full potential and complexity of academic inquiry.

Of course there are well-rehearsed arguments to the contrary. Noël Carroll articulates a common concern when he states that these 'theoretical excursions' are almost always dilettantish rather than rigorous, usually because they tend to rely upon second- or third-hand source material.[2] A decade before Carroll, Jonathan Ree was highly critical of a certain kind of interdisciplinarity he termed the *nouveau mélange*, which brings together material that is at best incompatible or at worst contradictory.[3] These arguments are not without foundation, but I remain concerned that they also make us over-defensive. In what follows, I hope to articulate some of the problems with our current theoretical approaches and to offer a sketch of alternative strategies. This essay is prompted by my work as an artist and as a teacher of practitioners rather than theorists. Within art, perhaps we can be a little less concerned with 'getting it right', overtly attempting to hold open a space in which uncertainty is privileged.

The theory and criticism of art is marked by a narrow orthodoxy of pseudo-interdisciplinarity that privileges the same few theories, and theorists, time and again. Victor Burgin's *The End of Art Theory* railed against the canon of established artistic 'masterpieces', observing that canonical works are 'consigned to perpetual exhumation'.[4] My sadness is that the new discourse Burgin laid out with such conviction almost twenty years ago has now congealed into our own canon of established theoretical masterpieces. Even at the time Burgin was writing his piece, he noted:

> The texts are looted of their terminology, which is then used to vacuously ornament the pages of conservative writings [...] Pages are now peppered with such terms as 'signifier', 'desire', 'drive', 'deconstruction' and so on — a roll call of the arrested terminological prisoners given meaningless labour in intellectual deserts'.[5]

It is still considered a 'good thing' by academics for art students to engage with this theoretical canon (and its descendants), but guidance is rarely offered as to what exactly they should do with it. Art students' anxieties seem primarily focused upon theory, and those anxieties are often aggravated by their teachers, some of whom fear this material (because they too had an art education that failed to properly explain its utility), while others are hidebound by an unduly reverential application of models from other fields (which are often incompletely understood), and yet others simply enjoy demonstrating a theoretical dexterity. In each case, they reinforce the idea of its difficulty.

If teachers explain something about the use of this theory, one of two approaches is usually followed. On the one hand, staff encourage students to read against the grain, a method that requires a level of academic confidence beyond many undergraduates. On the other hand, students perceive (through staff) that the work they make needs to be somehow 'about' the theoretical ideas they have encountered. This latter approach simply creates a defensive attitude in which students feel they have to 'justify' their work: it is as if we are telling them that without this theoretical material they can have little of interest to say. In any case, much theory and criticism of art tends to operate with a model of lack and disappointment concerned with how artists, artworks, critics, or theorists have failed. Students have frequently told me that they do not find this persuasive or helpful. Rather than opening up possibilities, it creates the expectation of having to defend whatever one does against all comers.

Students quickly perceive that there are preferred positions, readings, and opinions. They worry that transgression will result in their getting the art 'wrong' or will incur the wrath of their tutor (for which read poor marks). For some students certainties of interpretation are reassuring: they fear experiencing art without it having been pre-digested by criticism. The potential for rich and complex responses is seen as a significant difficulty rather than an aspiration. In addition, most theorizing of images and the visual realm has been marked by a deep mistrust of the object of study: images have become synonymous with seduction and misrepresentation. But like Barbara Maria Stafford, I believe that 'imaging [...] remains the richest, most fascinating modality for configuring and conveying ideas'.[6] I think it is time for art education and theory to offer a more positive and suggestive approach.

A key problem, however, is that most of my students don't actually go to see much art, except as convenient reproductions in library books or if a college trip is organized. I don't think this is simply to be put down to laziness, but rather that they actively prefer other forms, events, and phenomena. Although they are studying for a fine art degree, contemporary art seemingly fails to compel. My students obviously aren't alone in this, given the public debate in the early years of this century as to whether art is 'craftless tat' or 'cold, mechanical, conceptual bullshit'. The comments are from Ivan Massow, former Chairman of the ICA, and the then Culture Minister Kim Howells, respectively. (There is insufficient space here to explore the old arguments as to whether art is, has always been, or should be in crisis, though a lengthy debate throughout 2003 within the pages of *Art Monthly* explored precisely those issues and makes a worthwhile read.)[7] But even within the art world there is the sense that we are simply treading water. We need art and art criticism that can more fully challenge and engage students, artists, theorists, and public.

To want to study something we must be interested in it, and yet education is largely about losing or compromising one's interest, as Freud implies (according to Adam Phillips), and as I have witnessed daily.[8] Is it perhaps necessary to lose something in order to find it once more? In part I think this is true, but in our urgency to promote it as the main strategy for educational development I am concerned that we are close to suggesting that a kind of bereavement is good for you — surely a rather cruel approach. Phillips tells us that 'one of the first words in psychoanalysis for [...] interest was curiosity' (16), and, for him, curiosity is being alert to the things that uphold one's love of life. He goes further when he asserts that one of the aims of analysis is 'to free people to do nothing to the future but be interested in it' (32). I have a similar aim for art education.

In order to look forward, I first need to look back: curiosity has a history, one that is fascinatingly recounted in Barbara Benedict's book on the subject.[9] The word 'curiosity' stems from the Latin *curiosus*, meaning 'inquiring'. In a special issue of the journal *Word & Image* devoted to the subject, the art historian Peter Parshall defined curiosity as 'a state of mind and a condition of the emotions cultivated by those set on investigating the full scope of natural and human invention'.[10] It is the free-ranging method of inquiry that I find suggestive, and also the sense that such inquiry was not easily regulated. In the same issue of *Word & Image*, Christopher Wood observes that 'curiosity was the impulse to improper inquiry'.[11] The apparent impropriety of curiosity is remarked by St Augustine, who considered it a lust of the eyes, and Wood suggests that curiosity 'conspicuously resembled a sensual appetite'.[12]

Terry Eagleton reminds us that the aesthetic is 'a discourse concerned with the way reality strikes the body on its sensuous surface'.[13] The strength of art (and other cultural artefacts) lies in its potential to elicit an aesthetic affect. As a means of exploring the world we inhabit, this seems a profoundly powerful tool. The poet Fernando Pessoa may have declared that he had senses rather than a philosophy, but Susan Buck-Morss asserts that the aesthetic is not merely sensation, but also a 'fundamentally cognitive experience'.[14] She states that 'the critical power of art, or any cultural form, may not be perceived universally, but if it is perceived, it hits you in the gut', and goes on to suggest that this 'somatic' experience resists 'predatory reason' because it 'can't be stomached, gobbled up by the mind'. She claims that this 'non-digestible residue is food for critical cognition' (43).

On the face of it, this notion of a gut response is almost blasphemous within the contemporary university or art school context. But if we attend more closely to Buck-Morss's argument, we see that it is certainly not pre-critical or naive. Her suggestion is that artists and cultural producers ought to be concerned with providing, in whatever form, 'a somatic experience that is self-reflective — critical in the philosophical sense' (43). It is thus not mere sensation that is perceived by feeling, but actually a critical form of knowledge. Were we to speak more frankly about the complexities of the 'non-digestible residue' we would seem to have the basis for a more complex, subtle, and honest relationship to art.

In considering the sexual researches of children as Freud's apotheosis of curiosity, Phillips suggests that children do not sacrifice their lives to theory making, but 'their lives are made possible by it'.[15] He tells us that for Walter Pater (a figure newly rediscovered by a range of contemporary thinkers) the real interest 'was in what the art, and the life of the artist, could evoke in him; what he could use it to become'.[16] It is this forward-looking, 'prospective' interest (Phillips's term) that I think we ought to be pursuing in art and education in preference to the 'foreclosed' aspects of much art and academic study, which seem to discipline (and narrow) potential experience.[17]

How then can we develop our abilities (and those of our students) to be prospectively interested in the world? Jonathan Lear has suggested that we are hampered by an excess of 'knowingness',[18] which can problematically proscribe responses and ideas. I think we need to counter this. If I can practise my own contextually inappropriate *nouveau mélange* for a moment, I would like to juxtapose the Russian Formalist Viktor Shklovsky's idea of 'making strange' (*oestranenie*)[19] with Jonathan Culler's opinion that 'the works we allude to as theory have the power to make strange the familiar and to make readers conceive of their own thinking, behaviours and institutions in new ways'.[20] The idea of defamiliarization is not a new concept, but it is one we have rather put aside, perhaps in fear of its potential romanticism. Within what is frequently described as the knowledge economy, not immediately knowing or understanding is something to be concealed rather than positively experienced.

One mechanism for positively eliciting this strangeness is described by Jane Bennett as enchantment. She writes that enchantment is

> a surprising encounter, a meeting with something that you did not expect and [with which you] are not fully prepared to engage. Contained within this surprise state are (1) a pleasurable feeling of being charmed by the novel and as yet unprocessed encounter and (2) a more unheimlich (uncanny) feeling of being disrupted or torn out of one's default sensory-psychic-intellectual disposition.[21]

Bennett concludes that

> the overall effect of enchantment is a mood of fullness, plenitude, or liveliness, a sense of having one's nerves or circulation or concentration powers tuned up or recharged — a shot in the arm, a fleeting return to childlike excitement about life.

The effect of enchantment, then, is to reawaken interest. Her assertion that when one is enchanted one is actively engaged describes exactly the kind of state I would wish to see — but don't — in art galleries and universities.

What seems to be important about Bennett's work is that she is suggestive of what we might do with this engagement. Far from allowing a naive retreat from the world's problems, she offers the prospect of using enchantment as an effective counter to cynicism, despair, and passivity. She does not seek to re-enchant a disenchanted world, but to attend to existing instances of 'the marvellous erupting in the everyday', in the words of Jackson Lears.[22] His *Fables of Abundance* is a powerful study of advertising, and I find this a telling reference. In one example of a possible counter-story, Bennett's argument goes that as consumers we derive non-commercial value from consumption and advertisements, so that some of this pleasure may be susceptible to 'ethical redeployment'.[23]

Within recent academic history, pleasure has had pretty rough treatment. Horkheimer and Adorno describe it thus: 'pleasure always means not to think about anything [...] It is flight from the last remaining thought of resistance.'[24] The heady debates around pleasure initiated by Laura Mulvey and others meant it largely became the feeling that dared not speak its name. But Bennett seeks to mobilize the energies of our pleasures in order 'to exercise one's capacity to see things as otherwise than they are'.[25] She urges us to use our pleasure in order to fire our imagination: indeed, she sees this as an ethical responsibility.

Others have also argued that imagination might actually be a source of knowledge. Gregory Currie, in his essay 'Realism of Character and the Value of Fiction', says that 'in imagining things, one might thereby come to know (possibly other) things'.[26] Some academics have keenly pursued this strategy. Gregory Ulmer, for instance, has developed a pedagogic–critical method he terms 'heuretics' because he believes, 'learning is much closer to invention than to verification'. He complains that 'the modes of writing now taught in school tend to be positioned on the side of the already known rather than on the side of wanting to find out (of theoretical curiosity) and hence discourage learning how to learn'.[27]

I should like to conclude on this question of knowledge. Peter de Bolla's book *Art Matters* ends with an evocative consideration of wonder: a feeling very close to Bennett's 'enchantment'. What is interesting about wonder, according to de Bolla, is that 'it feels as if it comes [...] before knowledge, since as Socrates remarked, the primary motivation of wonder is the recognition of ignorance'.[28] De Bolla goes on to say that

> wonder requires us to acknowledge what we do not know or may never know, to acknowledge the limits of knowledge. It is, then, a different species of knowledge, a way of knowing that does not lead to certainties or truths about the world or the way things are.

I see this as a positive approach. I would urge you to remember that several of our academic terms originate in such uncertainty: our 'essay' comes from the French *essayer* — to try, and 'discourse' from its Latin root *discursus* — a going to and fro. It concerns me that universities no longer remember this. These terms suggest the potential for taking risks in our experiences and learning, pursuing our interests where we need to. They do not require us to be so defensive.

Peter Parshall has said that 'the curious frame of mind was an agitated and unstable universe, a place where conventional categories of understanding became blurred'.[29] It is now acceptable (and indeed fashionable) to be artistically or academically interdisciplinary, but current forms of interdisciplinarity seem fundamentally conservative, merely reiterating a familiar set of models. Under the guise of policing academic rigour, these 'master discourses' ultimately control the boundaries of what is 'thinkable'.

Just as the church frowned upon 'curiosity' as being contrary to a proper inquiry into God's universe, I fear one risks institutional excommunication in truly following one's curiosity as artist or academic. Adam Phillips has wondered 'whether knowing and understanding, however well done, should be the be-all and end-all'.[30] Within the arts and humanities at least, I am more concerned with being interesting, and interested, than with being right. Phillips's suggestion that it may be more interesting to have made something haunting than something true is in fact what drives me. It is heartening that wonder, curiosity, and enchantment are to be found once more as subjects proper to academic study, and I should like to propose that we might usefully develop them as methods, using the clues in work by Bennett, de Bolla, et al. The resulting open-mindedness may be a more compelling milieu for educating artists and bringing new audiences to our works of theory and practice. Speaking of psychoanalysis Phillips has said that it should aspire to develop languages that people find intriguing enough to want to learn, without being so impressed by them that they lose their own voices, and that this process should enable them to lose themselves in whatever makes them curious and makes them feel alive.[31] This lesson is one we would do well to heed.

Notes to Chapter 11

1. Adam Phillips, *Promises, Promises: Essays on Literature and Psychoanalysis*, 2nd edn (London: Faber and Faber, 2002), p. xiii.
2. Noël Carroll, 'Prospects for Film Theory: A Personal Assessment', in *Post-Theory: Reconstructing Film Studies*, ed. by David Bordwell and Noël Carroll (Madison: University of Wisconsin Press, 1996), pp. 37–68 (p. 41).
3. Jonathan Ree, 'Marxist Modes', in *Radical Philosophy Reader*, ed. by Roy Edgely and Richard Osborne (London: Verso, 1985), pp. 337–60 (p. 338).
4. Victor Burgin, *The End of Art Theory: Criticism and Postmodernity* (London: Macmillan, 1986), p. 159.
5. Ibid., p. 163.
6. Barbara Maria Stafford, *Good Looking: Essays on the Virtue of Images* (Cambridge: MIT Press, 1996), p. 4.
7. The debate begins with an article by Michael Archer, 'Crisis What Crisis?', *Art Monthly*, no. 264 (March 2003), 1–4.
8. Adam Phillips, *The Beast in the Nursery*, 2nd edn (London: Faber and Faber, 1999), p. 23.
9. Barbara Benedict, *Curiosity: A Cultural History of Early Modern Inquiry* (Chicago: University of Chicago Press, 2001).
10. Peter Parshall, 'Introduction', *Art and Curiosity in Northern Europe*, ed. by Peter Parshall (*Word & Image*, 11.4 (1995)), pp. 327–31 (p 327).
11. Christopher S. Wood, '"Curious Pictures" and the Art of Description', in *Art and Curiosity* (see Parshall, above), pp. 332–52 (p. 334).
12. Ibid., pp. 336–37.
13. Terry Eagleton, *The Ideology of the Aesthetic* (Oxford: Blackwell, 1990), p. 13.
14. Grant Kester, 'Aesthetics after the End of Art: An Interview with Susan Buck-Morss', *Art Journal*, 56.1 (1997), 38–45 (p. 39).

15. *The Beast in the Nursery*, p. 29.
16. *Promises, Promises*, p. 149.
17. Phillips, *The Beast in the Nursery*, 32.
18. Jonathan Lear, *Open Minded: Working Out the Logic of the Soul* (Cambridge, MA: Harvard University Press, 1998).
19. Viktor Shklovsky, *Theory of Prose* (Champaign, IL: Dalkey Archive Press, 1993).
20. Jonathan Culler, *On Deconstruction: Theory and Criticism after Structuralism* (London: Routledge, 1983), p. 9.
21. Jane Bennett, *The Enchantment of Modern Life: Attachments, Crossings and Ethics* (Princeton: Princeton University Press, 2001), p. 5.
22. Jackson Lears, *Fables of Abundance: A Cultural History of Advertising in America* (New York: Basic Books, 1994), p. 19, quoted in Bennett, *The Enchantment of Modern Life*.
23. *The Enchantment of Modern Life*, p. 129.
24. Max Horkheimer and Theodor Adorno, *Dialectic of Enlightenment* (New York: Herder and Herder, 1972), p. 144.
25. *The Enchantment of Modern Life*, p. 76.
26. Gregory Currie, 'Realism of Character and the Value of Fiction', in *Aesthetics and Ethics: Essays at the Intersection*, ed. by Jerrold Levinson (Cambridge: Cambridge University Press, 1998), pp. 161–81 (p. 161).
27. Gregory Ulmer, *Heuretics: The Logic of Invention* (Baltimore: Johns Hopkins University Press, 1994), p. xii.
28. Peter de Bolla, *Art Matters* (Cambridge, MA: Harvard University Press, 2003), p. 143.
29. 'Art and Curiosity', p. 327.
30. *Promises, Promises*, p. 173.
31. Ibid., p. xiv.

CHAPTER 12

❖

Loopholes in Performance

Anthony Gritten

Between the idea
And the reality
Between the motion
And the act
Falls the Shadow.

T. S. Eliot, 'The Hollow Men' (1925)

This chapter articulates a response to a central aspect of the history of music performance studies, which has witnessed a gradual shift in focus from music appreciation to the musical experience to the musical act. It is part of a project to understand the folk psychology of performing: 'what it feels like' to perform.[1] By this I mean the structures of belief, desire, and intention that provide the conditions of possibility for performing as the performer herself sees it. There has been a great deal of work recently on the meanings of performance,[2] on how it signifies,[3] and on how performers contribute to that signification,[4] but I am more interested in what evades such signifying processes and resists such an unduly hasty assimilation of performing to performance. This essay is less about the languages of music criticism and how they tackle performance, that most thorny of musical subjects, than about the dynamic object of such languages when performing is at issue.

I

In the modern era, and especially in our current period of accountability and transparency, the activity of performing music has frequently been conceived, in Taylorist fashion, as revolving around a 'contract'.[5] It has been taken gastronomically to be a matter of catering for and servicing the listener: the performer is accountable to the listener or the composer or both, and performing is accountable to performance — a singular event to the general case. According to this logic of representation, practice and theory, performance and criticism, doing and writing, are related and hence evaluated in terms of their mutual fidelity to one another. The greater theory's fidelity, the truer is its representation of practice; the greater practice's fidelity, the deeper is its theoretical and critical significance. (Such is the essence of critique.)[6]

I would like to suggest, though, that this logic is limiting and restrictive. My charge is that it fails to unfold the umbrella term Performance (capital P) into its constituent moments: 'performing', 'performance', and 'the performative'. Other relations are equally conceivable between performance and criticism, so we should avoid surreptitiously assimilating them and specifying the manner of their structural convergence. In search of a more 'benevolent demarcation'[7] of the two domains, I shall suggest that their relation is better described as a 'drift'[8] and that performing drifts away both from performance and from (its own) representation — from theory and criticism. More importantly, though, I shall argue that this term better describes the performer's *own* understanding of what it means to perform live.

II

Before exploring an alternative possibility for performing, we might ask, How does Performance as a cultural activity get forced into this position (if not ignored)?[9] Consider the chapter on 'Ornamentation and Improvisation' in Paul Henry Lang's symbolically titled *Musicology and Performance*.[10] Lang raises issues central to performing:

> Ornamentation and improvisation are a tentative and chaotic field in which composition, *ex tempore* invention, oral tradition, palaeography, folk music, organology, monophony, polyphony, motor urge, and the elemental desire to 'play' cross one another; for there are no fixed boundaries — the whole complex is constantly involved in the contradictory problem of what is spontaneous versus what is premeditated. (212)

Without much probing, we can see that Lang's conception of ornamentation presupposes a metaphysics of presence typical of his generation. An ornament, he writes, 'completes' and 'decorates' the text, and, since it 'is *added* to preexisting music, therefore it can also be dispensable' (210–11). The history of ornamentation, too, documents changing attitudes towards the relation between text and 'decoration', the dominant trajectory of the modern era having been towards the integration of ornament into text (218). Likewise with cadenzas: an improvised cadenza, Lang says, is a 'commentary or exegesis', and can be either a 'jarr[ing] interpolation' or an 'organic completion' of the movement to which it is appended (228). Lang's approach might help provide a cultural understanding of Performance derived from the historical logic of the work concept, but it is less useful for understanding what the performer does. We might counter that the work concept should be understood as a loose, open idea,[11] solving many of the problems infecting Lang's approach. After the horse has bolted, though, why shut the gate? For the performer has always and necessarily understood the work concept as loose and open (in so far as she has needed the work *concept*), and her fluid, pre-theoretical conception of it (if indeed 'conception' best describes her own sense of what she does) has always been central to a healthy culture of performance. Missing from Lang's approach is a dynamic conception of ornamentation as less an attribute of what the musical work 'is' than a relation of what the act of performing might 'become'. This is to reconfigure the practice of ornamentation as a mode of attention directed towards the work: in short, as a performative category. Immediately this splits what Lang calls Performance into the three moments mentioned above, and helps to deal with the actual performing 'of' such ornamentation, in which an element like improvisation and going by names like 'judgement' guides the musical act. That said, Lang's decision not to separate ornamentation from improvisation usefully highlights the performativity of ornamentation and the interdependence of improvisation and composition.[12]

A similarly problematic and equally representative example, this time from a philosopher rather than a musicologist, is provided by Stan Godlovitch's essay 'The Integrity of Musical Performance'.[13] Godlovitch itemizes the 'integrity conditions' of performance in a way that brings the 'identity conditions' familiar from Formalists like Peter Kivy close to performer-focused folk-psychological ideas of authenticity and cognitive issues of anxiety. As we might expect, though, almost every point in his framework is qualified with concessions to musical practice: 'The strictures upon continuity are not rigid', 'We must approach the notion of completeness cautiously', 'Here we charitably [*sic*!] extend the staffing framework of performance', 'Naturally [*sic*!], fine-grained distinctions in disruption exist which complicate my overall distinction', 'I've got some discretion';[14] and so on. My point concerns the function of these 'concessions' in the practice of performing. To be fair, this lies slightly outside Godlovitch's purview, since he is writing about the craft of performance rather than performing (my distinction, not his). Nonetheless, he would probably assert — in a swift denial of the claims of empirical psychology — that the concessions lead inevitably and unproblematically from his theory of performance to its practical embodiment, and automatically generate the transfer of force between the two domains. Common sense or the weight of experience may certainly tell the performer that many of these 'integrity conditions' are 'fine-grained' rather than 'rigid': however, she must also judge how and when to act with or without their guidance and constraint — if she considers them at all (Godlovitch notes elsewhere that 'someone performing sensitively might simultaneously be bored to distraction').[15] Musical judgements are not as easy in practice as they are in Godlovitch's representational framework, for it is unlikely that performing begins with clear distinctions that are somehow then (but when is 'then'?) muddied as the performer sets about her task. Nonetheless, the active and sometimes self-conscious embodiment of each singular judgement about such 'fine-grained distinctions' is an imperative weighing heavily upon the performer and her sense of what it means to perform.

The problematic elements of these two examples help to illustrate the way in which we might sidestep the conventional theories of Performance mentioned above. We are seeking to incorporate into performing the somewhat contrary idea that, as Lydia Goehr phrases it, 'the practice of music should remain imperfect in its ground precisely because that imperfection leaves open a space for those in the practice who act'.[16] This 'space', moreover, is by nature dynamic and born not of stasis and reification but of movement and flight.

III

In order to investigate this movement, we need to describe the dynamics of musical performativity. To emphasize performativity is not to seek the unmediated essence of performing (a chimera), but to explore the quality of performing we call 'liveness' or 'eventness': that towards which the performer aims and in the face of which the listener and critic respond.

Consider what Bakhtin calls the 'signatures' that subtend the act of performing. A signature is not a thing but a mode of attention or a posture: a judgement or an intention.[17] Adding a signature to a 'rough draft' of an act[18] is the means whereby the hero of a discourse (what we usually call the subject) engages live with what is already given, and hence the moment at which the ethical and aesthetic moments of her act converge. A signature inscribes temporality into the judgement which it literally author-izes, being that by which the commitment to judge is actualized, underwritten, and literally *given* embodiment. It is a step over the temporal 'threshold'.[19]

The performer maintains a relation 'with' her signatures and 'with' performativity in her culturally sanctioned 'performance space'.[20] This is part of the relation between performing and performance (which, we should note, is not the same as the relation between 'process' and 'product',[21] the idea of process still being heavily inflected by notions of what the listener hears and sees). Pursuing a course between 'human *judgement* [...] and the frothing sea of *contingency*',[22] performing requires qualities like engagement, trust, openness, empathy with the music[23] (or at least the capacity for it), and so on; the performer guesses (as well as knows), aims (as well as shoots), hopes (as well as predicts), takes risks (often calculated), and so on. Goehr has described her task as double-edged (hence the brackets in the previous sentence), by which she means that the performer seeks to negotiate a path between 'the perfect performance of music' and 'the perfect performance',[24] or what I have been calling performance with performing. This still leaves us with the question of how this 'task' (Bakhtin) is presented to her. Presentation being a temporal phenomenon,[25] let us consider the time of performing.

Time comes to the performer as a sequence of imperatives, each in the form of a recurrent question, 'What is it to perform music?'.[26] These imperatives literally take time to fulfil (whether or not elements of them have been rehearsed prior to the event),[27] but what kind of time is this? It cannot be simply or only measurable clock time, though the performer does have mediated access to this. Some psychologists refer to 'flow,' by which they mean that the performer 'is totally absorbed in an activity and there is a lack of self-consciousness, and an altered sense of time'.[28] Others speak of event time, the time of work lived through as a sequence of tasks and judgements, complete with — in fact, completed by — their signatures.[29] These judgements, though, differ from the pragmatic judgements of everyday life in that not only must they work when performing live (this is also true of everyday non-aesthetic reasoning), but they must fulfil the task assigned on the first — and only — attempt. For, unlike rehearsal of course, performing is an 'extreme' occasion[30] and an end in itself.[31] For example, an appropriate title for Jerrold Levinson's controversial book,[32] were it to be rewritten on behalf of the performer, would have to be something like 'Music in ... Just a Moment', since, as Bakhtin notes, 'the real centre of gravity of my own self-determination [as hero] is located solely in the future'[33] on the 'threshold' of time,[34] and it is the nature of this threshold that it 'opens onto an uncertain and contingent "afterwards"'.[35] It should be clear that this description of the performer's time, parallel to descriptions of musical practice as 'imperfect in its ground',[36] is intended to interpolate into the so-called passage or 'conversion' from cognitive representation to expressive performance[37] (sometimes conceptualized as a 'bridge')[38] elements of ambiguity, complexity, and indeterminacy, for these are arguably fundamental to the whole Western culture of creative Performance.

How does the performer live with and respond to this 'open' quality of performing? One answer is in terms of the tools, technologies, and skills that she acquires and uses. Some theories (Stravinsky's is one)[39] assert that, just as Plato's slave boy in the *Meno* doesn't initially know that he 'knows geometry' (knew it all along), so the performer needs just enough education to perform. Much musicology from the 1960s to the 1980s was like this, inspired as it was by the aesthetics of Stravinsky or Schoenberg (or both), and the backlash spearheaded by John Rink's seminal response in 1990 to Wallace Berry's *Musical Structure and Performance*[40] was refreshing, though predictable. Other theories employ knowledge as 'a *frame of reference* for [...] how [performers] go about their training and their job or pastime',[41] as a means of 'anticipat[ing] the social context of the performance and the inevitable physiological and psychological arousal that situation will bring'.[42] If, however, we wish to do justice to performing, by acknowledging the performer's own capacity to judge and admitting that some — if not many — things that happen live will not have been 'anticipated' (hence the imperative to judge), then we must rethink this blanket assertion, as some theories of performing have done, and suggest that, for the performer, knowledge is necessary but not sufficient. 'Rules', as Wittgenstein noted, 'leave loopholes open, and the practice has to speak for itself.'[43] Many writers have indeed considered this imperative that performing and the performer speak for themselves. Erwin Stein wrote of 'artistic sincerity'.[44] John Rink has described the matter as one of 'informed intuition'.[45] Richard Taruskin has invoked Trilling's notions of 'sincerity and authenticity'.[46] Jonathan Dunsby has written of the need for 'instinct balanced by intention'[47] and that, grounded in a 'fully integrated personality',[48] the performer must 'dare' to perform.[49] This is an important idea, more so than Dunsby was prepared to admit in *Performing Music*. As long ago as Aristotle, 'courage' was believed to be first in the list of virtues, the (transcendental) virtue which made the others possible.[50]

IV

This gives us some idea of the performer's major psychological investment in performance: that which goes by names like 'performativity', 'singularity', 'eventhood', 'eventness' — in short, performing live. The investment lies at the root of the common ailments of performance, physiological, behavioural, and mental: sweating, stress, stiffness, stage fright and anxiety, memory loss, and so on.[51] And it is the case whether or not performing is mediated by technology.[52] However, such an investment comes at a price, and it is this to which we now turn.

Consider Bakhtin again, this time on the asymmetrical flipside of signatures:

'loopholes'. The closest Bakhtin comes to an explicit definition is this paragraph:

> A loophole is the retention for oneself of the possibility of altering the ultimate, final meaning of one's own words. If a word retains such a loophole this must inevitably be reflected in its structure. This potential other meaning, that is, the loophole left open, accompanies the word like a shadow. Judged by its meaning alone, the word with a loophole should be an ultimate word and does present itself as such, but in fact it is only the penultimate word and places after itself only a conditional, not a final, period.[53]

According to Bakhtin, then, loopholes inflect the temporal character of a judgement. They are holes in the temporal fabric of the hero's discourse offering her possibilities and 'sideshadows'[54] by means of which she may avoid the finalization imposed upon her by others in the discourse and 'slip away and rise above her own consummatedness'.[55]

This is of 'enormous style-shaping significance'[56] for the performativity of judgements, the implication being that a temporal 'excess' within the very relation between self and other emerges in the (non-)form of loopholes.[57] When the hero gives her signature, loopholes close and process tends towards product, but when she keeps loopholes open she does so in order to retain for her act the possibility of 'openendedness, indecision, indeterminacy [...] through which we glimpse the future'.[58] The retention of open loopholes is, like a signature, a quite particular form of judgement responding explicitly to the potential meaning and significance of the act; however, unlike a signature, the very meaning — indeed, the very being — of the act is kept moving. It is not that open loopholes undermine signification per se, merely that they resist and delay any totalizing tendency to (claim to) provide all meaning and significance.

But this is not the whole story. It would be one-sided to use loopholes as a means of describing the intentional activity of the performer,[59] of articulating a phenomenology of time and action possessed by the subject/hero (which is where the first part of this chapter headed). Why is this? Bakhtin's paradigmatic 'word with a loophole' is the Underground Man's, in which the potentially reflexive self-consciousness of any utterance is elevated into a first principle. An everyday natural phenomenon — the withdrawal of certainty with time — is subjected to such extreme attention and second-guessing that it becomes pathological, a neurosis controlling his every move. Investing desire solely in the loopholes within his acts, the Underground Man mistakenly thinks that he can control them at will, that he can possess them as 'his'; yet his investment — what Bakhtin elsewhere describes as a '*movement* of consciousness'[60] — remains unfulfilled and unsublimated. Time's response is blank. In short, drifting anonymously through discourse, loopholes remain beyond the hero's control (even the grammar of their description emphasizes their anonymous exteriority). Just at the hero cannot lift himself up by his own hair (Bakhtin's metaphor), nor can he fully apprehend his own act as his: its loopholes always evade his grasp. The Underground Man can never have the last say.

It is becoming clear that the conventional support for the relation between performance and criticism, namely the 'chain of dependency [...] with the performer as the crucial link'[61] is less than secure. Furthermore, notions like the 'technological advantage'[62] of criticism of one musical party over another (even of the performer over himself) may be no more than wishful thinking, if not perverse. This, however, is not to undermine the numerous claims made by the study of Performance and by music criticism generally. In fact, it underwrites them with a much stronger sense of their fragile relation to the performer's act, not of performance, but of performing.

Yet, while 'performance is integral to the work',[63] performing is not. Performing drifts away from performance and in its wake appears a 'shadow', as Eliot noted in the epigraph to this essay.[64] One locus for this drift is the performer's body and its various structures and mechanisms both physiological and psychological, and these bear a painfully different significance for performer and listener.[65] Specifying the communicative 'circuits'[66] generated between performer and listener is thus too hasty, and it is more appropriate to ask how the terms performing, performance, and performative conjugate the same cultural phenomenon of Performance and how we might avoid conflating them.[67] The point is that, while signatures trace the outlines of the performer's live judgements, loopholes are cognitively opaque and unavailable for introspection, even to the performer herself, since it is they — not she — that make live performing live: the performative is not a human category and cares not for subjectivity. On the one hand, the performer is unaware while she performs of what makes *this* particular and unrepeatable live act of performing live; and yet, on the other hand, she becomes aware of her performing in so far as she approaches it as her own listener from outside. This, though, she comes to know, not as performing, but as performance: as her own first critic.

The performer's awareness of her 'own' performing thus involves a difficult paradox. We confront this by asking, not 'How does the performer know and use her loopholes?', but rather 'How can we account for the cultural assumption which ascribes to the performer such a transcendent feat of cognition?' (and therein lies a whole history of 'the Modern'). For if we are to follow Nicholas Cook's injunction to think performing (my term) more in terms of performing *from* a script than of the performing *of* a text,[68] then there is a necessary and affirmative consequence: performing *from* a script presupposes not merely a transcendence or outsideness of the performer with respect to her script (which is the locus of her expressive and signifying creativity), but an 'excess' or 'surplus' drift which she cannot master.[69] Hence: performing drifts away from performance.

V

This, of course, poses a difficulty for how performing, performance, and the performative are to be understood in relation to each other. Can they even be related? This difficulty also affects the domain of writing about music. What is music criticism to do? How is it to account for music performance without assimilating it to its own rightful domain of the literary? (And what would such an assimilation come to mean?) How might we do justice to the performer's signatures and their loopholes?

The issue at this point is, not that of how the performative signifies (which is a matter of and for performance), but that of its intensity. Steps in the right direction begin by focusing on what performing does, on what it 'sets in motion'.[70] This is not to say that we should avoid considering 'what' performance 'says' or 'means' (the domain of signification); indeed, far from it. Rather, we should also focus on (in fact, give priority to) the emergence of the actual event of performing. Here the achievements of empirical psychology are crucial.[71] Nevertheless, the point is not that the 'saying' and 'doing' of performing are in opposition and that, therefore, empirically based studies tell us the most about performing. Rather, at issue are the various drifts between the two domains, and we should understand that these drifts are as central to performing as they are to performance (the latter being that which is conventionally studied by both hermeneutics and empirical psychology). And performative drift cannot be measured; to 'measure' it would be to rewrite it into the domain of performance away from that of performing and to reduce its significance to that of nothing more than — significance. (All drift measures, in so far as it 'measures' anything, is the relation between time and the death drive.)

So: How is music criticism to acknowledge and measure up to the drift of performing? Adequation can no longer be an ideal, since the 'promise' of performance[72] held out to performing by theory, like a carrot to a donkey, cannot but fail (on its own reckoning) to break that promise and starve the donkey. It is no longer a question of dematerializing performance and making it signify.[73] According to Lyotard, we bear witness to the figural when asking 'Is it happening?', rather than 'What is happening?', which is to say, 'Whence performance?', rather than 'How can we read it?'.[74] However, because the question 'Is it happening?' focuses upon the emergence of the event as a socially embodied practice rather than its representation, this makes it difficult to trace the meanings and identities of the performer's experience of performing, if 'meaning', 'identity', and 'experience' are understood in the conventional sense as something 'signifying' and 'signified'; which is to say, if they are understood without the notion of a drift not just between signifier and signified (which is hardly a new idea), but alongside any such relation that might pertain between signifier and signified. As Lyotard remarks pertinently, 'One does not at all break with metaphysics by putting language everywhere.'[75] This is because the phrase I have just used ('the performer's experience of performing') is strictly speaking a non sequitur: it cannot be the performer who experiences performing but a listener (whether herself or another sitting more comfortably than she), and this listener experiences it as performance; the performer merely performs (!). Indeed, in so far as, 'requir[ing] no foundational unity',[76] performing necessarily bears witness to the irrepressible 'force'[77] of performativity, there can be no single unified 'identity' for musical performing, or by implication the performer herself (note that this does not mean 'no identity *tout court*', since there is always the safe route above performing of performance discourse and what it signifies). The act of performing is to the event of performance as 'figure' is to 'discourse' (Lyotard), as 'difference' is to 'identity' (Derrida), as 'saying' is to 'said' (Levinas), and as 'loophole' is to 'signature' (Bakhtin). The investment in performing live cannot be sublimated or receive catharsis, so music criticism should seek to invest its own energies elsewhere — first and foremost in its own act of literary writing.

VI

If I have unintentionally fetishized the semantics of those three p-words, then I hope that this nonetheless shows what is at stake. One of my intentions is to reinstate performing firmly back into the cultural dialectic, in the belief that it is a perpetually unrepresentable activity (not that it is mystical but simply that it drifts alongside the theatre of representation), and that this is what defines its (non-)relation both to the musical work and to its musical culture. Performing and performance 'dissimulate' each other. I have also argued that writing about performing should be held accountable, not for its mere fidelity to performing, but for what it literally makes of performing: perhaps such an activity of phrasing should be called 'ventriloquism'.[78] Although criticism cannot 'gain time'[79] from performing, it does create its own kind of creative time set over and against performing, and this is its value as a cultural activity. 'Snatching eternity from the jaws of evanescence',[80] as one musicologist has recently described performance criticism, doesn't have to be as apocalyptic as it sounds.

Notes to Chapter 12

1. Jonathan Dunsby, *Performing Music: Shared Concerns* (Oxford: Oxford University Press, 1995), back cover.
2. E.g. Christopher Small, *Musicking: The Meanings of Performing and Listening* (Hanover, CT: Wesleyan University Press, 1998).
3. E.g. Nicholas Cook, 'Analysing Performance and Performing Analysis', in *Rethinking Music*, ed. by Nicholas Cook and Mark Everist (Oxford: Oxford University Press, 1999), pp. 239–61.
4. E.g. Patrik N. Juslin, 'Communicating Emotion in Performance: A Review and a Theoretical Framework', in *Music and Emotion: Theory and Research*, ed. by Patrik N. Juslin and John A. Sloboda (Oxford: Oxford University Press, 2001), pp. 309–37; Eric Clarke, 'Expression in Performance: Generativity, Perception, and Semiosis', in *The Practice of Performance: Studies in Musical Interpretation*, ed. by John Rink (Cambridge: Cambridge University Press, 1995), pp. 21–54; Caroline Palmer, 'Mapping Musical Thought to Musical Performance', *Journal of Experimental Psychology*, 15 (1989), 331–46.
5. Timothy S. Hall, 'The Score as Contract: Private Law and the Historically Informed Performance Movement', *Cardozo Law Review*, 20 (May–July 1999), 1589–1614.
6. Jean-François Lyotard, *Libidinal Economy*, trans. by Iain Hamilton Grant (London: Athlone, 1993), p. 95.
7. Mikhail Bakhtin, 'From Notes Made in 1970–71', in *Speech Genres and Other Late Essays*, trans. by Vern McGee, ed. by Caryl Emerson and Michael Holquist (Austin: University of Texas Press, 1986), pp. 132–58 (pp. 136–37).
8. Jean-François Lyotard, 'Adrift', in *Driftworks*, trans. and ed. by Roger McKeon (New York: Semiotext(e), 1984), pp. 9–17 (pp. 9–10).
9. Anthony Pople, 'Analysis: Past, Present and Future', *Music Analysis*, 21/special issue (July 2002), 17–21 (p. 19).
10. Paul Henry Lang, *Musicology and Performance* (New Haven, CT: Yale University Press, 1997), pp. 210–31. Further references are given after quotations in the text.
11. Nicholas Cook, 'At the Borders of Musical Identity: Schenker, Corelli, and the Graces', *Music Analysis*, 18 (1999), 179–233.

12. Bruce Ellis Benson, *The Improvisation of Musical Dialogue: A Phenomenology of Music* (Cambridge: Cambridge University Press, 2003).
13. Stan Godlovitch, 'The Integrity of Musical Performance', *Journal of Aesthetics and Art Criticism*, 51 (1992–93), 573–87.
14. Ibid., pp. 574, 574, 575, 578, 578.
15. Stan Godlovitch, *Musical Performance: A Philosophical Study* (London and New York: Routledge, 1998), p. 127.
16. Lydia Goehr, *The Quest for Voice: Music, Politics, and the Limits of Philosophy* (Oxford: Oxford University Press, 1998), p. 173.
17. Mikhail Bakhtin, *Toward a Philosophy of the Act*, trans. by Vadim Liapunov, ed. by Vadim Liapunov and Michael Holquist (Austin: University of Texas Press, 1993), pp. 38–39.
18. Ibid., p. 44.
19. Mikhail Bakhtin, *Problems of Dostoevsky's Poetics*, trans. and ed. by Caryl Emerson (Minneapolis: Minnesota University Press, 1984), pp. 61, 63, 73, 170–76, 287.
20. Goehr, *The Quest for Voice*, pp. 148–49.
21. Jerrold Levinson, 'Evaluating Musical Performance', in *Music, Art, and Metaphysics: Essays in Philosophical Aesthetics* (Ithaca, NY: Cornell University Press, 1990), pp. 376–92 (p. 378); Nicholas Cook, 'Music as Performance', in *The Cultural Study of Music: A Critical Introduction*, ed. by Martin Clayton, Trevor Herbert, and Richard Middleton (New York: Routledge, 2003), pp. 204–14.
22. Dunsby, *Performing Music*, pp. 16, 12–14, 42, 58, 64.
23. Ibid., pp. 54, 85.
24. Goehr, *The Quest for Voice*, pp. 132–73.
25. Jean-François Lyotard, *The Differend: Phrases in Dispute*, trans. by Georges Van Den Abbeele (Minneapolis: Minnesota University Press, 1988), pp. 59–85.
26. Jean-François Lyotard, *The Inhuman: Reflections on Time*, trans. by Geoffrey Bennington and Rachel Bowlby (Cambridge: Polity Press, 1991), pp. 97, 128, 135; Goehr, *The Quest for Voice*, p. 170.
27. Godlovitch, *Musical Performance*, p. 49.
28. Mihalyi Csikszentmihalyi, *Flow: The Psychology of Optimal Experience* (New York: Harper and Row, 1990), quoted in Renée Cox Lorraine, *Music, Tendencies, and Inhibitions: Reflections on a Theory of Leonard Meyer* (Lanham, MD: Scarecrow Press, 2001), p. 93.
29. Alphonso Lingis, 'Catastrophic Times', in *Time and Value*, ed. by Scott Lash, Andrew Quick, and Richard Roberts (Oxford: Blackwell, 1998), pp. 16–31.
30. Edward W. Said, *Musical Elaborations* (London: Vintage, 1992), pp. 1–34.
31. Dunsby, *Performing Music*, p. 97; Godlovitch, *Musical Performance*, p. 29.
32. Jerrold Levinson, *Music in the Moment* (Ithaca, NY: Cornell University Press, 1997).
33. Mikhail Bakhtin, 'Author and Hero in Aesthetic Activity', in *Art and Answerability: Early Philosophical Essays by M. M. Bakhtin*, trans. by Vadim Liapunov, ed. by Michael Holquist and Vadim Liapunov (Austin: University of Texas Press, 1990), pp. 4–256 (p. 127).
34. Emmanuel Levinas, *Existence and Existents*, trans. by Alphonso Lingis (Dordrecht: Nijhoff, 1988), p. 99.
35. Lyotard, *The Inhuman*, p. 65.
36. Goehr, *The Quest for Voice*, p. 173; Andy Hamilton, 'The Art of Improvisation and the Aesthetics of Imperfection', *British Journal of Aesthetics*, 40 (2000), 168–85.
37. Stephen Davies, *Themes in the Philosophy of Music* (Oxford: Oxford University Press, 2003), p. 92.
38. Hilde Hein, 'Performance as an Aesthetic Category', *Journal of Aesthetics and Art Criticism*, 28 (1970), 381–86 (p. 383).
39. Igor Stravinsky, *Poetics of Music* (Cambridge, MA: Harvard University Press, repr. 1970), pp. 121–35.
40. John Rink, review of Wallace Berry, *Musical Structure and Performance*, *Music Analysis*, 9 (1990), 319–39.
41. Dunsby, *Performing Music*, p. 18.
42. Jane Davidson, 'Communicating with the Body in Performance', in *Musical Performance: A Guide*

to Understanding, ed. by John Rink (Cambridge: Cambridge University Press, 2002), pp. 144–52 (p. 144).

43. Ludwig Wittgenstein, *On Certainty*, trans. by Dennis Paul and G. E. M. Anscombe, ed. by G. E. M. Anscombe and G. H. von Wright (Oxford: Blackwell, 1969), §139.
44. Erwin Stein, *Form and Performance* (London: Faber and Faber, 1962), 11.
45. Review of Berry, *Musical Structure and Performance*, p. 324.
46. Richard Taruskin, *Text and Act: Essays on Music and Performance* (Oxford: Oxford University Press, 1995), Chapter 2.
47. Dunsby, *Performing Music*, pp. 67, 9, 45, 56, 88.
48. Ibid., p. 55; Stravinsky, *Poetics of Music*, p. 27.
49. Dunsby, *Performing Music*, p. 55.
50. Aristotle, *Nichomachean Ethics*, trans. by Martin Oswald (Indianapolis: Bobbs-Merrill, 1962), pp. 68–77.
51. Elizabeth Valentine, 'The Fear of Performance', in *Musical Performance* (see Davidson, note 42 above), pp. 168–82.
52. Philip Auslander, *Liveness: Performance in a Mediatized Culture* (New York: Routledge, 1999).
53. Bakhtin, *Problems of Dostoevsky's Poetics*, p. 233.
54. Gary Saul Morson, *Narrative and Freedom: The Shadows of Time* (New Haven, CT: Yale University Press, 1994), pp. 117–72.
55. Bakhtin, 'Author and Hero in Aesthetic Activity', p. 21.
56. Bakhtin, *Problems of Dostoevsky's Poetics*, p. 196.
57. Bakhtin, 'Author and Hero in Aesthetic Activity', p. 109.
58. Mikhail Bakhtin, 'Epic and Novel: Toward a Methodology for the Study of the Novel', in *The Dialogic Imagination: Four Essays by M. M. Bakhtin*, trans. by Caryl Emerson and Michael Holquist, ed. by Michael Holquist (Austin: University of Texas Press, 1981), pp. 3–40 (p. 16).
59. Henry Shaffer, 'Intention and Performance', *Psychological Review*, 83 (1976), 375–93.
60. Bakhtin, *Toward a Philosophy of the Act*, p. 36.
61. Dunsby, *Performing Music*, p. 42.
62. Anthony Pople, 'Systems and Strategies: Functions and Limits of Analysis', in *Theory, Analysis, and Meaning in Music*, ed. by Anthony Pople (Cambridge: Cambridge University Press, 1994), pp. 108–23 (p. 114 n. 15).
63. Davies, *Themes in the Philosophy of Music*, pp. 58–59.
64. Goehr, *The Quest for Voice*, p. 140.
65. Elaine Scarry, *The Body in Pain: The Making and Unmaking of the World* (Oxford: Oxford University Press, 1985); Elaine Scarry, *Resisting Representation* (Oxford: Oxford University Press, 1994); David Lidov, 'Mind and Body in Music', *Semiotica*, 66 (1987), 69–97.
66. Goehr, *The Quest for Voice*, p. 150.
67. Lyotard, *The Inhuman*, p. 4.
68. Cook, 'Music as Performance'.
69. Bakhtin, 'Author and Hero in Aesthetic Activity', pp. 12, 22–27; Bakhtin, *Problems of Dostoevsky's Poetics*, p. 299; Alphonso Lingis, *Phenomenological Explanations* (The Hague: Martinus Nijhoff, 1986), pp. 67–68; Nicholas Cook, 'Perception: A Perspective from Music Theory', in *Musical Perceptions*, ed. by Rita Aiello (Oxford: Oxford University Press, 1994), pp. 64–95 (p. 92).
70. Lyotard, *Libidinal Economy*, p. 51.
71. Eric Clarke and Jane Davidson, 'The Body in Performance', in *Composition — Performance — Reception: Studies in the Creative Process in Music*, ed. by Wyndham Thomas (Aldershot: Ashgate, 1998), pp. 74–92; *The Science and Psychology of Music Performance: Creative Strategies for Teaching and Learning*, ed. by Richard Parncutt and Gary E. McPherson (Oxford: Oxford University Press, 2002).
72. Godlovitch, *Musical Performance*, p. 19; Davies, *Themes in the Philosophy of Music*, p. 95.
73. Lyotard, *Libidinal Economy*, p. 45.
74. Lyotard, *The Inhuman*, Chapters 6, 7, 9, 11.
75. Jean-François Lyotard, *Discours, Figure* (Paris: Klincksieck, 1971), p. 14.
76. Susan Bernstein, *Virtuosity of the Nineteenth Century: Performing Music and Language in Heine, Liszt, and Baudelaire* (Stanford: Stanford University Press, 1998), p. 6.

77. Eric Clarke, 'Listening to Performance', in *Musical Performance* (see Davidson, note 42 above), pp. 185–96 (p. 190).
78. Alan Street, 'The Obbligato Recitative: Narrative and Schoenberg's Five Orchestral Pieces, Op. 16', in *Theory, Analysis, and Meaning in Music* (see Pople, note 62 above), pp. 164–83 (p. 183).
79. Lyotard, *The Differend*, p. xiv.
80. Cook, 'Music as Performance', p. 208.

CHAPTER 13

❖

Etymology and its Others

Daniel Blake Rosenberg

In the field of eighteenth-century letters, there is perhaps no text that better represents the ideal of interdisciplinarity than the *Encyclopédie* of Denis Diderot and Jean le Rond d'Alembert, nor is there another text that has attracted the same breadth of interdisciplinary attention among scholars. The *Encyclopédie* embodied the Enlightenment notion that knowledge should be accessible to all and that the details of every intellectual and technical specialization should be translatable into a general language. Diderot and d'Alembert considered contemporary boundaries between fields to be by and large irrational. And they envisioned their encyclopedia as a tool for crossing them.[1]

At the same time, the boundary-crossing project proposed by the Encyclopedists was in no way a call to scholarly anarchy. The same argument that rejected irrational boundaries was also a call to a new kind of disciplinarity. This is visible in the sharp distinction that the Encyclopedists drew between modern scientific disciplines and the erroneous and even 'superstitious' practices that they supplanted. The relationship between these two trajectories, toward disciplinarity and toward interdisciplinarity, gives rise to one of the central tensions of the *Encyclopédie*, and it is discussed at length both in the subject articles and in the theoretical articles that it contains. One of the notable places where this tension is at play is in the article on the science of *etymology*. For a variety of reasons, etymology had great relevance to Enlightenment philosophy, particularly to language origins theory after Condillac. Moreover, since the Middle Ages, etymology had claimed a privileged role in reconciling the languages of the different sciences and arts. That is to say, up to the eighteenth century, etymology had itself functioned as a kind of encyclopedic science. For these reasons, the article on etymology is a site that is particularly stressed in the *Encyclopédie*. Through it, the *Encyclopédie* takes a strong stand against this older encyclopedic tradition, and seeks to redefine etymology as a historical discipline with discrete rules and boundaries — as one discipline among others, shorn of its meta-disciplinary claims.

Taken in its broadest sense, the problem of discipline is as old as the problem of knowledge itself. In its original acceptation, *discipline* means learning. It is tied to the notion of apprenticeship and to the discipline of a specific teacher, whence the notion of discipline as stricture, correction, or authority. Over many centuries, the term took on the allied meaning of a specific approach to learning or of an objective field of knowledge intended by such an approach. Though we still use the term *disciple* to mean the student or follower of some particular person, the term *discipline* is now associated with general fields of study. Disciplinary practices are now more than ever structured by university departments, professional organizations, and specialist journals. But the term itself has taken on a more neutral meaning, as though differences among disciplines (such as history, art history, or literature) simply reflected differences among their objects.[2]

This modern sense of discipline did not appear all at once. As Donald Kelley has argued, notions of disciplinarity, no less than the various individual disciplines themselves, travelled on twisting and forking paths throughout the early modern period.[3] Following Aristotle, medieval philosophers envisioned a hierarchical organization of the arts and sciences. This perspective was at least partly supplanted during the Renaissance by the revival of a holistic ideal of the liberal arts. But neither framework proved successful at assimilating changes taking place during the sixteenth and seventeenth centuries, as is suggested by the stream of notable attempts to re-schematize and to re-hierarchize the fields of knowledge produced during the early modern period by such figures as Petrus Ramus, Konrad Gesner, and Francis Bacon, to name only a few.[4]

During the eighteenth century, conceptions of disciplines continued to change, as did the encyclopedic projects aimed at organizing them. This was made abundantly clear by Diderot and d'Alembert in their *Encyclopédie*.[5] In it, the hierarchical apparatus popularized by Francis Bacon is still present in the form of a chart that assimilates all the arts, sciences, and trades to a global hierarchical framework known as an encyclopedic tree. But, here, its status has been relativized. It now serves as only one possible system of organization among several that operate side by side, including the flat and arbitrary organizational system of the alphabetic dictionary and the multidimensional network of cross-references woven everywhere into the text.[6]

For Diderot and d'Alembert, this formal development responds to difficulties inherent in the development of knowledge itself. Progress in the arts, sciences, and trades implies the discovery of new objects and approaches and the further development of intellectual and practical specializations. In many cases, as disciplines advance, they grow apart, developing techniques, protocols, and languages that are less and less familiar to one another. For this reason, they argue, an encyclopedia can no longer be the work of an individual, even an individual of great genius. A modern encyclopedia, they explain, must be collaborative: the labour must be divided, and each field and subfield addressed by an expert.[7] Thus, while the *Encyclopédie* draws upon and encourages a movement toward the generalization of scientific concerns, it also understands itself to inhabit a world of increasing disciplinary specialization. When Diderot writes 'it is the special task of a philosophical century to attempt an *Encyclopedia*', he is saying two different things at once: that in the eighteenth century, modern science and philosophy have made the composition of a true encyclopedia possible for the first time; and that for the first time, they have made it necessary.[8]

The idea that words might serve as the material for a meta-discipline was not new in the eighteenth century, nor was the notion of an encyclopedic lexicon. These ideas were already embodied, for example, in the medieval *Etymologies* of Isidore of Seville. But their configuration and importance were very different from what we encounter in the eighteenth century.[9] As Michel Foucault has argued, for the Middle Ages and the Renaissance,

> language is not a totality of independent signs, a uniform and unbroken entity in which things could be reflected one by one, as in a mirror, and so express their particular truths. It is rather an opaque, mysterious thing, closed in upon itself, a fragmented mass, its enigma renewed in every interval, which combines here and there with the forms of the world and becomes interwoven with them.[10]

For this reason, according to Foucault, the early modern encyclopedia has a different form from the one that emerged during the Enlightenment. As he puts it, the aim of the pre-Enlightenment encyclopedia is not 'to reflect what one knows in the neutral element of language [...] [but] to reconstitute the very order of the universe by the way in which words are linked together and arranged in space'.[11]

For the Enlightenment, the nature of language was a crucial philosophical question. And language theory played a central role in the conception of the sciences and arts and their interrelationship. But, for the philosophers of the Enlightenment, etymology no longer functioned as a key to the world itself. On the contrary, the philosophers of the Enlightenment dismissed traditional etymologies as nothing more than 'cabalistical fictions'. And the entire enterprise was for a time left under a cloud. Writers such as Voltaire saw etymology as a case example of the sort of intellectual indiscipline against which the Enlighteners railed. According to these critics, with the traditional tools of etymology (free substitution of letters, connection of unrelated languages, anachronism, transformation through unlimited intermediary steps), one could easily prove that any word was related to any other. And even the most ardent practitioners of etymological analysis of the period considered it necessary to distinguish their projects from what they saw as the abuses of earlier etymological works.[12] Diderot and d'Alembert were no exception. Their *Encyclopédie* set out to rescue the practice of etymology for history, philosophy, and the other sciences that make use of its offices. It attempted to do this by defining etymology as a discipline, that is, by reining in both its discredited practices and its encyclopedic claims.

During the Enlightenment, words were increasingly studied in relation to other words rather than in relation to objects. This shift is marked in the clearest terms in the article on etymology written by the young economist Anne-Robert-Jacques Turgot for the *Encyclopédie*.[13] The first line of the article reads as follows: 'Words have no necessary relationship with the things that they express.'[14] Though Turgot's argument is entirely consistent with the prevailing Enlightenment language theories, it flies in the face of the grand etymological tradition described by Foucault. For Turgot, just as for Locke and Condillac, the linguistic sign embodies a primary negativity. Its essence is to have no essence. And its power as a representational and an analytic tool comes from precisely this. As Turgot argues, this is nowhere more evident than in mathematics — that most abstract and capable of symbolic languages.[15]

To emphasize the point, Turgot offers a parable of word origins in the form of the etymology of the word *falbala*. It is worth pausing over this etymology because in so many ways it violates expectations about the kind of narrative that should appear in a properly historical etymology. *Falbala* is French for a sort of trim often applied to petticoats and dresses during this period. If you are familiar with the fashions of the eighteenth century, you will have seen many different applications of the *falbala*. During the early part of the century, this sort of frill tended to migrate from the inside to the outside of the garment. At the same time, the petticoat was itself opened to display through a variety of styles and ruses, bringing the *falbala* to the centre of visual attention.

Falbala has cognates in several other languages, including *faldella* in Italian, *farbela* in Spanish, and *furbelow* in English. In French, the term was new in the seventeenth and eighteenth centuries and was often remarked upon, but its origin was not entirely clear. One contemporary etymology traces *falbala* to Turkish, drawing a parallel with the names of several other exotic novelties of the period including *sofa*, which had been so successfully transformed by Crébillon fils into a metonymy for the salacious and the unspoken.[16] Another derives it from the Latin *flabella* or fan. Still another traces it to *fald-plat*, the name for a pleated garment worn in Germany.[17] In other words, *falbala* provides an example of the very confusion and speculation that Turgot's approach to etymology was supposed to remedy.

But Turgot does little to clear up the confusion, and, arguably, his own fanciful contribution on this etymological question muddies the waters even more. According to Turgot, the word *falbala* is no more foreign to French than is frivolity itself. The term, he says, was invented as the result of a joke. As the story goes, a prince and courtier were traversing a market together one day, when the courtier remarked that in a market so prodigious, one might find anything one desired whether or not such a thing even existed. The prince took this pleasantry as a challenge. He made up a nonsense word, approached a seller, and asked her for it. 'Madame,' he said, pausing slightly as he was in the midst of inventing, 'do you sell any — um — *falbalas*?' The merchant responded without hesitation, 'Why, yes, Sire', and showed him some fabric. 'These are the very things that they call *falbalas*', she said. According to Turgot, the word was repeated in the market, and it soon entered general circulation. 'How many words', Turgot asks, 'owe their origin to circumstances so amusing and so likely to frustrate the wisdom of the etymologists?'[18]

Much of Turgot's conception of language is condensed in this brief parable. He argues here that the meaning of words is conventional, and that this is in some important way the case even at the moment of origin. Once the merchant and the prince agree that the term *falbala* refers to a piece of fabric, it does mean this for them. As the word enters general circulation, it comes to mean the same thing for society at large. There is more too. In this anecdote, Turgot situates words in a marketplace. Convention here does not arise from shared perception; rather, it is the result of negotiation between parties with different interests. These themes and arguments recur throughout Turgot's work, not least in his well-known writings on economics.[19]

In Turgot and in the *Encyclopédie* in general, the *falbala* is a figure for the nothingness that is language. *Falbala* is not just any term. It is an archetypal nonsense word. As we have seen in the various etymologies that it elicited, it almost irresistibly suggests the infantile and the exotic, conjuring fantasies of wilful courtiers, foreign luxuries, and the directionless inventiveness of play. As a thing, too, the *falbala* stretches the limits of meaningfulness. It is a term from fashion and ostentatiously so. It is a margin on a margin, an edge on an edge, a virtual scandal of nothingness. And it is telling that by the early nineteenth century, the term *falbala* had taken on the pejorative connotation of a 'pretentious ornament'.[20] The article on *falbalas* in the *Encyclopédie* is also telling in this regard. More than a simple definition, it amounts to a kind of theory of history.[21] According to the *Encyclopédie*, the *falbala* is that which is outside progress and the possibility of historical narration. It returns to fashion without reason or explanation.[22]

What is more, according to the Encyclopedists, *falbalas* emerge from or find their way to the most private places, places that cannot be named, paradigmatic nothings. In a move that foreshadows another telling discussion of the *falbala* in Rousseau's *Émile* (1762), the Encyclopedists here suggest that the *falbala* is the exemplary feminine object in that it names that thing which cannot be renounced by woman's desire.[23] In all these ways, the *falbala* embodies negativity itself. That is to say, in the terms of Turgot's language theory and that of the Encyclopedists, it is the archetypal sign. But, as Diderot argues, this presents a problem as well. The *falbala* is already so close to nothingness that it threatens to become incomprehensible. There is nothing natural in the term that would make it decipherable. Paradoxically, this least significant of things most demands an account in the *Encyclopédie*.[24]

What then has become of the encyclopedic ambitions of etymology? What of the notion that etymology provides a link to a pure language in which the relationship between words and things is motivated, direct, and unambiguous? It is unsurprising that a text on the theory of etymology would include an etymology of the word *etymology* itself and that such an etymology would at least try to address these questions. And Turgot's article does not disappoint. The word *etymology*, as Turgot notes, comes from the Greek roots *etumos* and *logos*. The basic etymological sense, then, is 'the true meaning of a word'.[25] And this is the sense in which the term was used throughout much of the medieval and the early modern periods. But in his account of the term, Turgot notes that, even very early on, it could be understood in more than one sense. He notes that its use by the Greeks was different from that of the Romans. According to Turgot, the Greeks had no comparative conception of languages. For them, there was only one true language. Thus, in Greek, *etymology* is equivalent to 'true meaning'. But Turgot argues that, for the Romans, the situation was different. From its very beginnings, Latin scholarship was marked by a consciousness of the difference between Greek and Latin and by the nuances of change and intellectual heritage. Thus, for the Romans, the term *etymology* comes to mean 'all inquiries into the origin of words', and it takes on a historical sense, allowing that words may legitimately change in meaning.[26] For Turgot, this conceptual evolution represents true progress, and this secondary and non-original etymology of *etymology* captures not just an origin but also a history worth recounting.

This move is striking in part because it provides a foundational narrative for an anti-foundational practice. It is also striking because it marks a full transition away from a mimetic notion of language and from the possibility of conceiving of etymology as a meta-disciplinary mode of thought. The epistemological shift that makes possible the interdisciplinarity of Diderot and d'Alembert at the same time enforces a discipline upon the possible claims of such practices as etymology. For this reason, I would argue that the rise of disciplinary and interdisciplinary thinking are part of the same historical movement during the eighteenth century. The two perspectives are different, but they exist in a shared ecology, each regulating and relying upon the other.

Though the particular institutional and epistemological issues that we face in academia today are different from those of the Enlightenment, I think that it would not be much of a stretch to make a parallel argument about our own period. And perhaps it might open some new avenues of investigation. It might, for example, shed some light on why a rhetoric of interdisciplinarity can be so universally successful in academia while interdisciplinary practice is so often excluded by institutional structures and paths. It might also lead us to ask historical questions about the emergence of the binary opposition of disciplinarity and interdisciplinarity.

It seems clear that our current discourse of interdisciplinarity emerged in response to the waning persuasive power of the great meta-discourses of the twentieth century including Marxism, psychoanalysis, and structuralism. And it seems important to recognize that this interdisciplinarity has its meaning only in relation to them. That is to say, our interdisciplinarity, like that of the Enlightenment, emerged as a rejection of specific and identifiable meta-disciplinarities rather than as a response to a dead end in disciplinary thinking. Conceiving of interdisciplinarity in this way, that is, as inter/disciplinarity, may help to explain why its critique of disciplines seems always so inconclusive. The two in fact are mirror images of one another. This is not to say that there is something inherently wrong with interdisciplinary strategies or with stretching the boundaries of disciplinary practice. On the contrary, it is to suggest that this can only be a beginning. I would propose that we aim to move beyond a binary critique of disciplinarity toward what Turgot would call a 'genealogy' of our inter/disciplinarity and of what it excludes.

Notes to Chapter 13

1. These are the central arguments of both the jointly authored 'Discours préliminaire' and Diderot's article, 'Encyclopédie', in *Encyclopédie, ou dictionnaire raisonné des arts, des sciences, et des métiers*, ed. by Denis Diderot and Jean le Rond d'Alembert, 17 vols (Paris: Briasson, 1751–65), I, i–lii; V (1755), 635–48. On the disciplinary and interdisciplinary dynamics of the *Encyclopédie*, see esp. *L'Encyclopédie: du réseau au livre et du livre au réseau*, ed. by Robert Morrissey and Philippe Roger (Paris: Honoré Champion, 2001), and Daniel Brewer and Julie Candler Hayes, *Using the 'Encyclopédie': Ways of Knowing, Ways of Reading*, *SVEC* 2002:05. For a longer discussion of this and other related issues, see Daniel Rosenberg, 'We Have Never Been Interdisciplinary: Etymology and Encyclopedism in the Eighteenth Century and Since', *SVEC* 2005:04, 3–22.
2. For a nuanced account of the meaning of 'discipline' in contemporary science, see Timothy Lenoir, *Instituting Science: The Cultural Production of Scientific Disciplines* (Stanford: Stanford University Press, 1997), pp. 45–74.

3. *History and the Disciplines: The Reclassification of Knowledge in Early Modern Europe*, ed. by Donald Kelley (Rochester, NY: University of Rochester Press, 1997), p. 2.
4. See the group of articles 'Early Modern Information Overload' by Daniel Rosenberg, Ann Blair, Brian Ogilvie, Jonathan Sheehan, and Richard Yeo, *Journal of the History of Ideas*, 64 (2003), 1–72.
5. Richard Yeo, *Encyclopaedic Visions: Scientific Dictionaries and Enlightenment Culture* (Cambridge: Cambridge University Press, 2001).
6. Diderot and d'Alembert, 'Discours préliminaire', p. xv; Diderot, 'Encyclopédie', pp. 640–41. For a longer discussion, see Daniel Rosenberg, 'An Eighteenth-Century Time Machine: The *Encyclopedia* of Diderot', in *Postmodernism and the Enlightenment: New Perspectives in French Intellectual History*, ed. by Daniel Gordon (New York: Routledge, 2001), pp. 45–66.
7. Diderot, 'Encyclopédie', pp. 635–36.
8. Ibid., p. 644.
9. E. R. Curtius, 'Etymology as a Category of Thought', in *European Literature and the Latin Middle Ages*, trans. by Willard R. Trask (Princeton: Princeton University Press, 1967), pp. 495–500; Howard Bloch, *Etymologies and Genealogies: A Literary Anthropology of the French Middle Ages* (Chicago: University of Chicago Press, 1983), esp. pp. 30–63; Nancy Struever, 'Fables of Power', *Representations*, 4 (1983), 108–27; Paul Zumthor, 'Etymologies', in *Langue, texte, énigme* (Paris: Éditions du Seuil, 1975), pp. 144–60.
10. Michel Foucault, *The Order of Things: An Archaeology of the Human Sciences* (New York: Vintage Books, 1973), pp. 34–35.
11. Ibid., pp. 37–38. In the same passage, Foucault notes, 'the use of the alphabet as an arbitrary but efficacious encyclopedic order does not appear until the second half of the seventeenth century'.
12. See, for example, Charles de Brosses, *Traité de la formation mécanique des langues et des principes physiques de l'étymologie*, 2 vols (Paris: Saillant, 1765), I, 32–35; and Antoine Court de Gébelin, *Monde primitif analysé et comparé avec le monde moderne*, 9 vols (Paris: the author and others, 1773–82), II (1774), 9. 'L'étymologie', de Brosses writes in a striking understatement, 'n'est pas un art inutile.' See also Daniel Rosenberg, 'A New Sort of Logick and Critick: Etymological Interpretation in Horne Tooke's *Diversions of Purley*', in *Language, Self, and Society: A Social History of Language*, ed. by Roy Porter and Peter Burke (Cambridge: Polity Press, 1991), pp. 300–30.
13. On the composition of the article, see Turgot, 'Étymologie', *Encyclopédie*, VI (1756), 111; see also notes by Anne-Robert-Jacques Turgot in *Oeuvres de Turgot*, ed. by Gustave Schelle, 5 vols (Paris: F. Alcan, 1913–23), I, 516–17, and the introduction and notes by Anne-Robert-Jacques Turgot in *Turgot: Étymologie*, ed. by Maurice Piron (Brugge: De Tempel, 1961), pp. v–xi, 99–100. On the personal tensions between Turgot and de Brosses around the question of etymology, see Th. Foisset, *Le Président de Brosses: histoire des lettres et des parlements au XVIIIe siècle* (Paris: Olivier-Fulgence, 1842). For a far-reaching account of Turgot's language theory, see Daniel Droixhe, *La Linguistique et l'appel de l'histoire (1600–1800): rationalisme et révolutions positivistes* (Geneva: Droz, 1978).
14. Turgot, 'Étymologie', p. 98. It is worth noting that this argument between de Brosses and Turgot operates as something like a primal scene for the internal history of linguistics. From Rasmus Rask on, nineteenth-century linguists would point back to Turgot as a true practitioner of linguistics *avant la lettre*. Indeed, Ernest Renan, founder of the Société Linguistique de Paris, would argue that Turgot was unique among eighteenth-century language theorists in this respect. Renan, *De l'origine du langage* (Paris: Lévy-Frères, 1848), pp. 41–42. Turgot's work is habitually promoted as 'prophetic' and removed from the context of eighteenth-century language theory, an ironic fate for the acknowledged pioneer of *historical method* in language studies.
15. Turgot, 'Étymologie', pp. 102–03.
16. Crébillon fils (Claude-Prosper Jolyot de Crébillon), *Le Sopha, conte moral* (1742).
17. These different accounts are summarized in both Gilles Ménage, *Dictionnaire étymologique de la langue françoise*, 2 vols, new edn (Paris, 1750), II, 293, and de Brosses, *Traité*, II, 465–66.
18. Turgot, 'Étymologie', p. 107.

19. See the remarkable discussions of the etymology of *monnaie* in Turgot's *Réflexions sur la formation et distribution des richesses* (1766) and 'Valeurs et monnaies', in Turgot, *Oeuvres*, II (1914), 533–601, and III (1919), 83–84. Here, Turgot makes a strongly counter-intuitive move, claiming that the contemporary meaning of *monnaie* is due not to its Latin root *moneta* but to the etymologically unrelated Latin term *pecunia*.
20. *Le Grand Robert de la langue française*, 2nd edn, ed. by Alain Rey, 9 vols (Paris: Le Robert, 1985), IV, 388. In 1711, it was already possible to speak of 'a lady who was at least ten years behind-hand in her dress, flounced and furbelowed from head to foot'. *The Spectator*, cited in C. Willett and Phillis Cunnington, *Handbook of English Costume in the Eighteenth Century* (London: Faber and Faber, 1957), p. 141.
21. 'Falbala', *Encyclopédie*, VI, 387: 'Cette grande roue du monde qui ramene tous les évenemens, ramene aussi toutes les modes, & fait reparoître aujourd'hui les *falbalas* avec plus d'éclat que jamais; les plus riches étoffes en sont ornées, les plus communes en reçoivent du relief, & toutes les femmes, les belles, les laides, les coquettes & les prudes, ont des *falbalas* jusque sur leurs jupons les plus intimes: les dévotes même en portent sous le nom de propreté recherchée: on renonce plus facilement au plaisir d'aimer qu'au desir de plaire.' The classic statements on the fashion cycle may be found in Alfred L. Kroeber and Jane Richardson, 'Three Centuries of Women's Dress Fashions: A Quantitative Analysis', *Anthropological Records*, 5 (1940), 111–54, and Roland Barthes, *The Fashion System*, trans. by Matthew Ward and Richard Howard (New York: Hill and Wang, 1983).
22. Philippe Perrot argues that the notion of the fashion cycle is in important ways new around 1700. Philippe Perrot, *Fashioning the Bourgeoisie: A History of Clothing in the Nineteenth Century*, trans. by Richard Bienvenu (Princeton: Princeton University Press, 1994), 17. See the critique of Perrot in Herbert Blau, *Nothing in Itself: Complexities of Fashion* (Bloomington: Indiana University Press, 1999), pp. 55–65, 88–94, and the very nuanced historical analysis in Jennifer Jones, '*Coquettes* and *Grisettes*: Women Buying and Selling in Ancien Régime Paris', in *The Sex of Things: Gender and Consumption in Historical Perspective*, ed. by Victoria de Grazia and Ellen Furlough (Berkeley: University of California Press, 1996), pp. 25–53.
23. *Oeuvres complètes: Jean-Jacques Rousseau*, ed. by Bernard Gagnebin and Marcel Raymond, 5 vols (Paris: Gallimard, 1959–95), IV: *Émile, ou de L'Éducation* (1969), pp. 706–07: '*Les enfans des deux séxes ont beaucoup d'amusemens communs et cela doit être; n'en ont-ils pas de même étant grands? Ils ont aussi des gouts propres qui les distinguent.* Les garçons cherchent le mouvement et le bruit; des tambours, des sabots, de petits carrosses. *Les filles aiment mieux ce qui donne dans la vüe et sert à l'ornement; des miroirs, des bijoux, des chiffons, surtout des poupées* [...]. Voyez une petite fille passer la journée autour de sa poupée, lui changer sans cesse d'ajustement, l'habiller, la deshabiller cent et cent fois, chercher continuellement de nouvelles combinaisons d'ornemens, bien ou mal assortis, il n'importe: les doigts manquent d'addresse, le goût n'est pas formé, mais déja le penchant se montre; dans cette éternelle occupation le tems coule sans qu'elle y songe, les heures passent, elle n'en sait rien, elle oublie les repas mêmes, elle a plus faim de parure que d'aliment: mais, direz-vous, elle pare sa poupée et non sa persone; sans doute; elle voit sa poupée et ne se voit pas, elle ne peut rien faire pour elle-même, elle n'est pas formée, elle n'a ni talent ni force, elle n'est rien encore; elle est toute dans sa poupée, elle y met toute sa coquéterie, elle ne l'y laissera pas toujours; elle attend le moment d'être sa poupée elle-même. *Voila donc un prémier goût bien décidé: vous n'avez qu'à le suivre et le régler. Il est sûr que la petite voudroit de tout son coeur savoir orner sa poupée, faire ses noeuds de manche, son fichu, son falbala, sa dentelle; en tout cela on la fait dépendre si durement du bon plaisir d'autrui qu'il lui seroit bien plus comode de tout devoir à son industrie.*' (My italics.)
24. Diderot, 'Encyclopédie', p. 646: ' A ceux qui y ont regardé avec dégoût certains traits historiques, la cuisine, les modes, *&c.* qu'ils ont oublié combien ces matieres ont engendré d'ouvrages d'érudition; que le plus succinct de nos articles en ce genre épargnera peut-être à nos descendans des années de recherches & des volumes de dissertations; qu'en supposant les savans à venir infiniment plus réservés que ceux du siecle passé, il est encore à présumer qu'ils ne dédaigneront pas d'écrire quelques pages pour expliquer ce que c'est qu'un *falbala ou qu'un pompon*; qu'un écrit sur nos modes, qu'on traiteroit aujourd'hui d'ouvrage frivole, seroit regardé dans deux mille ans, comme un ouvrage savant & profond, sur les habits François; ouvrage

très-instructif pour les Littérateurs, les Peintres & les Sculpteurs [...].' For a similar passage, see *Dictionnaire de l'Académie française*, 2nd edn, 2 vols (Paris, 1718), I, iii.

25. Turgot, 'Étymologie', p. 98.
26. Ibid.

CHAPTER 14

Yves Bonnefoy's *Récits en rêve*: The Intersection of Creativity and Critique

Victoria Best

As poet, critic, art historian, and translator, Yves Bonnefoy has always brought a certain aesthetic of convergence to bear on his work. Not only is his writing informed by his knowledge of art, philosophy, and modern theoretical criticism, but the critical discourses fundamental to these disciplines are equally in evidence in the hybrid genre of his poetry. Just as his poetic persona frequently stands on thresholds or in doorways, so the landscape of his poetic concerns is often the crossroads between creativity and critique. This is notably the case with his collected volume *Rue Traversière et autres récits en rêve*,[1] in which readings of Byzantine art, lyric expositions of form and colour, and imaginative improvisations on the theme of Saussurian linguistics are all incorporated into passages of prose poetry. However, while Bonnefoy is a poet keenly aware of the cultural context in which he writes, paradoxically he is opposed, in principle, to some of its major theoretical propositions. 'Ne faut-il pas se méfier de notre penchant à la théorie, que le rêve peut envahir, et que nos moyens d'appréhension limités risquent, tout simplement, de garder empiégé dans les lubies de l'époque?' [Shouldn't we be suspicious of our penchant for theory, which can so easily be taken over by our dreams, and which, quite frankly, our limited critical faculties run the risk of imprisoning in the passing fancies of our era?], he argues in a recent interview.[2] Bonnefoy's long-running debate with modern cultural theory is based on what would appear to be an unresolvable contradiction. His poetry is underpinned by an ardent belief in the notion of presence, which the critic John Jackson expresses thus: 'La présence, c'est le mode sur lequel l'unité de l'être ou du monde se révèle, en deça ou au-delà de la saisie conceptuelle que le langage peut en faire' [Presence is the mode in which the unity of being or the world reveals itself, up to and beyond the conceptual appropriations of it that language is able to make].[3] However, the theoretical climate in which Bonnefoy was (and is) working has been dominated by the wholesale deconstruction of presence. A chain of theorists, through Saussure and Barthes to Derrida and Lacan, have sought to expose the illusory nature of presence in language and, by association, in the postmodern decentred subject. John Jackson asks how it is possible then to validate the subjectively centred vision that is poetry, and replies: 'Mon hypothèse est que les récits en rêve de Bonnefoy sont la forme qu'il décida de donner comme réponse à ce défi' [My hypothesis is that the *récit en rêve* is the form that Bonnefoy decided to create as a response to this challenge].[4]

To write his dreams is to engage with representation at the intersection of self-presence and a radical internal alterity. Bonnefoy is exploring not only a different perspective on the self, but also a creative reformulation of the parameters of representation itself. Dreams offer him an understanding of narrative which relies on the logic of aesthetics rather than reason, where cause and effect, space and time, are radically reorganized. Yet he is not content simply to exploit the lyric potential of the dream landscape. In two creative passages that defy generic classification, 'Les Découvertes de Prague' (Discoveries in Prague) and 'Nouvelle suite de découvertes' (Further Discoveries), he details a '*rêverie*' that has fascinated him and then rereads it in a series of analyses that juxtapose critical acumen with poetic resonance. This is, I think, a moment of significant coincidence between creativity and critique, where it would seem that the translucent trajectory of presence is traced by, and engages with, the very critical methodology of which Bonnefoy declares himself suspicious. In the interplay between poetic self-creation and critical self-dissection in this particular work, there is, I would argue, much to explore in terms of both the practices of reading that the 'lubies' of our critical age have produced, and Bonnefoy's desire to move beyond our limited critical faculties in regard to the object of their inquiry: the much-disputed notion of presence.

The First *Rêverie*

In 1977 Bonnefoy committed to paper an idea which had been gestating inside him for some time. Its origin was an article he had read about the discovery of a bricked-up room in a chateau in Prague that contained numerous forgotten masterpieces. So evocative was this event and the *rêverie* it inspired that, many years later, Bonnefoy found himself compelled to confront and articulate his powerful response. Yet this response is already marked by alterity. Bonnefoy as author of the piece declares his position to be neither poet nor scribe, but somewhere between the two: 'Pour l'essentiel, toutefois, je crois être un témoin sérieux, et n'être donc qu'un témoin' [In any case, the most important thing is that I believe I am a sober witness, and thus nothing other than a witness] (44). In his fantasy, he imagines a historian being lowered on a rope into the newly discovered room, only to re-emerge claiming to have seen nothing. Later on, however, in a tense night-time conversation with his partner, he admits to her that he did indeed see the paintings but that he had been crippled by the fear they awoke in him. When pressed, he explains that this fear stems from their innate otherness, their difference: 'La différence, on ne peut pas la décrire. Ce n'est pas affaire de mots' [The difference cannot be described. It's not something words can do] (48). Ultimately he decides that this otherness is due to their absence from the world and the gaze. The sight has made him wonder whether the great works of art 'n'avait été que notre illusion' [have only ever been an illusion of ours] (50). As his partner protests he explains:

> Ils ont toujours été sous nos yeux. Et ils sont donc... notre rêve. Ils sont... ce que nous sommes. Tandis que ces autres, leur différence, c'est parce qu'ils ont été

> perdus, tous ensemble, parce qu'ils sont restés, comment dire, entre eux, dans le passé. Le passé est *autre*. (50)
>
> [They have always been before our gaze. And so they are ... our dream. They are ... what we are. While these other ones are different because they have been lost, all together, because they have remained, how shall I put it, alone together, in the past. The past is *other*.]

This poetic improvisation on a factual account comes to Bonnefoy as what he calls a *fait accompli*, as a whole and perfect piece, which he writes without altering a word. It is a poem, but it is also a 'parcelle de vie secrète' [a little piece of secret life] (42), owing to its status as dream. For Bonnefoy secondary revision is as much a part of the creativity of the act of dreaming as the *imprévisible* eruption of the dream images themselves. The *rêverie* has continually toyed with the formation and dissolution of images as the human mind perceives, projects, and reconstructs them. Language is as rich and overburdened with images as any more self-evidently visual art: 'Chaque phrase est un labyrinthe' [Each sentence is a labyrinth] (51). What Bonnefoy has produced is essentially a dream which he happens to have dreamt on paper, with all the enticing mystery of a dream and none of its ungraspable elusiveness. He therefore returns to his *rêverie* and begins to explore it, considering its genesis, analysing its symbolism, considering other fantasies it brings to mind. The result is a critique in two stages: he reaches preliminary conclusions about his self and his creativity before — once time has passed again — making a second productive return and digging even deeper into the poem as a cloudy mirror of his soul.

Bonnefoy is interested in what his *rêverie* reveals to him about himself, but I find myself particularly drawn to what this work has to say about the process of critical analysis. Essentially this is a prose poem which focuses on the mysteries and the beauties of the reading process. Creativity is always, from the start, a reading of something, in the sense that it is an enticing disquisition on an element of the human condition, though it is often aesthetically unclear exactly what the objects of its fantasies might be. Bonnefoy elegantly demonstrates how reading creative art offers the pleasure of deducing its foundations and significance, but he also shows that reading is an act of creativity in its own right, producing new enigmas as fast as it elucidates others. This confusion between the processes and the objects of inquiry is profoundly postmodern in its structure. Mark Currie identifies as fundamental to postmodern narrative theory 'the problem of whether literary meanings are discovered or invented by a critic — revealed or created in the act of reading'.[5] While for Bonnefoy revelation and creation are two sides of the same coin, both drawing from the well of human inspiration, it is interesting that he should engage in a process so aligned to Derridean methodology, and which has as one of its effects the undermining of presence in the way that it disputes the notion of the origin. This is most evident in the way that Bonnefoy tells us that his dream comes to him as a complete entity, yet he is compelled to break into it to analyse it, not once but twice, in order to draw out the significance it hides.

Structurally, we can see how Bonnefoy's *récit en rêve* appeals quite clearly to the Derridean economy of the supplement.[6] The supplement is the additional extra (in this case Bonnefoy's own rereading) that turns out always to be essential to the original project, and this again and again. The supplement is scandalous, according to Derrida, because it undermines any possible belief in wholeness, sufficiency or self-presence; the original, no matter how perfect it looks, can always be supplemented. As Christina Howells proposes,

> It describes the very being of the chain itself, with its structure of endless substitutions and its articulation of desire and languages. [...] The paradoxical structure of the supplement is not an accident, but an indication of the way in which presence is never really fully present, only represented.[7]

Literary criticism itself, then, conforms to the logic of the supplement, in that each additional reading becomes necessary to understanding the text, each reading is required to draw out what was already in the text but veiled, not quite present enough. Yet each additional reading is itself subject to the laws of representation, and therefore destined to be founded on absence and insufficiency.

Bonnefoy has a certain poetic awareness of his intent in pursuing a supplementary chain of critical inquiry: 'L'écriture, ce n'est qu'un sceau, bien souvent, qu'on appose sur un seuil: et si même le sceau a figure radieuse de seuil ouvert' [Often, writing is nothing other than a seal affixed across a threshold; and this even when the seal has the luminous radiance of an open doorway] (52), he declares, invoking the figure of the threshold once again at the point of intersection between creativity and critique. To embark on a series of supplementary analyses here is, despite its Derridean connotations, entirely in keeping with Bonnefoy's poetic endeavours. At the end of the *rêverie* he cries: 'Ah, toute évidence est énigme' (50), and in interview he discusses one form of critical inquiry which has maintained its status as culturally valid: that of interpreting historical evidence. Scholarly inquiry into the flaws and insufficiencies of previous acts of interpretation form an allegiance for him with the act of poetry. 'Dans les deux cas ne s'agit-il pas de délivrer une présence, une vie, des représentations inadéquates qui la recouvrent?' [Does it not concern in both cases the liberation of a presence, of a life, from the inadequate representations that have obscured it?].[8] For Bonnefoy the potential relentlessness of supplementarity is equally the endless inventiveness of a critical form of creativity. But this is a point to which I shall return. The *rêverie* points implicitly to another revelation concerning the act of criticism, but one which Bonnefoy himself does not spot. Bonnefoy is so busy analysing the dream for traces of his beloved presence that he does not realize that it perfectly articulates an anxiety of effective criticism even more fundamental than the anxiety of its own insufficiency. The historian's fear of the otherness of the paintings, to which he repeatedly and compulsively returns, is the *original motive for critical inquiry.* Identifying and naming otherness, expressing the specificity of difference, lies at the very heart of the critical act. How to make that unique difference communicable is the essential work of the critic. For Derrida, of course, difference is married to its own deferral; difference is fundamental, ever present, the structural underpinning of language, and yet it is also radically elusive. Bonnefoy would seem to agree to some extent; the terror of difference, or alterity, is that it cannot be named. Yet implicit within Bonnefoy's *rêverie* is the recognition that the very creativity of criticism is brought about by alterity's resistance to articulation.

The argument that I am developing here is that Bonnefoy and Derrida may not be so radically opposed as first indications suggest. The perpetual presence of difference is a form of presence to which even Derrida might subscribe, as would a certain radical alterity at the heart of the creative act which both invites and resists articulation. Furthermore, if we return to the understanding Bonnefoy has of the notion of presence we find that, as Jackson indicates, 'L'expérience de la présence est donc extérieure au langage, sinon étrangère à lui' [The experience of presence is therefore beyond language, if not alien to it].[9] Bonnefoy begins from the premise that presence and language are, I would suggest, like oil and water. They cannot infiltrate each other, but they are bound to the contours of each other. Furthermore, the experience of presence has, John Naughton argues, something in common with Barthes's *punctum*, or 'that wound which unsettles the culturally acquired, [...] that "seismical" experience which jars all our knowledge'.[10] Presence for Bonnefoy, then, is the mark of the heterogeneous in experience, not the flawless veneer of mimesis which Derrida is so keen to undermine. There is, then, no reason why Bonnefoy and Derrida should disagree so profoundly over the concept of presence in their structural understanding of the term. The difficulty must be seen to lie in the fantasies that inhabit their theoretical constructs; in other words, the difference of opinion is, I suggest, a mark of their presence in the act of creative critical inquiry.

The First Reading of the *Rêverie*

In his first analysis of his dream-text, written three months later, Bonnefoy hunts for the article about the chateau in Prague that provoked such a response in him. When he finds it, it is, of course, completely different from how he remembered it. Rather than being shut away in a lost basement room, the pictures were simply hanging on the walls, but their dusty, neglected condition meant they were overlooked. Bonnefoy argues that what he has taken away from the article is a certain symbolism, which he has transformed and clarified. His reading of his *rêverie* is profoundly psychoanalytic in tone and content, as the heterogeneous or densely symbolic elements of his dream lead him towards more authentic moments of self-presence through the discovery of an inner alterity. These lost pictures are structurally representative of the unconscious, of that which is shut away, and therefore terrifyingly different when glimpsed. But his transformation of the image tells him that he is seeking to deny the way that the unconscious is perpetually present in its absence: 'La galerie perdue, l'inconnu dont on ne veut pas, voici que j'apprends qu'ils sont dans chacun de nos mots, de nos desires, et troublent de leurs miroitements ou mirages notre conscience qui se croit libre' [The lost gallery, the undesirable unknown, turn out, I find, to be in every one of our words, our desires, and their reverberations and illusions trouble our consciousness which believes itself to be free] (59). The difference between his creative image of a bricked-up room in a chateau, and the reality of pictures present on the walls but unseen, certainly disturbs Bonnefoy. The former he associates with a kind of reassuring inner security system, the latter 'c'est au contraire ce qu'on cherche ne pas savoir, puisqu'il faut continuer à vivre' [it is, on the contrary, that which we seek not to know, because one must keep on living] (60). The presence of the unconscious unsettles Bonnefoy and causes him to ponder the disillusioning thought that we are 'troués de forces errantes, de pulsions qui ne savent rien' [shot through with erratic compulsions, with mindless drives] (60), and that his beloved notion of presence might be an impossible ideal. But to add my own supplementary analysis to Bonnefoy's critique, what is present here, if not present enough, is that like the lost pictures, like the unconscious itself, the self is always there in language, just unrecognized — or misrecognized. Bonnefoy's own excessive disappointment in the face of his unconsciously brilliant reminder of the unconscious is evidence enough of this. At this point he allows himself to be discouraged, to lack the courage of his convictions. After all, what are we to deduce from Bonnefoy's reading here other than the unarticulated belief that we are never more present than in our mistakes, our creative misrememberings, our eccentric transformations, our curious absences? The lacuna, *c'est moi.*

The other supplementary point that strikes me about Bonnefoy's analysis is that it occurs after a lapse of time. The reading he makes is possible only with the overview that three months' distance affords him. The supplement that is his critique, like any psychoanalytic analysis, is part of an ongoing history of supplements, in which a new reappraisal is due significantly to a new historical context for reading. Derrida, too, is interested in the process of psychoanalysis, partly because it obeys the logic of the supplement, in the way that the self-presence of the subject is asserted and fissured with each retelling of the past. Equally, the new version of events is radically informed by supposedly insignificant or irrelevant details of the old text which just turned out to be essential. As Howells points out,

> On the one hand, deconstruction is critical and analytical, decomposing and deconstituting what it explores; on the other, it involves disjunction and a belief in ultimate irreducibility. It shares with psychoanalysis the double motif of a search for the origin, combined with a perpetual deferring and dissociation.[11]

There is, perhaps, a certain paradoxical fixity about Derrida's thinking on the nodal points of dreams. The blind spot has a certain necessary irreducibility for him, which might last for ever, despite the relentless swathes of interpretation laid all about it. Derrida declares:

> What forever exceeds the analysis of the dream is indeed a knot that cannot be untied, a thread that, even if it is cut, like an umbilical cord, nevertheless remains forever knotted, right on the body, at the place of the navel. The scar is a knot against which analysis can do nothing.[12]

This would seem an over-corporeal metaphor for the grainy elusiveness of dreams, themselves the epitome of transformation and symbolic possibility. What Bonnefoy's analysis suggests here is that the movement from blindness to insight may well be simply the consequence of the passage of time. What cannot be seen in the present — and necessarily, through too close a proximity to the object of interpretation — will consolidate into a partial truth of self-presence in the future. Each significant moment in the future brings with it fresh insight, a new and unexpected glimpse of self-presence. The truth of psychoanalysis is that presence is not an answer, an entity that can be seen once and for all, rather it is like a shadow that becomes distinct in moments of intense illumination. Yet the repetitive temporality of insight makes analytical truth always historical, that's to say true in the moment of its conception, but issued with a best before date. And, indeed, six months later, Bonnefoy returns to add another layer, another supplement, of analysis to his text.

The First Rereading of the *Rêverie* and its Analysis

In this second analysis, Bonnefoy moves from locating the immanence of presence in images of the unconscious, to the immanence of presence in the divine. He focuses on the ambiguous reference in the original *rêverie* to 'quelque chose comme une forme' [something like a form] sensed in the darkness beyond the window where his lovers lie having their conversation. Bonnefoy wonders what it represents and then suggests: 'En tant qu'inachèvement, c'est-à-dire manque: "Dieu", aurais-je peut-être décidé' [As something unfinished, that is to say, as something lacking: "God", I would perhaps have decided]. This proposition is rejected, however, for 'c'est très profond en moi que je sens que ce qu'on nomme une foi m'est impossible' [I feel very deeply that what people call faith is impossible for me] (63). Although Bonnefoy discounts the possibility of 'God', his work is nevertheless bound up with the sublime in very particular ways. As Naughton indicates,

> A great part of the spiritual journey of Yves Bonnefoy will be devoted to mastering his thirst for an 'elsewhere', his natural tendency towards *excarnation* and flight. He will strive to see the incarnation of the divine in the real, in the present and unmistakeable moment.[13]

Such a dynamic finds elegant execution in this second analysis as Bonnefoy rejects the notion of an external deity and declares that 'cette présence incertaine encore mais évidement désirée, c'est une naissance, [...] une naissance qui soit divine — sauf que toute naissance est divine' [this presence, uncertain still but clearly desired, is a birth [...] a divine birth — except that all births are divine] (64). What could be more firmly incorporated, less theoretically abstract, more reassuringly real, than a baby? Bonnefoy remembers that he was able to write his *rêverie* because a real birth was impending; he was able to open himself up to articulating the fears about presence which the dream appeared to evoke, in the (unconscious) knowledge that he would be grounded in the real by a child. 'Toutes ces *Découvertes de Prague* ne furent que pour rêver qu'à ce "mauvais" inconnu, mirage né du vertige, se substitue cet autre inconnu, lui salvateur' [All these *Discoveries in Prague* were only dreamt so that in the place of this 'bad' unknown, a mirage caused by vertigo, a different unknown could be substituted, one that was salvationary] (65). Bonnefoy is delighted with this new insight, finding within it the solution to his sudden desire to transcribe his *rêverie*, to the evocative but opaque symbolism of the dream, and to his own uncertainties about the viability of the notion of presence. 'Qui peut penser longtemps qu'il n'est pas, s'il lui est donné de faire être?' [Who can think for any length of time that he doesn't exist, if he has been given the gift of creation?], he asks (65). The ending of this text, then, is redemptive, beautiful, and wholly questionable. It bothers Bonnefoy not one bit that the salvation of presence comes in the form of radical alterity that is the child, and his evocation of the divine clearly demands further consideration.

The first supplementary point to add to this analysis, then, is that, in order to reach a triumphant conclusion, Bonnefoy dispenses with the rigorous deconstructive analysis that characterized his previous reading. He embarks on a new process of reading which, although couched in the terms of analysis, is not analytic as such. Rather, Bonnefoy re-enters his *rêverie* seeking to communicate with it and hear its obscure messages, bringing his memories and emotions to the reading, rather than his powers of logic. This kind of textual appreciation reminded me of the distinction Bonnefoy himself made in an essay between Anglo-American and French schools of criticism.[14] Whereas Anglo-American criticism (according to Bonnefoy) treats poems like objects and searches for meaning, French critics respond to poetry as a form of activity, and attempt to relive the poet's unanalysable experience, to feel the dimension of what cannot be directly expressed. Bonnefoy's own act of communion with his work, and the spiritual encounter it represents, seem to me analogous in interesting ways to Georges Bataille's concept of 'inner experience'.[15] Drawing on the accounts of thirteenth-century Christian mystics, Bataille proposes a method of reading or experiencing shockingly violent and traumatic images that would not reduce them to the banalities and objectifications of language. By meditating on the image and identifying with the pain it represents, Bataille finds a way to experience a truth that language cannot tell. For Bataille this is a political activity, a way of inhabiting the irreducible otherness of the horrifying images of war and torture. But this notion of inner experience is undoubtedly also present in Bonnefoy's critique, if put to an entirely different use. I would like to suggest here that Bonnefoy's second reading of his work is 'mystical', in that the elements of the divine which characterize this analysis are appropriate because of its structural organization, not because of a faintly sentimentalized concept of giving birth. Derrida's understanding of the notion of God is useful here:

> God is the name and the element of that which makes possible an absolutely pure and absolutely present self-knowledge. From Descartes to Hegel and in spite of all the differences that separate the different places and moments in the structure of that epoch, God's infinite understanding is the other name for the logos as self-presence.[16]

To put God in the word is to give it divine plenitude, to sublimate the trace of the real into full and absolute presence. For Bonnefoy, the divinity bound up in the notion of the child is, I would suggest, a consequence of its ability to evoke a fullness of self-presence in Bonnefoy, and the presence of fullness in his *rêverie*. To find the child inhabiting the word is to recognize the divinity of the child — its ability, in other words, to make the dream intelligible and centred. This reading is *theological* because the presence Bonnefoy attributes to his work through this mystical union with the text and its associations is ultimately not a question of logical deduction, but of faith.

But, as in the case of the mystics, the plenitude of presence Bonnefoy experiences in his reading of the text comes at the price of paradox. His *rêverie* began by facing the anxiety caused by radical alterity; a fear that provoked the act of critical inquiry. Now he ends that inquiry with alterity reinstated, if neutralized, in the figure of the child. Most visionary and ecstatic mystics sought to move beyond textual representations of God to a more ineffable experience of communion with the divine. This is echoed in Bonnefoy's readings by a movement through close textual appreciation of his text to a more abstract encounter with the text's hidden recesses. For mystics, however, such a dynamic represented a movement from a given image to the experience, not of clarity and self-presence, but of the void, of ecstatic darkness. Hence a distinction was created in the modes of naming God between the cataphatic, in which names are positively attributed to the divine, and the apophatic, in which all attributes are 'unsaid' or denied in order to mark the illimitability of God's being. This movement from saying to unsaying in the face of radical otherness is intriguing, as is the need to name otherness temporarily in order to experience a more intense and complete union with the unknown in the subsequent act of unnaming. Bonnefoy's contemporary appropriation of the mystic's encounter with the unknown reorganizes its elements in evocative if confusing patterns. His *rêverie* opens with otherness that cannot be named, and which subsequently is named as the divine plenitude of the child, yet the holy grail of self-presence remains, to the external reader at least, elusive. By the end of the text Bonnefoy still appears to be standing in the darkness, even if he is at least ecstatic to be there. Perhaps we can consider the possibility that the alterity that haunts the passage is better understood as presence itself for Bonnefoy, and having sought and failed to place it in words, his final ecstasies are reserved for his reunion in its illimitable and nameless being for which the child is only a transient symbol.

In conclusion we can perhaps consider the seemingly heterogeneous reading processes that Bonnefoy employs, moving with comparative ease from the supplementarity of deconstruction, to the repetitive returns of psychoanalysis, to the blinding illuminations of mystical inner experience. If there is an innate coherency about their utilization, it is perhaps that all three processes have a dynamic in common. Deconstruction, psychoanalysis, and mysticism all seek a temporary symbolic appropriation of otherness, in order subsequently to unpick that symbolism and recognize the illimitability of the otherness they fail to describe. Hence the inevitable supplementarity of criticism, whereby each act of critique, each naming of textual otherness, is only a temporary and partial appropriation of the radical difference to itself of language and subjectivity which cannot ultimately be captured and understood. In this respect, the radical unknowability of otherness is one of the few things our secular culture still holds sacred.

Notes to Chapter 14

1. Yves Bonnefoy, *Rue Traversière et autres récits en rêve*, 2nd edn (Paris: Gallimard, 1992). Further references to this edition are given after quotations in the text.
2. Robert Kopp, 'Un entretien avec Yves Bonnefoy', *Magazine Littéraire*, no. 421 (June 2003), 22–27 (p. 26). Translations, unless otherwise stated, are my own.
3. John Jackson, *A la souche obscure des rêves: la dialectique de l'écriture chez Yves Bonnefoy* (Paris: Mercure de France, 1993), p. 60.
4. John Jackson, 'Yves Bonnefoy et la souche obscure des rêves', Postface to *Rue Traversière*, p. 209.
5. Mark Currie, *Postmodern Narrative Theory* (Basingstoke: Macmillan, 1998), p. 56.

6. For this understanding of the supplement I am drawing on Jacques Derrida, '... That Dangerous Supplement ...', in *Acts of Literature*, ed. by Derek Attridge (New York and London: Routledge, 1992), pp. 76–109.
7. Christina Howells, *Derrida: Deconstruction from Phenomenology to Ethics* (Cambridge: Polity Press, 1999), p. 58.
8. Kopp, 'Un entretien avec Yves Bonnefoy', p. 26.
9. Jackson, *A la souche obscure des rêves*, p. 60.
10. John Naughton, *The Poetics of Yves Bonnefoy* (Chicago and London: University of Chicago Press, 1984), p. 18.
11. Howells, *Derrida*, p. 120.
12. Jacques Derrida, 'Resistances', in *Resistances of Psychoanalysis*, trans. by Peggy Kamuf, Pascale-Anne Brault, and Michael Naas (Stanford: Stanford University Press, 1998), pp. 1–38 (p. 11).
13. Naughton, *The Poetics of Yves Bonnefoy*, p. 3.
14. Yves Bonnefoy, 'Critics: English and French and the Distance between Them', *Encounter* (July 1958), 39–45.
15. See for instance Bataille, *Guilty*, trans. by Bruce Boone (San Francisco: Lapis Press, 1988), or Bataille, *Inner Experience*, trans. by Leslie Anne Boldt (Albany: SUNY Press, 1988). My own reading is derived from Amy Hollywood's excellent analysis of Bataille in *Sensible Ecstasy: Mysticism, Sexual Difference and the Demands of History* (Chicago and London: University of Chicago Press, 2002), pp. 60–119.
16. Jacques Derrida, *Of Grammatology*, trans. by Gayatri Chakravorti Spivak (Baltimore: Johns Hopkins University Press, 1976), p. 98.

CHAPTER 15

On Touching: War, Art, and the Realm of the Senses

Santanu Das

In eighteenth-century Puisaux there lived an old man who was blind. When Diderot sought him out for illumination on the philosophy of the senses, he was full of sympathy for the old man's dark world. Asked whether he would like to be able to see, the old man replied: 'I would just as soon have long arms: it seems to me that my hands would tell me more about what happens on the moon that you can find out with your eyes and your telescopes.'[1]

The idea of the hand as more immediate and reliable than the eye, here articulated through the irrefutable, if tantalizing, logic of the blind, reaches across disciplines, cultures, and time.[2] It is through the sense of touch that we have access to the materiality of our own bodies, and of the world around us. A person may be born blind, deaf, and mute but in order to live, the skin — constituting twenty per cent of the body weight — must respond to touch. For Freud, the child's relationship to the mother's nipple is 'the prototype of every relation of love'; for Kristeva, the trauma of abjection lies in the tearing away from the maternal lining as the child learns to distinguish between the self and the world.[3] Language is born as the child cries out to the parent; language breaks down before the experience of physical pain, felt as hammering, burning, throbbing of nerve endings, an internalization of touch; and as a person dies, the skin becomes cold and inert, as if life lodged itself in the corpuscles of our skin. Fundamental to our ideas of self, touch is almost impossible to express: that is perhaps why the entry under touch, as Anzieu points out in *The Skin Ego*, is one of the longest in the English dictionary. In some ways, all our words are an attempt to *reach* out to people, showing how the most intimate form of communication underwrites language itself. And when words fail us — in times of illness, danger, or death — the body rushes in to fill the gap left by language: a clasp, a kiss, an embrace.

Even as Aristotle denigrated touch as the most lowly of the senses — a blow from which Western philosophy has not yet fully recovered — there has been a strong tradition that has championed touch as fundamental to aesthetic appreciation. In ancient Rome, Horace noted in *De arte poetica*, 'For yourselves, handle the Greek models by night, handle them by day'; in Victorian England, charged with the heady atmosphere of Oxford Hellenism, Walter Pater wrote lovingly, longingly, about the archaeologist Winckelmann caressing the Greek marbles with 'unsinged hands, with no sense of shame or loss'.[4] Yet touch defies the realm of representation. Unlike vision or sound, which can be preserved through photography or the phonograph, touch cannot be represented directly: it seems to break the realm of signification, losing its essence, changing its nature in the passage from the signified to the signifier. How can art and criticism bring the fierce interiority of the tactile within their fold? Is touch only a 'trace' in a painting such as Caravaggio's *The Doubting of Saint Thomas* (1601–02), or should a fuller appreciation of the painting include the phenomenology of reception in the way the *trompe l'oeil* effect turns our eyes into fingers and we try to penetrate the world of representation? In literary writing, Keats's 'This Living Hand' remains one of the most powerful evocations of touch, joining hand and script, tomb and flesh.[5] We are regularly 'touched' or 'moved' by literature, art, and music and yet, in the conventional languages of criticism, touch goes unnoticed, as if the all-pervasiveness of the skin has rendered it irrelevant.

Two questions will frame my inquiry in this chapter. First, I wish to argue that a 'heightened' responsiveness to and enjoyment of art — an affective understanding — has to accommodate the realm of the senses, and how a 'new' language of criticism may benefit from closer attention to the most intimate of the senses. Secondly, touch does not respect borders but spills over to the other senses and, in this regard, seems ideally suited for an interterdisciplinary examination: for touch to enter the realm of representation, it depends on a complex process of 'translation' that, as Mieke Bal notes, also characterizes transactions across disciplines.[6] In fact, an interdisciplinary investigation may provide fresh insights into the complex processes of the intersensorial, into the subtle negotiation between the eye, the ear, and the hand undertaken by us as we encounter different kinds of experience and art.

In order to address these issues, I shall focus on a particular historical event: the First World War. The historical and emotional resonances of that war take us, when we discuss the art it produced, beyond the confines of academic language into the realm of evocation and affect. Moreover, as I seek to demonstrate, the sense of touch is central to the experience of the First World War: from the visceral shock of the trench mud where the men floundered and drowned to the physical closeness among the soldiers as they huddled together against long winter nights and falling shells. After three weeks in the Somme, Wilfred Owen writes to his 'dearest mother': 'I have not seen any dead. I have done worse. In the dank air, I have perceived it, and in the darkness, felt.'[7] And a month before his death on the Sambre–Oise Canal bank, he writes to his fellow soldier-poet, Siegfried Sassoon:

> The boy on my side, shot through the head, lay on top of me, soaking my shoulder, for half an hour.
>
> Catalogue? Photograph? Can you photograph the crimson-hot iron as it cools from the smelting? This is what Jones's blood looked like, and felt like. My senses are charred.[8]

Owen lays claim on the haptic, trying to evoke the perilous intimacy of the moment by drawing on the flesh of the eye: 'crimson-hot iron'. Horror, pity, maternity, and a diffuse eroticism are fused and confused in that 'half an hour' of contact. In order to examine how tactual perception informs First World War art and gets 'translated' across disciplines, I shall consider a range of evidence: archival materials, painting, poetry, memoirs, and trench objects. I shall suggest that an interdisciplinary approach, rooted in a close, affective reading of texts, is not inimical to historical analysis but might illuminate more fully a particular time and culture. The word 'felt', key to Owen's letters both to his mother and to Sassoon, raises a fundamental problem of representation: how can writing transmit the processes of touch?

In the early decades of the twentieth century, the typewriter tore the writer's hand from the act of writing.[9] In today's world of computers, there is no tangible relationship between the hand that taps at the keyboard and the final printed page: technology rather than death seems to give the lie to any universal validity for Keats's 'this warm scribe my hand'.[10] But the connection between the writer and the writing remains infrangible in the world of the archives. We leaf through manuscripts, each alone, in palpable relation to past lives, past bodies. As we open the dark-brown pocket notebook of H. Gladstone, two loose pages — a small hand-drawn map and a diagram of a clock face with some Morse code signals — fall out of a curious little flap (Figure 15.1).[11] We come across a letter in the shape of an 'X' to symbolize a kiss, sent by G. W. Hayman to his wife Marie (Figure 15.2).[12] Opening the file of Private Bennett, we do not know what to examine first: a Certificate of Identity, torn at the edges; a soiled Field Service postcard stamped 16 November 1915, reporting the sender's admission to hospital; and a particularly grimy envelope, marked 'On Active Service' and stamped 16 December 1916, addressed to Mrs Bennett (Figure 15.3).[13] As we cautiously try to take the letter out of the envelope, our fingers encounter something leafy and crumbly: it is a bunch of blue and white flowers, the dried stalks still green, pressed onto the letter. 'These flowers from outside of our Hut', Bennett had lovingly written to his wife in blue ink on the Regiment paper as he pressed the flowers, stained with blobs of what may be trench mud. We carefully replace the flowers our intrusive fingers have pulled out of the envelope: the process is intimate and unsettling.

My point of entry into the relationship between touch and aesthetic representation in context of the First World War will be through John Singer Sargent's monumental war painting, *Gassed* (1918–19). The oil painting, commissioned for the Hall of Remembrance but now permanently housed in the Imperial War Museum, depicts the aftermath of a gas attack that the artist had witnessed the previous year in France: 'a harrowing sight,' Sargent wrote, 'a field full of gassed and blindfolded men'.[14] Ten blindfolded soldiers move haltingly in single file across the twenty-foot-long canvas, each touching the man in front. What each soldier perceives is what the hand feels — rucksack, rifle, or the rough uniform-clad body in front. The hand not only grasps or clutches; it enables each of the soldiers to think and plan the next step forward, gathering a disabled cluster of men into a neat line. The sense of touch defines space and guides the rhythm of the movement, as if new eyes have opened at the tip of the fingers.

Painting, like surgery, requires a rare coordination of eye and hand. Every fresh brush-stroke is an angling and guiding of touch on the canvas just as each little movement on the part of the blindfolded soldiers in the painting is sensed through the hand. The interruption of the desultory chain by the fourth soldier from the

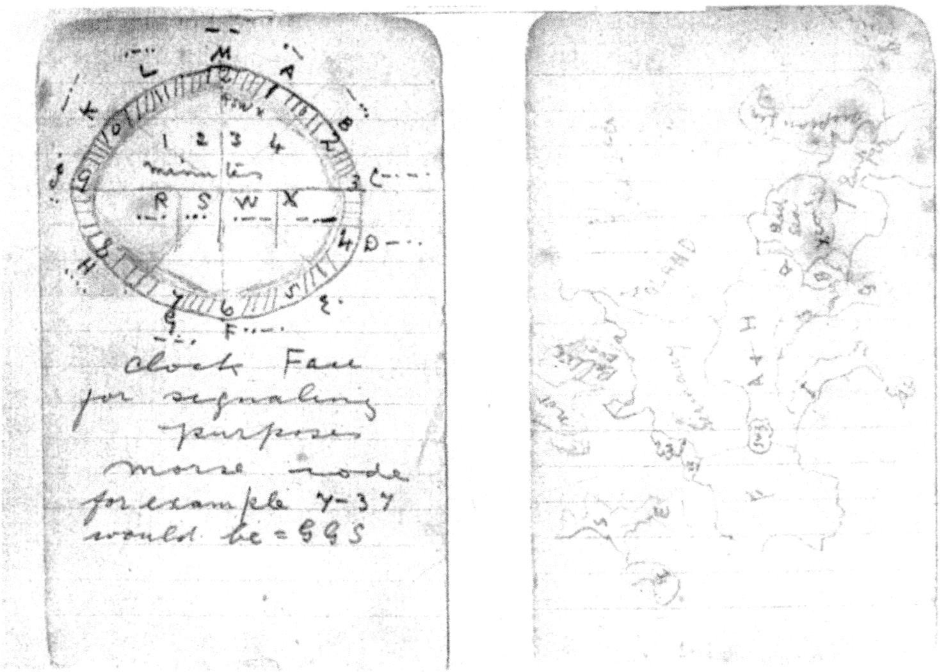

FIGURE 15.1. Diagram of a clock face with Morse code signals written beside the numbers, and hand-drawn map of Europe and from the diary of H. Gladstone. Imperial War Museum, London

end as he temporarily falls out of line draws attention to the centrality as well as the nakedness of the hand. The gesture is raw: the human subject is cast as a set of anxious limbs, thrust into a poorly delimited space like an exposed nerve; it evokes the vulnerability and disorientation of the human body in a dark world. The repetitive and trance-like figures establish a powerful rhythm across the pictorial space, as in a sculpted frieze, and can be compared to representations of the blind leading the blind (as in Bruegel's *The Parable of the Blind*) or the *Dance of Death*, which Singer's friend Vernon Lee employed in her allegory *The Ballet of the Nations* (1915). The most striking feature about the painting is the strange use of light: the spectacle of blindness is represented through the drama of chiaroscuro. Coming from no particular source, the greenish-beige light holds the soldiers and stills them in our minds in a moment of numbed serenity, as if in a flashback or a dream.

In *Ways of Seeing* (1977), John Berger writes evocatively about the importance of touch in painting. Discussing Holbein's *The Ambassadors* (1533), Berger notes: 'Every square inch of the surface of this painting, whilst remaining purely visual, appeals to, importunes, the sense of touch.'[15] Berger highlights a quality to which the art historian Alois Riegl, early in the twentieth century, powerfully drew attention, calling it the 'haptic' mode of representation: a quality of physical tactility that he noted in certain art traditions such as Egyptian and Islamic painting, late Roman

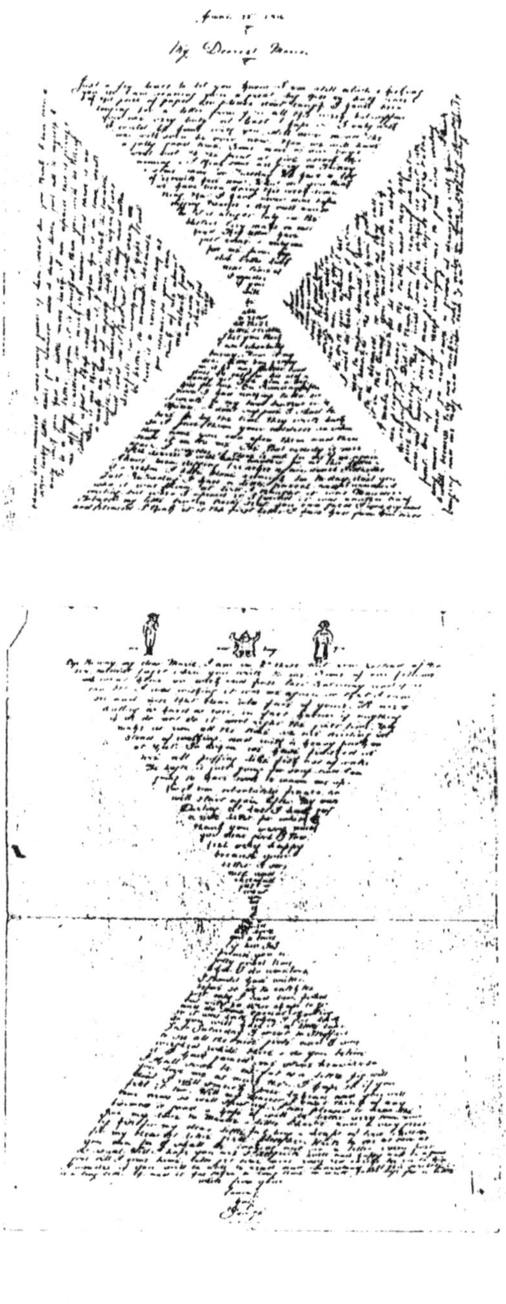

FIGURE 15.2. Letter in the shape of a kiss, from G. W. Hayman to his wife. Imperial War Museum, London

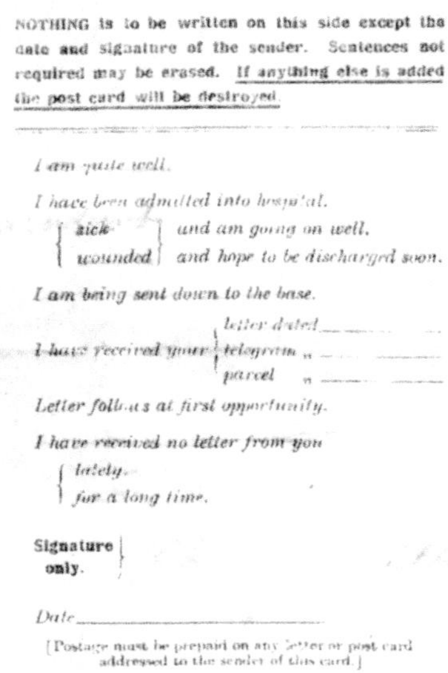

NOTHING is to be written on this side except the date and signature of the sender. Sentences not required may be erased. If anything else is added the post card will be destroyed.

I am quite well.

I have been admitted into hospital.

{ *sick* } *and am going on well.*
{ *wounded* } *and hope to be discharged soon.*

I am being sent down to the base.

I have received your { *letter dated* ___ / *telegram* " ___ / *parcel* " ___ }

Letter follows at first opportunity.

I have received no letter from you
{ *lately.* / *for a long time.* }

Signature only.

Date ___

[Postage must be prepaid on any letter or post card addressed to the sender of this card.]

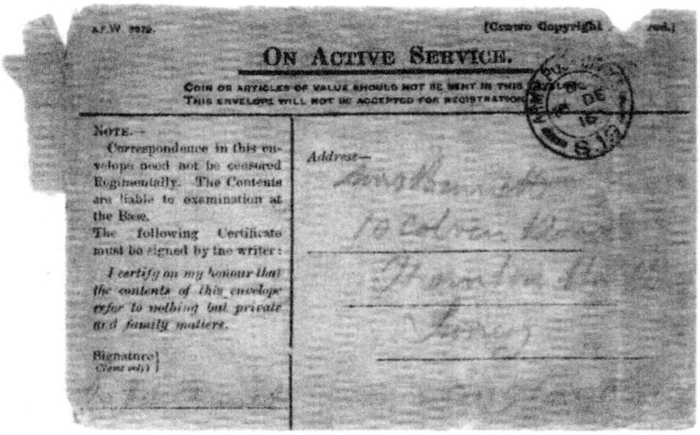

FIGURE 15.3. Items from the papers of Private G. H. Bennett: envelope addressed to his wife; Field Service postcard reporting his admission to hospital following an unspecified accident; part of a letter with flowers pressed onto the paper. Imperial War Museum, London

metalwork, and textile art.[16] In *Gassed*, the light itself may be said to have become haptic in the way the afternoon glow touches the soldiers. The horizontal brush-strokes evoke the texture of objects: the ropes, the folds of the threadbare fabric of the khaki, the life-size buttons and buckles, the straps and slings and military accoutrements, the soles of the shoes, the upturned hat; the light clings to the jumble of elbows and knees in foreshortened space. Yet the affective power of the painting lies in the way it dramatizes the disjunction between the viewer's visual sense of space and the soldiers' tactile space. In symmetrical contrast to the leg of the player about to kick the ball in the army match in the distant background, the third soldier lifts his foot far higher than is needed as he tries to negotiate the duckboard: blindness is inscribed most powerfully at the point when touch is anticipated as collision but is absent. In 'The Royal Academy', Virginia Woolf recalls how *Gassed* 'at last pricked some nerve of protest, or perhaps of humanity'. Referring to the raised foot, Woolf notes: 'This little piece of over-emphasis was the final scratch of the surgeon's knife which is said to hurt more than the whole operation.'[17] In Woolf's evocative account — as she plays on the relation between the surface of the canvas and the surface of the skin — the body of the painting and that of the viewer meet and move under the artist's hand: the 'little piece of over-emphasis' pricks the skin set between the viewer and the painting, and subjectivity bleeds.

FIGURE 15.4. John Singer Sargent, charcoal study for *Gassed* (1918–19). Imperial War Museum, London, Artists' Archives

The absence of vision is a source of trauma in war writings: the eyes of the soldiers that we meet in Owen, Sassoon, or Isaac Rosenberg are not blind but open and disoriented in the night. Sargent's grasp on trench reality is acute. In the dark, muddy, subterranean world of the trenches, the soldiers navigated space not through safe distance of the gaze but rather through the clumsy immediacy of tactile perception: 'grope', 'creep', 'crawl' are recurring verbs in trench narratives, showing the shift from the visual to the tactile. Sargent's *Gassed* may be read in conjunction with Owen's 'gas' poem, 'Dulce et Decorum Est'. In a letter to his mother, he writes: 'Here is a gas poem, done yesterday, (which is not private, but not final).'[18]

> Gas! Gas! Quick, boys! — An ecstasy of fumbling
> Fitting the clumsy helmets just in time;
> But someone still was yelling out and stumbling,
> And flound'ring like a man in fire or lime. ...
> Dim, through the misty panes and thick green light,
> As under a green sea, I saw him drowning.
> In all my dreams, before my helpless sight,
> He plunges at me, guttering, choking, drowning.
> [...]
> If you could hear, at every jolt, the blood
> Come gargling from the froth-corrupted lungs,
> Obscene as cancer, bitter as the cud
> Of vile, incurable sores on innocent tongues, —
> My friend, you would not tell with such high zest
> To children ardent for some desperate glory,
> The old Lie: Dulce et decorum est
> Pro patria mori.[19]

When we read the first stanza along with Sargent's *Gassed*, the resonance is striking: Sargent's soldiers seem to be moving through 'the misty panes and thick green light' while Owen's poem turns the reader into a viewer, enveloped by the 'green sea'. For both, light seems to 'thicken' and cling round the bodies. Yet the differences between the two are equally telling, especially in the manipulation of haptic space through vision and sound. If Sargent's canvas portrays the scene through the slightly distanced vision that can take in four layers of bodies — indeed, to absorb the full length of the painting, the stretch of fifty bodies, the spectator has to step back — the opening words ('Gas! Gas!') in Owen plunge us into the thick of action. Sargent's figures have a majestic, statuesque quality moving in slow time; Owen's figures enter the poem 'bent double' and 'curs[ing] through sludge' as he evokes the horrifically sensuous. Herein lies the difference between a state-commissioned, epic rendering of a battle scene and a personal lyric testimony: more crucially, the difference between a 62-year-old civilian painter and a 24-year-old soldier poet.

Can sound, like light and perspective, create the illusion of space and suggest the materiality of the body moving through it? In his intriguing book *What Makes Sound Patterns Expressive?* (1992), Reuven Tsur notes, 'Tactile metaphors such as sharp, piercing, thin, thick, heavy sounds are usually used to refer to some lowly differentiated, evasive, non-conceptual and continuous (i.e. noncategorical) qualities of sounds [...] Certain aspects of the physical signal are subliminally perceived and these aspects sometimes do reach consciousness, however faintly.'[20] Even if sound patterns, as Tsur suggests, fall on and are registered by the skin, what distinguishes poetry from other kinds of utterance is the use of rhythm. Is the 'tactile' dimension of poetic utterance to be found not only in external stimuli but also in an internal kinaesthetic quickening as the human heartbeat speeds up in an effort to 'match' the slightly faster poetic rhythm?[21] Metrical acceleration through spondees and exclamations, suggesting the sudden, altered rhythm of the bodies, is crucial to Owen's evocation of panic, but what sustains (or perverts?) it is a series of rather sensuous linguistic devices: sibilance, labials, vowel-modulation, rhyme. Is there a central disjunction between the body at war and the body of sound, just as Sargent's emollient contours partly aestheticize the haggard soldiers?

Mustard gas corrodes the body from within rather than ripping apart the flesh. The testimony of the gas attack moves accordingly from visual impressions to visceral processes; from sounds produced between the body and the world — fumbling, stumbling, flound'ring, drowning — to sounds within the body: coughing, guttering, choking, gargling. The word 'ecstasy' is ambiguous: how can a horrific gas attack, rooted in historical reality, induce ecstasy? In the muddy trenches of the First World War, do we find an experiential validation of Burke's idea of the 'sublime' where terror and pleasure meet? Yet what Owen describes is an immediate experience of horror rather than a spectacle of terror. Closer to Owen's time and temperament is Freud's suggestion that 'feelings of apprehension, fright or horror' have a 'sexually exciting effect' and that 'all comparatively intense affective processes, even terrifying ones, trench upon sexuality'.[22] Indeed, 'fumbling' has an erotic feel, especially in the context of Owen's long, tortured relation to hands and boys.[23] Yet, in a poem that explores the complicity of language in violence — the dangers of Horace's 'sweet' phrase, 'Dulce et decorum est'[24] — 'ecstasy' may stand in, consciously or unconsciously, for the perverse narrative impulse itself: poetic language, asked to describe violence, touches itself instead through alliteration and echo (ecstasy, clumsy, misty) and experiences exhilaration, replacing real-life horror with linguistic pleasure. Owen, thus criticizing the 'sweetness' of a particular poetic tradition, seems to be trapped insidiously in the 'sweetness' of the lyric form itself. For the excessive music of the rhyme, conspiring with sibilance and labials — as verbs are stretched beyond their bounds and an extra foot is left 'hanging' at the end of the lines (fumbling, stumbling, drowning) — creates a sonic realm that obscenely mimes, if not aestheticizes, the spectral space created round the charred body through its own jerky, erratic movements. But at the same time, the compulsive rhyme of the present continuous is intensely affective: it suggests the eternal 'now' of the trauma victim, doomed to a compulsion to repeat past experiences as the present.

In his poetry, Owen, through a strange manipulation of sound, creates linguistic-tactile fantasies, seducing us into moments we would otherwise flinch from: moments when limbs are sliced off ('limbs knife-skewed', 'shaved us with his scythe'), the flesh is ripped apart ('shatter of flying muscles', 'Ripped from my own back | In scarlet shreds', 'limped on, blood-shod'), or the mouth starts bleeding ('I saw his round mouth's crimson deepen as it fell', 'Nor what red mouths were torn to make their blooms').[25] A rigorous Protestant ethic, suppressed homoeroticism, and hatred of warfare combine to produce these tortured, almost sadomasochistic, images: the male body that cannot be touched, legally or morally, can only be mutilated in Owen's poetry. A visceral thrill as well as an acute physical empathy constitute the body in pain in Owen's poetry, hovering around moments when we no longer know where the *is* ends and the *was* begins. The perverse aestheticizing impulse is evident in 'Dulce et Decorum Est' in the savage juxtaposition of tongues: the excessive music of the lyric form and the actual lacerated tongue of the gas victim, his muteness while Owen rewrites Keats's 'palate fine' as the 'vile, incurable sores on innocent tongues'. It is important to note that the gas attack brings out, for Sargent and Owen, concerns specific to their craft: with Sargent, the focus is on the eyes; for Owen, it is on the tongue where lyric poetry has its origin.

Both Sargent and Owen point up a central paradox: the First World War ravaged the male body on an unprecedented scale but restored tenderness to touch in male relationships. In Sargent's painting, the sense of desolation is balanced by an Owenesque sense of community as the soldiers in the ground, to quote a line from 'Spring Offensive', 'leaning on the nearest chest or knees | Carelessly slept'.[26] The homoerotic undertones of trench life that Owen evokes would not be lost on this society artist who painted portraits of wealthy women for his living, and of young working-class men for pleasure, such as the *Nude Study of Thomas E. McKeller.* If we look at the figures on the ground, we do not know where one figure ends and the other begins: the folds of colour and of fabric hold within them the contours of the bodies as they touch and blend in a world of sensuous contact and comfort. In the trenches of the First World War, mutilation and mortality, darkness and the breakdown of language led to a new level of intimacy and intensity under which the carefully constructed mores of civilian society broke down. Men nursed and fed their friends when ill; they bathed together; they held each other as they danced, and in sleep, their bodies 'spooned' together (Figure 15.6).[27] There was also gender-bending: Jack, a soldier, must close his letter to Miss Williams as 'my wife is in bed & wants me to keep her warm but it is only a Palestine wife. another Sussex boy [...] It is very chilly at night right now. & it is nice to have someone to keep each other warm.'[28]

A new world of largely non-genital tactile tenderness was opening up in which pity, thrill, affection, and eroticism are fused and confused: it is this world that Sargent's painting explores. C. H. Cox remembers how his comrade 'laid back in my arms and his last words were for his mother as he died in my arms'.[29] These soldiers were often haunted by the *feel* of their comrades' bodies as life ebbed out and the warm mutuality of the embrace was lost for ever. The most evanescent of human senses, touch can be preserved only in memory and through language. Consequently, there is the urgent need within war writings to remember and re-present these moments, to evolve a literary language around touch. The writings of the soldier poets might be regarded as a phantasmatic space where they resurrect their dead comrades through language, infusing them with the warmth they had once known: 'I clasp his hand', 'For a moment, the touch | Of a warm hand', and 'I had clasped warm, last night'.[30] War literature is haunted by the sense of touch, from Rupert Brooke's 'linked beauty of bodies' to Siegfried Sassoon's 'my fingers touch

Figure 15.5. Men of the Duke of Wellington's Regiment after the capture of Marfaux on 23 July 1918, during the battles of the Marne. Photograph courtesy of the Imperial War Museum, London. Q6867

his face' to Robert Nichols's more sentimental 'My comrade, that you could rest | Your tired body on mine'.[31] Here, language functions almost as a skin, through which the absent comrade is reached, felt, embraced.

Of all the senses, touch is most closely associated with emotion and affect. When his beloved David was killed in the trenches, a devastated Sassoon wrote down in his diary:

> So, after lunch, I escaped to the woods above Sailly-Luarette, and grief had its way with me in the sultry thicket [...] And I lay there under the smooth bole of a beech-tree, wondering, and longing for the bodily presence that was so fair. [...] So I wrote his name in chalk on the beech-tree stem, and left a rough garland of ivy there, and a yellow primrose for his yellow hair and kind grey eyes, my dear, my dear. [...]
>
> For you were glad, and kind and brave;
> With hands that clasped me, young and warm.[32]

Memory of the beloved reverts to the intimacy of the caress. Literary pastoral provides Sassoon with a ritual of mourning: Keatsian sensuousness flows into and fuses with homoerotic longing and loss as Sassoon remembers, and tries to resurrect, through the ivy, the primrose, and finally through language, the 'bodily presence that was so fair'. In *A Lover's Discourse*, Roland Barthes notes: 'I enwrap the other in my words, I caress, brush against, talk up this contact.'[33] Can the rustle of language evoke what is longed for so poignantly and so irretrievably lost — the mutuality of the embrace? Indeed, Wilfred Owen's 'Futility' dramatizes this process in its most poignant and desolate form, beginning appropriately at a moment when the reciprocity of the gesture is denied:

> Move him into the sun —
> Gently its touch awoke him once,
> At home, whispering of fields half-sown,
> Always it woke him, even in France,
> Until this morning and this snow.
> If anything might rouse him now
> The kind old sun will know.
>
> Think how it wakes the seeds —
> Woke once the clays of a cold star.
> Are limbs, so dear achieved, are sides
> Full-nerved, still warm, too hard to stir?
> Was it for this the clay grew tall?
> — O what made fatuous sunbeams toil
> To break earth's sleep at all?[34]

The 'futility' arises out of Owen choosing the most caressive of lyric voices to portray a moment of unyielding touch. It is the force of this rejection that now leads Owen to stroke the male body with the most intangible of substances: light and language, playing on the vestigial relation between the sun, heat, and temperature. The meshing of the literal and the metaphoric aspects of the sun's 'touch' enables Owen to traverse a remarkable range of emotions and references within fourteen lines: nature and nostalgia, eros and geology, elegy and protest.[35]

Touch stubbornly adheres to live flesh and yet, through heat and temperature, it extends its reach; metaphors proliferate. We note in the use of 'woke' one of Owen's favourite techniques: repetition. But we know immediately that this is not actually repetition, for to repeat is not to repeat but to change: here 'woke' changes through panels of time, accretes in meaning from contact and consciousness to germination and genesis. At the level of sound, 'woke' works with 'sun', weaving itself into the rhyme scheme to produce new sound patterns: half-rhymes (sun–sown), assonance (sown–snow), alliteration (know–now), full-rhyme (snow–know). This constant echoing and mirroring is like the aural equivalent of loving contact and mutuality whose denial forms the core of the poem: for these sensuous folds of sound highlight by contrast the cold, unyielding body they contain. Owen circled the following lines in his manuscript, revising them repeatedly:

> Are ~~almost~~
> ~~Yet Are~~ limbs, perfect ~~at last~~, and sides
> ~~And heart still warm it cannot~~
> ~~Almost life-warm~~ ~~too hard~~ to stir ?
> Full-nerved, still-warm too hard[36]

The body contact established through the opening trochee 'move him' is pressed towards a tactual perception and evocation of texture and temperature through acute details (nerves, warm, hard) and linguistic energy; trochee, sibilance, caesura, long vowels are all marshalled in a single line in a final attempt at resuscitation, only to come up against the hardness of 't' and 'r'. The moment is also informed by some of the age-old narratives of animation: of Christ restoring eyesight through touch, of Pygmalion ('clay' brings in this reference) making the statue move, of Sleeping Beauty being kissed to life. The appeal of these legends and the poignancy of the poem lie in the irreducible fact that we have bodies, and our bodies need touch and intimacy in order to grow and develop and enter into meaningful relationships with each other.[37]

Touch, associated with love and care, is also the closest ally of their opposite: pain. Physical pain manifests itself through processes of touch, whether internal or external; in fact, the depth of association between the two can be seen in that both seem to defy language. In *The Body in Pain*, Elaine Scarry argues: 'Whatever pain achieves, it achieves in part through its unsharability, and it ensures this unsharability through its resistance to language.'[38] One of the main ways in which painful touch makes itself evident, manages to communicate its fierce interiority, is through the visual: the image of the wound. Indeed, First World War writings and art are haunted with description of wounds. The genre where it occurs with obsessive frequency is the memoir by the female nurses. Called upon to repair the shattered fragments of the male body away from the battlefields, these women who volunteered in thousands during the war provide some of the most moving accounts of the horrors of war. How can written prose — read from a book kept at arm's length, as opposed to immediate aural or visual stimulus — affect us bodily so that we wince and tighten? Consider the following example, a representative account of the nurses' experience from the final section of Enid Bagnold's *A Diary Without Dates* (1918), which records her nursing experience in the First World War:

> It was all very fine for the theatre people to fill his shoulder chockful of pluggings while he lay unconscious on the table; they had packed it as you might stuff linen into a bag: it was another matter to get it out.
>
> I did not dare touch his hand with that too-easy compassion which I have noticed here, or whisper to him, 'It's nearly over...' as the forceps pulled at the stiffened gauze. It wasn't nearly over.
>
> Six inches deep the gauze stuck, crackling under the pull of the forceps, blood and pus leaping forward from the cavities as the steady hand of the doctor pulled inch after inch of the gauze to the light. And when one hole was emptied there was another, five in all.
>
> Sometimes, when your mind has a grip like iron, your stomach will undo you; sometimes, when you could say 'To-day is Tuesday, the fifth of August,' you faint. There are so many parts of the body to look after, one of the flock may slip your control while you are holding the other by the neck. But Waker had his whole being in his hands, without so much as clenching them.
>
> When we had finished and Sister told me to wipe the sweat on his forehead, I did so reluctantly, as though one were being too exacting in drawing attention to so small a sign.[39]

What makes the above passage so very difficult — almost impossible — to read is the relentless precision of facts without any emotional outlet. What I wish to suggest is that such absence calls for an almost inversely proportional affective response from the reader. At work here is also a complex process of intersensoriality. The scene employs the art of the close-up: the gaze zooms, inch after inch, into the wound, turning the depiction into a relation between sight, touch, and the exposed flesh.

The wound makes external what is ineluctably internal and private: to see the wound is to feel the pain. Bagnold uses a structure of bodily damage and agency to break through the representational crisis and transmit pain. The witnessing body registers the horror through haptic vision as forceps 'pull' out 'stiffened' gauze from the six-inch-deep wounds, five in all. Penetration of Waker's body becomes a penetration of the readers' consciousness, only to leave us, like the nurse, with what Browning called 'the gaping impotence of sympathy'. The five gaping wounds, six inches deep, create a gap in comprehension as the mouth can only silently articulate horror. We experience an emotional vertigo in the act of witnessing, lurching between the twin acts of reaching out and looking away: there is at once a connection and a cut in the imagining. Physical pain obliterates the consciousness of everything apart from its own absolute reality: what about the witness, the young nurse who writes now and whose voice was so thoroughly choked then? As the measured shock of the clinical language passes to the hollow depth of the biblical echo — the five wounds of Christ or Saint Veronica wiping his brow — the two tiny gestures inscribing the self, 'I did not dare' and 'I did so reluctantly', reveal the terrible predicament of the witnessing subject. The unexpected metaphor of the 'flock' foregrounds this by an appeal to the reader: 'Sometimes, when your mind has a grip like iron, your stomach will undo you; [...] There are so many parts of the body to look after, one of the flock may slip your control while you are holding the other by the neck.' Is the nurse here about to faint? However, as we finish the paragraph, the body is reclaimed by Waker, his open fists eluding our grasp: the incommensurability of the body in pain, the unmaking of the world. The nurse as well as the reader is left with a crippling sense of inadequacy. Yet for that moment in the text, the three bodies — Waker's, the nurse-narrator's, and the reader's — are compacted through an act of visceral tightening.

This haptic gaze is realized at a literal, bodily level if we move to a different kind of evidence: trench objects and trench art displayed in war museums or exhibitions. In museums at Ypres or the Somme, or at the Imperial War Museum in London, we come across, along with war diaries and manuscripts, trench artefacts: a bloodstained map of Belgium found on the body of the poet Julian Grenfell, the Military Cross won by Wilfred Owen, the pocket watch of Edward Thomas. The hands of this watch are fixed at 7.36 a.m., a timeless testimony to Thomas's death in an explosion that left no visible marks on his body; a mute companion to the last, the clock had faithfully recorded the moment when its master's heart stopped beating.[40] Equally fascinating is the category of trench art: vases, model windmills, crucifix, ashtrays, and penknives that the soldiers made in trenches, in hospitals, or at home while on leave, out of shells, cartridges, and trench debris.[41] They are an astonishing array of objects, at once poignant and ironic in the way bullets and artillery shells — agents of destruction — are domesticated and imaginatively reconfigured into art with a physical link to the world of the trenches. These objects challenge our taxonomies of art, conflating meaning, memory, and materiality.

Why do these objects move and disturb us so much? They not only congeal time but also conceal processes of touch. The British Museum Reading Room ticket of Brooke, the pocket watch of Thomas, or the clock made from an exploded artillery-shell case evoke the body of the user or the maker, traces of hands, hidden but palpable.[42] Like the manuscripts that we examined, these objects have a precious, living quality, for they are the archives of touch and intimacy — the touch and use of their possessors in their early youths or in the trenches. But unlike manuscripts, such objects, preserved and exhibited behind glass-panels, cannot be touched: in museums, the thrill of touch is replaced, as Stewart has argued, by the proximity of our gaze. Our intent gaze is a ritual of curiosity and restraint. Many of these items are minute. We have to look at very close proximity, bringing the haptic within the visual: our fantasized touching of these objects constitutes the language of communication.

The understanding and appreciation of First World War art takes us well beyond the confines of academic interest into the area of evocation and affect: it also takes us into the etymological roots of the word 'aesthetics' ('aisthetikos': 'things perceptible by the senses'). The most intimate and immediate of the senses, touch can lead us directly into the processes of cognition and appreciation. A language across disciplines alerts us to the complex processes of translation in the processes of sensory perception, and helps us to discover shared impulses of pleasure before the narrowly specialized vocabulary of each discipline sets in. Mutual and non-teleological, forever roving and open-ended, touch can help us to understand art not as distant objects, fixed in time and place, but rather as a process of ongoing mutuality, a relationship that allows us to plunge once more, without embarrassment but with self-awareness, into the spell of the sensuous.

Notes to Chapter 15

Parts of this chapter were incorporated and expanded upon in my monograph *Touch and Intimacy in First World War Literature* (Cambridge: Cambridge University Press, 2005).

I gratefully acknowledge the Imperial War Museum, London, and its staff for their help and for permission to use some of their documents, photographs and sketches; and the copyright holders of private collections of letters kept at the IWM. Every effort has been made to trace copyright holders, and the author and the Imperial War Museum would be grateful for any information which might help to trace those whose identities or addresses are not currently known.

1. Denis Diderot, 'Letter on the Blind for the Use of Those Who See', trans. by M. Jourdain, in *Denis Diderot: Thoughts on the Interpretation of Nature and Other Philosophical Works*, ed. by David Adams (Manchester: Clinamen Press, 1999), pp. 147–200 (p. 153); also see Jacques Derrida's suggestive exploration of blindness in painting in *Memoirs of the Blind: The Self-Portrait and Other Ruins*, trans. by Pascale-Anne Brault and Michael Naas (Chicago: University of Chicago Press, 1993).
2. Gillian Beer notes, 'The hand is the most conscious, and at the same time the most intimate, point of contact between the individual and the surrounding world', 'Four Bodies on the Beagle: Touch, Sight, and Writing in a Darwin Letter', in *Textuality and Sexuality: Reading Theories and Practices*, ed. by Judith Still and Michael Worton (Manchester: Manchester University Press, 1993), pp. 116–32 (pp. 116–17). Some major works to address the issue of touch and human

subjectivity are Maurice Merleau-Ponty, *Phenomenology of Perception*, trans. by Colin Smith (London: Routledge, 1962); Ashley Montagu, *Touching: The Human Significance of the Skin* (New York: Columbia University Press, 1971); Didier Anzieu, *The Skin Ego*, trans. by Chris Turner (New Haven: Yale University Press, 1989); Ruth Finnegan, *Communicating* (London: Routledge, 2002). For the role of touch in aesthetic appreciation, see Gabriel Josipovici, *Touch* (New Haven: Yale University Press, 1996); Mieke Bal, *Quoting Caravaggio: Contemporary Art, Preposterous History* (Chicago: University of Chicago Press, 1999); Susan Stewart, *Poetry and the Fate of the Senses* (Chicago: University of Chicago Press, 2002).

3. Sigmund Freud, 'Infantile Sexuality', *The Standard Edition of the Complete Psychological Works*, trans. and ed. by James Strachey, 24 vols (London: Hogarth Press, 1953–74), VII (1953), 181–82; Julia Kristeva, *Powers of Horror: An Essay on Abjection*, trans. by Leon S. Roudiez (New York: Columbia University Press, 1982).
4. Aristotle, 'De anima', *The Basic Works of Aristotle*, ed. by Richard McKeon (New York: Random House, 1941), pp. 535–603; Horace, *Satires, Epistles, Ars Poetica*, trans. by H. Rushton Fairclough (Cambridge, MA: Harvard University Press, 1991), p. 472; Walter Pater, 'Winckelmann', in *The Renaissance: Studies in Art and Poetry*, rev. 2nd edn (London: Macmillan, 1877), pp. 177–232 (p. 222); see also Condillac, 'A Treatise on the Sensations', trans. by Franklin Philip in collaboration with Harlan Lane, in *Philosophical Writings of Étienne Bonnot, Abbé de Condillac*, 2 vols (Hillsdale, NY: Erlbaum, 1982–87), I, 155–339.
5. See Beer, 'Four Bodies', pp. 116–17; Stewart, *Poetry and the Fate of the Senses*, p. 161.
6. Aristotle, 'De anima': 'Whatever can be said of what is tangible, can be said of touch, and vice versa; if touch is not a single sense but a group of senses, there must be several kinds of what is tangible' (577). And again, 'Touch, indeed, discriminates more than one set of different qualities' (567). Mieke Bal emphasized the idea of 'translation' at the 2003 conference New Languages for Criticism.
7. Wilfred Owen, *Collected Letters*, ed. by Harold Owen and John Bell (London: Oxford University Press, 1967), p. 429; hereafter *CL*.
8. *CL*, p. 581.
9. See Martin Heidegger, *Parmenides*, trans. by Andre Schuwer and Richard Rojcewicz (Bloomington: Indiana University Press, 1992), pp. 81–82; see also Friedrich A. Kittler, *Discourse Networks 1800/1900*, trans. by Michael Metteer with Chris Cullens (Stanford: Stanford University Press, 1990).
10. 'The Fall of Hyperion: A Vision', in *John Keats: The Poems*, ed. by David Bromwich (London: Everyman's Library, 1992), p. 351.
11. H. Gladstone, 'Diary', Imperial War Museum (henceforth IWM), 86/2/1.
12. G. W. Hayman, 'Papers', IWM, 87/51/1.
13. G. H. Bennett, 'First World War Papers', IWM, Miscellaneous 12, Item 265.
14. The letter is quoted by Evan Charteris in his biography, *John Sargent* (London: Heinemann, 1927), p. 214.
15. John Berger and others, *Ways of Seeing* (London: BBC and Harmondsworth: Penguin Books, 1972), p. 90.
16. Alois Riegl, *Late Roman Art Industry* (1927), trans. by Rolf Winkes (1927; Rome: Bretschneider, 1985). Riegl writes in passionate detail about the the haptic quality of Egyptian art, which 'maintained as far as possible the appearance of a unified, isolated object adhering to the plane', as opposed to the optical, illusionist style of late Roman art in which objects relinquished a tactile connection to the plane. Also see Laura U. Marks, *Touch: Sensuous Theory and Multisensory Media* (Minneapolis: Minnesota University Press, 2002), pp. 4–5.
17. Virginia Woolf, 'The Royal Academy', *The Essays of Virginia Woolf*, ed. by Andrew McNeillie (London: Hogarth Press, 1986–), III: *1919–1924* (1988), pp. 89–94 (pp. 92–93). See also Charteris, *John Sargent*, pp. 213–16; Richard Cork, *A Bitter Truth: Avant-Garde Art and the Great War* (New Haven: Yale University Press, 1994), pp. 219–22.
18. *Wilfred Owen: Complete Poems & Fragments* (henceforth *CP&F*), ed. by Jon Stallworthy (Oxford: Oxford University Press, 1983), p. 140.
19. Ibid.
20. Reuven Tsur, *What Makes Sound Patterns Expressive? The Poetic Mode of Speech Perception* (Durham, NC, and London: Duke University Press, 1992).

21. Paul Fussell, *Poetic Meter and Poetic Form* (New York: Random House, 1966), p. 5.
22. Freud, 'Infantile Sexuality', p. 203.
23. See Santanu Das, '"Kiss me, Hardy": Intimacy, Gender, and Gesture in First World War Trench Literature', *Modernism/Modernity*, 9.1 (January 2002), 51–74 (p. 66).
24. In the letter to his mother Susan Owen describing the poem, he writes: 'The famous Latin tag [from Horace, *Odes*, III.ii.13] means of course It is sweet and meet to die for one's country. Sweet! And decorous!', *CL*, pp. 499–500.
25. *CP&F*, pp. 166, 165, 169, 178, 140, 123.
26. Ibid., p. 192.
27. Joanna Bourke, *Dismembering the Male: Men's Bodies, Britain and the Great War* (London: Reaktion Books, 1996), pp. 133–36.
28. Miss D. Williams, 'Papers', IWM, 85/4/1.
29. C. H. Cox, 'A Few Experiences of the First World War', IWM, 88/11/1.
30. Raymond Heywood,'My Pal', H .L. Simpson, 'Two Nights', A. Newberry Choyce, 'A May Morning', all quoted in *Lads: Love Poetry of the Trenches*, ed. by Martin Taylor (London: Duckworth, 1989), pp. 95, 109, 96.
31. Brooke, 'Fragment', in *The Collected Poems* (1929) (London: Papermac, 1987), p. 318; Sassoon, 'The Last Meeting', typescript, Cambridge University Library, Add. 7973, S51–end; Nichols, 'Casualty', in *Aurelia and Other Poems* (London: Chatto & Windus, 1920), p. 75.
32. Siegfried Sassoon, *Diaries 1915–1918*, ed. by Rupert Hart-Davis (London: Faber, 1983), pp. 44–45.
33. Roland Barthes, *A Lover's Discourse*, trans. by Richard Howard (1978; Harmondsworth: Penguin Books, 1990), p. 73.
34. *CP&F*, p. 158.
35. In a letter to his brother Harold, Owen mentions the 'brown scarf of sunshine' (*CL*, p. 407), a phrase that weaves itself into a rough draft of 'Disabled' ('scarfed with a sun-burn hand', *CP&F*, p. 353).
36. *CP&F*, p. **319**.
37. Also see Stewart, *Poetry and the Fate of the Senses*, pp. 165–70, for an exploration of some of these myths through the senses.
38. Elaine Scarry, *The Body in Pain: The Making and Unmaking of the World* (Oxford: Oxford University Press, 1985), p. 4.
39. Enid Bagnold, *A Diary Without Dates* (1918) (London: Virago, 1979), pp. 122–23.
40. These were exhibited in the Imperial War Museum exhibition 'Anthem for Doomed Youth: Twelve Soldier-Poets', held in September 2002. The exhibition had echoes of what Stephen Greenblatt has called the 'museum of resonance' in his influential essay, 'Resonance and Wonder', in *Learning to Curse: Essays in Early Modern Culture* (New York: Routledge, 1990), pp. 161–83. See also *Material Memories: Design and Evocation*, ed. by Marius Kwint, Christopher Breward, and Jeremy Aynsley (Oxford: Berg, 1999).
41. Nicholas Saunders, *Trench Art: A Brief History and Guide* (Barnsley: Leo Cooper, 2001).
42. Susan Stewart powerfully analyses our charged relation to museum objects in her chapter 'Facing, Touch and Vertigo' (pp. 145–85) in *Poetry and the Fate of the Senses* where she writes about 'the constant play among deixis, tact, proximity, and negation that is at work in the sensual creation and apprehension of all aesthetic forms' (p. 175).

CHAPTER 16

Snapshots from the Hereafter: Benjamin, Adorno, and the Critic as Photographer

Carolin Duttlinger

Photography is a recurrent and complex theme in the writings of Walter Benjamin and Theodor W. Adorno. Benjamin's work on the technical media and their impact on traditional art has been subjected to extensive critical scrutiny; while Adorno's critique of the culture industry has been equally well analysed, his particular engagement with photography has been somewhat overlooked.[1] Indeed, unlike Benjamin, Adorno is less concerned with the medium's cultural and historical dimensions than with its more abstract capacities as a metaphor for critical inquiry. As I shall demonstrate here, Adorno's particular angle on photography picks up and expands on a theme that is already present in Benjamin's writings: the notion of the critic as photographer. In this chapter, I shall illustrate how Benjamin's and Adorno's engagement with photography and criticism develops over the course of their extensive dialogue about the medium and its function within discourses of (literary) criticism and (political) critique. The ramifications of this exchange within their writings are multifaceted, subtle, and complex, and continue to have an impact on Adorno's work long after Benjamin's death in 1940. Indeed, although their reflections on the medium are firmly rooted in their specific historical-cultural context — the rise of Nazism, the experience of exile, and the question of the role of criticism in times of personal and political crisis — their engagement with photography as a model for criticism continues to hold relevance for questions of critical practice and methodology.

While Benjamin and Adorno treat photography as the subject of cultural or technological inquiry, they also adopt it as an epistemological paradigm which both symbolizes and shapes the critic's understanding of reality. Contrary to common conceptions of photography as an objective, unmediated form of representation, both writers deny the medium such immediacy, emphasizing instead its capacity for alienation, distortion, and fragmentation. They propose that photography can be mobilized to challenge not only conventional notions of representation but also, by extension, the social status quo. In this respect, it can serve to counter uncritical, and thus ideologically stabilizing, perspectives on reality.

To start with, I shall explore Benjamin's and Adorno's uses of photography as a paradigm of literary representation in their discussion of the works of Franz Kafka. They develop the notion of the writer Kafka as a 'photographer', and of the camera as a perspectival device which allows the translation of experience into the written text. For Benjamin, the interrelations between Kafka and photography also acquires a personal, identificatory dimension which becomes clear in his childhood memoirs. The ability of photography to mediate between criticism and autobiography is taken up by Adorno in his notion of the critic as photographer, a model which underpins both thinkers' writings on history and philosophy. In all of the above contexts, photography encapsulates a critical stance characterized by a mixture of distance and proximity, objectivity and distortion, intellectual detachment and personal involvement.

Reading Photography

A studio portrait of the writer Franz Kafka as a child taken around 1887 (Figure 16.1) assumes a particular role in Benjamin's critical as well as his personal, autobiographical writings. Benjamin discusses this image not only in his essay 'Franz Kafka: On the Tenth Anniversary of his Death' (1934) but also in two other texts: the essay 'Little History of Photography' (1931) and his childhood memoirs, *Berlin Childhood around 1900* (1932–38).[2] Benjamin's engagement with the photograph thus forms a point of convergence between his literary, media-historical, and autobiographical projects of the 1930s, illustrating his persistent concern with questions of selfhood in relation to wider technological and socio-historical developments. The recurrence of the Kafka photograph in Benjamin's autobiography suggests moreover that his theoretical interests at the time had a profoundly personal dimension as his role as an intellectual and his existence more generally were thrown into crisis.

At first sight, Benjamin's strategy of discussing a childhood photograph of the writer seems a rather peculiar move, given his otherwise text-based, non-biographical approach to Kafka's work. That said, Benjamin's account of the picture does not follow the conventions of a biographical or psychoanalytic reading; instead, he constructs the picture as a visual equivalent to Kafka's texts, a tableau which exemplifies and condenses central aspects of his writings. What is more, the fact that Benjamin explores the image in both the 'Kafka' and 'Photography' essays suggests that it holds some intrinsic significance not only for Kafka's texts but also for the history of photography and of the late nineteenth century more generally.[3] By reusing the same example in both essays, Benjamin suggests that developments in the fields of literature and photography should not be considered as unrelated but have to be seen in their interrelation, in their common rootedness in a cultural context which they reflect and — potentially — challenge or expose. For Benjamin, the nineteenth-century bourgeois photographic portrait acts both as the predecessor of twentieth-century mass culture and as its diametrical, pre-modern, opposite.

Benjamin seems at first to offer little more than a detailed, although highly evocative, description of the photograph. His account, however, establishes a dialectical relationship between the image and Kafka's texts:

Figure 16.1. Photograph of Franz Kafka, *c.* 1887.
Courtesy of Archiv Klaus Wagenbach, Berlin

> There is a childhood picture of Kafka; rarely has 'poor, brief childhood' been made into an image in a more touching way. It was probably made in one of those nineteenth-century studios whose draperies and palm trees, tapestries and easels, placed them somewhere between a torture chamber and a throne room. At the age of about six, the boy presents himself in a sort of winter garden landscape, wearing a tight, heavily lace-trimmed, almost embarrassing child's suit. Palm branches loom in the background. And as if to make these upholstered tropics still more sultry and sticky, the subject holds in his left hand an oversized, wide-brimmed hat of the type worn by Spaniards. Immeasurably sad eyes reign over the landscape which is predestined to them and into which the shell of a large ear is listening. (BG II.2, 416 / BE II, 800; translation amended)

The phrase 'poor, brief childhood' (*arme kurze Kindheit*) with which Benjamin introduces his account of the photograph is taken from Kafka's short story 'Josefine, the Singer or the Mouse People' (1924), and acts as a kind of caption for the picture. Benjamin's notion that this formulation has been 'made into' a photograph suggests an inherent, paradoxical link between Kafka's last completed prose work and a portrait taken over thirty-five years earlier. Text and image exist in a mutual, albeit indeterminate, relationship. This correlation concerns not only the photograph's content but also the mode of its technological production: in its extreme brevity, Kafka's literary conception of childhood mirrors the act of photographic recording, which entails the arrest of temporal continuity into a static, atemporal image. In his description, moreover, Benjamin constructs the photograph as an allegory of Kafka's texts which reflects their underlying concerns on both an individual, psychological and a socio-historical level.

What, then, are the characteristics of this photographic childhood that Benjamin detects in Kafka's image? The photograph's touching (*ergreifend*) character stems from the boy's palpable alienation from the studio context. The child Kafka seems lost among the draperies, palm trees, tapestries, and easels that surround him, an effect which is increased by his stuffy ornate suit and large Spanish hat. In its pompous eclecticism, the studio resembles a stage set where the sitter is not the protagonist but merely another decorative prop.[4] Some elements of the picture, however, counter the impersonality of this scenario. Benjamin singles out the boy's large ear and 'immeasurably sad eyes' whose size and uncontainable, excessive melancholy disrupt the picture's carefully staged set-up.[5] Despite his forceful insertion into the studio context, the child is not merely the deaf and blind object of the viewer's gaze but maintains a degree of agency as the perceptive observer of his surroundings.

Benjamin's emphasis on Kafka's melancholic gaze gains a particular significance against the backdrop of his study *The Origin of German Tragic Drama* (1925), in which he describes melancholy as the emotional disposition characteristic of German Baroque drama. He argues that this literary genre embodies a melancholic gaze which has a mortifying effect on the perceived sights, draining them of any inherent life and thereby transforming them into dead objects ready for aesthetic appropriation: 'When the object becomes allegorical under the melancholic gaze, when it is drained of life and transformed into something dead preserved for eternity, then it lies in front of the allegorical writer, at his disposal for better or for worse' (BG I.1, 359). The melancholic's mortifying gaze entails the fixation of the perceived reality and its transformation into a static tableau — a process which bears a striking resemblance to the act of photographic recording.[6] Indeed, Kafka's 'immeasurably sad eyes' are assigned a similar photographic capacity within Benjamin's writings. Alienated from the photographic scenario, Kafka becomes in turn the melancholic photographer of the studio environment — and, one might add, of his socio-cultural context more generally. Despite his exposure to the mechanical gaze, Kafka appears as an active, perceptive observer whose eyes 'reign over the landscape which is predestined to them' (BG II.2, 416 / BE II, 800; translation amended). The boy's gaze is at once a reflection of the restrictive social conventions and expectations embodied in the bourgeois portrait and the means by which he establishes his future mastery as a writer, a mastery over a reality from which he is simultaneously alienated and to whose power structures he is subjected.

In his discussion of Kafka's childhood portrait, Benjamin first articulates the notion of the writer as photographer, a theme which will permeate both his and Adorno's writings. Subsequently, this photographic perspective also comes to be associated with that of the critic and thus gain an identificatory function for both thinkers.

In a letter of 17 December 1934, Adorno first gestures towards this figurative equivalence of photography and criticism in his response to the manuscript of Benjamin's essay. From the very start, Adorno singles out Benjamin's exploration of photography as evidence of a 'correlation in the philosophical centres' of their respective critical approaches.[7] To illustrate this claim, Adorno develops his own interpretation of Kafka in the light of photography:

> May I present you my earliest, nine-year-old attempt at interpreting Kafka: that he was a photograph of worldly life taken from the perspective of the redeemed, of which nothing is visible in the picture but the corner of the black cloth, while the horribly distorted optic of the image is no other than that of the obliquely positioned camera itself.[8]

In this quasi-theological scenario, Adorno uses photography as a figure for the seemingly familiar but deeply disturbing and alienating character of Kafka's texts. Despite its 'redeemed', transcendental position, this 'obliquely positioned camera' does not provide a corrective, harmonizing perspective but instead produces only a radically, even horribly, distorted image of the world. This sight, which indicates the irreducible difference between the perspectives of the immanent and the transcendental, has its correlative in a physical flaw of the resulting image: the corner of the photographer's cloth, which is visible in the photograph and which acts as a material trace of the conditions of its production.

Central to Adorno's model of the writer as photographer is the mixture of distance and proximity that characterizes the photographic gaze. On the one hand, Kafka the photographer is radically detached from the recorded scene through his 'redeemed', elevated position, a spatial (and existential) distance which is enforced by the mode of recording; the camera acts as a mediating device, a mechanical barrier between viewer and reality. On the other hand, the camera also negates any sense of distance, bringing the viewer into — often unsettling — proximity to the recorded scene. Benjamin comments on this effect of photography to reveal the 'optical unconscious' of reality, that is, to expose unknown and alienating perspectives, details or microstructures (BG II.I, 371). The photographic gaze is at once telescopic and microscopic, and in both capacities it alienates the viewer from the recorded reality. It is in this respect that the camera can acquire a critical, political function in that it shatters any ideologically constructed image of reality as an orderly, coherent entity, exposing underlying rifts, hierarchies, and power structures.[9]

Fairy-Tale Snapshots: The Photography of Memory

Benjamin's engagement with the Kafka photograph is not limited to his theoretical writing. In the winter of 1932–33, he pursued a very different project in which he again turned to this particular image: his childhood memoirs *Berlin Childhood around 1900*. Among anecdotal accounts of places, objects, and individuals that shaped the narrator's upbringing, the text contains a section in which Benjamin recounts how he had his picture taken as a child. His account portrays this experience as disconcerting and alienating, thus echoing the sentiment that he elsewhere discerns in Kafka's portrait. What is more, Benjamin even inserts the description of this particular image into his memoirs, appropriating it as one of his own childhood photographs. To start with, the adult narrator describes the existing photograph, commenting on the saddening gaze 'which penetrates me from the child's face lying in the shadow of an indoor palm tree'. In the following, more detailed description, however, he switches to a first-person narrative account of the actual recording, thus putting himself in the place of the young Kafka:

> I am standing there bareheaded, my left hand holding a giant sombrero which I dangle with studied grace. My right hand is occupied with a walking stick, whose curved handle can be seen in the foreground while its tip remains hidden in a cluster of ostrich feathers spilling from a garden table. (BG IV.I, 261 / BE III, 392)

This passage closely resembles the description in Benjamin's essay on Kafka, providing an even more detailed account of the photographic set-up. In the course of his repeated engagement with Kafka's portrait, it appears to have acquired a highly personal significance, allowing him to recognize his own childhood experiences in the image of another Jewish writer of bourgeois origins.

The implications of Benjamin's act of imposture for his understanding of Kafka and for his autobiography are manifold and cannot be pursued here in full. Suffice it to say that Benjamin, owing to his persecution during the Nazi era, was acutely aware of the use of the photographic medium for purposes of identification and surveillance.[10] The winter of 1932–33, when *A Berlin Childhood* was mostly composed, marked the onset of Nazism, and after completing the first version Benjamin went into exile in Paris. His childhood memoirs are thus the account of an era whose very foundations were being destroyed at the time he was writing. Given his own subjection to the racial politics of the Third Reich, Benjamin's move to replace his own photograph with that of Kafka moreover forms part of a general strategy which underpins his memoirs: the deletion of identifiable physiognomic features from the text.[11] In this respect, Benjamin's identification with Kafka also has a second, both personal and symbolic significance, as it marks the melancholic adoption of a face which has already been erased, the identification with the fellow Jew and writer who has already gone to his death.

The symbolic equivalence which Benjamin perceived between his own position and that of the young Kafka would later be tacitly repeated by Adorno. In an afterword written for the first publication of *A Berlin Childhood* in book form (1950), Adorno returns to his notion of the writer as photographer of reality, this time in relation to Benjamin rather than Kafka:

> The fairy-tale photographs of 'A Berlin Childhood' — they are not only debris seen from the bird's-eye perspective of the long-past life but also snapshots taken from this lofty state, recorded by the aeronaut who moves [*bewegte*] his models to stand amicably still. (AG 20.1, 172)

Adorno's reading of the memoirs is underpinned by a series of contrasts between the modern and the archaic, past and present, stasis and movement. The genre of the fairy tale situates the recorded images within an idyllic past, a notion that contrasts with the technological mode of their recording. This mixture of tradition and modernity is echoed in the notion of the photographer as 'aeronaut', a term which was used as early as the eighteenth century in relation to hot-air balloons[12] but which also alludes to the modern technology of aerial photography. The reference to the fairy-tale photographs taken from the aeronaut's lofty position invests the photographs with a light-hearted character which is, however, countered by their association with the 'debris' of the past. The photographer relates to his subject matter with a mixture of proximity and distance, through a process of recollection that detaches him from the experiences he so vividly describes. This past is remembered in a discontinuous, fragmentary way reminiscent of Benjamin's writings on allegory and melancholy. Through their episodic structure, Benjamin's memoirs resemble an album of self-contained snapshots in which the vividness of the individual images is the expression of the writer's melancholic recollection, the photographic arrest of the images of his past.

As in the case of Benjamin's 'Kafka' essay, Adorno again brings out the implicit photographic model that underlies Benjamin's writing. By returning to the image of the writer as photographer, Adorno establishes a link between Benjamin's memoirs and his critical engagement with Kafka, suggesting that both writer and critic pursue their subject in a similar manner. However, while the photographer Kafka looks down on earth from the perspective of redemption, the aeronaut Benjamin is only provisionally suspended from the recorded scene in his hot-air balloon, an antiquated vehicle whose fragility is evident when contrasted with the modern aerial technologies of transport and warfare. The precarious position of their photographer makes the idyllic fairy-tale 'images' of *A Berlin Childhood* into the harbingers of terror and destruction.

In the following section I shall turn to another manifestation of the theme of the critic as photographer which, once again, underpins both Benjamin's and Adorno's works. Here, the paradigm of photography becomes associated with more general epistemological, methodological, and political questions about the role of criticism and the possibility of (historical) knowledge. What underlies the approach of both thinkers is the function of criticism in times of political and personal crisis.

Redeemed Perspectives?

Alongside his literary and autobiographical writings, Benjamin was occupied, in the last decade of his life, with the so-called *Arcades Project*, an exploration of nineteenth-century culture from a materialist historical perspective. In his last essay, 'On the Concept of History' (1940), which acts as a theoretical backdrop to this study, Benjamin reconsiders photography as a model for critical analysis. In his notes he writes:

> The tradition [*Überlieferung*] of bourgeois society can be compared to a camera. The bourgeois critic looks into it just like the layman who enjoys the colourful images viewed through the aperture. The materialist dialectician operates with it. His aim is to arrest [*festzustellen*, also 'to state']. He might focus on a larger or a smaller section, might choose a brighter political or a more subdued historical lighting — in the end, he presses the button and takes the picture. (BG I.3, 1164–65)

The photographic medium enables the dialectical historian to highlight and to emphasize certain aspects of the recorded events. Instead of merely using the camera as a perspectival device, he 'operates' with it and adopts a more selective stance towards the recorded reality. Most importantly, Benjamin discards the notion of history as a continuous, teleological entity — the colourful images seen by the bourgeois historian who does not press the button — in favour of a conception of history as a series of unrelated snapshots determined by the viewer's critical perspective. Photography thus acts not as a direct depiction of the past but rather as a model for the process of transmitting historical knowledge (*Überlieferung*).

This photographic model of historical analysis also underpins the essay itself. 'On the Concept of History' not only takes up the notion of history as a series of discontinuous snapshots, but also bears a close affinity to Benjamin's critical engagement with the Kafka photograph. Once again, he uses an image to illustrate his theoretical argument, and even though this picture is not a photograph, his argument returns to notions of fragmentation, mortification, and arrest which already inform his engagement with the Kafka portrait.

Central to Benjamin's argument is the notion that the past cannot be perceived or analysed as a continuous entity but has to be approached as a series of isolated and shock-like 'constellations' determined by the observer's present perspective and situation (BG I.2, 703 / BE IV, 396). This conception becomes particularly apparent in the famous ninth thesis about the 'Angel of History', a figure which encapsulates Benjamin's concept of history as well as of the role of the materialist historian. His account is inspired by Paul Klee's watercolour *Angelus Novus*, a picture that he owned alongside a copy of Kafka's childhood photograph.[13] The close link between the two images is reflected not only in their ownership but also in Benjamin's respective textual accounts: while his description of the photograph in the 'Kafka' essay reads 'There is a childhood picture of Kafka' (BG II.2, 416 / BE II, 800), the account of the painting opens with the sentence, 'There is a picture by Klee called *Angelus Novus*' (BG I.2, 697 / BE IV, 392). In both cases, Benjamin uses the non-specific term *Bild*, a strategy which distracts from their particular representational nature. This generalizing tendency is amplified by the parallel formulation 'There is' which lends a sense of vagueness and uncertainty about the spatial and ontological status of the images.

Indeed, the parallels between the two passages also extend to the details of Benjamin's description. In 'On the Concept of History' he writes: '[The picture] shows an angel who looks as if he were about to move away from something he is staring at. His eyes are gaping, his mouth is open, and his wings are spread' (BG I.2, 697 / BE IV, 392; translation amended). As in his earlier account of Kafka's 'immeasurably sad eyes', Benjamin puts particular emphasis on the Angel's wide-open eyes; while, in the photograph, the boy's eyes correspond to his large ear, here this correlation recurs in the sight of the Angel's open mouth. Indeed, the gaze of Klee's Angel, like that of the child Kafka, has the mortifying effect of melancholy, transforming history into a tableau of destruction: 'Where *we* perceive a chain of events, *he* sees one single catastrophe which perpetually heaps debris upon debris' (BG I.2, 697 / BE IV, 392; translation amended).

If the child Kafka thus acts as Benjamin's melancholic alter ego in his memoirs, then the Angel of History with his arresting gaze appears as an embodiment of the historian as photographer. Both adopt the kind of reifying perspective which freezes reality into one catastrophic tableau. As a model for critical practice, however, the Angel — like the child Kafka — is deeply ambiguous: despite the arresting force of his gaze, he is ultimately merely the passive observer of the catastrophes of history, unable to intervene in its endless chain of destruction:

> The angel would like to stay, awaken the dead, and make whole what has been broken to pieces. But a storm is blowing from Paradise and has got caught in his wings; it is so strong that the angel can no longer close them. This storm drives him irresistibly into the future, to which his back is turned, while the pile of debris in front of him grows toward the sky. What we call progress is *this* storm. (BG I.2, 697–98 / BE IV, 392–93)

The above passage exemplifies both the extreme consequences and the ultimate impasse of Benjamin's concept of the critic as photographer. The backward-directed gaze of the Angel perceives history as a static tableau of perpetual destruction which leaves no space for an alternative, positive projection of the future. This photographic conception of the past eclipses the possibility of an emancipatory vision essential for constructive criticism and political resistance. On a personal level, the melancholic fatalism expressed in this passage provides an acute image of Benjamin's desperate circumstances at the time which would lead to his suicide in September 1940.

As in the previous cases, Benjamin's photographic conception of criticism is again echoed by Adorno. Several years after Benjamin's death, Adorno once more takes up this model in his essay collection *Minima Moralia: Reflections from Damaged Life*, written in 1944–47 during his exile in the USA. As in Benjamin's 'On the Concept of History', the photographic paradigm is not made explicit but becomes clear within the trajectory of Benjamin's and Adorno's dialogue on the topic, in this case harking back to their exchange about Kafka.

Minima Moralia can be described as a series of philosophical snapshots; short pieces on literature, music, and philosophy alternate with observations about modern life and popular culture. Like Benjamin's late projects, the collection is informed by a discernible resistance to argumentative coherence and a movement towards brevity and fragmentation. In *Minima Moralia*, the theme of a 'damaged life' overshadowed by Nazism as well as by the de-individualizing effects of capitalist mass culture is illuminated from a variety of different perspectives and reflected in its argumentative structure which prevents a teleological, coherent argument. In the final text, Adorno reflects on this form of writing in a piece on the role of 'philosophy [...] in the face of desperation'.[14] His argument echoes a much earlier remark: his notion of Kafka the photographer, which he had developed over fifteen years earlier. As Adorno writes in *Minima Moralia*, philosophy in times of crisis

> would be the attempt to view all things as they present themselves from the perspective of redemption. Realization has no light but the one which shines onto the world from the direction of redemption [...]. Perspectives must be constructed which displace and estrange the world, exposing it, with its rifts and crevices, as impoverished and disfigured as it will appear one day in the messianic light.[15]

The critical perspective described in this passage mirrors Adorno's earlier comment on Kafka as a photographer who records worldly life from the perspective of redemption. Once again, this vision is characterized by distortion and displacement, thus recalling Kafka's obliquely positioned camera. As in the case of Benjamin's Angel of History, the snapshots of reality recorded by the critic 'in the face of desperation' have nothing in common with the false harmony and synthesis projected by political ideology: they expose instead the rifts and crevices of modern society. The critic operating with his camera produces an objective picture by remaining true to the underlying, infernal state of society, even if these images seem alienating and distorting to the eyes of the uninitiated viewer.

As Adorno comments, the adoption of such a perspective is essentially a simple task. It merely requires a reversal of the existing categories, the transformation of the negative into the positive photograph. At the same time, however, such an image is impossible to record, because it requires a standpoint which is detached from worldly life while simultaneously being 'struck by the same disfigurement and impoverishment from which it strives to escape'.[16] In a movement that begins with the notion of Benjamin as the endangered aeronautic photographer of his childhood, Adorno comes to problematize the notion of critical detachment which he had earlier constructed as the basis of both Kafka's literary oeuvre and Benjamin's memoirs. The photographic paradigm now comes to symbolize the impossibility of such a critical perspective and remains at best an imaginary supplement for the critic's flawed, insufficient faculties in the age of instrumentalized reason.

In Benjamin's and Adorno's works, the photographic paradigm becomes a model for criticism which engages with its object through a mixture of proximity and detachment. The camera mediates between the critic and his or her object of analysis, putting into focus certain configurations but also distancing the viewer from the recorded sights. If the camera thus provides a model for criticism, it also acts as its prosthesis and even as a shield which protects the critic from the traumatic engagement with reality — a shield, however, which repeatedly collapses, exposing the precarious condition of criticism in times of political crisis. This is particularly clear in the case of Benjamin's Angel of History, whose gaze becomes the signature of trauma, of the critic's inability to escape the harrowing conditions which underlie his enterprise. Adorno, in turn, constructs a provisional alternative to this stance, a perspective which illuminates the flaws of the existing world from the detached viewpoint of a better one. Ultimately, however, the prospect of an alternative perspective in *Minima Moralia* is thwarted by the same problem as that which besets Benjamin's melancholic photographer: the realization that such a detached outlook would be an evasive and ultimately impossible move in the face of political adversity.

At the same time, however, the camera is a tool which reveals the critic's own determination by his historical, political, and personal circumstances. Ultimately, the camera of criticism works both ways: directed at the outside world, it also offers an image of the photographer who looks through its aperture, exposing the resulting image and its distortions as a reflection of his gaze. Just as Benjamin recognizes his personal experiences in the photograph of the young Kafka, both his and Adorno's texts act as snapshots of their authors' own perspectives and predicaments.

Notes to Chapter 16

1. On Benjamin, see for example Eduardo Cadava, *Words of Light: Theses on the Photography of History* (Princeton: Princeton University Press, 1997); on Adorno, see Heinz Steinert, *Culture Industry*, trans. by Sally-Ann Spencer (Cambridge: Polity Press, 2003).
2. References to Benjamin's works will be given to both the German original and — where applicable — the English Harvard edition. References to the *Gesammelte Schriften*, ed. by Rolf Tiedemann and Hermann Schweppenhäuser, 7 vols, paperback edn (Frankfurt a.M.: Suhrkamp, 1991), will be abbreviated BG; references to the English translations in the *Selected Writings*, ed. by Michael W. Jennings, 4 vols (Cambridge, MA, and London: Belknap Press/Harvard University Press, 1996–2003), will be abbreviated BE.
3. For a comparison between the two passages, see BG II.1, 375 / BE II, 515 and BG II.2, 416 / BE II, 800.
4. This reifying effect also entails an uncanny reversal of animate and inanimate elements; not only is the child exposed to the gaze of the camera, but this tendency is also echoed in the phrase 'palm branches loom in the background' (BG II.2, 416 / BE II, 800), with the German verb *starren* meaning both to stare and to be stiff: the surrounding objects are invested with an unsettling perceptual agency which heightens the overall sense of reifying exposure.
5. On Benjamin's discourse on the body and the role of seeing and hearing in his autobiographical writings, see Gerhard Richter, *Walter Benjamin and the Corpus of Autobiography*, Kritik: German Literary Theory and Cultural Studies (Detroit: Wayne State University Press, 2000). As Gabriel Josipovici notes, Benjamin's account 'brings out clearly [...] the horror of being looked at which was such an important element in Kafka's character'. *The Lessons of Modernity* (Basingstoke: Macmillan, 1987), p. 4.

6. Indeed, Hubertus von Amelunxen argues that Benjamin's study on German Baroque drama 'comes closer to the essence of photography than those of his writings which explicitly deal with the technical media'; 'Skiagraphia — Silberchlorid und schwarze Galle: Zur allegorischen Bestimmung des photographischen Bildes', in *Allegorie und Melancholie*, ed. by Willem van Reijen (Frankfurt a.M.: Suhrkamp, 1992), pp. 90–108 (p. 96).
7. Theodor W. Adorno and Walter Benjamin, *Briefwechsel 1928–1940*, ed. by Henri Lonitz (Frankfurt a.M.: Suhrkamp, 1994), p. 90; *The Complete Correspondence 1928–1940*, ed. by Henri Lonitz, transl. by Nicholas Walker (Cambridge: Polity Press, 1996), p. 66.
8. Ibid.
9. In his later essay 'Notes on Kafka' (1953), Adorno further pursues this notion of the photographic character of Kafka's texts which he discerns in Kafka's use of serial replication both on the level of characters — the uncanny doubles and triplets that populate his works — and on the level of narrative structures where set-ups and events repeat themselves. Theodor W. Adorno, *Gesammelte Schriften*, ed. by Rolf Tiedemann, 20 vols (Frankfurt a.M.: Suhrkamp, 1970–90), x.1, 264. References to this edition will be given using the abbreviation AG. English translation of the essay in Theodor W. Adorno, *Prisms*, trans. by Samuel and Shierry Weber (Cambridge, MA: MIT Press, 1981), pp. 243–71 (p. 253). Another photographic feature is the sudden arrest of the narrative into sharply defined, highly detailed tableaux: 'Eternalized gestures in Kafka are the momentaneous brought to a standstill. The shock is like a surrealist arrangement of that which old photographs convey to the viewer' (AG x.1, 263; *Prisms*, pp. 252–53).
10. In 'The Paris of the Second Empire in Baudelaire', Benjamin writes: 'Technical measures had to come to the aid of the administrative control process. [...] The invention of photography was a turning point in the history of this process. It was not less significant for criminology than the invention of the printing press was for literature. Photography made it possible for the first time to preserve permanent and unmistakable traces of a human being. The detective story came into being when this most decisive of all conquests of a person's incognito had been accomplished. Since that time, there has been no end to the efforts to capture [*dingfest machen*] a man in his speech and actions' (BG i.2, 550 / BE iv, 26–27).
11. The history of *A Berlin Childhood* illustrates Benjamin's concern to maintain his 'autobiographical incognito'. Benjamin published most chapters individually under the pseudonym Detlev Holz in the *Frankfurter Zeitung*. See Rolf Tiedemann, 'Nachwort', in Walter Benjamin, *Berliner Kindheit um neunzehnhundert: Gießener Fassung* (Frankfurt a.M.: Suhrkamp, 2000), pp. 113–26 (p. 124). In the later versions of the text written in exile in Paris, Benjamin incorporated this strategy of authorial incognito into the work: while the 'Mummerehlen' chapter formed the first section of the earliest version of the text, the recently recovered so-called *Gießener Ausgabe* (1932–33), it was later moved towards the end of the text in the *Fassung letzter Hand* from 1938, where the account of the photographs is left out altogether (cf. BG vii.1, 417–18 / BE iii, 374–75).
12. Harro Segeberg, *Literatur im technischen Zeitalter: Von der Frühzeit der deutschen Aufklärung bis zum Beginn des Ersten Weltkriegs* (Darmstadt: Wissenschaftliche Buchgesellschaft, 1997), pp. 38–39.
13. *Walter Benjamin 1892–1940*, ed. by Rolf Tiedemann, Christoph Gödde, and Henri Lonitz (= *Marbacher Magazin*, no. 55 (1990)), p. 246.
14. AG iv, 281; Theodor W. Adorno, *Minima Moralia: Reflections from Damaged Life*, trans. by E. F. N. Jephcott (New York: Verso, 1978), p. 247.
15. AG iv, 281; *Minima Moralia*, p. 247.
16. AG iv, 281; *Minima Moralia*, p. 247.

CHAPTER 17

❖

Faith and Doubt: An Alternative Dialectic

Patrick Gray

In Plato's *Republic*, Socrates casts a cold eye on art. We may love it, but even so it is a pernicious distraction from the truth. It does not present a thing as it is or even an imitation of it, but at best an imitation of an imitation. According to Socrates, the bed 'the painter makes' imitates the bed 'the carpenter makes', the bed that we would call the 'real' bed: a solid, life-size piece of furniture. This bed, however, is also an imitation. The 'real' bed is something else, something altogether different. According to Socrates, the bed 'the carpenter makes', the material bed, 'imitates' or 'resembles' the 'form' of the bed, 'bedness', so to speak: the invisible, intangible 'idea' of a bed. Socrates calls this the bed 'in nature', that is, the 'real' bed, 'which we might say God makes'.

As a form of imitation, art seems to Socrates inevitably, irredeemably reductive. A two-dimensional painting cannot fully, adequately represent a three-dimensional bed. It distorts and simplifies, capturing one angle and ignoring others, favouring a single, biased, incomplete perspective. So also, Socrates insists, material objects fall short of what they imitate: ideas. The bed the carpenter makes is not the real bed, but at best a cheap knock-off or sham substitute. The real bed is the bed God makes: the idea of a bed.

According to Socrates, the philosopher sees clearly, figuratively speaking, because he escapes matter altogether and engages solely with ideas. The carpenter, however, like the artist, sees dimly. He sees the shadows of things, not the things themselves, because he sees with his eyes, not with his mind. He is trapped in matter or worse, in imitations of matter, in art. Matter leads us away from ideas, and art leads us further still. Art therefore is all in all harmful: 'imitative poetry' (lit. imitative 'making') 'ruins listeners' minds'. What then are we to do? Socrates' conclusion is notorious. Art should be forbidden or at least, strictly censored. The republic cannot allow it.[1]

Plotinus, founder of neo-Platonism, reverses Socrates' interpretation of art. According to Plotinus, 'the arts are not to be slighted on the ground that they create by imitation of natural objects'. The arts 'give no bare reproduction of the thing seen, but go back (lit. 'run back up') to the ideas from which Nature itself derives'.[2] Socrates is precisely wrong. Art leads towards ideas; poetry improves the mind.

Art is to be cherished, encouraged, and defended as the natural complement of philosophy, and champions of art such as Sidney in his *Defense of Poesy* and Shelley in his *Defence of Poetry* draw upon neo-Platonic thought to defend their craft against Platonic counterclaims. Poets, moreover, are not the only neo-Platonists. In his *Introduction to the Philosophy of Fine Art*, Hegel likewise uses Plotinus' metaphysics to reconcile art and philosophy.

Plato, Aristotle, and Plotinus each distinguish ideas from matter. Ideas are abstract, universal, and incorporeal; matter is concrete, particular, and corporeal. Where, however, do ideas exist? Plato believes that ideas exist outside matter. They are immaterial; they have no location. Aristotle believes that Plato's objective ideas exist in matter, giving it definition. They are the forms, the essences, of things. Plotinus believes like Aristotle that ideas exist in matter as forms, but also like Plato that they exist outside matter as what we would call, 'ideas': thoughts. Ideas exist free from matter in our minds. They are 'ideas', not in Plato's strange, free-floating sense, but in our familiar, mind-bound sense. That said, Plotinus's ideas are not subjective. They do not depend on us. Plotinus represents a turning point or inclusive transition between the wholly objective ideas of Plato and Aristotle and the wholly subjective ideas of Nietszche. Ideas exist in our minds, but they also exist outside our minds in matter and, Plotinus would add, in other, better minds: angelic minds, divine minds. We do not create ideas; we observe them. In *A New Mimesis*, A. D. Nuttall makes this clear: 'The neo-Platonist who locates reality in an ulterior world of forms and the naturalist who locates reality in the here and now are both using "reality" in the same sense.'[3] Ideas exist 'out there' in reality before they exist 'in here' in our perceptions of it.

Hegel elaborates upon Plotinus's belief in the twofold, complementary existence of ideas in matter and in minds, linking the two types of existence, subjective and objective, by cause and effect. Ideas exist as forms of matter because Hegel's idiosyncratic, impersonal God, the so-called 'World-Soul', expresses them as such. The World-Soul wants to become aware of itself, to apprehend its own ideas, and to do so it must express them outside itself, outside its mind in matter. It cannot be conscious of itself unless it becomes something other than itself, so it puts itself, the ideas in its mind, outside itself: 'out there'.

The World-Soul expresses its ideas in the world; so also, on a smaller scale, the artist expresses his ideas in art. In his *Introduction to the Philosophy of Fine Art,* Hegel explains that art 'imparts' to matter a 'higher reality, born of mind'. It 'pervades what is sensuous with mind'. Art is 'an evolution of the notion [i.e. 'the universal'] *out of* itself, an alienation from itself towards the sensuous'. The artist puts his ideas outside himself in order to become conscious of them.[4]

Do the artist's ideas correspond, however, to anything outside the artist's mind? Hegel does not address this problem. What if the artist is wrong? What if the 'abstract law' the artist expresses does not, in truth, hold true? What if such 'a kind of man' would not 'probably or necessarily say or do' 'such or such'? Art does not express universals. It expresses beliefs about universals. It expresses 'abstract law' not necessarily as it is but rather as it is believed to be: as it appears diversely, not necessarily in the mind of God, but in the mind of Shakespeare, Michelangelo, or some other mortal.

Literature, Hegel proposes, is a translation from one language, the general, into another, the specific. Literature translates beliefs about universals into imaginary particulars, hypothetical abstract laws into realistic instances, and abstract ideas into concrete objects. What then is literary criticism? How does it differ, if at all, from simple appreciation? 'Artistic contemplation differs from theoretical consideration by the scientific intelligence, in cherishing interest for the object as an individual existence, and not setting to work to transmute it into its universal thought and notion' (71–72). Here we have a hint. According to Hegel, 'theoretic contemplation of things' seeks to be 'acquainted with them in their universality', to find their 'law', to conceive of them 'in terms of their notion'. Hegel calls the 'satisfaction' of this 'theoretic interest' 'the work of science'. We might call it the work of the literary critic. The critic starts 'from the sensuous thing in its individuality', but 'transforms it within the mind, making a concrete object of sense into an abstract matter of thought'. If literature is a translation, literary criticism is a back-translation. The critical mind undoes the 'alienation' towards 'the sensuous' which the artistic mind 'evolved' out of itself, 'recognizing itself in its alienation in the shape of feeling and the sensuous, in its other form, by transmuting the metamorphosed thought back into definite thought, and so restoring it to itself' (70–71, 23).

Translation is a tricky business, however. A word in one language may not correspond exactly to a single, precise equivalent in another language. The Latin word *fama*, for example, can be translated as 'rumour', 'reputation', 'fame', or many other English words. To choose one meaning is to lose others. English is more precise; *fama* in English loses a certain ambiguity, a certain tension. Like Latin, literature resists translation. Its concrete language does not correspond one-to-one with the abstract language of criticism. What it states in particulars can be, in universals, confusing, ambiguous, or outright contradictory: *simul pro simul contra*. 'We are at once met by the remark that the manifold feelings and ideas, which art aims at provoking or reinforcing, intersect and contradict, and by mutual interference cancel one another' (90).

Edmund Spenser sets up Book I of *The Faerie Queene* as a straightforward allegory. 'A faire Ladye in mourning', 'riding' like Christ 'on a white Asse', arrives at the court of the Queen of the Fairies and tells her that her father and mother have been 'shut up in a brasen castle' for 'many years' by 'an huge dragon'. The 'lovely Ladie', Una, is the Christian church. Her father, 'the king of *Eden*', is Adam; her mother, Eve. They represent by synecdoche their progeny as well: fallen man. The dragon is Satan; the 'brasen castle', their prison, is the consequence of the Fall: the postlapsarian world of sweat, suffering, and so forth. The Queen of the Fairies grants the quest to the 'Redcrosse Knight', 'Holinesse', and he rides forth with Una to fight the 'Dragon horrible'.[5]

The Redcrosse Knight runs into trouble, however. On the way to Una's homeland, he and Una meet an 'old man', a 'Hermit': Archimago. Spenser, we know, is Protestant; Archimago is Catholic. He tells the Redcrosse Knight 'of Saints and Popes', and tosses in, 'evermore', 'an *Ave-Mary* after and before'. Straightaway we are on the alert. Archimago, we discover, is a 'guilefull great Enchaunter'.[6] When the Redcrosse Knight and Una are asleep, he calls 'out of deepe darknesse dred'

> Legions of Sprights, the which like little flyes
> Fluttring about his ever damned hed,
> A-waite whereto their service he applyes.[7]

Archimago commands these 'Sprights' to appear to the Redcrosse Knight as dreams of Una being unfaithful to him: 'false shewes' to 'abuse his fantasy'. When the Redcrosse Knight wakes, Archimago shows him the thing itself: the 'wanton lust and lewd embracement' of two spirits whom, 'with charmes and hidden artes', he has made to resemble Una and 'a young Squire'. The Redcrosse Knight, 'yblent' with 'rage', rides off and leaves Una, 'forsaken Truth', to fend for herself, a falling in instead with a new lady, Duessa: 'faire falsehood'. Duessa is 'a goodly Lady clad in scarlet red', with 'a *Persian* mitre on her hed':

> The sole daughter of an Emperour
> He that the wide West under his rule has,
> And high hath set his throne, where *Tiberis* doth pas.[8]

The Emperor of the West is the Pope. Duessa, his daughter, is Catholic doctrine. Who or what then is Archimago? Commentators on Spenser's *Faerie Queene* tend to interpret him as a symbol of the Catholic clergy: a Catholic 'miracle worker' or false teacher, a 'Catholic enchanter'. This is true. Archimago, however, is also something else.[9]

Torquato Tasso claims in his 'Allegory of the Poem' that his epic poem *Gerusalemme liberata* represents the pursuit of 'happiness', Jerusalem (sc. heaven, the 'new Jerusalem'), by a single man, a Christian army. The 'less noble soldiers' represent the body; the 'princes', 'the faculties of the soul'. The army struggles externally against 'the enemies and disasters and accidents of adverse fortune' and internally against itself in a psychomachia, a clash of 'princes', a 'combat with the rational faculty ['Goffredo'] waged by the concupiscible faculty ['Tancredi'] and the irascible faculty ['Rinaldo']'.[10]

Tasso's 'Allegory of the Poem' sets up a useful distinction between 'external' and 'internal' 'impediments'. Spenser, like Tasso, presents his epic as a psychomachia: a battle in the soul. The Redcrosse Knight, 'Holinesse', struggles against internal impediments: 'Orgoglio' (Italian, pride), for example, a 'Gyaunt proud', 'horrible and hye', 'stalking' with 'sturdie steps', and 'Despaire', a 'cursed man' 'low sitting on the ground' in a 'darksome cave', 'musing full sadly in his sullein mind'. Spenser does include some external impediments, however. The 'dreadfull Dragon' at the end of Book I, Satan, is not something within the mind, native to it, betraying it. It attacks from without.

Archimago is more complicated. He is a saboteur, so to speak, as well as a siege engine, attacking from within as well as from without. He is an external enemy, the Catholic clergy, and also, like Tasso's 'sorcerer', Ismeno, an 'internal impediment': the imagination, Aristotle's *phantasia*, a faculty of the mind known in the Renaissance as, variously, 'fantasy' or 'fancy'. In Book II of *The Faerie Queene* Spenser indulges in a long allegorical set-piece: the House of Alma. The house represents the body. Alma, its mistress, represents the soul: Latin, *anima*. Her courtiers represent the various faculties of the mind. 'Eumnestes', for example, represents memory: 'an old old man, halfe blind', ensconced, 'decrepit', amid books, records, and genealogies. One of these courtiers, Phantastes, eerily resembles Archimago. Archimago's 'study' is full of 'Legions of Sprights', 'like little flyes', 'Fluttring about his ever damned hed'. Phantastes' 'chamber' is full of 'flyes', 'like many swarmes of Bees'. This time, however, the 'Sprights' are identified: they are 'fantasies', Aristotle's *phantasiai*, images, or *phantasmata* (lit. ghosts, spectres, phantoms). They are the insubstantial images imagination presents to the mind: 'dreames', 'visions', and 'opinions unsound'.

> All the chamber filled was with flyes,
> Which buzzed all about, and made such sound,
> That they encombred all mens ears and eyes,
> Like many swarmes of Bees assembled round,
> After their hives with honny do abound:
> All those were idle thoughts and fantasies,
> Devices, dreames, opinions unsound,
> Shewes, visions, sooth-sayes, and prophesies;
> And all that fained is, as leasings, tales, and lies.[11]

An 'internal' interpretation of Archimago is not altogether new. James Nohrnberg tells us that Archimago 'acts [...] the part' of 'the fallen imagination'.[12] Sean Kane calls Archimago 'the dark voice of tendencies within the victim himself, an inclination to fantasy': 'Spenser links doctrinal heresy so closely with the psychology of the disturbed soul that it becomes impossible to tell if external agents of temptation or the fallen faculties themselves are the causes of Redcrosse's undoing.'[13] External and internal interpretations of Archimago are not cosily complementary, however. Archimago as a Catholic priest is anti-Catholic. Archimago as imagination is anti-Protestant.

According to Catholics, the Church is the criterion of the truth. According to Protestants, each individual conscience is its own criterion of truth. The head-to-head rivalry of these two epistemologies in the Reformation opened what Richard Popkin calls 'Pandora's box': the Sceptics' 'problem of the criterion'. A criterion cannot be defended but by reference to some other, more fundamental criterion. What criterion, however, could be more fundamental than either the Church or the individual conscience? The floor had collapsed beneath their feet.[14]

The problem of the criterion affected intellectual tactics. Rather than defending their own criteria, Reformation and Counter-Reformation theologians attacked their opponents' criteria. In *Hamlet in Purgatory*, Stephen Greenblatt gives us a hint of what these attacks were like. Protestant preachers called Catholic beliefs 'men's fantasies', 'feigned fantasies', 'the gross abuses of fantastic brains', and so on.[15]

Greenblatt asks but does not altogether answer an important question. 'Why were people like Tyndale, Latimer, and Donne confident that their sharp weapon would not turn against their own beliefs?'[16] The Protestant accusation, 'imagination', could be turned against the accuser. In *Twelfth Night*, Shakespeare shows us the form and pressure of a Catholic counterattack. Shakespeare's stage 'Puritan', Malvolio, misinterprets a forged, cryptic letter as a noblewoman's confession of her love for him while two noblemen, his enemies, look on and laugh. 'Look how imagination blows him!' one exclaims. Shakespeare suggests that the God-given inspiration guiding Protestant reading, the Puritan's inner light, might be a will-o'-the-wisp. It might be nothing more than his own imagination.[17]

What is Archimago? His dual interpretation, internal and external, seems to be what 'the deconstructive critic seeks to find': Derrida's 'aporia'. J. Hillis Miller calls it 'the element in the system studied which is alogical, the thread in the text in question which will unravel it all, or the loose stone which will pull down the whole building'.[18] If Archimago is a Catholic priest, his deceitful 'Hypocrisy' calls Catholic epistemology into doubt. The Church cannot be trusted. If he is the imagination, his ability to deceive 'Holinesse' undermines the foundation of Protestant epistemology: the reliability of individual interpretation of Scripture. He threatens Protestant faith in our ability to distinguish human imagination from divine illumination.

A deconstructionist critic such as Miller would discover in Archimago an 'aporia', an 'impasse of thought', or a 'boggling of the mind': the simultaneous presence of two meanings which are 'irreconcilable'.[19] He would demonstrate how *The Faerie Queene*, like every other 'text', 'performs [...] its own self-dismantling': 'it says two entirely incompatible things at the same time'.[20]

A New Critic such as Cleanth Brooks would find Archimago a 'paradox', an 'ambiguity', or an 'irony': a 'complex of attitudes'. He would show how the paradox is solved, the tension is worked out, and the stress is resolved. He would describe Archimago as a Hegelian synthesis of antitheses. He would demonstrate how *The Faerie Queene*, like every other poem, is an 'achieved harmony', a 'pattern of resolutions and balances and harmonizations': an 'organic unity'.[21]

The characteristic critical languages of New Criticism and Deconstruction stand in point-for-point contrast: 'paradox' vs. 'aporia', 'irony' vs. 'impasse', 'resolution' vs. 'dissemination', 'unity' vs. 'undecidability'. Each school has its shibboleths. Such terms, however, have fallen out of favour. We are reluctant to use them, because we recognize that they carry with them, whether we like it or not, certain dubious assumptions about literature. The New Critic assumes that it is unified; the deconstructionist assumes that it is not.

According to Coleridge, every good work of literature is an 'organic unity'. Each detail of a poem is an integral part of a total gestalt, like a facet of a diamond or an instrument in an orchestra. New Critics agree. In any great poem there is '*one* great conception', one 'essential principle', a 'unity of feeling': the 'Matrix', Coleridge calls it, 'arranging and disciplining' 'Thoughts'. Apparent contrariety enlivens real unity. Anti-belief is, to borrow Hegel's term, *aufgehoben* (lit. 'nullified'). Its conflict with belief expresses belief.[22]

Deconstructionists such as Miller argue 'you can't take it for granted that a good work of literature is organically unified'.[23] They find no '*one*' conception, no single 'Matrix', but conceptions and anti-conceptions, Matrices and anti-Matrices: mutually contradictory 'strata' or 'strands'. As matter and anti-matter collide, explode, and leave nothing, so belief and anti-belief 'deconstruct' each other.

Apparent unity 'disseminates' into real contrariety: 'undecidability'. Literature dismantles itself. Positive and negative charges attract each other, come into contact, and neutralize each other. An initial shock is all: no charge, no electricity remains. Literature expresses no belief.

Is there a Via Media between New Criticism and Deconstruction? Is it possible, that is, to acknowledge both unity and contrariety, without subsuming one into the other? Is it possible that literature both is and is not unified? Deconstruction opens a way forward. According to J. Hillis Miller, 'deconstructive reading' is not 'a free-for all'. We are not 'free to make any reading whatsoever'; 'When one speaks of undecidability as a feature of deconstructive criticism, one doesn't mean a free-for-all but a very precise identifiable movement back and forth among possibilities.'[24] What is Archimago's import? What does his duplicity communicate? Spenser might mean that we should not trust Catholic priests. He might mean that we should not trust ourselves. He does not mean, however, that we should all buy white elephants, or set fire to our desks. Literature does not mean, as, say, Stanley Fish might maintain, whatever the reader might want it to mean. Miller says straight out:

> I can't make George Eliot's *Middlemarch* or Stevens' 'The Rock' mean anything that I want it to mean. Such a text [...] may be complicated, heterogeneous, enigmatic, but that doesn't make it disappear or free me to make it mean anything I want. This fact preserves the possibility of saying to somebody, 'You're wrong in this case'.[25]

Literature is determinate. It is A and not-A. It is not, however, in addition to A and not-A, B and not-B, C and not-C, and so on ad infinitum. It is 'undecidable', but it is not indeterminate.

Derrida describes Deconstruction as 'a double gesture, a double science, a double writing'.[26] When he reads philosophers, he finds 'two interpretations'.[27] M. H. Abrams calls them reading$_1$ and reading$_2$: 'A text must be read determinately [reading$_1$] in order to be disseminated [reading$_2$] into an undecidability that never strikes completely free of its initial determination; deconstruction [reading$_1$] can only subvert the meanings of a text that has always already been construed [reading$_2$].'[28] Derrida constructs before he deconstructs; he 'construes' before he 'disseminates'.

In *Of Grammatology*, Derrida presents a double reading of Rousseau's *Essay on the Origin of Language.* He begins by telling us what 'Rousseau affirms [...] unambiguously', what 'Rousseau says [...] clearly', and so on. Such reading, he says, is an 'indispensable guardrail'. It is 'not easy', however, and 'requires all the instruments of traditional criticism'. The reader must 'recognize and respect all its classical exigencies': 'Without this recognition and this respect, critical production would risk developing in any direction at all and authorize itself to say anything.'[29] Having established reading$_1$, Derrida reveals that it is a 'strategic', 'provisional' interpretation, and moves on to a new, 'critical' interpretation: reading$_2$. He identifies 'strands' in Rousseau's *Essay* which contradict reading:[30]

> Derrida's reading$_2$ of Rousseau [...] repeatedly uncovers an opposition of meanings between what Rousseau 'wishes to say' and what 'he says without wishing to say it', or between what Rousseau 'declares' and what the text 'describes' without Rousseau's wishing to say it.[31]

Deconstruction, in practice, if not always in theory, gives two determinate, if contradictory, interpretations: A and not-A. $Reading_I$ and $reading_2$ are 'absolutely irreconcilable', according to Derrida.[32] They are, however, Miller says, 'identifiable'. The text is undecidable, but undecidable in a certain, precise way. Its 'aporia' can be distinguished from other *aporiai*. We can see which impasse we are in, even if we cannot get out it. The sides of the *abyme* are, moreover, distinct. One emerges before the other. One is salient, pre-eminent, manifest, obvious, in-our-faces; the other is elusive, receding, shadowy, hidden, slipping away from us even as we look at it. One, it seems, is the thing itself; the other is its shadow.

What is the relationship of $reading_I$ and $reading_2$? Perhaps we should, with due respect, let go of Abrams's useful but clunky terminology. If we call $reading_I$ 'belief', and $reading_2$ 'anti-belief', we capture their polar opposition. An author's anti-belief is the converse of his belief. He communicates both simultaneously; his belief, however, is more obvious than his anti-belief. What is 'anti-belief', however, if not doubt? If we call belief 'faith', and anti-belief 'doubt', adopting *pro tempore* a different vocabulary or alternative dialectic, the language of theology, we open up an interesting, absorbing, untapped resource: theological speculation about the nature of belief.

What is the relationship of faith and doubt? Christian accounts of early Christianity in the New Testament offer an interesting insight. Faith and doubt coexist. Each of the Synoptic Gospels, Matthew, Mark, and Luke, tells the story of a boy possessed by a 'mute spirit', whose father takes him to Jesus to be healed. 'If you can do anything,' the man says, 'have compassion on us and help us.' Jesus answers, 'If you can believe, all things are possible to him who believes.' 'Immediately' the father cries out, 'Lord I believe; help thou my unbelief!' Jesus casts the spirit out of the boy, and helps him to stand and walk. Afterwards, the disciples of Jesus come to him 'privately'. The boy's father had asked them to cast out the spirit before he asked Jesus, but they had not been able to do it. 'Why could we not cast it out?' they ask. Jesus answers, 'Because of your unbelief.'[33]

The story of the 'mute spirit' showcases two remarkable, counter-intuitive characteristics of the relationship of faith and doubt. Belief and 'unbelief' coexist within a single instant, a single sentence, a single cry: 'Lord I believe; help thou my unbelief!' Faith and doubt exist not in alternation but rather simultaneously — or at least, as near simultaneously as a single voice can say them. $Reading_2$ follows $reading_I$ in the mind of the critic, but not necessarily in the mind of the author. Are we to suppose that the disciples did not believe at all, when Jesus reproves them for 'unbelief'? No. Doubt ebbs and flows; in some sense, however, it is always present, even at the height of faith. It is the trace of the other in the selfsame; the shadow of the thing itself. 'Unbelief', moreover, can be found both high and low, in 'the disciples' as well as 'the people'. No one, no saint, no apostle, no disciple, is free from doubt. In his sermon on Jesus's rebuke of his disciples, St Augustine asks a pointed question. 'If the Apostles were unbelievers, who is a believer? What must the lambs do, if the rams totter?'[34] Some theologians go further. Just before Jesus dies on the cross, he cries out, 'My God, My God, why have You forsaken Me?'[35] What is the meaning of this lament, if not that Jesus himself doubts? According to a contemporary Orthodox theologian, Bishop Kallistos of Diokleia, Jesus takes upon himself not only the physical suffering of mankind, but also its mental suffering: doubt, despair, and 'spiritual death'.

> We cannot begin to explain how it is possible for One who is Himself the living God to lose awareness of the Divine Presence. But this at least is evident. [...] At this moment Jesus is truly experiencing the spiritual death of separation from God. Not only does He shed His blood for us, but for our sakes He accepts even the loss of God.[36]

Modern saints and mystics attest to an ineradicable presence of doubt within the most ardent, heartfelt, and manifest faith: a persistent commingling of shadow and light. In 2002 the postulator of Mother Theresa's cause, Father Brian Kolodiejchuk MC, published *The Soul of Mother Theresa: Hidden Aspects of her Interior Life*.[37] In private letters to her spiritual directors, Mother Theresa reveals that the last part of her life was a 'dark night of the soul'. Upon leaving her convent for the streets of India, she was tormented by doubt, loneliness, and feelings of abandonment: 'that terrible pain', she writes, 'of loss, of God not wanting me, of God not being God, of God not really existing'.

> The missionary foundress who called herself 'God's pencil' was not the God-intoxicated saint many of us had assumed her to be. We may prefer to think that she spent her days in a state of ecstatic mystical union with God, because that would get us ordinary worldlings off the hook. How else could this unremarkable woman, no different from the rest of us, bear to throw her lot in with the poorest of the poor, sharing their meager diet and rough clothing, wiping leprous sores and enduring the agonies of the dying, for so many years without respite, unless she were somehow lifted above it all, shielded by spiritual endorphins?[38]

Mother Theresa's namesake, Ste Thérèse of Lisieux (1873–97), also struggled with doubt. From Easter 1896 until her death from tuberculosis in 1897, she seemed 'to hear the darkness mocking her':

> You are dreaming about the light; [...] you believe that one day you will walk out of this fog that surrounds you! Advance, advance; rejoice in the death which will give not what you hope for but a night still more profound, the night of nothingness.[39]

Doubt cuts both ways, however. Ste Thérèse believes in God and doubts that he exists: her anti-belief or 'unbelief' is belief in 'nothingness'. Sartre believes in nothingness and doubts that that is all there is; his anti-belief or 'unbelief' is belief in 'something'. In his early novel *La Nausée* he is troubled by 'something', 'a funny little meaning', 'the real secret of existence'.

> The park smiled at me. [...] The smile of the trees, of the clump of laurel bushes, *meant* something; that was the real secret of existence. I remembered that one Sunday, not more than three weeks ago, I had already noticed in things a sort of conspiratorial air. [...] You could have sworn that things were thoughts that stopped half way, [...] with a funny little meaning that went beyond them. That little meaning annoyed me [...]. I left, I came back to the hotel, and there you are, I wrote.[40]

Sartre sinks into doubt, flounders for a moment, and resurfaces. He leaves the park and goes home to write *La Nausée*.

Sartre's Sunday morning in the park is a photo-negative of St Peter's night 'tossed by waves' on the Sea of Galilee. Each of the Synoptic Gospels tells the story: the disciples are asleep on a boat 'in the middle of the sea'. The winds are 'contrary' and the boat is 'tossed by waves'. Even so, Jesus comes to them, in the middle of the night, 'the fourth watch', 'walking on the sea'. The disciples are afraid, but Jesus reassures them, 'It is I.'

> And Peter answered Him and said, 'Lord, if it is You, command me to come to You on the water.' So He said, 'Come.' And when Peter had come down out of the boat, he walked on the water to go to Jesus. But when he saw the wind was boisterous, he was afraid; and beginning to sink he cried out, saying, 'Lord, save me!' And immediately Jesus stretched out His hand and caught him, and said to him 'O you of little faith, why did you doubt?' And when they got into the boat, the wind ceased. Then those who were in the boat came and worshipped Him, saying, 'Truly You are the Son of God.'[41]

The most familiar relationship of faith and doubt in literature is this type of sinking and resurfacing. An author entertains a doubt for a time, then rejects it. The pattern can be seen at its most basic in ballads, blues songs, and action movies: the bad guy triumphs for a while, then gets his comeuppance. The good guy wins in the end. The author asks himself a question (Wouldn't it be fun to be an outlaw?) and answers it (No, outlaws get killed by the sheriff.). Shakespeare lets us befriend Falstaff, 'a goodly portly man', 'sweet Jack Falstaff', 'of a cheerful look', then banishes him: a 'villainous abominable misleader of youth', 'a fool and jester', 'surfeit-swell'd'.[42] Milton paints Satan as an epic hero, an Achilles, a Greek god, then finally as a toad.

Milton shows us Satan before he shows us Christ. Likewise, Spenser shows us his bad magician, Archimago, before he shows us his good magician, Merlin. The cowboy in the black hat shoots up the town; then, and only then, does the cowboy in the white hat ride in. Spenser introduces a problem (What if conscience is nothing other than imagination?) then provides its solution (No, conscience is something other than imagination.). Archimago is not all there is; Merlin is also available, and Merlin is trustworthy.

In some of his other, minor poetry, *The Shepheardes Calender* and *The Teares of the Muses*, Spenser develops a distinction between good poets and bad poets. Bad poets, 'wanting due intelligence', make 'a monster of their fantasie'. They 'fling' 'rymes at randon', 'the fruitfull spawne of their ranke fantasies'.[43] Good poetry is 'poured forth into the witte by a certaine ενθουσιασμός, and celestiall inspiration'.[44] The good poet is 'ravished with a Poeticall furie', a 'divine' 'rage'. Like a prophet, like a 'Priest', he is 'inspired from above'.[45] The good poet creates by inspiration; the bad poet, by imagination. Spenser's distinction between good poets and bad poets sheds light on his distinction between Archimago and Merlin. Archimago works upon the 'fantasy', at night, upon sleeping victims, like dreams; Merlin works by *enthousiasmos*, like a prophet. Spenser calls him 'the Prophet', and shows him prophesying to Britomart, a virtuous lady, the 'conquests' of her 'Ofspring': the 'kings' of the 'Britons'. 'Overcomen of the spirites powre', Merlin speaks in 'suddein fit, and half extatick stoure'.[46]

Archimago deceives; Merlin reveals the truth. The shield he makes for King Arthur is 'all of Diamond perfect pure and cleene', a defense against 'magick arts': 'all that was not such, as seemd in sight, | Before that shield did fade, and suddeine fall'. Merlin also makes a 'glassie globe' for King Ryence, a 'looking glasse', which is able 'to shew in perfect sight, | What ever thing was in the world contaynd': 'Ne ought mote pas, | Ne ought in secret from the same remaynd'.[47]

Merlin, however, eerily resembles Archimago. Archimago lives 'downe in a dale', 'far from resort of people'; Merlin lives 'in a deep delve, farre from the vew of day, | That of no living wight he mote be found'. Archimago has 'legions of Sprights' 'fluttering about his ever damned head'; Merlin is 'with his sprights encompast round'. In his 'hideous hollow cave' there are a 'thousand sprights'. Both of them use writing to bind spirits to their service. Spenser describes Archimago in 'his study' composing 'verses'.

> When all drownd in deadly sleepe he findes,
> He to his study goes, and there amides
> His Magicke bookes and artes of sundry kindes,
> He seeks out mighty charmes, to trouble sleepy mindes.
> Then choosing out few words most horrible,
> (Let none them read) thereof did verses frame,
> With which and other spelles like terrible,
> [...]
> he cald out of deep darknesse dred
> Legions of Sprights.

Britomart discovers Merlin 'writing strange characters on the ground, | With which the stubborn feends he to his service bound'. What is still more interesting, however, is that Spenser includes Merlin's magic, 'prophesies', like Archimago's magic, 'dreames', in his list of the 'flyes', the 'fantasies', which, like the 'Sprights' in Archimago's 'study', and the 'sprights' in Merlin's 'balefull Bowre', fill the chamber of Phantastes.

> All those were idle thoughts and fantasies,
> Devices, dreames, opinions unsound,
> Shewes, visions, sooth-sayes, and prophesies;
> And all that fained is, as leasings, tales, and lies.

Merlin himself is 'not the sonne | Of mortall Syre', but rather, 'wondrously begotten' by 'false illusion of a guilefull Spright, | On a faire Ladie Nonne'.[48]

Spenser makes Merlin and Archimago so alike because he cannot altogether escape his doubt, 'unbelief', or anti-belief that Archimago and Merlin, imagination and divine illumination, might be one and the same. Spenser says of Archimago that 'he could take | As many formes and shapes in seeming wise' as '*Proteus*' himself. Conscience might be fantasy in another, different, still subtler disguise: revelation itself.[49]

Spenser's doubt does not make *The Faerie Queene* 'undecidable', however. Spenser is a Protestant; his faith in divine illumination is apparent. His doubt complicates the poem, enriches it, enlivens it, and gives it its electricity. What it does not do, however, is dissolve it into neutrality. Spenser's faith and his doubt are 'irreconcilable' and, moreover, unequal. The light outshines the darkness; the positive charge outweighs the negative; the current flows past the eddy.

The countercurrent of doubt is tenacious, however. Spenser addresses it but does not altogether dispel it. The relationship of faith and doubt is, on the surface, alternation but, still deeper, simultaneity. Doubt is always there. This specter, phantom, or ghostly reminder of another belief, the belief we have not chosen, is frightening, but also perhaps reassuring.

In this doubt, the other belief or 'unbelief' that haunts our belief, we find something lost, at times, in current critical debate: the possibility of agency. No belief can completely dominate our minds; because its opposite is always there, whispering to us, soliciting our attention and waiting to be chosen. Shakespeare banishes Falstaff, but he could have called him back; he was not far away: 'ten mile', no more. The next play could have been different. No 'discourse' can overwhelm us, because its opposite, an anti-discourse, is there, too; always there, at all times, however hard we work to dispel it. Why we choose one and not the other remains a mystery.

Why do we choose what we choose? Despite the best efforts of theologians, philosophers, psychologists, and sociologists, despite Calvin, Marx, Freud, and Foucault, the problem remains unsolved. It may well be insoluble. Why does Spenser choose Protestantism rather than Catholicism? Who knows? It is a mystery. Perhaps it is best to leave it so. Perhaps for us, as literary critics, it is enough, and more than enough, to describe faith and doubt, belief and unbelief, $reading_1$ and $reading_2$, and leave literature at that; to describe actions, in all their complexity, and leave motivations alone; to describe a given work of art and leave its causes as they are: unknown.

Notes to Chapter 17

1. Plato, *Republic 10*, trans. with commentary by Stephen Halliwell (Warminster: Aris & Phillips, 1988), §§595–97.
2. Plotinus, *Enneads*, v.8.1, trans. by Stephen MacKenna, 4th edn (London: Faber, 1969).
3. A. D. Nuttall, *A New Mimesis* (London: Methuen, 1983), p. 64.
4. G. F. W. Hegel, *Hegel: Introductory Lectures on Aesthetics*, transl. by Bernard Bosanquet (first published 1886 as *The Introduction to Hegel's Philosophy of Fine Art*); edited and with an introduction and commentary by Michael Inwood (Harmondsworth: Penguin Books, 1993), pp. 16, 22–23. Further references to this edition are given after quotations in the text.
5. Edmund Spenser, *The Faerie Queene*, I. 12. 26, in *The Works of Edmund Spenser: A Variorum Edition*, ed. by Edwin Greenlaw, Charles Grosvenor Osgood, and Frederick Morgan Padelford (Baltimore: Johns Hopkins University Press, 1932–57), I; see also p. 169.
6. *The Faerie Queene*, I. I. 34–35; see also p. 19.
7. *The Faerie Queene*, I. I. 38.
8. Ibid., I. I. 46, I. 2. 3, 5, 8, 22; see also pp. 31, 19.
9. Douglas Brooks-Davies, 'Archimago', in *The Spenser Encyclopedia*, ed. by A. C. Hamilton (Toronto: University of Toronto Press, 1990), p. 53.
10. 'Tasso's Allegory of *Gerusalemme Liberata*', trans. by L. F. Rhu, in L. F. Rhu, *The Genesis of Tasso's Narrative Theory: English Translations of the Early Poetics and a Comparative Study of their Significance* (Detroit: Wayne State University Press, 1993), pp. 157–59.
11. *The Faerie Queene*, II. 9. 50–51.

12. James Nohrnberg, *The Analogy of the Faerie Queene* (Princeton: Princeton University Press, 1976), p. 130.
13. Sean Kane, *Spenser's Moral Allegory* (Toronto: University of Toronto Press, 1989), pp. 36, 40.
14. Richard Popkin, *The History of Scepticism from Erasmus to Spinoza* (Berkeley: University of California Press, 1979), pp. 1–17.
15. Stephen Greenblatt, *Hamlet in Purgatory* (Princeton: Princeton University Press), pp. 36–37.
16. Ibid., p. 49.
17. William Shakespeare, *Twelfth Night*, II. 5. 42–43, ed. by J. M. Lothian and T. W. Craik (London: Methuen, 1975).
18. J. Hillis Miller, 'Stevens' Rock and Criticism as Cure, II', in *Theory Now and Then* (London: Harvester Wheatsheaf, 1991), pp. 117–32 (p. 126).
19. J. Hillis Miller, 'On Edge: The Crossways of Contemporary Criticism', ibid., pp. 171–200 (p. 176); J. Hillis Miller, 'How Deconstruction Works', ibid., pp. 293–95 (p. 294).
20. Miller, 'Stevens' Rock, II', p. 117; J. Hillis Miller, 'Deconstructing the Deconstructors', in *Theory Now and Then*, pp. 95–110 (p. 107).
21. Cleanth Brooks, 'The Heresy of Paraphrase', in *The Well-Wrought Urn: Studies in the Structure of Poetry* (1947) (London: Dobson, 1968), pp. 157–76 (pp. 159, 166).
22. *The Collected Works of Samuel Taylor Coleridge*, 16 vols (London: Routledge and Kegan Paul; Princeton: Princeton University Press, 1969–2002), V.1: *Lectures 1808–1819 on Literature*, ed. by R. A. Foakes (1987), pp. lxvii, 126, 358, 513; see also VII: *Biographia Literaria*, ed. by James Engell and W. Jackson Bate (1983), VII.1, p. lxxii, VII.2, 13, 16.
23. Miller, 'On Edge', p. 193.
24. Ibid., pp. 195–96.
25. Ibid., p. 196.
26. Jacques Derrida, 'Signature Event Context', *Glyph*, 1 (1977), 172–97 (p. 195); cited in M. H. Abrams, 'Construing and Deconstructing', in *Doing Things with Texts* (London: Norton, 1989), pp. 297–332 (p. 304).
27. Jacques Derrida, 'Structure, Sign, and Play in the Discourse of the Human Sciences', in *The Language of Criticism and the Sciences of Man: The Structuralist Controversy*, ed. by Richard Macksey and Eugenio Donato (Baltimore: Johns Hopkins University Press, 1970), pp. 247–72 (p. 264); cited in Abrams, 'Construing and Deconstructing', p. 304.
28. Ibid., 310.
29. Jacques Derrida, *Of Grammatology*, trans. by Gayatri Chakravorty Spivak (Baltimore: Johns Hopkins University Press, 1976), pp. 173, 184, 158–59; cited in Abrams, 'Construing and Deconstructing', pp. 305, 413n.
30. Derrida, *Of Grammatology*, pp. 99, 149, 200, 237, 240, 245.
31. Abrams, 'Construing and Deconstructing', pp. 306–07.
32. Derrida, 'Structure, Sign, and Play', p. 264; cited in Abrams, 'Construing and Deconstructing', p. 304.
33. Mark 9. 14–24; Matthew 17. 14–20.
34. St Augustine, *Sermons*, 30: 'On the New Testament', §1 <http://www.newadvent.org/fathers/160330.htm> [accessed 7 August 2007]
35. Matthew 27. 46.
36. Bishop Kallistos of Diokleia, *The Orthodox Way* (Crestwood, NY: St Vladimir's Seminary Press), p. 80.
37. Issued in four instalments by the ZENIT news agency, November–December 2002.
38. Carol Zaleski, 'The Dark Night of Mother Teresa', *First Things*, no. 133 (May 2003), 24–27 (pp. 24–25).
39. Ibid., pp. 26–27.
40. Jean-Paul Sartre, *Nausea*, trans. by Robert Baldick (London: Penguin Books, 2000), p. 193.
41. Matthew 14. 22–33.
42. William Shakespeare, *King Henry IV, Part 1*, II. 4. 416–17, 456, 469, ed. by A. R. Humphreys (Walton on Thames: Thomas Nelson, 1960); William Shakespeare, *King Henry IV, Part 2*, V. 5. 48, 50, ed. by A. R. Humphreys (Walton on Thames: Thomas Nelson, 1966).
43. Edmund Spenser, *The Teares of the Muses*, ll. 556–58, 321–22, in *The Works of Edmund Spenser: A Variorum Edition*, VIII: *The Minor Poems, Part Two* (1947).

44. 'Argument', 'E.K.', in 'October', *The Shepheardes Calender*, in *The Works of Edmund Spenser: A Variorum Edition*, VII: *The Minor Poems, Part One* (1943), p. 95.
45. 'Glosse', 'E.K.', ibid., pp. 102n, 103n, 100n.
46. Spenser, *The Faerie Queene*, III. 3. 21, 23, 50.
47. Ibid., I. 1. 33, 35; III. 2. 18–21.
48. Ibid., I. 1. 34, III. 3. 7, I. 1. 38, III. 3. 8–9, I. 1. 36–38, III. 3. 14, II. 9. 51, III. 3. 13.
49. Ibid., I. 2. 10.

CHAPTER 18

Literature and the Theory of Games: Kleist's *Verlobung in St Domingo* as an Example

Tim Mehigan

for Gerhard Neumann

In recent times, the theory of games has received application in many areas of economics, and some areas of the political and social sciences. It has proved to be a useful tool in modelling outcomes that assume a level of rational motivation among actors in a variable context of contingency. For this reason, the scenarios modelled by game theory are not objectively true or essentially real, although they arise from assumptions about real, living actors. Rather, they aim to predict the likely future behaviour of such actors under the limited conditions that hold for a given 'game situation'. This game situation is necessarily formal and abstract in nature, although it is easily applied to 'live' contexts in which it is operative. These might have to do with stock-market speculation, gambling, voter behaviour, or even procreation. At least as far as the last is concerned, the statistical fact that males and females are encountered in roughly equal abundance over the earth's surface has been interpreted as a strategic response to a set of biological and environmental factors within the game situation of life itself. In this case, human beings are the players and nature is the underlying rationality that constrains them and informs their actions (the view that nature is rationally directed was established in Western thinking during the Enlightenment). The great leap forward entailed in the thinking of Darwin, therefore, was to shift the focus of analysis away from biological actors and subjects towards a new idea of environment arguably consonant with game-theoretical assumptions.[1]

I

A game can be defined as any situation in which participants are bound to one another in a context of strategic interdependence.[2] In such circumstances, the behaviour of one participant or player depends on decisions or moves made by the other players. These moves are accompanied by rewards or pay-offs; the pay-offs are part of the game and define its structure. A pay-off is a condition of the game that helps manage the risk that the game, by its very nature, brings with it; one might say, therefore, that the pay-off attenuates contingent risk without ever being able to do away with it altogether. Despite the pay-offs, or indeed because of them, psychological uncertainty remains a given of the game situation. Uncertainty attaches above all to a lack of knowledge about the moves of other players. The promise of game theory is that the aspect of risk arising from the behaviour of players in a situation of strategic interdependence can be measured or mathematically quantified at each stage of the game, thus making it possible for all players to commit to action based on an understanding of how the game is played. Such understanding is predicated on a certain level of rational motivation in the structure of the game. The rational motivation of players is defined as the tendency of individual players to act in their own enlightened self-interest[3] or to favour the assumption of what has been called 'common knowledge rationality'.[4] Since the moves of participants in the game can be expressed as mathematical quantities, game theory in the social sciences is closely allied to, if not identical with, rational choice theory.[5]

The main aspects of a game situation are revealed in the prisoners' dilemma, a classic illustration of game theory first discussed by the Rand[6] Corporation scientists Merrill Flood and Melvin Dresher in 1950.[7] As for many games, the entire set of conditions governing the playing of the game is made clear to the players in advance of playing the game. For this reason the prisoners' dilemma is referred to as a game of complete information. The game goes as follows: two suspects are arrested and charged with a crime (it doesn't matter what crime). The police do not have sufficient evidence to convict the suspects, unless at least one of them confesses. The police take the suspects to separate cells and explain what consequences will follow the actions that they take. If neither confesses to the crime, then both will be convicted of a minor offence and sentenced to one month in jail. If both confess then both will be sent to jail for six months. If one confesses but the other does not, then the confessor will be released immediately but the other will be sentenced to nine months in jail — six for the crime, three for obstructing the course of justice. A bi-matrix table is used to represent the strategies outlined in this game (see Table 18.1). Each player has two strategies available: confess (or fink); not confess (or remain mum). Thus, if prisoner 1 chooses mum and prisoner 2 chooses fink, then prisoner 1 receives the pay-off −9 (representing nine months in jail) and prisoner 2 receives the pay-off 0 (representing immediate release). If, however, both decide to remain mum, then their pay-off is twice −1 (standing for one month in jail for both prisoners).

	P2 mum	*P2 fink*
P1 mum	−1, −1	−9, 0
P1 fink	0, −9	−6, −6

TABLE 18.1. The prisoners' dilemma: strategies used by two prisoners, with outcomes

Clearly, not all choices lead to optimal outcomes in the game. If, for example, one prisoner decides to play fink, then the other would prefer to play fink and so be in jail for six months (to remain mum would incur a pay-off of nine months). Similarly, if one prisoner plays mum, then the other would prefer to play fink and so be released immediately. Despite this overall strategic uncertainty, there is a best response possible in a given game. This response arises from a rational selection where neither player will regret her or his choices.[8] Such a response, which would be strategically stable or self-enforcing, can be called a Nash equilibrium, after its discoverer, the American John Nash, who later shared in the award of a Nobel Prize for his achievement.[9] As Hargreaves Heap and Varoufakis point out, 'Nash strategies are the only rationalisable ones which, if implemented, confirm the expectations on which they were based'.[10] In the prisoners' dilemma, the Nash equilibrium would be represented by the −1, −1 outcome, representing the decision of both prisoners to remain mum about the crime. To reiterate:

> As long as [...] conventions suggest to all parties what their role is to be [i.e. how they should play the game], and as long as parties obey conventions in their own self-interest as defined by the payoffs given by the game model, then conventional behaviour should be a Nash equilibrium. And analysing the situation using the notion of a Nash equilibrium will give an outer bound to the set of possibly 'stable' conventions.[11]

When players obey conventions in order to maximize the benefits for all players, the game is referred to as a cooperative game and is governed by cooperative game theory. In this case the unit of analysis is usually the group. When the individual player is concerned with doing as well as possible for her- or himself within the rules and possibilities provided for in the game, and when such individual behaviour constitutes the basic unit of analysis, the game is said to be governed by non-cooperative game theory.[12] When the participants in the prisoners' dilemma play the game non-cooperatively and do not disclose their choices to the other participant, no Nash equilibrium will necessarily result from the game. In this case, the risk element in the game rises and the pay-offs (and they can be of a negative nature) rise along with it.

II

Game theory may properly be considered an invention of the twentieth century. It cannot usefully be separated from statistical analysis and probability theory, which arose in the last decades of the nineteenth century, along with the industrialization of the European societies whose study they aimed to facilitate. Game theory therefore takes its place alongside other theories of behaviour and society that are pre-eminently modern, if the defining attribute of modernity is taken to be contingency, as the German sociologist Niklas Luhmann and others have argued.[13] Contingency, according to Luhmann, is anything that is 'neither necessary nor impossible',[14] that is, anything that is governed by the idea that an outcome could always be other than it is. Contingent views about self and society can be traced back to the paradigm shift in human understanding suddenly felt across a range of areas of human thinking and endeavour at the end of the eighteenth and the beginning of the nineteenth century. The older paradigm, which lost relevance in what Luhmann calls 'old European' society, was conditioned by essentialist views based on an assumption about the coincidence of thought and being in the world. Such a coincidence had long given grounds for views of a religious nature that assumed a divine presence in the world. Although the coming of contingent understanding which displaced these views has a long genesis in European thinking, it does not significantly pre-date the sixteenth century, and is closely associated with the important eighteenth-century thinkers, the Scottish sceptic David Hume, and the Prussian Immanuel Kant. Kant, according to his own testimony, indeed, was awakened from a 'dogmatic slumber' as a result of Hume's critique of rational precepts.[15] Another similarly awakened, although not by Hume in the first instance,[16] was the writer Heinrich von Kleist, who also went through a conceptual shift of a significant dimension in his early twenties after a protracted encounter with the philosophy of Kant.[17]

While it is not my purpose here to reconstruct in detail those epistemological aspects of game theory that are consonant with the rise of contingent awareness, I do mean to suggest the importance of the underlying paradigm shift which accompanies it and which has been popularly dated from 1800,[18] if only because it impacted heavily on the thinking of Kleist, one of the first game theorists *avant la lettre* of the modern age,[19] and perhaps the first of modern literature. A second aim of this paper is to suggest the utility of game theory for the general study of literature — a utility that, perhaps surprisingly, has scarcely ever been remarked upon.

Kleist's stories have usually been seen as a fascinatingly opaque, even suggestively malevolent, portrayal of an internal world that has entirely lost its rational underpinnings.[20] They therefore give evidence of the failure of Enlightenment values to sustain positions presupposing the self-evidence of reason, that is, the coincidence of reason and being, in the world. While there may be some truth to such views, they imply or even openly state that Kleist abandoned the project of reason at the centre of the Enlightenment,[21] and that, accordingly, rational positions no longer have any currency in the world. Such views would move Kleist in the direction of other views of his day, such as those espoused by the German Romantics, who were equally rationally sceptical in outlook, if not openly hostile to the Enlightenment project of reason. What I would prefer to suggest is that rationality remains an important constitutive element overall in Kleist's works, but it has been transferred from the level of individuals, who no longer absolutely command it, to the overall game situation itself. The 'critical deficit' in the secondary literature on Kleist, accordingly, appears to be a general failure to define and account for the precise type of rationality that, importantly, is still encountered in Kleist's imaginative world.[22] This critical deficit is in part made good in a set of contributions gathered together in a recent publication under the title of *Heinrich von Kleist und die Aufklärung*. Kleist, in the opinion of many of the contributors to that volume of research, while by no means a rationalist, appears to be anything but a committed anti-rationalist either[23] — a point which I believe is made obvious by the application of game theory to his work.

Early research demonstrated conclusively that the narrative model for Kleist's stories is an unheard-of or unprecedented event ('unerhörte Begebenheit')[24] — an event of a nature such as that which Goethe considered elemental to the form of the novella.[25] This event erupts upon the settled world of human understanding in the stories and precipitates a new quality of strategic interdependence for the story's participants. The unheard-of event might be an unexpected 'move' of nature, as is the case with the earthquake in *Das Erdbeben in Chili,* or some form of intervention of a person who turns out to be a player, as in the example of the Junker Wenzel von Tronka in the story *Michael Kohlhaas,* who suddenly erects a 'Schlagbaum' or barrier on his property and without warning levies a punitive tax on all those, including the trader Kohlhaas, who pass across his territory. What is important for the game-theoretical perspective is that the unheard-of event in each of the stories establishes a heightened level of risk for participants, and accordingly changes their behaviour. In fact, the unheard-of event both creates the game situation and recasts each story as a non-cooperative game of incomplete information, where each participant must negotiate her or his moves without any certainty about the motivation of other participants. Kleist, indeed, goes to great pains to undermine the strategic links between participants that would otherwise lead to cooperative alliances among participants or, conceivably, to a Nash equilibrium, the stable outcome of the game situation. Despite such preponderant instability, the game itself retains a rational appearance, since there are still pay-offs for behaviour at every stage of the game and a rational outcome is still provided for in the structure of the game.

III

In *Die Verlobung in St Domingo* — a story based on actual historical events of 1803–04 — civil war has broken out between the French colonizers of the Caribbean island of Santo Domingo and the island's indigenous inhabitants. As a result of an uprising that has witnessed the appropriation of farms and territory and a slaughter of whites by blacks, a force of thirty thousand black troops, under the command of the renegade Frenchman General Dessalines, is rapidly moving across the island in order to storm the capital, Port au Prince, the last bastion of French power on the island. The small party of Gustav von der Ried, an officer in the French army, who is Swiss by birth, must reach the capital before the arrival of General Dessalines's troops in order to effect an escape from the island. Gustav, the leader of the party, leaves his twelve compatriots by a wooded pond at nightfall and makes for a nearby house, where he attempts to secure food and overnight lodgings for his party. What Gustav doesn't know is that the house he happens upon belongs to the black man Congo Hoango, a former slave of the French plantation owner Guillaume de Villeneuve who treacherously slew de Villeneuve after hostilities began, despite many acts of kindness shown to him by the benevolent plantation owner over many years. Congo Hoango, in the meantime, has forcibly taken over the plantation and dedicated his life to the murder of all colonizers still left on the island. He has taken the mulatto Babekan as his concubine and has also taken in her daughter Toni, a mestiza, fathered by a Frenchman in Paris, who is accordingly lighter-skinned. The game whose context is shaped by the murder of the plantation owner, the story's unheard-of event, involves Gustav and his party on one side, and Congo Hoango, Babekan, and Toni on the other. Survival is the pay-off at every stage of this cut-throat game of non-cooperation.[26] The optimal strategy of one side is the killing or at least neutralization of the other, since this will guarantee the survival of one party, but such neutralization would not be the Nash equilibrium position in the game, as we shall see.

Two absences are apparent at the start of the game, and they condition its structure: Congo Hoango is away on a mission in support of the cause of General Dessalines, leaving Babekan (whose name means 'fortress') and her daughter Toni alone in the house; Gustav's party is holed up in its hideaway in the forest by the pond, thus leaving Gustav as the vanguard and lone promoter of the Swiss party's cause. Since neither side, by virtue of these absences, is able to exert dominance over the other, the game must be played on the assumption of dissimulation, very much like a game of poker. This point is made at the outset by Babekan, who indicates the need for 'List und [der ganze] Inbegriff jener Künste, die die Notwehr dem Schwachen in die Hände gibt' (165) (it is to be noted that this statement about the importance of dissimulation is, in the context of the story, itself a dissimulation). The first consequence of this strategy of dissimulation is that neither side knows the real motivation of the other, or, indeed, the true identity of the third player, the mestiza Toni, who starts the game on the black side. Since Toni has an African mother and a French father, she is at once black and white. She thus becomes the crucial player in the game, whose choices can tip the balance of the game in favour of one side or the other. In fact, the game may be understood as a struggle to establish a durable alliance with this third player, whose ultimate allegiance becomes the real focus of the game.

Interest in the allegiance of the third player is heightened still further by the question of racial identity. Since identity is linked to the moves the players make in the game, perceptions about racial origin assume importance for the players in assessing the strategy of the game. Indeed, for many interpreters, these perceptions are what the story is really about.[27] Certainly they help account for its startlingly modern appearance. From the perspective of the African, the European is imperialistic and destructive of natural values in a way that no act of kindness can make up for. Congo Hoango's murder of the plantation owner de Villeneuve is consonant with this idea. Black, therefore, must always oppose the moves of white in the game situation. From the reverse perspective, the African is heathen and treacherously dismissive of the humanistic values of tolerance and compassion at the centre of European civilization. Since tolerance is indicated in this position, we can only say that white does not directly oppose the moves of black, unless black is treacherous, in which case white must then oppose black. Such is the case in the story related by Gustav about the young negress who, through dissimulation, infected a white planter, her former owner, with yellow fever. Gustav renders this perspective clear at a crucial moment when doubts about Toni's allegiance are raised at a critical moment in the story: 'Die Rache des Himmels, meinte er, indem er sich mit einem leidenschaftlichen Ausdruck erhob, würde dadurch entwaffnet: die

Engel selbst, dadurch empört, stellten sich auf Seiten derer, die Unrecht hätten, und nähmen, zur Aufrechterhaltung menschlicher und göttlicher Ordnung, ihre Sache!' (171). Such passages represented a problem for early research on Kleist, since they were understood literally and enlisted in support of an essentialist account of humanistic values[28] or, alternatively, the Christian morality on which they were allegedly based.[29] Later scholarship understood them as contributions to a complicated dialogue about the Enlightenment and historicized them.[30] In neither category, however, are they completely subsumable. Rather, such passages are part of a discussion about contingency that has rendered all values precisely that: values or strategic positions to be taken up in a game situation where even the angels themselves can 'take sides'.

Die Verlobung in St Domingo can therefore be understood as a game with a bi-matrix structure in which neutralization of the opponent is the preferred outcome of one side; survival is the pay-off at each stage of the game. The game reveals an underlying contingency in the sense that the critical player, Toni, is both white and black and so without any predictable or necessary allegiance.[31] Allegiance, in her case, is pledged 'decisionistically', in response to the overall game situation. That Toni is the uncommitted third participant in the game does not gainsay its bi-matrix structure. Elsewhere, moves of such a third participant are normally ascribed in game theory to the position of 'nature'. Since Toni's true allegiance is a question of a decision not finally knowable to the other participants, the two sides of the bi-matrix, those occupied by Gustav and Babekan, have no choice but to 'trust' or 'distrust' Toni. Whether they trust or distrust at a particular stage of the game will determine the moves they make in the game; however, only trust can ensure that the game goes to the next stage, and only distrust can end it. The game, accordingly, moves ahead in a bifurcated pattern where trust, the '1' position in the game, continues the game, and distrust, the '0' position, at any stage would end it. This is made clear at the end of the game when Toni declares: 'du hättest mir nicht mißtrauen sollen' (193). The only way that Toni's decision, and perhaps her underlying motivation, can be known is by way of 'backwards induction',[32] that is, through a process of reasoning which assesses her choices from the end of the game back to its beginning. It is only by backwards induction, too, that any final assessment can be made about the level of rationality in the game. This, then, is Kleist's ultimate 'coup': rationality is no longer an a priori question, based on a complete knowledge of the game situation before the fact of human experience, but can only be established a posteriori in the light of actual moves undertaken by players in the game. It is in this undoing of Kant's Copernican project of reason — a project predicated on the idea that rational judgements can be made on the basis of assumptions which precede the fact of human experience — that we find Kleist's true answer to Kant. Kleist's answer to Kant therefore involves relativization of the claims of cognitive reason to provide an a priori guide for human behaviour, and moves other aspects of the humanist project, such as those factors that underpin contingent agreements, to the forefront.

IV

The game of trust at the heart of *Die Verlobung in St Domingo* moves ahead in distinct stages. The first stage begins with Gustav's arrival at the house and his reception by Babekan and Toni, and extends to the point of his first close contact with Toni. In this part of the story, the rules of the game are described, including the game's reliance on dissimulation. That there are no durable values which can serve the players as a guide to action is suggested in the difficulty of assessing origins: Toni is of mixed race, Babekan is a mulatto with a Cuban father (and therefore not unambiguously African); even Gustav himself, although white, is Swiss and as such not clearly in opposition to the moves of black. The game unfolds in response to assumptions that the players make about these origins, and what the origins ultimately stand for.

The second stage in the game is introduced by a substory, which is related by Gustav as a subgame[33] expressing a Nash equilibrium. Since the equilibrium it specifies represents a best reply to the players of that subgame, it can also be termed a subgame perfect (Nash) equilibrium.[34] In this subgame, Gustav's former lover Mariane Congreve saved him from the guillotine during events accompanying the French Revolution by denying knowledge of him under duress. This move in the subgame of trust had the highest possible positive pay-off for Gustav, since it ensured his survival, and the highest possible negative pay-off for Mariane, since she thereby succumbed to the guillotine. (If it can be assumed that Mariane's playing fink would have led to the death of both Gustav, as the exposed traitor of the revolutionary cause, and Mariane, as his accomplice, then Mariane's denial of Gustav which saves his life was also one of two Nash equilibrium outcomes of the game — the other being Gustav's death as a result of playing fink.) This subgame has instructional value for Toni, since it exactly mirrors her position in the main trust game — a game that, similarly, must also be played on the basis of the dissimulated identity of one player. The direct effect of this interpolated subgame is that it precipitates a decisive move by Toni, who subsequently makes love to Gustav and so indicates her trust of him. An act of trust, therefore, moves the game to the next stage, and has the direct pay-off of survival for all participants.

At this next stage of the game a new story is related, also by Gustav. It introduces a second subgame that sets up a counter-position to the story about Mariane Congreve. The new story tells of the slave girl who lures her former slave owner into a trap, where the decision to trust through an act of love, or, better, lovemaking, has the highest possible negative pay-off for the one who trusts, namely his death as a result of infection with yellow fever. Here trust does not lead to a perfect Nash equilibrium outcome. This position could have been reached only as a result of a decision not to trust. This second subgame of complete information therefore relativizes the information of the first subgame, and adds an implicit level of risk to moves that assume trust without the factor of dissimulation.

Toni's next move in the game must take account of the sudden return of Congo Hoango and the suspicions of her mother, who now suspects that Toni has had intimate contact with Gustav (Babekan, it is to be noted, has not been a recipient of the information about dissimulated motives in the second subgame about the slave girl). These events mean that she must practise a decisive act of dissimulation that both allays these suspicions in one direction, and promotes the survival of Gustav, whom it is now clear she truly loves, in the other. She achieves this by tying up Gustav while he sleeps in his room, thus giving the appearance of collusion with the moves of black, while at the same time rushing out to meet Gustav's party in the forest, intercepting a note issued by Babekan that would have lured the party into a trap. This enables Gustav's party to arrive with stealth, overcome Hoango and Babekan, quell the resistance of Hoango's encampment at the house, and liberate Gustav. What it fails to forestall, however, is Gustav's next move, which follows the logic not of the first subgame of trust, but of the second, on the presumption that Toni has treacherously betrayed him and ultimately proved to be a colluder on the black side. This move, which sees him murder Toni before he is in possession of complete information about her motives, is a decision irrevocably to mistrust that ends the game, and, in a postscript or coda to the game, ends his own life as well.

V

What, then, is to be said about *Die Verlobung in St Domingo* after this application of game-theoretical assumptions to the story? The most obvious thing that arises from viewing the story from the perspective of game theory relates to its overriding context of contingency. The story is revealed not only as a non-essentialist account of a contingent world, but also as a world that has nevertheless not abandoned rationality in any sceptical turn from it. Rather, the rationality we observe in the story is embedded in the highly symmetrical nature of its game structure; it is not pre-eminently encountered in the motivation of the figures, who, under certain circumstances, indeed, must favour strategies of non-rational behaviour in seeking to maximize their pay-offs in the game. To this extent, therefore, a game-theoretical approach helps us evaluate, and perhaps see the purpose of, the disparity between form and content long held to be characteristic of Kleist's fiction. The early critic Hermann Davidts is but one of many commentators struck by the highly organized, formalistic nature of Kleist's narratives on the one hand, and their subject matter on the other, where confusion, tragic misunderstandings and quirks of fate reign supreme.[35] In fact, one of the insights to be drawn from this reading of *Die Verlobung in St Domingo* is the difficulty that attends action in the world, precisely because the rational construction of events by the characters on a formal level of thought is unable to brook the complex 'content' of the world which such thought addresses. Kleist thereby relativizes the Enlightenment project of reason, which had insisted that the world could be known through the operation of a type of predictive cognitive schematism. Kleist does not conclude that rational action is impossible in the world. He does, however, draw attention to the issue of complexity and to the means by which it can be brokered beyond reversion to a transparent rationalism. This is underscored in the denouement of *Die Verlobung*, where the rationally minded European Gustav is unable to comprehend the strategies of the Afro-European Toni, though she never failed to have Gustav's best interests at heart. Kleist's point is to underscore the importance of following mixed strategies of both a rational and non-rational nature. While Nash equilibrium outcomes draw on the enlightened self-interest of players and require a 'common knowledge rationality' to sustain them, Kleist's narratives also 'load the dice' against responses founded on a simple predictive rationality. His stories thus point to the value of other, longer-term strategies in effecting equilibrium outcomes in the game situation. Such outcomes, of course, do not finally end the game so much as stabilize it at a point of incompletion. Thus we might conclude that game theory, in its preference for Nash equilibria, is inherently more conserving of the project of life than the novella, which, at least on the evidence of *Die Verlobung in St Domingo*, is strikingly at odds with it.

Notes to Chapter 18

1. Shaun P. Hargreaves Heap and Yanis Varoufakis discuss the theory of natural selection in the context of game theory in *Game Theory: A Critical Introduction* (London and New York: Routledge, 1995), pp. 228, 230.
2. Mary Ann Dimand and Robert W. Dimand, *A History of Game Theory*, I: *From the Beginnings to 1945* (London, New York: Routledge, 1996), p. 2.
3. The assumption that actors act out of 'enlightened self-interest' is basic to game theory; see e.g. Ken Binmore, *Game Theory and the Social Contract*, I: *Playing Fair* (Cambridge, MA, and London: MIT Press, 1994), p. 17.
4. This is a term used by Hargreaves Heap and Varoufakis, *Game Theory*, p. 23.
5. As Behnegar points out, rational choice theory represents 'the continuation of the tendency of modern social science following modern natural science to understand complex wholes in light of their simple elements.' See Nasser Behnegar, *Leo Strauß, Max Weber, and the Scientific Study of Politics* (Chicago and London: University of Chicago Press, 2003), p. 24.
6. As Hargreaves Heap and Varoufakis explain, 'Rand' stands for 'r[esearch] and d[evelopment]', *Game Theory*, p. 50.
7. See William Poundstone, *Prisoner's Dilemma: John von Neumann, Game Theory and the Puzzle of the Bomb* (New York: Anchor Books, 1993), pp. 8–9. As Poundstone argues, Flood and Dresher's work was strongly influenced by Neumann and Oskar Morgenstern, who had published their *Theory of Games and Economic Behavior* (Princeton: Princeton University Press, 1944) six years earlier.
8. Hargreaves Heap and Varoufakis, *Game Theory*, p. 50.
9. The 2001 Hollywood film *A Beautiful Mind* discusses aspects of Nash's life, including his contribution to game theory.
10. Hargreaves Heap and Varoufakis, *Game Theory*, p. 53.
11. David M. Kreps, *Game Theory and Economic Modelling* (Oxford: Clarendon Press, 1990), p. 35.
12. Ibid., p. 11.
13. Niklas Luhmann, 'Contingency as Modern Society's Defining Attribute', in *Observations on Modernity* (1992), trans. by William Whobrey (Stanford: Stanford University Press, 1998), pp. 44–62.
14. Ibid., p. 45.
15. As Kant said in the preface to the *Prolegomena*: 'Ich gestehe frei: die Erinnerung des David Hume war eben dasjenige, was mir vor vielen Jahren zuerst den dogmatischen Schlummer unterbrach und meinen Untersuchungen im Felde der spekulativen Philosophie eine ganz andere Richtung gab'; *Kants Werke: Akademie-Textausgabe*, ed. by Preußische Akademie der Wissenschaften, 11 vols (Berlin: Walter de Gruyter, 1968), IV, 260.
16. Although certainly indirectly, as I have argued in '"Betwixt a false reason and none at all": Kleist, Kant, Hume, and the "Thing in Itself"', in *A Companion to the Works of Heinrich von Kleist*, ed. by Bernd Fischer (Rochester, NY: Camden House, 2003), pp. 165–88.

17. For a discussion of Kleist's 'Kant crisis' and the views it has elicited in the critical literature, see Tim Mehigan, 'Kleist, Kant und die Aufklärung', in *Heinrich von Kleist und die Aufklärung*, ed. by Tim Mehigan (Rochester, NY: Camden House, 2000), pp. 3–21.
18. See among others Friedrich Kittler, *Aufschreibesysteme 1800/1900* (Munich: Wilhelm Fink, 1985).
19. Ken Binmore's application of game theory to Thomas Hobbes's *Leviathan* and other contractual theorists such as Rousseau, however, suggest that game theory is also encountered in the thinking of early political theorists of the modern age; *Game Theory and the Social Contract*, I.
20. Denys Dyer's discussion of Kleist's stories is but one of many approaches that highlight the irrationality of the world Kleist portrays; see Dyer, *The Stories of Kleist* (London: Duckworth, 1977), esp. pp. 151–69.
21. Bernd Fischer speaks of the 'Skepsis an der Ratio' that has long dominated readings of Kleist in the secondary literature: see Fischer, *Ironische Metaphysik: die Erzählungen Heinrich von Kleists* (Munich: Wilhelm Fink, 1988), p. 13.
22. For this reason, approaches, such as Fischer's, that emphasize the insoluble nature of the dilemmas thrown up by Kleist's stories (see Fischer, *Ironische Metaphysik*, p. 160) fail to give a full account of Kleist's critique of rational understanding.
23. See especially the contributions of Hans-Jochen Marquardt, 'Heinrich von Kleist: die Geburt der Moderne aus dem Geiste "neuer Aufklärung"', and David Roberts, 'Kleists Kritik der Urteilskraft: zum Erhabenen in *Das Erdbeben in Chili*', in *Heinrich von Kleist und die Aufklärung* (see Mehigan, note 17 above), pp. 22–45, 46–57.
24. See Dyer, *The Stories of Kleist*, pp. 150–00.
25. Johann Peter Eckermann, *Gespräche mit Goethe in den letzten Jahren seines Lebens*, ed. by Fritz Bergemann, 2 vols (Frankfurt: Insel, 1981), I, 207–08: 'denn was ist eine Novelle anders als eine sich ereignete, unerhörte Begebenheit'.
26. Babekan alludes to survival as a pay-off in the following way: 'Beim Himmel, diese deine Erklärung rettet ihm für heute das Leben!': *Heinrich von Kleist: Sämtliche Werke und Briefe*, ed. by Helmut Sembdner, 2 vols (Darmstadt: Wissenschaftliche Buchgesellschaft, 1983), II, 178. Further references to this edition and volume are given after quotations in the text.
27. See, for instance, Susanne Zantop, 'Changing Color: Kleist's *Die Verlobung in St Domingo* and the Discourses of Miscegenation', in *A Companion to the Works of Heinrich von Kleist* (see Fischer, note 16 above), pp. 191–208.
28. Among the many early adherents of this approach, Günter Blöcker's may be considered representative: *Heinrich von Kleist oder das absolute Ich* (Berlin: Argon, 1960).
29. Such is the nature of Gerhard Fricke's existentialist approach, first published in 1929, which was highly influential for later Kleist scholarship: *Gefühl und Schicksal bei Heinrich von Kleist* (Darmstadt: Wissenschaftliche Buchgesellschaft, 1963).
30. Fischer's analysis is a good example of such approaches: 'Kleists Erzählungen [können] durchaus historisch als Auseinandersetzung mit dem herrschenden Paradigma seiner Zeit (das vielleicht immer noch am treffendsten mit dem epochalen Schlagwort Idealismus gefaßt wird) begriffen werden, dessen Grenzen er im ironischen Experiment aufzuzeigen vermag, ohne sie freilich [...] grundsätzlich überschreiten zu können'; Fischer, *Ironische Metaphysik*, p. 12.
31. Toni is only half as black as her mulatto mother Babekan. This has significance for Herbert Uerlings, who has argued that the lightness of Toni's skin means that her blush can be decoded by the male as a cipher of sexual desire. See Herbert Uerlings, *Poetiken der Interkulturalität: Haiti bei Kleist, Seghers, Müller, Buch und Fichte* (Tübingen: Niemeyer, 1997), p. 43.
32. Hargreaves Heap and Varoufakis offer a useful discussion of 'backwards induction', *Game Theory*, pp. 80–85.
33. A subgame is a subset of an extensive game that starts from a 'node' in the game and feeds information back into a player's 'information partition'. For a discussion, see Hargreaves Heap and Varoufakis, *Game Theory*, pp. 82–83.
34. Ibid., p. 83.
35. See Hermann Davidts, *Die novellistische Kunst Heinrichs von Kleist* (Hildesheim: Gerstenberg, 1973).

CHAPTER 19

❖

Towards Discursive Discipline: Dance beyond Metaphor in Critical Writing

Lucia Ruprecht

This chapter argues for more discipline in the use of 'dance' as a trope in criticism. Following a strand in recent dance studies which questions the undifferentiated application of dance as metaphor for the mobility of signification or gender, it reclaims a more elaborate vision of bodily movement.[1] To this end it proposes to rethink the critical vocabulary of instability by closely reading two passages of deconstructive criticism by Paul de Man and Jacques Derrida, who both employ the metaphor of dance for developing their argument. In order to demonstrate what can be gained from reinstating dance as an object of analysis, the focus then turns to the bodily practice at the root of the metaphor. I shall illustrate instances of this practice by looking at the work of two choreographers chosen for their engagement in highly original modes of discursive interaction with their own medium: William Forsythe and his choreographic tool *Improvisation Technologies*, and Thomas Lehmen and his conceptual choreography *Schreibstück* (*Writing Piece*). By opening up more productive views on dance as concept and as object of critical writing, I aim to show that a critical analysis of the tropes of criticism is an essential part of the challenges and chances of in(ter)disciplinary theory.

One aspect of interdisciplinary work in the humanities is certainly the interdisciplinary character of theory itself; I refer here to a definition of theory by Jonathan Culler which is useful because it is both precise and general. Theory may be defined as the name for an unbounded corpus of works

> that succeed in challenging and reorienting thinking in domains other than those to which they ostensibly belong because their analyses of language, mind, history, or culture offer novel and persuasive accounts of signification, make strange the familiar and perhaps persuade readers to conceive of their own thinking and the institutions to which it relates in new ways.[2]

It is this cross-fertilization of thought between the disciplines that Clifford Geertz draws attention to as early as 1983. He ponders the rising 'recourse to the humanities for explanatory analogies in the social sciences' which is visible in the revised style of the discourse in social studies that incorporates more and more terms derived from forms of cultural performance — 'theatre', 'text', or 'game' — and traces how these terms alter the ways we think about society.[3] More recently, Mieke Bal turned the exploration of such borrowings, and their bearing on critical language, into an integral part of her theoretical approach. One of the distinguishing features of her project of cultural analysis is the attention to 'travelling' concepts as the main agents of exchange between different domains of critical inquiry. Concepts in Bal's sense are theories *en miniature*, which through their travels across history, practices, and disciplines change, and in so doing resist any stable positioning. In order to unfold their potential for critical analysis, and indeed to enter the critical endeavour, concepts have to be under constant scrutiny, so that the analysis of an object always also implies the analysis of its own instruments of investigation. Thus concepts are able to further communication in the academic or public discourse and enhance communication with the object, which is the main performer of scrutiny; in Bal's words:

> Theory here is not an instrument of analysis, to be 'applied' to the art object, supposedly serving it but in fact subjecting it. Instead, it is a discourse that can be brought to bear on the object at the same time as the object can be brought to bear on *it*.

Definition is thus more about 'meaningful' than about 'correct' use of concepts; it is not a once-and-for-all achievement, but an activity — maybe *the* activity of a theoretical approach to culture — that renegotiates concepts in the dialogue between critics (the notion of 'critic' may be taken in a wide sense here), and between the critic and her object.[4] This dialogue implies a destabilization, if not reversal, of the positions of subject and object, since the 'object' starts actively to shape the theory, rather than merely suffering the theoretical application. Theory negotiates transposable languages within a framework of mutual corrections, and it is not least a discursive discipline of continuous attention, reflection, and differentiation of concepts that makes critical writing worthwhile.

This attention, reflection, and differentiation will be devoted, in the following, to the use of 'dance' in critical writing, that is, theoretical writing which is not criticism of dance, but criticism of literature or culture. Indeed, one of the aims of this chapter is to stimulate the engagement with dance and dance criticism by other disciplines, and to show how this engagement might modify their critical languages. If not as a concept in any rigorous sense, theoretical writing indubitably employs 'dance' as a 'convenient metaphor' for various forms of movement, and not least 'for spontaneity, frivolity, and the inexpressible'.[5] Its most significant journey is not the travelling between uses within criticism, but that between practice and theory, turning the manifold styles, techniques, and forms of dancing into the metaphor dance, which is then substituted for various theoretical concepts of critical discourse. This process has three implications: the theoretical use of 'dance' is based on a generalization; the general term is summoned up to illustrate more abstract vocabularies; and, most fundamentally, theoretical writing is metaphorical writing. Again Bal's work provides the cues here: while she has pointed out how the concept of metaphor works as an appropriate 'metaphor of theory-in-general', and furthermore 'why it makes sense to consider theoretical concepts as metaphors',

I would like to cast light on the substitution of various concepts — or metaphors — with a single metaphor. While Bal accentuates the cognitive potential of metaphors, the substitution I am interested in is first of all of rhetorical, rather than cognitive, value, and its metaphorical surplus of meaning operates ideologically (reductive, generalizing) rather than theoretically (tolerating complexity): instead of productively bringing 'two frames of reference', the literal and the figurative, 'into collision' through a strictly speaking false assertion of identity, and thus promoting reflection, it simplifies and romanticizes the theoretical concept.[6] However, although failing to specify or analyse the object, the use of 'dance' tells us something about the effect of metaphorical assertions, about their intended or unintentional strategic potential, and therefore brings us back to the classical rhetorical paradigm of persuasion: metaphors are never innocent, and are 'much more tenacious than facts'.[7] An exploration of dance as a metaphor in the theoretical language of deconstruction may illustrate these claims.

In 'Semiology and Rhetoric', the programmatic first chapter of *Allegories of Reading*, Paul de Man makes a case for his emphasis on the undecidable, aporetic structure of linguistic meaning by analysing the end of W. B. Yeats's poem 'Among School Children'. The paradoxical figure of the rhetorical question which concludes the poem acts as a model example of ambiguity. This paradoxical figure, however, emerges within one of the best-known poetic appearances of dance:

> O chestnut-tree, great-rooted blossomer,
> Are you the leaf, the blossom or the bole?
> O body swayed to music, O brightening glance,
> How can we know the dancer from the dance?[8]

An isolated look at the final question exposes the impossibility of deciding between the literal and the figurative meaning of the line. The figurative meaning, here, plays along with the rhetorical function of language, which for de Man pertains both to a system of tropes and to persuasion and speech acts. 'How can we know the dancer from the dance?' as rhetorical question seen in context, then, continues the imagery of the preceding lines by stating the potential unity between experience and reflection, agent and activity, signifier and signified. The literal meaning, in contrast, which in de Man's terminology belongs to the grammatical function of language, takes the question at face value, as asking with some urgency how we can possibly avoid identifying what cannot be identified. Rhetoric and grammar, although closely intertwined, undermine each other. This instance is shown as paradigmatic for literary language, which is in a state of permanent self-contestation. Literature thus undoes claims for authority both literary and critical that draw on the continuity of form with meaning, of perception with knowledge and on the hermeneutic power of interpretation, claims that testify to what de Man calls aesthetic ideology. While this ideology may be described as the tyranny of decidability and definiteness, literature and criticism — 'the difference between them being delusive' — are both languages of undecidability, and therefore forms of critique of ideology.

Reading de Man's chapter as a literary text, then, one wonders why the author highlights a sequence on dance for pursuing his explorations of the rhetorical question, which he starts, by the way, with an example from the everyday use of this device. The end of 'Semiology and Rhetoric' is revealing. After his skilful unravelling of the unreliability of language, de Man declares: 'The resulting pathos is an anxiety (or bliss, depending on one's momentary mood or individual temperament) of ignorance.'[9] Bliss, in fact, seems to be unconvincing, given that the weight of anxiety is enhanced by the use of the word pathos, which resounds with suffering. I would like to argue that dance functions as a strategic metaphor here, professing, through the performative rather than the constative dimension of de Man's writing, a light-heartedness ('O body swayed to music, O brightening glance') which in a literal rhetoric of romanticism declares undecidability a blissful state of unrestrained mobility. It is as if the author needed the recourse to poetry in order to bear the poetic, in order to cope with the terror of the unknown, of not-yet and never-reliably-realizable meaning.[10] Faithful to the theoretical programme, de Man's 'Aesthetic Formalization: Kleist's "Über das Marionettentheater"' extends the metaphor of dance to the opposite of what it had represented before, to the 'fencing match' of formalizing interpretation. Undoing the earlier romanticized use in the new context, 'Aesthetic Formalization' relentlessly declares the metaphor to denote a spectacle of death, an 'ultimate trap as unavoidable as it is deadly'. The unavoidability of the trap of interpretation thus leads back to the anxiety of ignorance, and to the need for the act of making sense, even if this act can be a harmful demand that implies the 'dismemberment of language'.[11] De Man's elegant play with the metaphor of dance, ranging from graceful mobility to deathly performance, certainly illustrates the literary quality of the author's criticism. Yet instead of analysing undecidability, it simplifies and strategically promotes the author's values. Reading de Man with his own technique against himself, one cannot fail to acknowledge that the metaphor introduces an ideological element to his texts, thus betraying a gap between their presumed intentions and their tropological imagery. More importantly, however, it tells us something about the unsettling effect of a theoretical stance that argues for the political and ethical relevance of aporias, an effect which is evident, after all, in the many hostile, self-defensive reactions to deconstructive thought. The author himself gives voice to this anxiety in the face of undecidability, and uses the metaphor of dance both to gloss over it and to name its consequences.

Dance as showcase of the incalculable figures in an equally prominent manner in 'Choreographies', Jacques Derrida's interview with Christie V. McDonald. Encircling its subject in tentative steps and moves rather than directly addressing the questions, the interview is a virtuoso illustration of its epigraph attributed to the revolutionary anarchist Emma Goldman (1869–1940), who is supposed to have said of the feminist movement: 'If I can't dance I don't want to be part of your revolution.' It investigates the difficulty of reconciling two inherently different logics of thought: feminism as a political project in need of identities and essences that enable a liberating agency, and deconstruction as a denial of the possibility of such identities and essences.[12] Derrida thus answers the question about how he would describe 'woman's place' by questioning the need for a stable place in the first instance. Undoubtedly aware of 'the possibilities for misquotation and misinterpretation', he asks: 'Why must there be a place for woman? And why only one, a single, completely essential place?' Throughout the interview, he avoids being pinned down himself while lucidly unfolding the metaphorical realm of dance, which serves as the only positioning of woman within the non-position of constant movement: 'The most innocent of dances would thwart the *assignation à résidence*, escape those residences under surveillance; the dance changes place and above all changes *places*.' Suggesting at the beginning of the interview that his answers should be taken as dancerly improvisations, he at once reflects upon and performs femininity-as-movement, which then leads towards an increasing attention to movement as such. 'Dance' is both the exchange between the varying 'rhythms' of the two sexes and the desire to 'escape the combinatory itself', to enter into a 'multiplicity of sexually marked voices' beyond homosexuality and heterosexuality, and in so doing to invent 'incalculable choreographies' of sexual indeterminacy.[13]

While gender-theoretical rereadings of Derrida's deconstructive argument have been undertaken, I would like to linger on the use of 'improvisation' and 'choreography' here.[14] Derrida characterizes his improvisations as the opposite of 'calculated premeditation', as essayistic, momentary dances. This accent on the incalculable also extends to his understanding of choreography as 'mobile', made of random, transient arrangements and rearrangements of polysexual marks. The meanings of 'mobile', 'dance', 'improvisation', and 'choreography' become interchangeable; moreover, they do not specify in any sense the practical and strategic moves of a feminist revolution — an issue the interviewer is clearly concerned with — but shift it towards a queer cultural critique of theoretical phallogocentrism as the 'complicity of Western metaphysics with a notion of male firstness'.[15] Indicating the interaction of temporality and spatiality in dynamic constellations, the tropes come to signify the chance movement of *différance* that pertains to both the time and the space of language.[16] Metaphorically representing deconstructive thought as movement, they are particularly evocative since they also echo the movement of the metaphorical transference. Moreover, the tropes reflect upon their own status as metaphors whose signification is in permanent flux: 'dance', 'improvisation', and 'choreography' are substituted for 'movement', 'femininity', and 'sexual indeterminacy'; they also replace 'text' and 'reading'. The latter analogy is of specific interest because it recalls de Man's use of dancerly vocabulary. Derrida correlates the hermeneutic practice of arresting 'the text in a certain position, thus settling on a thesis, meaning or truth' with the stable placement of essentialized femininity, and with the truth value in Western discourse, which brings us back to the need 'to assuage [...] hermeneutic anxiety'.[17] Echoing de Man's recourse to Yeats, he treats the unease of permanent displacements through the uplifting metaphorical language of dance.

'Choreographies' uses the vocabulary of dancerly movement for reasons of style and strategy rather than for actually making use of the specific potential of this vocabulary. Contrary to its suggestive title, it promotes a decidedly non-choreographic understanding of dance. Physical movement, however, can be both rebellious and submissive, so that choreography is essential once one is genuinely interested in any specific agency of dance. Pacing out the same contrast between 'place' and 'dance', Henrik Ibsen's 1879 play *A Doll's House* reads like a backdrop to the interview. The heroine Nora's tarantella unfolds its complex emancipatory dynamic not merely because it is a dance, but by means of its powerful choreography. Derrida's resistance to any clear-cut topography of femininity that unavoidably recalls woman's place as being 'in the home' or 'in the kitchen' is prefigured in the play; yet the liberating dance is situated both outside and within the patriarchal economy, as a performance of rebellion staged as an act of discipline and obedience. Hence Nora performs her violent tarantella apparently to allure her husband and convince him that all his dance-masterly qualities are needed to dictate her movements; yet the excess of her submissive over-achievement of the set task foresees Nora's final move of slamming the door behind her when leaving her domestic life.

However, theoretical writing, not least the more recent language of performativity, is replete with non-choreographic views of dance.[18] Given that 'dance', if not shifted towards the agony of an interpretative pas de deux with death as in de Man's essay on Kleist, represents the very mobility at the heart of poststructuralist thought, one feels inclined to ask why it is that writers turn to this and not to other forms of movement. Why not 'walking, marching and swimming' as Janet Wolff wonders?[19] It seems that imagery which is able to express a critique of stasis is not enough. Dance attracts certain assumptions: lacking systematic documentation, it is perceived as spontaneous or chaotic; being non-verbal or pre-verbal, it challenges the symbolic order of language; playful and evanescent, it seems to subvert or escape from power.[20] While Wolff argues that dance, through being seen as creative and liberating, provides metaphors that 'operate automatically as critical theory', the examples of theoretical writing which have been analysed here suggest a more differentiated perspective.[21] Indeed, de Man's and Derrida's texts show that the vocabulary of dance functions so well because of its rhetorical, rather than conceptual, quality, persuading the reader of critical claims through opening up an appealing metaphorical realm of affective and aesthetic experience. This poetic quality of deconstructive criticism testifies to a double agency: by producing readings which are themselves literary and in need of a reading, deconstruction dismantles the making of sense through interpretation; at the same time, its poetic suggestiveness sustains our faith in powerful words — like dance.[22]

Personal perceptions of dance and dancing, whether as viewer or practitioner, underpin the effectiveness of the metaphor. This use of dance, then, is not about the object as such, but all about the critic's relation to this object, which is traditionally seen as extraordinarily resistant to theory. While the vocabulary of dance tells us much about the writer's experience of the object, and of the effect of metaphorical substitutions, it also silences this object through generalizing, simplifying, and romanticizing uses. However, dance requires theory precisely because it often appears to evade the intellectual grasp. There is a fundamental remoteness between the physicality of dance and the abstractions of critical writing. Verbal language is in general closer to what we may call the production and identification of meaning, whereas dance is associated, in the first place, with the production of 'presence'.[23] By presence I do not mean the revelation of a metaphysical truth on stage, but very concretely the experience of dance as event for both the performer and the spectator, as the performance or the witnessing of the enactment of physical effort in the here and now. The critic feels that she cannot do justice to this experience through a style of interpretation that is mainly concerned with the intellectual identification of meaning through interpretation, since this style is unable to reach the intensity of the affective and physical responses to the event. Presence-production and meaning-production are of course always interlinked, and their respective weights vary in different texts and different dance pieces; however, the distinction between presence and meaning is useful because it helps to explain why theoretical writing turns to dance in a poetic rather than a critical way, drawing on it as a metaphor and not as an object for analysis.

Yet despite being a form of cultural performance which is perceived as recalcitrant and difficult, dance is embedded in discursive and cognitive structures that can be analysed to productive effect. Indeed, among the most exciting research on dance is the investigation of movement and cognition carried out, for instance, at the University of Cambridge in 2003–04 in a joint research project of the choreographer Wayne McGregor and a group of collaborating scientists from the fields of cognitive psychology and neuroscience to inquire into connections between choreographic processes and the study of movement and the brain or mind. Moreover, dance studies have done much to denaturalize and historicize the modes in which the body signifies through performance. One aspect of this endeavour is the exploration of the culturally and historically varying techniques of bodily movement.[24] One quickly starts to see here that dance as a physical technique is characterized not by limitless transgressions, which 'carry, divide, multiply the body of each "individual"', to quote Derrida, beyond the context of his queer utopia, but by the finitude of bodily experience.[25] Dance always involves 'the acknowledgement of some point beyond which the dancer cannot go', whether this be the restrictions of physical capacity and of anatomy, or the prescribed moves of a choreography.[26] Looking at two examples of actual dance practice, I shall thus address the object, or more succinctly the activity at the base of the metaphor, on its own terms, and try to tell 'the dancer from the dance'. The following introduction to aspects of the work of William Forsythe, director of the Frankfurt Ballet until 2004 and now leading the Forsythe Company, and to a project by the Berlin-based choreographer Thomas Lehmen have been singled out as casting light on recent developments in those elements of dance which figured prominently in de Man's and Derrida's texts: interpretation, improvisation, and choreography. While both texts remain in the metaphorical circuit of the opposition between fixture and flux, definiteness and undecidability, the work of the choreographers shows a surprising and counter-intuitive intermingling of the calculated with the incalculable, of flux not despite or against, but because of fixture.

What is improvisation? At first sight, improvisation calls up the idea of a free, unforeseeable action that does not follow any prior plan or structure.[27] This action is meant to allow for the discovery of movement which cannot be choreographed and thus for the emergence of the new as in the context of Derrida's incalculable 'improvisations' of gender. Spontaneous and transient, improvisation is a process of constant figuration and refiguration. The study of improvisational processes in dance has however taught us that it is not the absence of any plan or structure, but indeed the interaction of a certain freedom of choice with the creation of limits — points in space, the concentration on specific qualities of movement, or the visualization of shapes or images — which produces the most original results. This is because the body needs stimulation and challenge in order not to fall back on known patterns of movement that occur with persistence once there are no restrictions from the outside. Productive improvisation therefore includes a choreographic element. Departing from these insights, and from the wish to make the improvisational process communicable, William Forsythe has developed a method of describing and encouraging improvisation which is available in a version for the public on the CD-ROM *Improvisation Technologies: A Tool for the Analytical Dance Eye*. This method reflects Forsythe's deconstructive approach to the 'language' of classical dance. Ballet can be described as a system with a certain vocabulary (elements of movement), grammar (rules of connecting and directing movement), and syntax (the actual combinations of movements). The choreographer is not interested in ballet as a historical ritual, but as a process of thinking or 'writing' — as opposed to the semantic unity of a text — which implies that dance becomes a syntactical operation characterized by choice, combination, dissection, and recombination. Therefore movement is 'the subject' of his works 'rather than a medium for a presumed narrative, musical analogy, or "meaning" existing somewhere "behind" the choreography'.[28]

Forsythe and his dancers find new 'ways of imagining the geometric relationships between different parts of the body as they move' by reassessing classical conventions like turnout (the rotation of the leg in the hip joint), verticality, balance, gravity, and spatial orientation. This process becomes accessible through the CD-ROM, which visualizes the principles of the generation of movement. Visualization is the key term here, since *Improvisation Technologies* is a dance school that is at the same time a school of seeing. It 'explains the basics of seeing motion by leaving traces', borrowing, in a complementary move to the texts investigated above, linguistic vocabulary to describe dance metaphorically: 'It's about a way of feeling and sensing spaces for the individual dancer, and so it's about inscription and how to write clearly this way.' There is for example one series of short demonstrations on the CD-ROM that is called 'rotating inscription', which introduces different modes of 'room writing' or 'drawing', 'u-ing' and 'o-ing', using the shapes of letters for capturing movement traces (Figure 19.1). The CD-ROM is thus a tool that visualizes the ephemeral drawings produced by movement in space, groups them according to their characteristics, and develops an analytical language for their description. To quote Forsythe again, it is

> maybe less about how to improvise than about how to analyse when you're improvising. If you are dancing, how do you actually say what happened? The technique is one way of taking mental note of what just happened to you while improvising.[29]

Forsythe's technique of analysing and describing movement creates a structure or

Figure 19.1. Demonstration of rotating inscription, from CD-ROM *Improvisation Technologies* by William Forsythe. © ZKM | Zentrum für Kunst und Medientechnologie Karlsruhe

a supply of options within which new movement can emerge, and helps to detect the complex operations within the dancing body, making them communicable to oneself, to other dancers and to the public.

Dance as communication between performer and audience, and between choreographer and performer, is of equal importance to the work of Thomas Lehmen. All his pieces are concerned with transcending conventional forms of dance spectacle, investigating the roles of choreography, interpretation, and performance. Choreography as the art of composing dances traditionally implies the creation by a single person of movement material which is then passed on to the interpreters. Lehmen's *Schreibstück*, in contrast, is a choreographic experiment that radically challenges expectations of authorship in dance: by separating the authorial (conceptual) from the choreographic (pragmatic) function of the maker of dances, Lehmen renounces the privileges of the creator. He is the author of a script that functions as a score of different tasks and guidelines for three choreographers, who realize the instructions with three dancers each (Figure 19.2). The script specifies certain factors, among them timing and spacing, while prescribing nothing about the actual transposition of the score into movement. It does, however, assign certain sequences to verbal interaction with the public, which is thus made aware of its participation in the event. The three versions are combined over two days to create

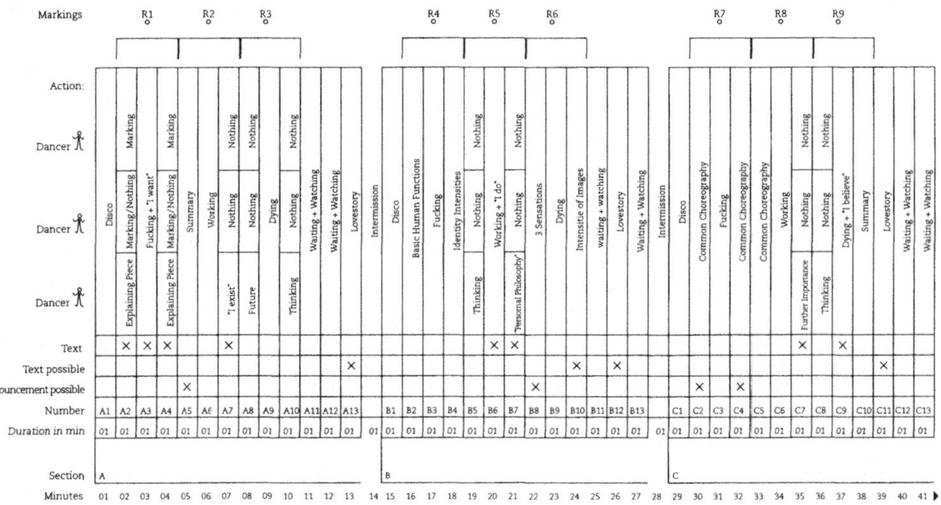

FIGURE 19.2. Score of *Schreibstück*. © Thomas Lehmen

a piece that figures the canonical performance of the different solutions. Again we are confronted with the interaction of improvisation and frames, with agency within a given structure, options and choice: Lehmen creates an interpretative 'thinking-space [...] which is not occupied by fixed significations' for choreography.[30] It is up to the choreographers how they represent such tasks as 'disco', 'identity intensities', 'waiting and watching', 'common choreography', or 'nothing'. Since its premiere in Berlin in 2002, which involved the choreographers Mart Kangro (Tallinn), Martin Nachbar (Berlin), and Sónia Baptista (Lisbon), *Schreibstück* has been performed by different choreographers and dancers at many dance festivals throughout Europe.

Lehmen thus introduces a new partition into the economy of dance production, passing on the full choreographic responsibility to the performers and thereby revaluing interpretation as a creative activity in its own right. This becomes evident in performances that are always, from the start, three readings of a given text, each viable on its own while also entering into productive interplay with the other versions. Both Lehmen and Forsythe work with the figure of a 'framed' mobility which offers itself to the critical grasp: Forsythe with a method of analysable and communicable improvisation by which new choreography may emerge, Lehmen with a concept of creation within guidelines that allow, through the dissociation of elements during the process of production, the reflection and discussion of authorship, choreography, interpretation, and performance. Their dances therefore may indeed be called upon in order to sharpen our understanding and our imagination of processes of figuration, of the materialization of the new, and of the undecidability between equally valid interpretations of a text; they do so, however, through operations too complex to be grasped in the notion of a general sense of movement. Like the poetic richness of deconstructive readings, which are themselves in need of a reading, these dances dismantle the desire for definiteness in the act of making sense, while engaging in a communicative project that turns them into both agents and objects of theory.

Notes to Chapter 19

This article was written with the generous support of a Junior Research Fellowship at Churchill College, Cambridge.

1. See Susan Leigh Foster, 'Choreographies of Gender', *Signs*, 24.1 (1998), 1–33; Janet Wolff, 'Dance Criticism: Feminism, Theory and Choreography', in *Resident Alien: Feminist Cultural Criticism*, ed. by Janet Wolff (Cambridge: Polity Press, 1995), pp. 68–87; more generally Catherine Nash, 'Performativity in Practice: Some Recent Work in Cultural Geography', *Progress in Human Geography*, 24 (2000), 653–64.
2. Jonathan Culler, 'Literary Theory', in *Introduction to Scholarship in Modern Languages and Literatures*, ed. by Joseph Gibaldi, 2nd edn (New York: Modern Languages Association of America, 1992), pp. 201–35 (p. 203).
3. Clifford Geertz, 'Blurred Genres: The Refiguration of Social Thought', in *Local Knowledge: Further Essays in Interpretive Anthropology* (New York: Basic Books, 1983), pp. 19–35 (p. 23).
4. See Mieke Bal, *Travelling Concepts in the Humanities: A Rough Guide* (Toronto: University of Toronto Press, 2002), pp. 61, 17.
5. Foster, 'Choreographies of Gender', p. 20.
6. Mieke Bal, 'Scared to Death', in *The Point of Theory: Practices of Cultural Analysis*, ed. by Mieke Bal and Inge E. Boer (Amsterdam: Amsterdam University Press, 1994), pp. 32–47 (pp. 34, 40).
7. Paul de Man, 'Semiology and Rhetoric', in *Allegories of Reading* (New Haven: Yale University Press, 1979), pp. 3–19 (p. 5); see also Jonathan Culler, 'The Turns of Metaphor', in *The Pursuit of Signs: Semiotics, Literature, Deconstruction* (London: Routledge and Kegan Paul, 1981), pp. 188–209 (p. 208).
8. William Butler Yeats, 'Among School Children', in *Poetry in English: An Anthology*, ed. by M. L. Rosenthal (New York: Oxford University Press, 1987), pp. 784–86 (p. 786).
9. De Man, 'Semiology and Rhetoric', pp. 11, 19.
10. See Adam Phillips, 'Poetry and Psychoanalysis', in *Promises, Promises: Essays on Literature and Psychoanalysis* (London: Faber and Faber, 2000), pp. 1–34 (pp. 22–23).
11. Paul de Man, 'Aesthetic Formalization: Kleist's "Über das Marionettentheater"', in *The Rhetoric of Romanticism* (New York: Columbia University Press, 1984), pp. 263–90 (p. 290).
12. The interview, which was published for the first time in 1982, prognosticates the move from feminism and gender studies to postfeminism and queer theory which developed through the 1980s and 1990s.
13. Jacques Derrida and Christie V. McDonald, 'Choreographies: Interview', in *Feminist Interpretations of Jacques Derrida*, ed. by Nancy J. Holland (University Park: Pennsylvania State University Press, 1997), pp. 23–41 (pp. 23, 24, 27, 28, 40).
14. See Foster, 'Choreographies of Gender', p. 27; Wolff, 'Dance Criticism', pp. 78–87.
15. Derrida and McDonald, 'Choreographies: Interview', pp. 24, 29.
16. See Jacques Derrida, 'Différance', in *Margins of Philosophy*, trans. by Alan Bass (New York: Harvester Wheatsheaf, 1982), pp. 1–27.
17. Derrida and McDonald, 'Choreographies: Interview', p. 29.
18. See Foster, 'Choreographies of Gender', p. 26.
19. Wolff, 'Dance Criticism', p. 79.
20. See Nigel Thrift, 'The Still Point: Resistance, Expressive Embodiment and Dance', in *Geographies of Resistance*, ed. by Steve Pile and Michael Keith (London: Routledge, 1997), pp. 124–51; Foster, 'Choreographies of Gender', p. 17; Wolff , 'Dance Criticism', pp. 79–80.
21. Wolff, 'Dance Criticism', p. 80.
22. See Phillips, 'Poetry and Psychoanalysis', pp. 21, 26.
23. On this understanding of 'presence' and 'meaning' with regard to opera, see Hans Ulrich Gumbrecht, 'Produktion von Präsenz, durchsetzt mit Absenz: über Musik, Libretto und

Inszenierung', in *Ästhetik der Inszenierung*, ed. by Josef Früchtl and Jörg Zimmermann (Frankfurt a.M.: Suhrkamp, 2001), pp. 63–76.

24. See Susan Leigh Foster, 'Dancing Bodies', in *Meaning in Motion: New Cultural Studies of Dance*, ed. by Jane C. Desmond (Durham, NC: Duke University Press, 1997), pp. 235–57.
25. Derrida and McDonald, 'Choreographies: Interview', p. 40.
26. Susan Bordo, *Unbearable Weight: Feminism, Western Culture, and the Body* (Berkeley: University of California Press, 1993), p. 228.
27. See Friederike Lampert, 'Tanzimprovisation auf der Bühne: Entdeckung von Nicht-Choreografierbarem', in *Tanz, Theorie, Text*, ed. by Gabriele Klein and Christa Zipprich (Münster: Lit, 2002), pp. 445–56.
28. William Forsythe, *Improvisation Technologies: A Tool for the Analytical Dance Eye* (Karlsruhe: ZKM; Cologne: German Dance Archive, 1999), pp. 36–37.
29. Ibid., pp. 36, 16.
30. Thomas Lehmen, 'Well, I'm an artist, and I can write whatever I want and in whatever form I want', in *Schreibstück* (ISBN 3–00–009996–4, distributed by the author), passage 4 [unpaginated].

CHAPTER 20

❖

Interdisciplinarity and Public Engagement

Katy Price

This article was written in 2003, and several contexts where critical practice might find fresh resources have gathered momentum during the intervening period. These include the development of creative practice as research, new initiatives for supporting live literature, and further involvement of humanities organizations in science outreach. Fortunately, critical discussions arising from these and other fora are not confined to subspecialists in, say, creative practice, community arts, or literature and science. Yet the potential contribution of English studies and related forms of criticism to ongoing debates regarding the scope and limits of public engagement and the diversity of ends that 'engagement' may serve remains to be realized. A fuller recognition of activities related to public engagement, as part of research assessment across the disciplines, is needed.

The New Languages for Criticism project is committed to 'comparative thinking within a wider interdisciplinary perspective' and to 'elaborating links and conceptual interfaces between different forms of cultural expression'; alongside this commitment the project involves people whose research 'reaches beyond the academic domain in an effort to stimulate critical thinking in the wider public arena'. The In(ter)discipline conference itself reiterated this dual commitment, aiming to 'stimulate discussion about the kinds of critical languages used within the scholarly as well as the public sphere, and the linguistic challenge that represents an increasingly interdisciplinary research culture within the modern Humanities'.[1] What connections exist between the commitment to interdisciplinarity and engagement with 'critical thinking in the wider public arena', and why might such connections be worth pursuing?

At the conference I was invited to respond to papers by Marilyn Strathern and Gillian Beer. Both papers were full of engaging material, but the combination struck me as being especially fruitful because the questions about interdisciplinarity raised by Marilyn Strathern in 'Commons and Borderlands' began to find answers in the *critical style* exemplified by Gillian Beer's 'Island Encounters'.[2] This is not surprising since Strathern began with a set of questions raised in an earlier essay by Beer herself, about the possibility and the procedure of interdisciplinary work.[3] Such questions are especially pertinent now that 'interdisciplinarity' has begun to attract funding and institutional support for its own sake. The existence of the Centre for Research in the Arts, Social Sciences and Humanities (CRASSH) itself and of numerous other initiatives reinforces the feeling that we have had more than enough specialization of knowledge, and that the most fruitful developments often arise through exchange between disciplines. But increasing recognition of the benefits of interdisciplinary work carries a requirement to think even more carefully about how and why it is done, to question the aims, the style, and the audience of interdisciplinary work. There are three basic motivations for incorporating some form of wider public outreach or engagement within any project: because public funding may be necessary, because the project may reflect on life beyond the academy, and because explanation to those who are not involved discourages practitioners from taking the value of their work for granted. It is important that the motivation is not simply financial, for two reasons: the need to consider public engagement is not proportional to the amount of funding, and expression of the value of research and education *solely* in terms of investment and marketing is inappropriate. Projects that cannot be evaluated in conventional economic terms have an even more pressing requirement to consider questions of public outreach, to explain why value should be accorded to activities that cannot be contained within prevailing systems of valuation, and to communicate any challenge to those systems that the project may present.

Responding with eloquent despair to the January 2003 UK Government White Paper on 'The Future of Higher Education', Stefan Collini confronted the 'market language' of economic benefit and competition pervasive in contemporary education policy, and observed that 'the populist language that dominates so much discussion in contemporary market democracies is not well adapted to justifying public expenditure in other than economic or utilitarian terms'. Collini went on to observe that 'scholarship in the humanities [...] which has no direct economic utility, scarcely figures in the White Paper, so preoccupied is it with science seen as a source of technological applications'.[4] Doubting whether 'any government will have the political courage to declare a university education a social good the cost of which each generation helps to bear for its successors', Collini outlined the implications of such a move, noting that it would entail not only 'acknowledging the limits of justifications couched exclusively in terms of economic prosperity' but, 'perhaps more difficult still, [...] accepting that there are some kinds of intellectual enquiry that are goods in themselves, that need to be pursued at the highest level, and that will almost certainly continue to require a certain amount of public support'. Such inquiries, he concludes, 'may now form a relatively minor part of the activities carried on in universities, and it is much easier, using economic and utilitarian arguments, to justify the other activities; but they remain indispensable'. If it is borne in mind that 'goods in themselves' may be found across the spectrum of disciplines (whatever the White Paper says, we all know that there is more to scientific work than technological application), Collini's conclusion invites further discussion of the claim to indispensability. And going into more detail about what makes a given area of academic research indispensable implies being able to communicate the goods to those who are not already engaged in it (presumably those who are so engaged are already persuaded). This external constituency includes academics working in other fields, and perhaps 'indispensable' simply means 'indispensable within the context of higher education'. But if it requires public support then it makes sense at least to think about wider audiences. The very necessary struggle against populist rhetoric carries with it the risk that we will neglect questions of public engagement, and I would like to suggest that successful resistance to the hazards of populism demands a greater, not lesser, consideration of public engagement on the part of academic researchers.

Interdisciplinary work seems an obvious place to turn for clues as to how these aims might be pursued. If a form of inquiry is a good in itself then that 'good' may well be transferable between contexts of inquiry. Even without the set of initial motivations for outreach outlined above, we might expect such transfer or collaboration to entail, as a matter of course, greater accessibility and explication of jargon, techniques, and findings. Concepts and procedures from different disciplines have to be explained in non-specialist terms in order to facilitate work between specialist areas in the first place, so interdisciplinary research might constitute an automatic first step towards public engagement. But Strathern sounded a warning note when she found this expectation functioning as a 'rhetorical elision found in government and other public statements, between being able to deal with materials in an inter-disciplinary way and being able to communicate to anyone (stakeholders)'. In other words, 'Interdisciplinarity is seen as the first move towards general intelligibility.' As Strathern's paper showed, however, the assumption of such a move can work to undermine genuine interdisciplinarity. Revealing the more complex senses of ownership that qualify the attribution of a natural or given intelligibility to interdisciplinary work, she identified two pressures that characterize the modern university: 'undivided outcomes' and 'undivided origins'. Each of these can undermine public access to knowledge, either by creating 'a new form of monstrous self-referentiality' or through the assertion of ownership of knowledge. These amount to little more than two versions or reassertions of specialism in the name of interdisciplinarity.

Thinking more carefully about how interdisciplinarity works in practice, it may be more effective to retain and cultivate specialist skills and knowledge instead of abandoning specialization only to have it spring up again in the counterproductive forms identified by Strathern. As Beer observes, 'Our initiating professional skills are diverse. We should beware, it seems to me, in the pleasure of learning new practices, of renouncing or undervaluing our long learnt skills.'[5] Fruitful interdisciplinary work is just as much about knowing where your strengths lie, what your own training amounts to, as it is about crossing boundaries and so forth. The adjective 'interdisciplinary' gains significance when it refers to a specific context or project, and may be weakened if taken to refer to an end in itself. Beer's 'long learnt skills' are immediately specified: for 'those trained in literary studies', she observes, it is 'our skill as questioning *readers*' that counts.[6] With the critical skills of questioning readers in mind, I would like to consider the relationship between public engagement and interdisciplinarity in more detail. What is it about literary reading that makes it a fruitful contribution to interdisciplinary work? And what features of literary criticism yield effective terms for engagement with wider public audiences? Both questions put the identity and function of literary criticism under pressure. Can the consideration of either one help with thinking about the other? Is there a more fruitful connection to be exploited between public accessibility and interdisciplinarity than the rhetorical elision identified by Strathern?

My starting point for the public engagement question is a challenge issued by Catherine Belsey in May 2000 to colleagues working in English studies. 'What is the public standing of English studies?' she asked; 'Where is English in the media? What does anyone know about us, except what they remember from school (spelling tests) or what they read in the Sunday papers (book reviews)?'[7] Suggesting that we 'begin by learning from the scientists', Belsey pointed to the need for 'a committee to promote the public understanding of English studies and bring what we do to the attention of the media. We need prizes for the best popular expositions of aspects of our work.' The public standing of any type of academic work does not begin with a blank slate; it is inevitably bound up with the publishing industry, with institutional developments, and with government policy. Observing that 'the research assessment exercise has taught us to look first to university presses and academic journals' for publication of work in English studies, Belsey made the following recommendations:

> We should approach BBC2 and Channel 4 with good ideas. We should write for trade publishers. And above all, we should put pressure on successive RAE panels to endorse these plans and to recognize the worth of popularization in all its forms.

Since 2000 there has been a significant amount of activity contributing to the public standing of English studies. The issue was immediately and explicitly taken up by the Council for College and University English, with the Chair's Report for that year referring to Belsey's appeal and expressing the 'hope that in future CCUE can take a lead in presenting our subject to a wider audience'.[8] The following year further progress was noted, with proposals for a 'sponsored prize for scholarship in English', for articles in the national press, and for collaborative conferences stressing 'the importance of work in English to topics of wide public interest' (literature and medicine, and literature and biography were key themes here).[9] The major funding body for academic work in this area, the British Academy, includes as one of its main objectives the promotion of 'public understanding of research and scholarship'; a Public Understanding and Activities Committee was founded in 1998–99. From 1998 an annual keynote British Academy Lecture has been held, 'intended to address a wider audience than the purely scholarly and to advance public understanding of the subjects the Academy exists to promote'.[10] In June 2002 the British Academy organized an event with the Institute of Contemporary Arts on 'Reclaiming Literature'; open to everybody and featuring high-profile academics and writers, this event aimed 'to examine (and to try to improve) the relationship between academic literary criticism and criticism in the media'.[11]

The year 2000 also saw the establishment of the English Subject Centre as part of the Learning and Teaching Support Network.[12] Aiming to 'support all those who teach in Higher Education English by a variety of means and activities', the Centre focuses on the needs of the academic English community rather than on any explicit public outreach programme, but this certainly does not entail a neglect of wider public engagement issues. Taking up the directorship of the Centre in 2003, Ben Knights described the Centre's priorities for 2003–04 as including 'development of work across the secondary / tertiary divide [...]; promoting the public understanding of English Studies; and helping colleagues to explore the pedagogic implications of the growth of creative writing programmes'.[13] The commitment of Centre staff to supporting and developing English in practice puts them in a key position with regard to the shifting nexus of interests — publishing, policy, and instutional development — that is vital to the profile of any academic discipline. The English Subject Centre was no sooner founded than its sharing of interests with related bodies such as the English Association and CCUE was formalized with the creation of the Common English Forum, created at the end of 2000 with the announcement that 'English language associations are joining forces in an effort to improve public understanding of English'.[14]

Finally, it is worth noting the continued contribution of such bodies as the English Association and the English and Media Centre, whose main objectives are to promote English in educational contexts and to support students and teachers; as with the English Subject Centre these objectives entail a significant interest in issues of wider public engagement. The English Association in particular is actively involved in engagement with younger readers through the primary journal *English 4–11*; English Association North, a distinct organization, publishes *The Reader*, containing articles and reviews 'about writing worth reading' and promoting enjoyment of literature to readers at large, along with discussions about access to literature and personal accounts from readers with diverse experiences and interests. The BBC TV series 'The Big Read', screened from October to December 2003, has served a related function, reaching a wide audience and including links to local reading groups and courses.

Two years after Belsey's article appeared in the *Times Higher Education Supplement* a further appeal was published in the same paper, this time by Bob Eaglestone.[15] This reiterated some of Belsey's main points, including the comparison with public understanding of science movements, the idea that 'English offers a unique and important way to understand contemporary problems', and that there is a good deal more to the subject than 'higher gossip about nice novels'. This last point is, Eaglestone maintains, reflected in the new criteria for AS and A2 English, which show 'how profoundly the subject has changed — it is as much about "different interpretations of literary texts by different readers" and the "contexts in which literary texts are written and understood" as about "great books"'. But, he adds, 'this change [...] seems to have gone nearly unnoticed in the wider world'. Belsey and Eaglestone share a concern with the 'huge gulf between what goes on in English departments and the public understanding of English, between what students and academics actually do and what the media presents us as doing', while Eaglestone identifies this gulf as a product of 'theory wars' over the past two decades, a neglect of public outreach resulting from tension between high theorists and traditionalists, each defending their own specialist concerns. The proposed solution is, again, to follow the example of science; Eaglestone notes that 'since the mid-1980s, a cadre of well-informed and dedicated science journalists and academics committed to the public understanding of science have worked to make such things as the human genome and relativity part of our everyday language', and concludes that only with a similar movement committed to the public understanding of English can the gulf be crossed.

There is a potential gap, and scope for misunderstanding, between these two appeals for direct engagement published in the *THES* and the actual practices that are being developed by the organizations listed above. In practice the commitment to raising public awareness of English studies is not treated in isolation but is pursued in conjunction with the promotion of English as a subject within the curriculum and as a route to rewarding careers, with work on broadening access to higher education, and with efforts to raise public awareness of the humanities in general through publications, fellowships, public talks, and media appearances. Arching over this set of related aims is the recognition that English is a very popular subject, with high take-up at A-level and university, along with a conviction that the value of literary study is already widely acknowledged. In this context the comparison with science might reasonably be taken by those committed to work in this area as a misrepresentation of the situation and even as an unwarranted accusation that they are not getting anything done to promote public awareness. Not everything that contributes to greater 'public understanding' sports that label, and conversely not everything taking place under that label actually achieves very much towards the stated end.

Two questions about terms need clarifying here. First there is the issue of whether 'public understanding' is the best term to use. In 2000 the British Academy's Public Understanding and Information Officer changed his job title to External Relations Officer, but his role remained the same: 'to increase public awareness and understanding of the value of the humanities and social sciences and their contribution to the intellectual and cultural life of the nation'.[16] Reference to 'the nation' here denotes the working sphere of the British Academy but, particularly in the context of literary study, this concern with 'the intellectual and cultural life of the nation' has further connotations that are reinforced by such terms as 'public understanding'. Briefly, such phrases immediately bring to mind the cultural mission on which the institutional development of English studies depended, first in the context of the British Empire in India, and then as humanizing, liberal discipline at home. Increasing recognition in recent decades of the role played by these interests in the foundation of English studies has affected the practice of criticism; it is not simply a matter of exposing the imposition of values implicit in the work of earlier critics, but entails continuing recognition of the extent to which our own practices are indebted to these founding contexts and the implications for how our work relates to contemporary audiences. Terms like 'public understanding' have a tendency to diffuse this set of concerns, a tendency running counter to the very careful consideration that both Belsey and Eaglestone have given to these matters in their own introductory books about criticism.[17]

The use of 'public understanding' was, presumably, employed in both *THES* appeals in recognition of the increasing prominence and effectiveness of science communication movements. This association, as I have noted, may tend to alienate further those best placed to collaborate in promoting criticism to wider public audiences, by carrying the implication (intended or incidental) that in contrast to their counterparts in science they do not care about wider outreach. The comparison with science may strike many of those working in English studies as an invidious one; after all, the value of literary study has long been described in terms running counter to those used (or assumed to be used) in the promotion of science. Again, this is a theme which goes right back to the beginnings of academic criticism; it is inevitably tangled up with the 'cultural mission' theme and must be treated with equal care.[18] We can no more discard comparisons and connections with the sciences than we can ignore the value-laden character of criticism; both issues have long been and still are integral to the public face of criticism and their implications are likely to undermine any efforts to broaden the constituencies of criticism if they are not made explicit.

While granting that the comparison with science and its communication cannot be ignored, it is worth noting that even among science communication experts there are doubts about the term; these range from Richard Dawkins fulminating against vulgarization to debates in science outreach circles about effective public engagement. An eloquent if somewhat partial spokesperson, Dawkins associates 'Public Understanding of Science' in general with dumbing down, and worries that the promotion of science as 'fun' will send 'the wrong signals and might attract people to science for the wrong reasons'. Such 'calculated dumbing down' is, he warns, 'the worst: condescending and patronizing'.[19] At the other end of the spectrum of debate, discussions at the British Association's 2002 Festival of Science reflected a 'feeling [...] that PUS has had its day'.[20] The *Financial Times* reported:

> Scientists are now realising it embodies a condescending attitude: that the public is bound to support the work of scientists, if only it can be made to understand what it is. The new watchword is PEST — public engagement in science and technology.

This newspaper report was triggered by a press release from the science minister Lord Sainsbury, stating:

> We have moved decisively away from the era in which it was enough for science communicators simply to educate the public about science and its benefits. What is needed now is an effective two-way dialogue and debate between those who do scientific research and the public.[21]

The movement away from a 'deficit model' of science communication and towards public engagement had been debated among science communication professionals for at least three years before this appeal, both at meetings (some involving Sainsbury himself) and on the PSCI-COM electronic discussion forum.[22]

Science communication movements may not provide the most appropriate models for public outreach in English studies but the broader issues and the diversity of approaches found within these debates do represent a valuable resource for those interested in conveying the indispensability of any type of academic research to a wider audience. The preliminary survey given above, of existing work relating to the public profile of English studies since 2000, presents a promising picture, with key lobbying bodies such as CCUE expressing their commitment and with new organizations (principally the English Subject Centre) in a good position to mediate the complex of interests relating to outreach issues. Yet the promotion of English studies through existing channels still leaves plenty of scope for engagement beyond the 'natural audience' of literary criticism. Raising the profile of English studies does not inevitably facilitate the engagement of wider audiences in key issues or important developments in academic criticism. The phrase 'public understanding of English studies' masks this gap and, by meaning different things in different contexts, has a tendency to divide the development of English as a subject from public engagement with critical practice just when these two interests can most benefit from working together.

This brings me to the second point about terminology, the distinction between 'English studies' and 'criticism'. In its broadest sense 'English studies' represents a curricular and institutional subject area, while 'criticism' encompasses the techniques taught and developed within that subject. We generally take exams in, and create departments of, English, while teaching and developing critical skills. 'English studies' has tended to admit material from beyond its habitual curricular area (films, postcolonial literature and philosophy, for instance), while 'criticism' has gone out looking for new material to apply itself to and new questions to ask about existing material. This distinction is not intended to imply that English studies or students are passive while criticism and critics are active, but rather to convey a sense of English studies as living in buildings and pedagogical communities and syllabuses; entities that criticism also inhabits while having a tendency to crop up elsewhere: in other arts and languages but also (and this is crucial to the outreach question) in other lives and locations not usually associated with critical development. If critical skills help to make English studies indispensable, then engagement with wider audiences with regard to their role within and beyond the subject is not simply an optional, worthwhile extra; it is vital to the continued indispensability of the subject. As I have suggested, the implication of criticism in the values of those who practise it, and the relationship between their work and those involved in scientific developments, are integral to such engagement.

So far I have been sketching parameters for public engagement with criticism. If this has been fairly done, the zone we have to work with lies between the rejection of populism and the neglect of broader public audiences, between direct outreach and the less direct implications of subject development, and between vulgarization and the imposition of values. This space is, not surprisingly, characterized by questions rather than answers: What is criticism? What and whom it is for? How do we go about it? Such questions might seem a hopeless basis for fresh engagement with wider audiences. Surely the first step towards greater public interest in any activity or profession is a clear message telling people what that activity consists of and what it can achieve. Promoting criticism along the lines just described sounds like trying to sell umbrellas with holes in for better viewing of the weather. But such self-reflexive questioning has always been one of the key strengths of criticism; we have never really been in the umbrella business. Every textual encounter is potentially as much a test of the critical approach adopted as it is of the writing in question. And it is this potential for critical development that is most evident when criticism is deployed in an interdisciplinary context. Applying the skills of the questioning reader to materials from the history of science, from philosophy or from anthropology does not merely yield new perspectives on those other disciplines, it also changes the procedures and the temper of the critic. Questioning reading remains the core skill, but the kind of questions posed, the sphere and the manner of their posing are likely to shift. This is not to claim that criticism works best as a colonizing enterprise, bringing new areas under its questioning control, but to suggest that we view it as a partnership endeavour, less centralized and more inclined to engage with different local settings. All disciplines ask questions, but the key characteristics of critical questioning are this self-reflexivity and the shifting tendency it engenders. Not that other disciplines are never self-reflexive or adaptive, but criticism specializes in disturbing the conditions for questioning. Critics have been taught to do this by poets, novelists, and dramatists, and as criticism engages with other genres and materials this learning process continues.

I started by asking two questions: What is it about literary reading that makes it a fruitful contribution to interdisciplinary work? and What features of literary criticism yield effective terms for engagement with wider public audiences? This essay has focused on the second question, and I have only begun to approach the first. But it is becoming clear that these questions may be more effectively linked when they are turned round: what can criticism gain from engagement with other disciplines and with wider public interests? Instead of treating the wider public as an additional discipline or field, to which critical skills can be offered and from which additional material for critical treatment may be appropriated, we might be better off thinking about what our own critical practices can continue learning from participation in different contexts. Rather than going about trying to convince people beyond the natural audience of criticism that critical reading can change your life, it could be more effective to consider the ways in which your life changes your criticism. The difference I am trying to get at here is more a question of emphasis than a clear-cut distinction between *modi operandi*. It consists of thinking about how critical practice relates to the rest of one's life, and writing criticism that knows its author is alive.

To conclude this very preliminary discussion of interdisciplinarity and public engagement I would like to come back to the suggestion made right at the beginning, that answers might be found in critical style or form. As any critic knows, there is a good deal more to form than decoration of a message; style and disposition have at least as much to do with content as with packaging. This means that the form of critical writing can be its most powerful asset, not so much in terms of making the questions posed accessible to more readers but in inspiring further questioning, in passing on the questioning habit. Critical form is in itself (or can be) an effective, ongoing, and committed means of engagement with new audiences, or of fresh engagement with familiar ones. Critical style is not just a matter of personality, persuasion, or taste; it can reflect and effect lasting exchange between different areas of concern. For instance, the choice of critical metaphor, phrasing, or attitude can make all the difference between simply dismissing the values or concerns of a former age or a different culture, and understanding how those values operate, the complications that ensue from our encounter with them. Ultimately this leaves the reader of criticism with more options when thinking about how and what to read in future. Similar issues of style or form can hinder or facilitate partnership arrangements between habitual critical beats and alternative fields or interests, again opening up the options.

I began by following Marilyn Strathern's cue and suggesting that interdisciplinarity is not an automatic gateway to enhanced public accessibility. I would like to conclude by remembering that different disciplinary specialisms constitute publics in themselves. Engagement with these audiences enables criticism to develop in ways that can more fruitfully result in stylistic or temperamental adaptations than in direct appropriation of new domains or terminology for criticism. Engagement with wider public audiences represents an equally significant area of development and continued critical learning; less a realm for outreach than a source of potential and valuable developments in temperament and style. New styles do not guarantee new readers, but the desire for new readers and the development of new critical styles go hand in hand, as interdisciplinary criticism continues to demonstrate. And the more contact there is between the way we write criticism and the work being done by such bodies as the English Subject Centre and the English Association, the better placed critics will be for fruitful public engagement. Abandoning the term 'public understanding' is a small first step towards a more effective working relationship between subject development and forms of academic criticism that are increasingly engaged with diverse readers.

Notes to Chapter 20

I am very grateful to Catherine Belsey, Helen Lucas, and Judy Simons for answering my queries and for drawing my attention to important resources and perspectives in the course of researching this chapter. The views about public understanding expressed here are my own.

1. <www.crassh.cam.ac.uk/projects/newlangs.html> and <www.crassh.cam.ac.uk/events/events2003/newlangsconf.html> [accessed 29 December 2003].
2. Marilyn Strathern's paper formed the springboard for her book *Commons and Borderlands: Working Papers on Interdisciplinarity, Accountability and the Flow of Knowledge* (Wantage: Sean Kingston, 2004); Gillian Beer's paper was published in revised form as 'Island Bounds', in *Islands in History and Representation*, ed. by Rod Edmond and Vanessa Smith (London: Routledge, 2003), pp. 32–42.
3. Gillian Beer, 'Forging the Missing Link: Interdisciplinary Stories', in *Open Fields: Science in Cultural Encounter* (Oxford: Clarendon Press, 1996), pp. 115–45 (p. 115).
4. Stefan Collini, 'HiEdBiz', *London Review of Books*, 6 November 2003, pp. 3, 9.
5. Beer, 'Forging the Missing Link', p. 116.
6. Ibid. (emphasis in original).
7. Catherine Belsey, 'The Power of a Profile', *Times Higher Education Supplement* (hereafter *THES*), 5 May 2000, p. 16.
8. Judy Simons, 'Chair's Annual Report, 1999–2000', Council for College and University English (hereafter CCUE) <www.ccue.ac.uk> [accessed 29 December 2003].
9. Rick Rylance, Chair's Report, 2000–2001, CCUE <www.ccue.ac.uk> [accessed 29 December 2003].
10. British Academy Review, July 1998 — July 1999 <www.britac.ac.uk/pubs/review/01–9899/07-lectures.html> [accessed 29 December 2003].

11. British Academy, news and reports, 24 May 2002 <www.britac.ac.uk/news/release.asp?NewsID=66> [accessed 29 December 2003]. In November 2002 the British Academy hosted a further 'Public Understanding' event, 'Is There a Crisis of Truth in the Humanities?'
12. The Learning and Teaching Support Network (known from 1 May 2004 as the Higher Education Academy) consists of twenty-four Subject Centres; the English Subject Centre differs from the other Centres in that, rather than being established through an institutional bidding process, it was set up as a partnership between Royal Holloway, King's College London, and CCUE. Ben Knights, 'Introduction from the Director' <www.english.ltsn.ac.uk/aboutus/director.htm> [accessed 29 Dec 2003; no longer available].
13. Ben Knights, 'Editorial', *English Subject Centre Bulletin*, no. 6 (October 2003) <www.english.heacademy.ac.uk/archive/publications/bulletins/bulletin6.pdf> [accessed 29 Dec 2003].
14. Harriet Swain, 'English Fears Set Forum in Motion', *THES*, 1 December 2000, p. 6.
15. Bob Eaglestone, 'Lit Critters Need Selling', *THES*, 21 June 2002, p. 23.
16. Jonathan Breckon, 'External Relations', British Academy Review, January–July 2000 <www.britac.ac.uk/pubs/review/03–00a/07-external.html> [accessed 29 December 2003].
17. Catherine Belsey, *Critical Practice*, 2nd edn (London: Routledge, 2002); Robert Eaglestone, *Doing English*, 2nd edn (London: Routledge, 2002).
18. One very fruitful approach is found in the work of Jeff Wallace, particularly his article '"Taking Possession of the Ordinary Man's Mind": Literary Studies and the History of Science', *Literature and History*, 1 (1990), 58–74. Wallace's reconstruction of F. R. Leavis's use of history of science has clear implications for claims to interdisciplinarity in present-day criticism. John Guillory's challenging account of the more recent Sokal affair explores the historical relations between criticism and social science, stressing the continued impact of this neglected theme on the public standing of academic criticism. See 'The Sokal Affair and the History of Criticism', *Critical Inquiry*, 28 (2002), 470–508.
19. Richard Dawkins, *Unweaving the Rainbow* (London: Penguin Books, 1998), pp. 21–24.
20. Clive Cookson, 'Scientists Prepare to Experiment with Public Opinion', *Financial Times*, 17 September 2002, p. 6.
21. 'Science Communication Study', DTI press release 10 September 2002, P/2002/568.
22. The PSCI-COM archives are at <www.jiscmail.ac.uk/lists/psci-com.html>.

BIBLIOGRAPHY

Works Cited

Abraham, Gerald, *Chopin's Musical Style* (London: Oxford University Press, 1939)

Abrams, M. H., 'Construing and Deconstructing', in *Doing Things with Texts* (London: Norton, 1989), pp. 297–332

Adorno, Theodor W., *Aesthetic Theory*, trans. and ed. by Robert Hullot-Kentor (Minneapolis: University of Minnesota Press, 1997)

——'Commitment', in *Can One Live after Auschwitz? A Philosophical Reader*, ed. by Rolf Tiedemann, trans. by Shierry Weber Nicholson (Stanford: Stanford University Press, 2003), pp. 240–58

——*Gesammelte Schriften*, ed. by Rolf Tiedemann, 20 vols (Frankfurt a.M.: Suhrkamp, 1970–90)

——*Minima Moralia: Reflections from a Damaged Life*, trans. by E. F. N. Jephcott (New York: Verso, 1978)

——'Notes on Kafka', in *Prisms*, trans. by Samuel and Shierry Weber (Cambridge, MA: MIT Press, 1981), pp. 243–71

——and Benjamin, Walter, *Briefwechsel 1928–1940*, ed. by Henri Lonitz (Frankfurt a.M.: Suhrkamp, 1994)

Agamben, Giorgio, 'The End of the Poem', in *The End of the Poem: Studies in Poetics*, trans. by Daniel Heller-Roazen (Stanford: Stanford University Press, 1999)

——'Noten zur Geste', in *Postmoderne und Politik*, ed. by Jutta Georg-Lauer (Tübingen: Edition Diskord, 1992), pp. 97–107

Alexandrescu, Sorin, 'Le Discours étrange, à propos de *La Nuit* de Maupassant', in *Sémiotique narrative et textuelle*, ed. by Claude Chabrol (Paris: Larousse, 1973), pp. 55–95

Alphen, Ernst van, *Caught by History: Holocaust Effects in Contemporary Art, Literature, and Theory* (Stanford: Stanford University Press, 1997)

——*Francis Bacon and the Loss of Self* (London: Reaktion Books, 1992)

Amelunxen, Hubertus von, 'Skiagraphia — Silberchlorid und schwarze Galle: zur allegorischen Bestimmung des photographischen Bildes', in *Allegorie und Melancholie*, ed. by Willem van Reijen (Frankfurt a.M.: Suhrkamp, 1992), pp. 90–108

Anzieu, Didier, *The Skin Ego*, trans. by Chris Turner (New Haven: Yale University Press, 1989)

Archer, Michael, 'Crisis What Crisis?', *Art Monthly*, no. 264 (March 2003), 1–4

Aristotle, 'De anima', *The Basic Works of Aristotle*, ed. by Richard McKeon (New York: Random House, 1941), pp. 535–603

——*Nichomachean Ethics*, trans. by Martin Oswald (Indianapolis: Bobbs-Merrill, 1962)

Augustine, St, *Sermons*, 30: 'On the New Testament', <http://www.newadvent.org/fathers/160330.htm> [accessed 7 August 2007]

Auslander, Philip, *Liveness: Performance in a Mediatized Culture* (New York: Routledge, 1999)

Bagnold, Enid, *A Diary Without Dates* (1918) (London: Virago, 1979)

Bakhtin, Mikhail, 'Author and Hero in Aesthetic Activity', in *Art and Answerability: Early Philosophical Essays by M. M. Bakhtin*, trans. by Vadim Liapunov, ed. by Michael Holquist and Vadim Liapunov (Austin: University of Texas Press, 1990)

——'Epic and Novel: Toward a Methodology for the Study of the Novel', in *The Dialogic Imagination: Four Essays by M. M. Bakhtin*, trans. by Caryl Emerson and Michael Holquist, ed. by Michael Holquist (Austin: University of Texas Press, 1981), pp. 3–40

——'Forms of Time and of the Chronotope in the Novel', in *The Dialogic Imagination: Four Essays by M. M. Bakhtin*, trans. by Caryl Emerson and Michael Holquist, ed. by Michael Holquist (Austin: University of Texas Press, 1981), pp. 84–258

——'From Notes Made in 1970–71', in *Speech Genres and Other Late Essays*, trans. by Vern McGee, ed. by Caryl Emerson and Michael Holquist (Austin: University of Texas Press, 1986)

——*Problems of Dostoevsky's Poetics*, trans. and ed. by Caryl Emerson (Minneapolis: Minnesota University Press, 1984)

——*Toward a Philosophy of the Act*, trans. by Vadim Liapunov, ed. by Vadim Liapunov and Michael Holquist (Austin: University of Texas Press, 1993)

Bal, Mieke, *Double Exposures: The Subject of Cultural Analysis* (New York: Routledge, 1996)

——*Louise Bourgeois' Spider: The Architecture of Art-Writing* (Chicago: University of Chicago Press, 2001)

——*Narratology: Introduction to the Theory of Narrative*, 2nd edn (Toronto: University of Toronto Press, 1997)

——*Quoting Caravaggio: Contemporary Art, Preposterous History* (Chicago: University of Chicago Press, 1999)

——*Reading 'Rembrandt': Beyond the Word–Image Opposition* (Cambridge and New York: Cambridge University Press, 1991)

——'Religious Canon and Literary Identity', *lectio difficilior*, 2000.2 (September 2000) <http://www.lectio.unibe.ch/00_2/htm>

——'Scared to Death', in *The Point of Theory: Practices of Cultural Analysis*, ed. by Mieke Bal and Inge E. Boer (Amsterdam: Amsterdam University Press, 1994), pp. 32–47

——*Travelling Concepts in the Humanities: A Rough Guide* (Toronto: Toronto University Press, 2002)

Barthes, Roland, *The Fashion System*, trans. by Matthew Ward and Richard Howard (New York: Hill and Wang, 1983)

——*A Lover's Discourse*, trans. by Richard Howard (1978; Harmondsworth: Penguin Books, 1990)

Bataille, Georges, *Guilty*, trans. by Bruce Boone (San Francisco: Lapis Press, 1988)

——*Inner Experience*, trans. by Leslie Anne Boldt (Albany: SUNY Press, 1988)

Beer, Gillian, 'Forging the Missing Link: Interdisciplinary Stories', in *Open Fields: Science in Cultural Encounter* (Oxford: Clarendon Press, 1996), pp. 115–45

——'Four Bodies on the Beagle: Touch, Sight, and Writing in a Darwin Letter', in *Textuality and Sexuality: Reading Theories and Practices*, ed. by Judith Still and Michael Worton (Manchester: Manchester University Press, 1993), pp. 116–32

——'Island Bounds', in *Islands in History and Representation*, ed. by Rod Edmond and Vanessa Smith (London: Routledge, 2003), pp. 32–42

Behnegar, Nasser, *Leo Strauß, Max Weber, and the Scientific Study of Politics* (Chicago and London: University of Chicago Press, 2003)

Belsey, Catherine, *Critical Practice*, 2nd edn (London: Routledge, 2002)

——'The Power of a Profile', *Times Higher Education Supplement*, 5 May 2000, p. 16

Benedict, Barbara, *Curiosity: A Cultural History of Early Modern Inquiry* (Chicago: University of Chicago Press, 2001)

Benjamin, Walter, *Gesammelte Schriften*, ed. by Rolf Tiedemann and Hermann Schweppenhäuser, 7 vols, paperback edn (Frankfurt a.M.: Suhrkamp, 1991)

——*Selected Writings*, ed. by Marcus Bullock and others, 4 vols (Cambridge, MA, and London: Belknap Press/Harvard University Press, 1996–2003)

BENNETT, JANE, *The Enchantment of Modern Life: Attachments, Crossings and Ethics* (Princeton: Princeton University Press, 2001)

BENSON, BRUCE ELLIS, *The Improvisation of Musical Dialogue: A Phenomenology of Music* (Cambridge: Cambridge University Press, 2003)

BERGER, JOHN, and others, *Ways of Seeing* (London: BBC; Harmondsworth: Penguin Books, 1972)

BERNSTEIN, SUSAN, *Virtuosity of the Nineteenth Century: Performing Music and Language in Heine, Liszt, and Baudelaire* (Stanford: Stanford University Press, 1998)

BETTELHEIM, BRUNO, *The Uses of Enchantment: The Meaning and Importance of Fairy Tales* (New York: Knopf, 1976)

BHABHA, HOMI K., *The Location of Culture* (New York: Routledge, 1994)

BINMORE, KEN, *Game Theory and the Social Contract*, I: *Playing Fair* (Cambridge, MA, and London: MIT Press, 1994)

BLAU, HERBERT, *Nothing in Itself: Complexities of Fashion* (Bloomington: Indiana University Press, 1999)

BLOCH, HOWARD, *Etymologies and Genealogies: A Literary Anthropology of the French Middle Ages* (Chicago: University of Chicago Press, 1983)

BLÖCKER, GÜNTER, *Heinrich von Kleist oder das absolute Ich* (Berlin: Argon, 1960)

BOLLA, PETER DE, *Art Matters* (Cambridge, MA: Harvard University Press, 2003)

BOLTER, JAY DAVID, and GRUSIN, RICHARD, 'Remediation', *Configurations*, 4 (1996), 311–58

BONNEFOY, YVES, 'Critics: English and French and the Distance between Them', *Encounter* (July 1958), 39–45

——*Rue Traversière et autres récits en rêve*, 2nd edn (Paris: Gallimard, 1992)

BORDO, SUSAN, *Unbearable Weight: Feminism, Western Culture, and the Body* (Berkeley: University of California Press, 1993)

BORGES, JORGE LUIS, 'Blindness', *The Total Library: Non-Fiction 1922–1986*, trans. by Esther Allen and others (London: Penguin Books, 2001), pp. 473–83

——'Poema de los dones', *El hacedor* (1960), in *Obra poética, 1923–1977* (Madrid: Emecé/ Alianza, 1993), p. 119

BORMANN, HANS-FRIEDRICH, 'Theatralität als Vorschrift: zu Michael Frieds Kunst und Objekthaftigkeit', in *Diskurse des Theatralen*, ed. by Erika Fischer-Lichte and others (Basel and Tübingen: Francke, 2004)

BOURKE, JOANNA, *Dismembering the Male: Men's Bodies, Britain and the Great War* (London: Reaktion Books, 1996)

BOWIE, MALCOLM, *Freud, Proust and Lacan: Theory as Fiction* (Cambridge: Cambridge University Press, 1987)

BRANDSTETTER, GABRIELE, 'Aufführung und Aufzeichnung: Kunst der Wissenschaft?', in *Kunst der Aufführung — Aufführung der Kunst*, ed. by Erika Fischer-Lichte, Clemens Risi, and Jens Roselt (Berlin: Theater der Zeit, 2004), pp. 40–50

BRECHT, BERTOLT, 'A Short Organum for the Theatre', in *Brecht on Theatre: The Development of an Aesthetic*, ed. and trans. by John Willett (New York: Hill and Wang, 1964), pp. 179–205 (first publ. as 'Kleines Organon für das Theater', *Sinn und Form*, special issue: Bertolt Brecht (1949))

BRECKON, JONATHAN, 'External Relations', British Academy Review, January–July 2000 <www.britac.ac.uk/pubs/review/03–00a/07-external.html> [accessed 29 December 2003]

BREWER, DANIEL, and HAYES, JULIE CANDLER, *Using the 'Encyclopédie': Ways of Knowing, Ways of Reading*, *SVEC* 2002:05

British Academy Review, July 1998 — July 1999 <www.britac.ac.uk/pubs/review/01–9899/07-lectures.html> [accessed 29 December 2003]

British Academy, news and reports, 24 May 2002 <www.britac.ac.uk/news/release.asp?NewsID=66> [accessed 29 December 2003]
BROOKE, RUPERT, 'Fragment', in *The Collected Poems* (1929) (London: Papermac, 1987), p. 318
BROOKS, CLEANTH, 'The Heresy of Paraphrase', in *The Well-Wrought Urn: Studies in the Structure of Poetry* (1947) (London: Dobson, 1968), pp. 157–76
BROOKS-DAVIES, DOUGLAS, 'Archimago', in *The Spenser Encyclopedia*, ed. by A. C. Hamilton (Toronto: University of Toronto Press, 1990), p. 53
BROSSES, CHARLES DE, *Traité de la formation mécanique des langues et des principes physiques de l'étymologie*, 2 vols (Paris: Saillant, 1765)
BUCHLOH, BENJAMIN H. D., 'Gerhard Richters *Acht Grau*: zwischen Vorschein und Glanz', in *Gerhard Richter: Acht Grau*, ed. by the Solomon R. Guggenheim Foundation (New York: Guggenheim Museum Publications, 2002), pp. 13–29
BURGIN, VICTOR, *The End of Art Theory: Criticism and Postmodernity* (London: Macmillan, 1986)
CADAVA, EDUARDO, *Words of Light: Theses on the Photography of History* (Princeton: Princeton University Press, 1997)
CARROLL, NOËL, 'Prospects for Film Theory: A Personal Assessment', in *Post-Theory: Reconstructing Film Studies*, ed. by David Bordwell and Noël Carroll (Madison: University of Wisconsin Press, 1996), pp. 37–68
CASERIO, ROBERT, *The Novel in England, 1900–1950: History and Theory* (New York: Twayne, 1999)
CHARLESWORTH, J. J., 'The Dysfunction of Criticism', *Art Monthly*, no. 269 (September 2003), 1–4
CHARTERIS, EVAN, *John Sargent* (London: Heinemann, 1927)
CLARK, ADRIAN, review of Mel Gooding, *Ceri Richards* (Moffat: Cameron & Hollis 2002), *British Art Journal*, 4.2 (summer 2003), 99
CLARKE, ERIC, 'Expression in Performance: Generativity, Perception, and Semiosis', in *The Practice of Performance: Studies in Musical Interpretation*, ed. by John Rink (Cambridge: Cambridge University Press, 1995), pp. 21–54
——'Listening to Performance', in *Musical Performance: A Guide to Understanding*, ed. by John Rink (Cambridge: Cambridge University Press, 2002), pp. 185–96
——and DAVIDSON, JANE, 'The Body in Performance', in *Composition — Performance — Reception: Studies in the Creative Process in Music*, ed. by Wyndham Thomas (Aldershot: Ashgate, 1998), pp. 74–92
COLERIDGE, SAMUEL TAYLOR, *The Collected Works*, 16 vols (London: Routledge and Kegan Paul; Princeton: Princeton University Press, 1969–2002)
COLES, ALEX, 'The Bathroom Critic', *Art Monthly*, no. 263 (February 2003), 7–10
COLLINI, STEFAN, 'HiEdBiz', *London Review of Books*, 6 November 2003, pp. 3, 9
CONDILLAC, ABBÉ DE, 'A Treatise on the Sensations', trans. by Franklin Philip in collaboration with Harlan Lane, in *Philosophical Writings of Étienne Bonnot, Abbé de Condillac*, 2 vols (Hillsdale, NY: Erlbaum, 1982–87), I, 155–339
COOK, NICHOLAS, 'Analysing Performance and Performing Analysis', in *Rethinking Music*, ed. by Nicholas Cook and Mark Everist (Oxford: Oxford University Press, 1999)
——'At the Borders of Musical Identity: Schenker, Corelli, and the Graces', *Music Analysis*, 18 (1999), 179–233
——'Music as Performance', in *The Cultural Study of Music: A Critical Introduction*, ed. by Martin Clayton, Trevor Herbert, and Richard Middleton (New York: Routledge, 2003)
——'Perception: A Perspective from Music Theory', in *Musical Perceptions*, ed. by Rita Aiello (Oxford: Oxford University Press, 1994), pp. 64–95

COOKSON, CLIVE, 'Scientists Prepare to Experiment with Public Opinion', *Financial Times*, 17 September 2002, p. 6

CORK, RICHARD, *A Bitter Truth: Avant-Garde Art and the Great War* (New Haven: Yale University Press, 1994)

CRAMER, FRANZ ANTON, 'Wie darf ich Tanz verstehen?', *ballettanz*, 2003.3 (March), 28–31

CRÉBILLON FILS (Claude-Prosper Jolyot de Crébillon), *Le Sopha, conte moral* (Gaznah [Paris]: Imprimerie du [...] Sultan des Indes, 1742)

CSIKSZENTMIHALYI, MIHALYI, *Flow: The Psychology of Optimal Experience* (New York: Harper and Row, 1990)

CULLER, JONATHAN, 'Literary Theory', in *Introduction to Scholarship in Modern Languages and Literatures*, ed. by Joseph Gibaldi, 2nd edn (New York: Modern Languages Association of America, 1992), pp. 201–35

—— 'The Turns of Metaphor', in *The Pursuit of Signs: Semiotics, Literature, Deconstruction* (London: Routledge and Kegan Paul, 1981), pp. 188–209

CUNNINGHAM, MICHAEL, *The Hours* (London: Picador, 1999)

CURRIE, GREGORY, 'Realism of Character and the Value of Fiction', in *Aesthetics and Ethics: Essays at the Intersection*, ed. by Jerrold Levinson (Cambridge: Cambridge University Press, 1998), pp. 161–81

CURRIE, MARK, *Postmodern Narrative Theory* (Basingstoke: Macmillan, 1998)

CURTIUS, E. R., 'Etymology as a Category of Thought', in *European Literature and the Latin Middle Ages*, trans. by Willard R. Trask (Princeton: Princeton University Press, 1967), pp. 495–500

DAS, SANTANU, '"Kiss me, Hardy": Intimacy, Gender, and Gesture in First World War Trench Literature', *Modernism/Modernity*, 9.1 (January 2002), 51–74

DAVIDSON, JANE, 'Communicating with the Body in Performance', in *Musical Performance: A Guide to Understanding*, ed. by John Rink (Cambridge: Cambridge University Press, 2002), pp. 144–52

DAVIDSON, JUSTIN, 'Philharmonic Benefits its Audience, Too', *Newsday*, 22 September 2001

DAVIDTS, HERMANN, *Die novellistische Kunst Heinrichs von Kleist* (Hildesheim: Gerstenberg, 1973)

DAVIES, STEPHEN, *Themes in the Philosophy of Music* (Oxford: Oxford University Press, 2003)

DAWKINS, RICHARD, *Unweaving the Rainbow* (London: Penguin Books, 1998)

DELEUZE, GILLES, *Cinema 1: The Movement-Image*, trans. by Hugh Tomlinson and Barbara Habberjam (Minneapolis: University of Minnesota Press, 1986)

DE MAN, PAUL, 'Aesthetic Formalization: Kleist's "Über das Marionettentheater"', in *The Rhetoric of Romanticism* (New York: Columbia University Press, 1984), pp. 263–90

—— 'Semiology and Rhetoric', in *Allegories of Reading* (New Haven: Yale University Press, 1979), pp. 3–19

DEPARTMENT OF TRADE AND INDUSTRY, 'Science Communication Study', press release 10 September 2002, P/2002/568

DERRIDA, JACQUES, 'Différance', in *Margins of Philosophy*, trans. by Alan Bass (New York: Harvester Wheatsheaf, 1982), pp. 1–27

—— *Memoirs of the Blind: The Self-Portrait and Other Ruins*, trans. by Pascale-Anne Brault and Michael Naas (Chicago: University of Chicago Press, 1993)

—— *Of Grammatology*, trans. by Gayatri Chakravorti Spivak (Baltimore: Johns Hopkins University Press, 1976)

—— 'Resistances', in *Resistances of Psychoanalysis*, trans. by Peggy Kamuf, Pascale-Anne Brault, and Michael Naas (Stanford: Stanford University Press, 1998), pp. 1–38

—— 'Signature Event Context', *Glyph*, 1 (1977), 172–97

——'Structure, Sign, and Play in the Discourse of the Human Sciences', in *The Language of Criticism and the Sciences of Man: The Structuralist Controversy*, ed. by Richard Macksey and Eugenio Donato (Baltimore: Johns Hopkins University Press, 1970), pp. 247–72
——'... That Dangerous Supplement ...', in *Acts of Literature*, ed. by Derek Attridge (New York and London: Routledge, 1992), pp. 76–109
——and MCDONALD, CHRISTIE V., 'Choreographies: Interview', in *Feminist Interpretations of Jacques Derrida*, ed. by Nancy J. Holland (University Park: Pennsylvania State University Press, 1997), pp. 23–41
Dictionnaire de l'Académie française, 2nd edn, 2 vols (Paris, 1718)
DIDEROT, DENIS, 'Encyclopédie', in *Encyclopédie, ou dictionnaire raisonné des arts, des sciences, et des métiers*, ed. by Denis Diderot and Jean le Rond d'Alembert, 17 vols (Paris: Briasson, 1751–65), V (1755), 635–48
——'Letter on the Blind for the Use of Those Who See', trans. by M. Jourdain, in *Denis Diderot: Thoughts on the Interpretation of Nature and Other Philosophical Works*, ed. by David Adams (Manchester: Clinamen Press, 1999), pp. 147–200
——and D'ALEMBERT, JEAN LE ROND, 'Discours préliminaire', in *Encyclopédie, ou dictionnaire raisonné des arts, des sciences, et des métiers*, ed. by Denis Diderot and Jean le Rond d'Alembert, 17 vols (Paris: Briasson, 1751–65), I, i–lii
DIMAND, MARY ANN, and DIMAND, ROBERT W., *A History of Game Theory*, I: *From the Beginnings to 1945* (London, New York: Routledge, 1996)
DROIXHE, DANIEL, *La Linguistique et l'appel de l'histoire (1600–1800): rationalisme et révolutions positivistes* (Geneva: Droz, 1978)
DUNSBY, JONATHAN, *Performing Music: Shared Concerns* (Oxford: Oxford University Press, 1995)
DYER, DENYS, *The Stories of Kleist* (London: Duckworth, 1977)
EAGLESTONE, ROBERT, *Doing English*, 2nd edn (London: Routledge, 2002)
——[as EAGLESTONE, BOB], 'Lit Critters Need Selling', *Times Higher Education Supplement*, 21 June 2002, p. 23
EAGLETON, TERRY, *The Ideology of the Aesthetic* (Oxford: Blackwell, 1990)
ECKERMANN, JOHANN PETER, *Gespräche mit Goethe in den letzten Jahren seines Lebens*, ed. by Fritz Bergemann, 2 vols (Frankfurt: Insel, 1981)
ECO, UMBERTO, *The Search for the Perfect Language*, trans. by James Fentress (Oxford: Blackwell, 1995)
EINSTEIN, ALFRED, *Mozart: His Character, his Work*, trans. by Arthur Mendel and Nathan Broder (New York: Oxford University Press, 1945)
EISENSTEIN, SERGEI, *The Film Sense*, trans. and ed. by Jay Leyda (London: Faber, 1943)
——'Through Theatre to Cinema', *Focus on Film and Theatre*, ed. by James Hurt (Englewood Cliffs, NJ: Prentice Hall, 1974), pp. 116–29
'Evidentia, Evidenz', in *Historisches Wörterbuch der Rhetorik*, ed. by Gerd Ueding, 7 vols (Tübingen: Niedermeyer, 1992–), III (1996), 33–47
FINNEGAN, RUTH, *Communicating* (London: Routledge, 2002)
FISCHER, BERND, *Ironische Metaphysik: die Erzählungen Heinrich von Kleists* (Munich: Wilhelm Fink, 1988)
FOISSET, TH., *Le Président de Brosses: histoire des lettres et des parlements au XVIIIe siècle* (Paris: Olivier-Fulgence, 1842)
FORSYTHE, WILLIAM, *Improvisation Technologies: A Tool for the Analytical Dance Eye* (Karlsruhe: ZKM; Cologne: German Dance Archive, 1999)
FOSTER, SUSAN LEIGH, 'Choreographies of Gender', *Signs*, 24.1 (1998), 1–33
——'Dancing Bodies', in *Meaning in Motion: New Cultural Studies of Dance*, ed. by Jane C. Desmond (Durham, NC: Duke University Press, 1997), pp. 235–57
FOUCAULT, MICHEL, *The Order of Things: An Archaeology of the Human Sciences* (New York: Vintage Books, 1973)

FREUD, SIGMUND, 'Infantile Sexuality', in *The Standard Edition of the Complete Psychological Works*, trans. and ed. by James Strachey, 24 vols (London: Hogarth Press, 1953–74), VII (1953), 181–82
——'The Question of Lay Analysis' (1926), in *The Standard Edition of the Complete Psychological Works*, trans. and ed. by James Strachey, 24 vols (London: Hogarth Press, 1953–74), XX (1959), 183–258
FRICKE, GERHARD, *Gefühl und Schicksal bei Heinrich von Kleist* (1929) (Darmstadt: Wissenschaftliche Buchgesellschaft, 1963)
FUSSELL, PAUL, *Poetic Meter and Poetic Form* (New York: Random House, 1966)
GANNON, MARY, 'Critics on Reviews', *Poets & Writers*, 31.5 (September–October 2003), 54–61
GÉBELIN, ANTOINE COURT DE, *Monde primitif analysé et comparé avec le monde moderne*, 9 vols (Paris: the author and others, 1773–82)
GEERTZ, CLIFFORD, 'Blurred Genres: The Refiguration of Social Thought', in *Local Knowledge: Further Essays in Interpretive Anthropology* (New York: Basic Books, 1983), pp. 19–35
GODLOVITCH, STAN, 'The Integrity of Musical Performance', *Journal of Aesthetics and Art Criticism*, 51 (1992–93), 573–87
——*Musical Performance: A Philosophical Study* (London and New York: Routledge, 1998)
GOEHR, LYDIA, *The Quest for Voice: Music, Politics, and the Limits of Philosophy* (Oxford: Oxford University Press, 1998)
GREEN, HENRY, *Loving, Living, Party Going* (1939) (Harmondsworth: Penguin Books, 1993)
GREENBLATT, STEPHEN, *Hamlet in Purgatory* (Princeton: Princeton University Press)
——'Resonance and Wonder', in *Learning to Curse: Essays in Early Modern Culture* (New York: Routledge, 1990), pp. 161–83
GREENFIELD, SUSAN, *The Private Life of the Brain* (London: Penguin Books, 2001)
GUILLORY, JOHN, 'The Sokal Affair and the History of Criticism', *Critical Inquiry*, 28 (2002), 470–508
GUMBRECHT, HANS ULRICH, 'Produktion von Präsenz, durchsetzt mit Absenz: über Musik, Libretto und Inszenierung', in *Ästhetik der Inszenierung*, ed. by Josef Früchtl and Jörg Zimmermann (Frankfurt a.M.: Suhrkamp, 2001), pp. 63–76
——and others, 'Emergence: A Manifesto for Risk Taking Interdisciplinarity' (unpublished document in possession of Gabriele Brandstetter, 2002)
HABERMAS, JÜRGEN, 'What Is Universal Pragmatics?', in *Communication and the Evolution of Society*, trans. by Thomas McCarthy (London: Heinemann, 1979), pp. 1–68
HAGSTRUM, JEAN H., *The Sister Arts: The Tradition of Literary Pictorialism and English Poetry from Dryden to Gray* (Chicago: University of Chicago Press, 1958)
HALL, TIMOTHY S., 'The Score as Contract: Private Law and the Historically Informed Performance Movement', *Cardozo Law Review*, 20 (May–July 1999), 1589–1614
HAMILTON, ANDY, 'The Art of Improvisation and the Aesthetics of Imperfection', *British Journal of Aesthetics*, 40 (2000), 168–85
HANSEN, MARK B. N., 'Affect as Medium, or the "Digital-Facial-Image"', *Journal of Visual Culture*, 2 (2003), 205–28
HARGREAVES HEAP, SHAUN P., and VAROUFAKIS, YANIS, *Game Theory: A Critical Introduction* (London and New York: Routledge, 1995)
HARTER, DEBORAH, *Bodies in Pieces: Fantastic Narrative and the Poetics of the Fragment* (Stanford: Stanford University Press, 1996)
HEDLEY, ARTHUR, *Chopin* (London: Dent, 1963)
HEGEL, G. F. W., *The Philosophy of Fine Art*, transl. by Bernard Bosanquet (1886; ed. and with intro. by Michael Inwood, Harmondsworth: Penguin Books, 1993)

HEIDEGGER, MARTIN, *Being and Time*, trans. by John Macquarrie and Edward Robinson (New York: Harper and Row, 1962)
——*Parmenides*, trans. by Andre Schuwer and Richard Rojcewicz (Bloomington: Indiana University Press, 1992)
HEIN, HILDE, 'Performance as an Aesthetic Category', *Journal of Aesthetics and Art Criticism*, 28 (1970), 381–86
HEINE, HEINRICH, *Poetry and Prose*, ed. and trans. by Frederick Ewen (New York: Citadel Press, 1948)
HIGGINS, DICK, 'Intermedia', *Leonardo*, 34 (2001), 49–54
HOLLYWOOD, AMY, *Sensible Ecstasy: Mysticism, Sexual Difference and the Demands of History* (Chicago and London: University of Chicago Press, 2002)
HOOKER, C. W. R., *What is the Fourth Dimension? Reflections Inspired by a Pair of Gloves* (London: A. & C. Black, 1934)
HORACE, *Satires, Epistles, Ars Poetica*, trans. by H. Rushton Fairclough (Cambridge, MA: Harvard University Press, 1991)
HORKHEIMER, MAX, and ADORNO, THEODOR, *Dialectic of Enlightenment* (New York: Herder and Herder, 1972)
HOWELLS, CHRISTINA, *Derrida: Deconstruction from Phenomenology to Ethics* (Cambridge: Polity Press, 1999)
HUXLEY, ALDOUS, *Brave New World* (1932), with Introduction by David Bradshaw (London: Vintage, 2004)
JACKENDOFF, RAY, *Foundations of Language: Brain, Meaning, Grammar, Evolution* (Oxford: Oxford University Press, 2002)
JACKSON, JOHN, *A la souche obscure des rêves: la dialectique de l'écriture chez Yves Bonnefoy* (Paris: Mercure de France, 1993)
——'Yves Bonnefoy et la souche obscure des rêves', Postface to *Rue Traversière et autres récits en rêve*, 2nd edn (Paris: Gallimard, 1992), p. 209
JACOBUS, MARY, 'Prometheus on the Couch: Wilfred Bion and the Language of Terror' (lecture, 14 July 2003, School of Criticism and Theory, Cornell University)
JAMESON, FREDRIC, *The Political Unconscious: Narrative as a Socially Symbolic Act* (Ithaca, NY: Cornell University Press, 1981)
JANSSENS, ANN VERONICA, *Une image différente dans chaque oeil / A Different Image in Each Eye*, ed. by Laurent Jacob, French trans. by Daniel Vander Gucht (Liège: Espace 251 Nord, 1999)
JONES, JENNIFER, '*Coquettes* and *Grisettes*: Women Buying and Selling in Ancien Régime Paris', in *The Sex of Things: Gender and Consumption in Historical Perspective*, ed. by Victoria de Grazia and Ellen Furlough (Berkeley: University of California Press, 1996), pp. 25–53
JOSIPOVICI, GABRIEL, *The Lessons of Modernity* (Basingstoke: Macmillan, 1987)
——*Touch* (New Haven: Yale University Press, 1996)
JUSLIN, PATRIK N., 'Communicating Emotion in Performance: A Review and a Theoretical Framework', in *Music and Emotion: Theory and Research*, ed. by Patrik N. Juslin and John A. Sloboda (Oxford: Oxford University Press, 2001), pp. 309–37
KALLBERG, JEFFREY, 'Chopin's March, Chopin's Death', *19th-Century Music*, 25 (2001–02), 3–26
KALLISTOS OF DIOKLEIA, BISHOP, *The Orthodox Way* (Crestwood, NY: St Vladimir's Seminary Press)
KANE, SEAN, *Spenser's Moral Allegory* (Toronto: University of Toronto Press, 1989)
Kants Werke: Akademie-Textausgabe, ed. by Preußische Akademie der Wissenschaften, 11 vols (Berlin: Walter de Gruyter, 1968)
KAZAN, FRANCESCA, 'Description and the Pictorial in *Jacob's Room*', *ELH*, 55 (1988),

701–19

Keats, John, 'The Fall of Hyperion: A Vision', in *John Keats: The Poems*, ed. by David Bromwich (London: Everyman's Library, 1992), p. 351

Kellaway, Kate, 'Hatchet Man', *Observer*, 23 November 2003, Review section, pp. 1–2

Keller, Evelyn Fox, *Making Sense of Life: Explaining Biological Development with Models, Metaphors, and Machines* (Cambridge, MA: Harvard University Press, 2002)

Kelley, Donald, ed., *History and the Disciplines: The Reclassification of Knowledge in Early Modern Europe* (Rochester, NY: University of Rochester Press, 1997)

Kelly, Michael, ed., *Encyclopedia of Aesthetics*, 4 vols (New York and Oxford: Oxford University Press, 1998)

Kester, Grant, 'Aesthetics after the End of Art: An Interview with Susan Buck-Morss', *Art Journal*, 56.1 (1997), 38–45

Kittler, Friedrich, *Aufschreibesysteme 1800/1900* (Munich: Wilhelm Fink, 1985); as *Discourse Networks 1800/1900*, trans. by Michael Metteer with Chris Cullens (Stanford: Stanford University Press, 1990)

Kleist, Heinrich von, *Sämtliche Werke und Briefe*, ed. by Helmut Sembdner, 2 vols (Darmstadt: Wissenschaftliche Buchgesellschaft, 1983)

Kohon, Gregorio, ed., *The Dead Mother: The Work of André Green* (London: Taylor & Francis, 2005)

Kolodiejchuk, Father Brian, *The Soul of Mother Theresa: Hidden Aspects of her Interior Life*, issued in four instalments by the ZENIT news agency, November–December 2002

Kopp, Robert, 'Un entretien avec Yves Bonnefoy', *Magazine Littéraire*, no. 421 (June 2003), 22–27

Kramer, Lawrence, *Classical Music and Postmodern Knowledge* (Berkeley: University of California Press, 1995)

Kreps, David M., *Game Theory and Economic Modelling* (Oxford: Clarendon Press, 1990)

Kristeva, Julia, *Black Sun: Depression and Melancholia*, trans. by Leon S. Roudiez (New York: Columbia University Press, 1992)

——*Powers of Horror: An Essay on Abjection*, trans. by Leon S. Roudiez (New York: Columbia University Press, 1982)

Kroeber, Alfred L., and Richardson, Jane, 'Three Centuries of Women's Dress Fashions: A Quantitative Analysis', *Anthropological Records*, 5 (1940), 111–54

Kwint, Marius, Breward, Christopher, and Aynsley, Jeremy, eds, *Material Memories: Design and Evocation* (Oxford: Berg, 1999)

La Beaumelle, Agnès de, ed., *Alberto Giacometti: Le dessin à l'œuvre* (Paris: Gallimard/Centre Pompidou, 2001)

Lakoff, George, *Women, Fire, and Dangerous Things: What Categories Reveal about the Mind* (Chicago and London: University of Chicago Press, 1987)

——and Johnson, Mark, *Metaphors We Live By* (Chicago and London: University of Chicago Press, 1980)

Lampert, Friederike, 'Tanzimprovisation auf der Bühne: Entdeckung von Nicht-Choreografierbarem', in *Tanz, Theorie, Text*, ed. by Gabriele Klein and Christa Zipprich (Münster: Lit, 2002), pp. 445–56

Lang, Paul Henry, *Musicology and Performance* (New Haven, CT: Yale University Press, 1997)

Laplanche, Jean, and Pontalis, Jean-Baptiste, *The Language of Psychoanalysis*, trans. by Donald Nicholson-Smith (London: Karnac Books, 1988)

Lear, Jonathan, *Open Minded: Working Out the Logic of the Soul* (Cambridge, MA: Harvard University Press, 1998)

Lears, Jackson, *Fables of Abundance: A Cultural History of Advertising in America* (New York: Basic Books, 1994)

Le Goff, Marcel, *Jorge Luis Borges: l'univers, la lettre et le secret* (Paris: Harmattan, 1999)
Lehmen, Thomas, *Schreibstück* (ISBN 3–00–009996–4, distributed by the author)
Lenoir, Timothy, *Instituting Science: The Cultural Production of Scientific Disciplines* (Stanford: Stanford University Press, 1997)
Levinas, Emmanuel, *Existence and Existents*, trans. by Alphonso Lingis (Dordrecht: Nijhoff, 1988)
Levinson, Jerrold, 'Evaluating Musical Performance', in *Music, Art, and Metaphysics: Essays in Philosophical Aesthetics* (Ithaca, NY: Cornell University Press, 1990), pp. 376–92
——*Music in the Moment* (Ithaca, NY: Cornell University Press, 1997)
Lewis, Wyndham, *Blasting and Bombardiering* (1937) (London: Calder and Boyars, 1967)
Lidov, David, 'Mind and Body in Music', *Semiotica*, 66 (1987), 69–97
Lingis, Alphonso, 'Catastrophic Times', in *Time and Value*, ed. by Scott Lash, Andrew Quick, and Richard Roberts (Oxford: Blackwell, 1998)
——*Phenomenological Explanations* (The Hague: Martinus Nijhoff, 1986)
Lord, Catherine M., *The Intimacy of Influence: Narrative and Theoretical Fictions between the Novels of George Eliot, Virginia Woolf and Jeanette Winterson* (Amsterdam: ASCA Press, 1999)
Lorraine, Renée Cox, *Music, Tendencies, and Inhibitions: Reflections on a Theory of Leonard Meyer* (Lanham, MD: Scarecrow Press, 2001)
Luhmann, Niklas, 'Contingency as Modern Society's Defining Attribute', in *Observations on Modernity* (1992), trans. by William Whobrey (Stanford: Stanford University Press, 1998), pp. 44–62
Lyotard, Jean-François, 'Adrift', in Jean-François Lyotard, *Driftworks*, trans. and ed. by Roger McKeon (New York: Semiotext(e), 1984), pp. 9–17
——*The Differend: Phrases in Dispute*, trans. by Georges Van Den Abbeele (Minneapolis: Minnesota University Press, 1988)
——*Discours, Figure* (Paris: Klincksieck, 1971)
——*The Inhuman: Reflections on Time*, trans. by Geoffrey Bennington and Rachel Bowlby (Cambridge: Polity Press, 1991)
——*Libidinal Economy*, trans. by Iain Hamilton Grant (London: Athlone, 1993)
McLuhan, Marshall, *Understanding Media: The Extensions of Man* (New York: McGraw-Hill, 1964)
Mandelstam, Osip, 'Conversation about Dante', in *Osip Mandelstam: The Collected Critical Prose and Letters*, ed. by Jane Gary Harris, trans. by Jane Gary Harris and Constance Link (London: Collins Harvill, 1991), pp. 397–442
Marks, Laura U., *Touch: Sensuous Theory and Multisensory Media* (Minneapolis: Minnesota University Press, 2002)
Marquardt, Hans-Jochen, 'Heinrich von Kleist: die Geburt der Moderne aus dem Geiste "neuer Aufklärung"', in *Heinrich von Kleist und die Aufklärung*, ed. by Tim Mehigan (Rochester, NY: Camden House, 2000), pp. 22–45
Marrati, Paola, *Gilles Deleuze: cinéma et philosophie* (Paris: PUF, 2003)
Mehigan, Tim, '"Betwixt a false reason and none at all": Kleist, Kant, Hume, and the "Thing in Itself"', in *A Companion to the Works of Heinrich von Kleist*, ed. by Bernd Fischer (Rochester, NY: Camden House, 2003), pp. 165–88
——'Kleist, Kant und die Aufklärung', in *Heinrich von Kleist und die Aufklärung*, ed. by Tim Mehigan (Rochester, NY: Camden House, 2000), pp. 3–21
Ménage, Gilles, *Dictionnaire étymologique de la langue françoise*, 2 vols, new edn (Paris, 1750)
Merleau-Ponty, Maurice, *Phenomenology of Perception*, trans. by Colin Smith (London: Routledge, 1962)
Miller, J. Hillis, 'Deconstructing the Deconstructors', in *Theory Now and Then* (London:

Harvester Wheatsheaf, 1991), pp. 95–110
——'How Deconstruction Works', in *Theory Now and Then* (London: Harvester Wheatsheaf, 1991), pp. 293–95
——'On Edge: The Crossways of Contemporary Criticism', in *Theory Now and Then* (London: Harvester Wheatsheaf, 1991), pp. 171–200
——'Stevens' Rock and Criticism as Cure, II', in *Theory Now and Then* (London: Harvester Wheatsheaf, 1991), pp. 117–32
MONEGAL, EMIR RODRÍGUEZ, *Jorge Luis Borges: biographie littéraire* (Paris: Gallimard, 1983)
MONTAGU, ASHLEY, *Touching: The Human Significance of the Skin* (New York: Columbia University Press, 1971)
MORRISSEY, ROBERT, and ROGER, PHILIPPE, eds, *L'Encyclopédie: du réseau au livre et du livre au réseau* (Paris: Honoré Champion, 2001)
MORSON, GARY SAUL, *Narrative and Freedom: The Shadows of Time* (New Haven, CT: Yale University Press, 1994)
NAIR, RUKMINI BHAYA, *Lying on the Postcolonial Couch: The Idea of Indifference* (Minneapolis: University of Minnesota Press, 2002)
NASH, CATHERINE, 'Performativity in Practice: Some Recent Work in Cultural Geography', *Progress in Human Geography*, 24 (2000), 653–64
NAUGHTON, JOHN, *The Poetics of Yves Bonnefoy* (Chicago and London: University of Chicago Press, 1984)
NEUMANN, GERHARD, 'Theatralität der Zeichen', in *Szenographien: Theatralität als Kategorie der Literaturwissenschaft*, ed. by Gerhard Neumann, Caroline Pross, and Gerald Wildgruber (Freiburg i.Br.: Rombach, 2000), pp. 65–112
NEUMANN, JOHN VON, and MORGENSTERN, OSKAR, *Theory of Games and Economic Behavior* (Princeton: Princeton University Press, 1944)
NICHOLS, ROBERT, 'Casualty', in *Aurelia and Other Poems* (London: Chatto & Windus, 1920), p. 75
NICOLSON, HAROLD, *Public Faces* (1932) (Harmondsworth: Penguin Books, 1944)
NOHRNBERG, JAMES, *The Analogy of the Faerie Queene* (Princeton: Princeton University Press, 1976)
NUTTALL, A. D., *A New Mimesis* (London: Methuen, 1983)
ORWELL, GEORGE, *Down and Out in Paris and London* (London: Gollancz, 1933)
OWEN, WILFRED, *Collected Letters*, ed. by Harold Owen and John Bell (London: Oxford University Press, 1967)
——*Complete Poems & Fragments*, ed. by Jon Stallworthy (Oxford: Oxford University Press, 1983)
——*Poems*, British Library, Add. MS 43720
PALMER, CAROLINE, 'Mapping Musical Thought to Musical Performance', *Journal of Experimental Psychology*, 15 (1989), 331–46
PARNCUTT, RICHARD, and MCPHERSON, GARY E., eds, *The Science and Psychology of Music Performance: Creative Strategies for Teaching and Learning* (Oxford: Oxford University Press, 2002)
PARSHALL, PETER, 'Introduction', *Art and Curiosity in Northern Europe*, ed. by Peter Parshall (= *Word & Image*, 11.4 (1995)), pp. 327–31
PATER, WALTER, 'Winckelmann', in *The Renaissance: Studies in Art and Poetry*, rev. 2nd edn (London: Macmillan, 1877), pp. 177–232
PECK, DALE, *Hatchet Jobs: Writings on Contemporary Fiction* (New York and London: New Press, 2004)
PEEREN, ESTHER, 'Bakhtin and Beyond: Conceptualizing Identity through Popular Culture' (doctoral thesis in preparation, University of Amsterdam, ASCA)
PEIRCE, CHARLES SANDERS, 'Logic as Semiotic: The Theory of Signs', in *Semiotics: An*

Introductory Anthology, ed. with introduction by Robert E. Innis (Bloomington: Indiana University Press, 1985), pp. 4–23
PERROT, PHILIPPE, *Fashioning the Bourgeoisie: A History of Clothing in the Nineteenth Century*, trans. by Richard Bienvenu (Princeton: Princeton University Press, 1994)
PETERS, SIBYLLE, 'Performative Writing 1800/2000? Evidenz und Performanz in der medialen Refiguration des Wissens', in *Performativität und Ereignis*, ed. by Erika Fischer-Lichte and others (Basel and Tübingen: Francke, 2003), pp. 99–116
PHILLIPS, ADAM, *The Beast in the Nursery*, 2nd edn (London: Faber and Faber, 1999)
——'Poetry and Psychoanalysis', in *Promises, Promises: Essays on Literature and Psychoanalysis* (London: Faber and Faber, 2000), pp. 1–34
——*Promises, Promises: Essays on Literature and Psychoanalysis*, 2nd edn (London: Faber and Faber, 2002)
PISTERS, PATRICIA, *The Matrix of Visual Culture: Working with Deleuze in Film Theory* (Stanford: Stanford University Press, 2003)
PLATO, *Republic*, trans. by Robin Waterfield (Oxford and New York: Oxford University Press, 1998)
——*Republic 10*, trans. with commentary by Stephen Halliwell (Warminster: Aris & Phillips, 1988)
PLOTINUS, *Enneads*, v.8.1, trans. by Stephen MacKenna, 4th edn (London: Faber, 1969)
POPKIN, RICHARD, *The History of Scepticism from Erasmus to Spinoza* (Berkeley: University of California Press, 1979)
POPLE, ANTHONY, 'Analysis: Past, Present and Future', *Music Analysis*, 21/special issue (July 2002), 17–21
——'Systems and Strategies: Functions and Limits of Analysis', in *Theory, Analysis, and Meaning in Music*, ed. by Anthony Pople (Cambridge: Cambridge University Press, 1994), pp. 108–23
POUNDSTONE, WILLIAM, *Prisoner's Dilemma: John von Neumann, Game Theory and the Puzzle of the Bomb* (New York: Anchor Books, 1993)
REE, JONATHAN, 'Marxist Modes', in *Radical Philosophy Reader*, ed. by Roy Edgely and Richard Osborne (London: Verso, 1985), pp. 337–60
REISZ, KAREL, and MILLAR, GAVIN, *The Technique of Film Editing*, 2nd edn (Guildford: Focal Press, repr. 1991)
RENAN, ERNEST, *De l'origine du langage* (Paris: Lévy-Frères, 1848)
REY, ALAIN, ed., *Le Grand Robert de la langue française*, 2nd edn, 9 vols (Paris: Le Robert, 1985)
REYNOLDS, TERI, 'Case Studies in Cognitive Metaphor and Interdisciplinary Analysis: Physics, Biology, Narrative' (unpublished doctoral dissertation, Columbia University, New York, 2000)
RHU, L. F., trans., 'Tasso's Allegory of *Gerusalemme Liberata*', in L. F. Rhu, *The Genesis of Tasso's Narrative Theory: English Translations of the Early Poetics and a Comparative Study of their Significance* (Detroit: Wayne State University Press, 1993), pp. 157–59
RICHTER, GERHARD, *Acht Grau*, ed. by the Solomon R. Guggenheim Foundation (New York: Guggenheim Museum Publications, 2002)
——*Walter Benjamin and the Corpus of Autobiography*, Kritik: German Literary Theory and Cultural Studies (Detroit: Wayne State University Press, 2000)
RICOEUR, PAUL, *Time and Narrative*, trans. by Kathleen (McLaughlin) Blamey and David Pellauer, 3 vols (Chicago: University of Chicago Press, 1984–88)
RIEGL, ALOIS, *Late Roman Art Industry*, trans. by Rolf Winkes (1927; Rome: Bretschneider, 1985)
RINK, JOHN, review of Wallace Berry, *Musical Structure and Performance*, *Music Analysis*, 9 (1990), 319–39

ROBERTS, DAVID, 'Kleists Kritik der Urteilskraft: zum Erhabenen in *Das Erdbeben in Chili*', in *Heinrich von Kleist und die Aufklärung*, ed. by Tim Mehigan (Rochester, NY: Camden House, 2000), pp. 46–57

RODOWICK, D. N., *Gilles Deleuze's Time Machine* (Durham, NC: Duke University Press, 1997)

RORTY, RICHARD, *Contingency, Irony and Solidarity* (Cambridge: Cambridge University Press, 1989)

ROSEN, CHARLES, *The Classical Style: Haydn, Mozart, Beethoven* (London: Faber and Faber, 1971)

ROSENBERG, DANIEL, and others, 'Early Modern Information Overload', *Journal of the History of Ideas*, 64 (2003), 1–72

——'An Eighteenth-Century Time Machine: The *Encyclopedia* of Diderot', in *Postmodernism and the Enlightenment: New Perspectives in French Intellectual History*, ed. by Daniel Gordon (New York: Routledge, 2001), pp. 45–66

——'A New Sort of Logick and Critick: Etymological Interpretation in Horne Tooke's *Diversions of Purley*', in *Language, Self, and Society: A Social History of Language*, ed. by Roy Porter and Peter Burke (Cambridge: Polity Press, 1991)

——'We Have Never Been Interdisciplinary: Etymology and Encyclopedism in the Eighteenth Century and Since', *SVEC* 2005:04, 3–22

ROUSSEAU, JEAN-JACQUES, *Oeuvres complètes*, ed. by Bernard Gagnebin and Marcel Raymond, 5 vols (Paris: Gallimard, 1959–95), IV: *Émile, ou de L'Éducation* (1969)

RYLANCE, RICK, Chair's Report, 2000–2001, Council for College and University English (CCUE) <www.ccue.ac.uk> [accessed 29 December 2003]

SADIE, STANLEY, *Mozart Symphonies* (London: Ariel Music, 1986)

SAID, EDWARD W., *Musical Elaborations* (London: Vintage, 1992)

SARTRE, JEAN-PAUL, *Nausea*, trans. by Robert Baldick (London: Penguin Books, 2000)

SASSOON, SIEGFRIED, *Diaries 1915–1918*, ed. by Rupert Hart-Davis (London: Faber, 1983)

——'The Last Meeting', typescript, Cambridge University Library, Add. 7973, S51–end

SAUNDERS, NICHOLAS, *Trench Art: A Brief History and Guide* (Barnsley: Leo Cooper, 2001)

SCARRY, ELAINE, *The Body in Pain: The Making and Unmaking of the World* (Oxford: Oxford University Press, 1985)

——*Resisting Representation* (Oxford: Oxford University Press, 1994)

SCHENKER, HEINRICH, 'Rameau oder Beethoven? Erstarrung oder geistiges Leben in der Musik?', in *Das Meisterwerk in der Musik*, 3 vols (Munich, 1925–30), III, 11–24

SEEL, MARTIN, 'Inszenieren als Erscheinenlassen: Thesen über die Reichweite eines Begriffs', in *Ästhetik der Inszenierung*, ed. by Josef Früchtl and Jörg Zimmermann (Frankfurt a.M.: Suhrkamp, 2001), pp. 48–62

SEGEBERG, HARRO, *Literatur im technischen Zeitalter: von der Frühzeit der deutschen Aufklärung bis zum Beginn des Ersten Weltkriegs* (Darmstadt: Wissenschaftliche Buchgesellschaft, 1997)

SHAFFER, HENRY, 'Intention and Performance', *Psychological Review*, 83 (1976), 375–93

SHAKESPEARE, WILLIAM, *King Henry IV, Part 1*, ed. by A. R. Humphreys (Walton on Thames: Nelson, 1960)

——*King Henry IV, Part 2*, ed. by A. R. Humphreys (Walton on Thames: Nelson, 1966)

——*Twelfth Night*, ed. by J. M. Lothian and T. W. Craik (London: Methuen, 1975)

SHKLOVSKY, VIKTOR, *Theory of Prose* (Champaign, IL: Dalkey Archive Press, 1993)

SIEPMANN, JEREMY, *Chopin: The Reluctant Romantic* (Boston: Northeastern University Press, 1995)

SILVERMAN, KAJA, 'How to Stage the Death of God', in *Eija-Liisa Ahtila: Fantasized Persons and Taped Conversations* (Helsinki: Museum of Contemporary Art, 2002), pp. 182–96

——*The Threshold of the Visible World* (New York: Routledge, 1996)

——*World Spectators* (Stanford: Stanford University Press, 2000)

SIMONS, JUDY, 'Chair's Annual Report, 1999–2000', Council for College and University English (CCUE) <www.ccue.ac.uk> [accessed 29 December 2003]

SMALL, CHRISTOPHER, *Musicking: The Meanings of Performing and Listening* (Hanover, CT: Wesleyan University Press, 1998)

SPENSER, EDMUND, *The Works of Edmund Spenser: A Variorum Edition*, ed. by Edwin Greenlaw, Charles Grosvenor Osgood, and Frederick Morgan Padelford (Baltimore: Johns Hopkins University Press, 1932–57)

SPIELMANN, YVONNE, 'Aesthetic Features in Digital Imaging: Collage and Morph', *Wide Angle*, 21.1 (January 1999), 131–48

SPIVAK, GAYATRI CHAKRAVORTI, 'Translator's Preface and Afterword to Mahasweta Devi's *Imaginary Maps*' and 'Subaltern Talk', in *The Spivak Reader*, ed. by Donna Landry and Gerald MacLean (New York: Routledge, 1996), pp. 267–86, 287–308

STAFFORD, BARBARA MARIA, *Good Looking: Essays on the Virtue of Images* (Cambridge: MIT Press, 1996)

STEIN, ERWIN, *Form and Performance* (London: Faber and Faber, 1962)

STEINERT, HEINZ, *Culture Industry*, trans. by Sally-Ann Spencer (Cambridge: Polity Press, 2003)

STENGERS, ISABELLE, ed., *D'une science à l'autre: des concepts nomades* (Paris: Éditions du Seuil, 1987)

STEVENS, DENIS, ed., *L'Orfeo, favola in musica da Claudio Monteverde*, corrected edn (London: Novello, 1968)

STEWART, SUSAN, 'Facing, Touch and Vertigo', in *Poetry and the Fate of the Senses* (Chicago: University of Chicago Press, 2002), pp. 145–85

——*Poetry and the Fate of the Senses* (Chicago: University of Chicago Press, 2002)

STRATHERN, MARILYN, *Commons and Borderlands: Working Papers on Interdisciplinarity, Accountability and the Flow of Knowledge* (Wantage: Sean Kingston, 2004)

STRAVINSKY, IGOR, *Poetics of Music* (Cambridge, MA: Harvard University Press, repr. 1970)

STREET, ALAN, 'The Obbligato Recitative: Narrative and Schoenberg's Five Orchestral Pieces, Op. 16', in *Theory, Analysis, and Meaning in Music*, ed. by Anthony Pople (Cambridge: Cambridge University Press, 1994), pp. 164–83

STRUEVER, NANCY, 'Fables of Power', *Representations*, 4 (1983), 108–27

SWAIN, HARRIET, 'English Fears Set Forum in Motion', *Times Higher Education Supplement*, 1 December 2000, p. 6

SYLVESTER, DAVID, *About Modern Art: Critical Essays, 1948–97*, 2nd [updated] edn (London: Pimlico, 1997)

——*Looking at Giacometti* (New York: Owl Books, 1997)

SZENDY, PETER, *Écoute: une histoire de nos oreilles*, with foreword by Jean-Luc Nancy (Paris: Éditions de Minuit, 2001)

TARUSKIN, RICHARD, *Text and Act: Essays on Music and Performance* (Oxford: Oxford University Press, 1995)

TAYLOR, MARTIN, ed., *Lads: Love Poetry of the Trenches* (London: Duckworth, 1989)

THRIFT, NIGEL, 'The Still Point: Resistance, Expressive Embodiment and Dance', in *Geographies of Resistance*, ed. by Steve Pile and Michael Keith (London: Routledge, 1997), pp. 124–51

TIEDEMANN, ROLF, 'Nachwort', in Walter Benjamin, *Berliner Kindheit um neunzehnhundert: Gießener Fassung* (Frankfurt a.M.: Suhrkamp, 2000), pp. 113–26

——, GÖDDE, CHRISTOPH, and LONITZ, HENRI, eds, *Walter Benjamin 1892–1940* (= *Marbacher Magazin*, no. 55 (1990))

TOVEY, DONALD F., *A Companion to Beethoven's Pianoforte Sonatas* (London: Associated Board, 1931)

——*Essays in Musical Analysis*, 6 vols (London: Oxford University Press, 1935–39), I: *Symphonies*

TSUR, REUVEN, *What Makes Sound Patterns Expressive? The Poetic Mode of Speech Perception* (Durham, NC, and London: Duke University Press, 1992)

TURGOT, ANNE-ROBERT-JACQUES, 'Étymologie', *Encyclopédie, ou dictionnaire raisonné des arts, des sciences, et des métiers*, ed. by Diderot and d'Alembert, 17 vols (Paris: Briasson, 1751–65), VI (1756), III

——introduction and notes in *Turgot: Étymologie*, ed. by Maurice Piron (Brugge: De Tempel, 1961), pp. v–xi, 99–100

——*Réflexions sur la formation et distribution des richesses* (1766) , in *Oeuvres de Turgot*, ed. by Gustave Schelle, 5 vols (Paris: F. Alcan, 1913–23), II (1914)

——'Valeurs et monnaies', in *Oeuvres de Turgot*, ed. by Gustave Schelle, 5 vols (Paris: F. Alcan, 1913–23), III (1919), 83–84

TYSON, ALAN, *Mozart: Studies of the Autograph Scores* (Cambridge, MA: Harvard University Press, 1987)

UERLINGS, HERBERT, *Poetiken der Interkulturalität: Haiti bei Kleist, Seghers, Müller, Buch und Fichte* (Tübingen: Niemeyer, 1997)

ULLRICH, WOLFGANG, *Die Geschichte der Unschärfe* (Berlin: Wagenbach, 2002)

ULMER, GREGORY, *Heuretics: The Logic of Invention* (Baltimore: Johns Hopkins University Press, 1994)

VALENTINE, ELIZABETH, 'The Fear of Performance', in *Musical Performance: A Guide to Understanding*, ed. by John Rink (Cambridge: Cambridge University Press, 2002), pp. 168–82

WALL, KATHLEEN, 'Significant Form in *Jacob's Room*: Ekphrasis and the Elegy', *Texas Studies in Literature and Language*, 44 (2002), 302–23

WALLACE, JEFF, '"Taking Possession of the Ordinary Man's Mind": Literary Studies and the History of Science', *Literature and History*, 1 (1990), 58–74

WEINRICH, HARALD, *Tempus: besprochene und erzählte Welt*, 5th edn (Stuttgart: Kohlhammer, 1994)

WESCHER, HERTA, *Collage*, trans. by Robert E. Wolf (New York: Harry Abrams, 1968)

WESEMANN, ARND, 'Warum Tanz verstehen?', *ballettanz*, 2003.3 (March), 36–37

WILDGRUBER, GERALD, 'Theorie und Chor', in *Szenographien: Theatralität als Kategorie der Literaturwissenschaft*, ed. by Gerhard Neumann, Caroline Pross, and Gerald Wildgruber (Freiburg i.Br.: Rombach, 2000), pp. 391–452

WILLETT, C., and CUNNINGTON, PHILLIS, *Handbook of English Costume in the Eighteenth Century* (London: Faber and Faber, 1957)

WINNICOTT, D. W., 'Home Again' (1945), in *The Child and the Outside World*, ed. by Janet Hardenberg (London: Tavistock, 1957)

——'Integrative and Disruptive Factors in Family Life' (1957), in *The Family and Individual Development* (London: Tavistock, 1965)

WITTGENSTEIN, LUDWIG, *On Certainty*, trans. by Dennis Paul and G. E. M. Anscombe, ed. by G. E. M. Anscombe and G. H. von Wright (Oxford: Blackwell, 1969)

——*Philosophical Investigations*, 2nd [bilingual] edn, trans. by G. E. M. Anscombe (New York: Macmillan, 1958)

——*Zettel*, ed. by G. E. M. Anscombe and G. H. von Wright, trans. by G. E. M. Anscombe (Berkeley: University of California Press, 1970)

WOLFF, JANET, 'Dance Criticism: Feminism, Theory and Choreography', in *Resident Alien: Feminist Cultural Criticism*, ed. by Janet Wolff (Cambridge: Polity Press, 1995), pp. 68–87

WOOD, CHRISTOPHER S., '"Curious Pictures" and the Art of Description', in *Art and Curiosity in Northern Europe*, ed. by Peter Parshall (= *Word & Image*, 11.4 (1995)), pp. 332–52

Woolf, Leonard, *The Journey not the Arrival Matters: An Autobiography of the Years 1939–1969* (London: Hogarth Press, 1969)
Woolf, Virginia, *Between the Acts* (London: Hogarth Press, 1941)
——*Jacob's Room* (London: Vintage, 2000)
——'The Royal Academy', *The Essays of Virginia Woolf*, ed. by Andrew McNeillie (London: Hogarth Press, 1986–), III: *1919–1924* (1988), pp. 92–93
——*A Writer's Diary* (London: Triad Grafton, 1978)
Wortelkamp, Isa, *Sehen mit dem Stift in der Hand: die Aufführung im Schriftzug der Aufführung* (Freiburg i.Br.: Rombach, 2006)
Yeo, Richard, *Encyclopaedic Visions: Scientific Dictionaries and Enlightenment Culture* (Cambridge: Cambridge University Press, 2001)
Zaleski, Carol, 'The Dark Night of Mother Teresa', *First Things*, no. 133 (May 2003), 24–27
Zantop, Susanne, 'Changing Color: Kleist's *Die Verlobung in St Domingo* and the Discourses of Miscegenation', in *A Companion to the Works of Heinrich von Kleist*, ed. by Bernd Fischer (Rochester, NY: Camden House, 2003), pp. 191–208
Zaslaw, Neal, *Mozart's Symphonies: Context, Performance Practice, Reception* (Oxford: Clarendon Press, 1989)
Zumthor, Paul, 'Etymologies', in *Langue, texte, énigme* (Paris: Éditions du Seuil, 1975), pp. 144–60

Further Reading

BAL, MIEKE, *The Mottled Screen: Reading Proust Visually* (Stanford: Stanford University Press, 1997)

BARTHES, ROLAND, *La Chambre claire: note sur la photographie* (Paris: Gallimard, 1980)

—— *The Rustle of Language*, trans. by Richard Howard (Berkeley: University of California Press, 1989)

BEER, GILLIAN, *Virginia Woolf: The Common Ground* (Edinburgh: Edinburgh University Press, 1996)

BEGBIE, JEREMY, *Theology, Music and Time* (Cambridge: Cambridge University Press, 2000)

BERGER, JOHN, 'Against the Great Defeat of the World', in *The Shape of a Pocket* (London: Bloomsbury, 2001), pp. 207–19

BOGUE, RONALD, *Deleuze on Music, Painting, and the Arts* (New York: Routledge, 2003)

BOLTER, JAY DAVID, and GRUSIN, RICHARD, 'Immediacy, Hypermediacy, Remediation', in *Remediation: Understanding New Media* (Cambridge, MA, and London: MIT Press, 2000), pp. 20–52

BOWIE, MALCOLM, *Psychoanalysis and the Future of Theory* (Oxford: Blackwell, 1993)

BRONFEN, ELISABETH, Introduction to Virginia Woolf, *Jacob's Room* (London: Vintage, 2000), pp. xi–xix

BURGIN, VICTOR, ed., *Thinking Photography* (London: Macmillan, 1982)

BUTLER, JUDITH, *The Psychic Life of Power* (Stanford: Stanford University Press, 1997)

BUTT, JOHN, *Playing with History: The Historical Approach to Musical Performance* (Cambridge: Cambridge University Press, 2002)

CALVINO, ITALO, *Six Memos for the Next Millennium* (London: Cape, 1992)

CLARKE, ERIC, and COOK, NICHOLAS, eds, *Empirical Musicology: Aims, Methods, Prospects* (Oxford: Oxford University Press, 2004)

CLASSEN, CONSTANCE, *Worlds of Sense: Exploring the Senses in History and Across Cultures* (London: Routledge, 1993)

CLAYTON, MARTIN, HERBERT, TREVOR, and MIDDLETON, RICHARD, eds, *The Cultural Study of Music: A Critical Introduction* (New York: Routledge, 2003)

CRARY, JONATHAN, *Suspensions of Perception: Attention, Spectacle, and Modern Culture* (Cambridge, MA: MIT Press, 1999)

CULLER, JONATHAN, *On Deconstruction: Theory and Criticism after Structuralism* (London: Routledge, 1983)

CUMMING, NAOMI, *The Sonic Self: Musical Subjectivity and Signification* (Bloomington: Indiana University Press, 2000)

DENORA, TIA, *Music in Everyday Life* (Cambridge: Cambridge University Press, 2000)

DERRIDA, JACQUES, *Le Toucher: Jean-Luc Nancy* (Paris: Galilée, 2000)

DYER, GEOFF, *Out of Sheer Rage: In the Shadow of D. H. Lawrence* (London: Little, Brown, 1997)

FUSSELL, PAUL, *The Great War and Modern Memory* (New York: Oxford University Press, 1975)

HATTEN, ROBERT S., *Interpreting Musical Gestures, Topics, and Tropes: Mozart, Beethoven, Schubert* (Bloomington: Indiana University Press, 2004)

HEJINIAN, LYN, *The Language of Inquiry* (Berkeley: University of California Press, 2000)

KAHN, DOUGLAS, *Noise, Water, Meat: A History of Sound in the Arts* (Cambridge, MA: MIT Press, 1999)

KITTLER, FRIEDRICH, 'The Perspective of Print', trans. by Geoffrey Winthrop-Young and Michael Wutz, *Configurations*, 10 (2002), 37–50

LANGER, SUSANNE K., *Feeling and Form: A Theory of Art* (London: Routledge & Kegan Paul, 1953)

——— *Mind: An Essay on Human Feeling*, 3 vols (Baltimore: Johns Hopkins University Press, 1967–82), II (1972)

LYOTARD, JEAN-FRANÇOIS, *The Postmodern Condition: A Report on Knowledge*, trans. by Geoff Bennington and Brian Massumi (Minneapolis: University of Minnesota Press, 1984)

MERLEAU-PONTY, MAURICE, *The Visible and the Invisible*, ed. by Claude Lefort, trans. by Alphonso Lingis (Evanston, IL: Northwestern University Press, 1992)

NANCY, JEAN-LUC, *Corpus* (Paris: Métailié, 2000)

——*Noli me tangere: essai sur la levée du corps* (Paris: Bayard, 2003)

RABB, JANE M., ed., *Literature & Photography: Interactions 1840–1990: A Critical Anthology* (Albuquerque: University of New Mexico Press, 1995)

RAHN, JOHN, *Music Inside Out: Going Too Far in Musical Essays* (Amsterdam: G+B Arts International, 2001)

SCHER, STEVEN, ed., *Music and Text: Critical Inquiries* (Cambridge: Cambridge University Press, 1992)

SCHWARZ, DAVID, ANAHID, KASSABIAN, and SIEGEL, LAWRENCE, eds, *Keeping Score: Music, Disciplinarity, Culture* (Charlottesville: University Press of Virginia, 1997)

SOLNIT, REBECCA, *A Field Guide to Getting Lost* (New York: Viking, 2005)

SPITZER, MICHAEL, *Music as Philosophy: Adorno and Beethoven's Late Style* (Bloomington: Indiana University Press, 2006)

WINTER, JAY, *Sites of Memory, Sites of Mourning: The Great War in European Cultural History* (Cambridge: Cambridge University Press, 1995)

ZBIKOWSKI, LAWRENCE M., *Conceptualizing Music: Cognitive Structure, Theory, and Analysis* (New York: Oxford University Press, 2002)

SUBJECT INDEX

INDEX OF NAMES AND TEXTS

Printed in Great Britain
by Amazon

42640375R00150